MW00846487

CAMBRIDGE SERIES ON
HUMAN–COMPUTER
INTERACTION 7

Extra-Ordinary Human–Computer Interaction

Cambridge Series on Human–Computer Interaction

Managing Editor
Professor John Long, Ergonomics Unit, University College, London

Editorial Board
Dr. P. Barnard, Medical Research Council, Applied Psychology Unit, Cambridge, England
Professor T. Bosser, Westphalian Wilhelms University at Munster, Institute for Pure and Applied Psychology, Munster, Germany
Professor W. Buxton, Computer Systems Research Institute, University of Toronto, Canada
Dr. S. Card, Xerox Palo Alto Research Center, Palo Alto, California
Dr. J. M. Carroll, Virginia Polytechnic Institute, Blacksburg, Virginia
Professor Joelle Coutaz, Computer Science Department, IMAG-LGI, University of Grenoble, France
Professor J. Grudin, Information and Computer Science Department, University of California at Irvine
Dr. T. Landauer, Bellcore, Morristown, New Jersey
Professor J. Lansdown, CASCAAD, Middlesex Polytechnic, England
Professor T. W. Malone, Sloan School of Management, MIT, Cambridge, Massachusetts
Professor H. Thimbleby, Department of Computing Science, University of Stirling, Scotland
Professor T. Winograd, Department of Computer Science, Stanford University, California

Titles in the series
1. J. Long and A. Whitefield, eds. *Cognitive Ergonomics and Human–Computer Interaction*
2. M. Harrison and H. Thimbleby, eds., *Formal Methods in Human–Computer Interaction*
3. P. B. Andersen, *The Theory of Computer Semiotics*
4. J. M. Carroll, ed., *Designing Interactions: Psychology at the Human–Computer Interface*
5. J. Darragh and I. Witten, *The Reactive Keyboard*
6. S. Greenberg, *The Computer User as Toolsmith*
7. A. D. N. Edwards, *Extra-Ordinary Human–Computer Interaction*
8. K. Y. Lim and J. Long, *The MUSE Method for Usability Engineering*
9. G. Marchionini, *Information Seeking in Electronic Environments*
10. P. Thomas, ed., *The Social and Interactional Dimensions of Human–Computer Interfaces*

Extra-Ordinary Human–Computer Interaction

Interfaces for Users with Disabilities

Edited by

Alistair D. N. Edwards

Department of Computer Science
University of York, York, England

CAMBRIDGE
UNIVERSITY PRESS

Published by the Press Syndicate of the University of Cambridge
The Pitt Building, Trumpington Street, Cambridge CB2 1RP
40 West 20th Street, New York, NY 10011-4211, USA
10 Stamford Road, Oakleigh, Melbourne 3166, Australia

© Cambridge University Press 1995

First published 1995

Printed in the United States of America

Library of Congress Cataloging-in-Publication Data
Extra-ordinary human–computer interaction : interfaces for users with
disabilities / [edited by] Alistair D.N. Edwards.
p.   cm. – (Cambridge series on human–computer interaction : 7)
Includes index.
ISBN 0-521-43413-0 (hardback)
1. Human–computer interaction.   I. Edwards, Alistair D. N.
II. Series.
QA76.9.H85E97   1995
004'.01'9–dc20   94-22940
                                                                      CIP

A catalog record of this book is available from the British Library.

ISBN 0-521-43413-0 hardback

In memory of

David Purvis
who was indirectly responsible for the creation of this book

Contents

List of figures and tables   *page* ix
Preface   xv
Acknowledgments   xviii
List of contributors   xix
Trademarks   xxiii

Section 1: Introductions   1

1   **Extra-ordinary human–computer interaction**   3
    Alan F. Newell

2   **Computers and people with disabilities**   19
    Alistair D. N. Edwards

Section 2: Case studies   45

3   **An evaluation of the PRC Touch Talker with Minspeak: Some lessons for speech prosthesis design**   47
    Gary W. Strong

4   **Outspoken software for blind users**   59
    Alistair D. N. Edwards

5   **Intelligent systems for speech and language impaired people: A portfolio of research**   83
    Alan F. Newell, John L. Arnott,
    Alistair Y. Cairns, Ian W. Ricketts, and
    Peter Gregor

6   **Predictive interfaces: What will they think of next?**   103
    Saul Greenberg, John J. Darragh,
    David Maulsby, and Ian H. Witten

Section 3: Research   141

7   **Modeling and analysis of dyslexic writing using speech and other modalities**   145
    Jerome Elkind and Jeff Shrager

8   Giving Candy to children: User-tailored
     gesture input driving an articulator-based
     speech synthesizer   169
     Randy Pausch and Ronald D. Williams

9   Reading and pointing – New interaction
     methods for braille displays   183
     Gerhard Weber

10   Metaphors for nonvisual computing   201
     Elizabeth D. Mynatt and W. Keith Edwards

11   Multiple modalities in adapted interfaces   221
     Alistair D. N. Edwards, Ian J. Pitt,
     Steve A. Brewster, and Robert D. Stevens

12   Travel alternatives for mobility impaired
     people: The Surrogate Electronic Traveler
     (*Set*)   245
     Robert C. Williges and Beverly H. Williges

13   Input and integration: Enabling technologies
     for disabled users   263
     Robin Shaw, Anne Loomis, and E. Crisman

Section 4: Practice   279

14   Treat people like computers? Designing
     usable systems for special people   283
     Harold Thimbleby

15   Interfacing online services, alternative inputs,
     and redundant displays   297
     Norman Coombs

16   Producing a text-to-speech synthesizer for use
     by blind people   307
     Paul Blenkhorn

17   A physical skills based strategy for choosing
     an appropriate interface method   315
     Sherry Perdue Casali

18   Technology for people with special needs:
     HCI design issues   343
     Kate Howey

19   Resources   361
     Alistair D. N. Edwards and Rex Hancock

Index   375

Figures and tables

Figures

2.1   Matching the user to the interface   *page* 23

3.1   View of the Touch Talker   51

3.2   The Touch Talker in use with the user leaning over to see the   53
      display

3.3   Carrying the Touch Talker while using the walker   54

4.1   The keypad as used by Outspoken   62

4.2   A typical Macintosh screen which could be accessed through   64
      Outspoken

4.3   An icon which might have to be "pronounced" by Outspoken   67

4.4   A dialogue which might be scanned by Outspoken   68

4.5   A menu which has been pulled down by the user pressing the   70
      DRAG/RELEASE key once

4.6   An "empty" wastebasket icon   72

4.7   The bulging wastebasket icon, signifying that it contains   72
      (recoverable) files

4.8   A Macintosh window displaying files represented as icons   74

4.9   The same files as in the window in Figure 4.8, but now given a   75
      different representation

4.10 By reshaping the window shown in Figure 4.9, it can be made   75
      easier to use

4.11 A dialogue which has been redesigned to make it more   78
      compatible with Outspoken

5.1   Research into an integrated communication system for   86
      disabled people at the Microcomputer Centre, Dundee
      University

5.2.   Pal as a window on the screen of the word processor   87

5.3   Chat discussion stage control screen   90

5.4   Chat control screen for opening and closing a conversation   91

6.1   The potential savings of a predictive system, showing   104
        cognitive–physical trade-offs

6.2   Using RK-button, the Unix version of the Reactive Keyboard   109

6.3   Using RK-pointer, the Macintosh version of the Reactive   111
        Keyboard

6.4   Overview of the Reactive Keyboard system   113

6.5   Menu trees generated by uniform and probability subdivision 116

6.6   Workbench in use, showing the main Workbench window and   121
        two pop-up windows

6.7   Example of operating the Autoprogramming Calculator for   126
        various values of x

6.8   Using Basil to align a set of boxes   130

6.9   Tools attempted in sorting by height   134

7.1   The Hayes and Flowers model for the writing process, with the 153
        addition of text production and capture processes

7.2   Model of expert transcription typing in flow chart form   155

7.3   Flow model of transcription typing by dyslexic subject   157

7.4   Partial flow model of K's use of the DragonDictate speech   159
        recognizer for transcription

7.5   Flow model of collaborative transcription in which K dictated 162
        text to a human transcriber

7.6   Postulated flow model of K's use of the DragonDictate speech 164
        recognizer

8.1   The human vocal tract   171

8.2   Two-dimensional tongue position grid   173

8.3   The experimental setup   175

8.4	Target curves	176
8.5	Tracker space to device space	177
8.6	Mapping to a target surface	177
8.7	From surface to two signals	179
9.1	Examples of six-dot and eight-dot braille	184
9.2	The representation of digits in European and American braille	185
9.3	A single spring-loaded electromagnetic braille pin	188
9.4	Design of DeWulf's Braille Mouse	189
9.5	Elements of an eight-dot braille display	191
9.6	Filtering output and duplicating it	194
9.7	A two-line braille display with routing keys	196
9.8	Snapshot of Word 5.0 with graphical elements	198
10.1	A typical graphical user interface	203
11.1	The Soundtrack screen layout, a grid of auditory windows	222
11.2	The Soundtrack auditory File menu	223
11.3	The two-dimensional layout of targets	228
11.4	Targets laid out as a one-dimensional menu	228
11.5	A typical line graph	240
12.1	Design characteristics of the Set hardware/software configuration	251
12.2	Systems approach to the iterative design of Set	253
13.1	Diagram of the basic EWCI concept	264
13.2	State diagram of the FSA for a user with control of a single eyelid	268
13.3	One level of the simulation software	270

13.4   What an icon screen might look like for a typical set of   274
       peripherals linked to the computer for control

13.5   Second level interaction   275

17.1   Schematic diagram of the proposed selection system   320

Tables

2.1   Persons with moderate physical disabilities have difficulty using   36
       input devices and controls

2.2   Some people with severe physical disabilities cannot use   37
       standard input devices

2.3   Some people with visual impairments cannot see lettering and   38
       symbols on keyboard, equipment, or screen because it is too
       small or has low contrast

2.4   Some people are blind and cannot use standard visually based   39
       output and input devices and indicators

2.5   Some people with hearing disabilities cannot hear auditory   40
       output at normal volume levels or at all

2.6   Some people with seizure disorders are sensitive to certain   40
       flicker frequencies which can cause them to go into seizure

2.7   Some design features or changes would greatly reduce the cost   41
       or difficulty third-party manufacturers and agencies encounter in
       developing special access devices and materials

6.1   Summary of five predictive interfaces   106

6.2   Retrieval and update algorithms for assigning probabilities   118

7.1   Typical rates for producing text by a dyslexic and a non-dyslexic   149
       in three activities using four methods for capturing text

10.1   Characteristics of real rooms   211

10.2   Comparing real rooms and Audio Rooms   214

11.1   Target location speeds for auditory location under different   227
       conditions

11.2   Comparison of the two speech and nonspeech targeting speeds   229

11.3   Results of the UnMouse experiments   233

12.1 Conferencing technology 247

12.2 Preliminary taxonomy of information tasks and task activities 256
performed in electronic offices

12.3 Communication media appropriate for group work 257

13.1 FSA state transition matrix for Figure 13.2 269

17.1 Description of subject sample 325

17.2 Action categories and associated descriptors 326

17.3 Action categories and attribute levels for the reach subtests 327

17.4 Multiple regression equation for each input device 331

17.5 Distribution of scores for the disabled subject sample for the 333
tablet relevant subtests

17.6 Distribution of scores for the disabled subject sample for the 333
tablet relevant subtests

17.7 Summary of decision guidelines 335

17.8 Pearson Product Moment correlation coefficients of actual 337
performance versus predicted performance, using regression
equations

17.9 Pearson Product Moment correlation coefficients of actual 338
performance versus predicted performance, using estimated
weights

Preface

This book is a product of the growing realization that the discipline of human–computer interaction (HCI) must broaden its horizons to encompass all potential computer users, including those who have conditions which would generally be labeled as *disabilities*. (This thesis is expounded much more fully and eloquently in Chapter 1.) Once that fact is recognized, it is clear that a gap exists in that there are no books covering this aspect of HCI. Thus I set about identifying authors with the expertise to write such a book. As many of them as possible were gathered together at two workshops, one held in York, England, and the other held as part of ACM's (Association for Computing Machinery) Chi conference in New Orleans.

As Bob and Beverly Williges point out in Chapter 12, computers manipulate information, and information is essentially of the mind and can be processed by people regardless of physical or sensory limitations. Another interesting opportunity is that computers can be used as prostheses to help people who have cognitive disabilities to manipulate information. This aspect is also part of Elkind and Shrager's work in Chapter 7. So, for as long as the personal computer has been in existence, people have realized its potential as a prosthesis to ameliorate the handicapping effects of some people's disabilities. However, most of this work has been carried out by individuals working in isolation, often literally working in their garages. The common scenario is that a person with an interest in computers has met an individual with a disability and seen the potential for putting the computer to good use. He or she has then produced some aid and supplied it to that person and that is the end of the story. The experience has not been shared with anyone else – for example by publishing. The workshops and this book are an attempt to redress that situation. They are an opportunity to bring people working in this field together – under the auspices of the HCI establishment.

Whom is this book about?

The writer of any book on technology faces the problem of volatile material; the book can soon appear dated by the technology it describes. However, the writers of this book also face another and similar hazard in that the term used to describe the subject user group also changes as a matter of fashion. At the time this book was written, in the early 1990s, there was a movement advocating "political correctness" in language. The aims of those who advocate this approach to language are laudable. They wish to reduce the negative associations of conditions – such as those classed as disabilities – by defining new positive terms to describe them.

What is really required is a change in attitude and not just a change of language. For instance, if being blind were not considered by most (sighted) people to be a wholly negative condition, but rather a *state* – with advantages and disadvantages – then people would be less likely to object to being so described. If a person is willing to be described as *blind,* others will understand fairly precisely what is meant, which is not true if the term "visually inconvenienced" is used.

The problem with using "politically correct" language is that one rapidly descends into euphemism.[1] When a new term is introduced, many people will not understand it, and as they learn its meaning, it will have to be replaced. In this way a cycle is created which is hard to break.

Of course, language is powerful and must be used with care. For instance, to say that someone *suffers* from a hearing loss is rather more value laden than simply saying that the person has a hearing loss. While any kind of labeling can be counterproductive, inappropriate descriptions can be dangerously misleading or simply offensive. At the same time, language is constantly changing, so that the word "cripple" was once considered a precise medical term but is now considered inaccurate and offensive. So it is that now terms such as "physically disabled" are considered inappropriate by some people, who prefer descriptions such as "physically challenged." In this book we have tried to avoid any obviously offensive language; we take care to remember that we are talking about people, hence "disabled people" and not "the disabled." Furthermore the English language differs on the two sides of the Atlantic, no less in this field than in most. Thus, "visual impairment" refers to what Britons understand to be "partial sight." I hope that no one will be unduly perturbed by any of the language we use. If they are, I apologize.

Whom is this book for?

It is traditional for authors and publishers to suggest that any given book is suitable for the widest possible audience, so it would be no surprise if at this point I suggested that this volume should be read by *anyone* who is involved in human–computer interaction. However, in this case I really believe this to be true. As described in several places in the book, a significant proportion of the population have some form of disability. Whenever anyone designs a piece of information technology, there is therefore a high probability that people with disabilities will want or need to access that technology. In general it is the decisions designers make when they are *not* thinking about the needs of disabled

---

[1] This point was best described by David Lunney in an electronic discussion on the Internet.

people which have the greatest effect on them.[1] So even if you do not envisage ever designing a system to be used specifically by people with identifiable disabilities, reading this book may make you a little more conscious of the effects design decisions you make may have on that group of users.

To be more specific, the main audience for this book is intended to be human–computer interface designers who have recognized the need to be aware of the needs of exceptional users when they develop interfaces. This may result, for instance, from their need to comply with legislation, so that interfaces which they would at one time have developed purely for mainstream users must now also accommodate those with special needs.

Chapter 1 gives a broad introduction to the interaction between HCI development and the accommodation of users with extra-ordinary needs and sets out the broad philosophy of the book. Chapter 2 fills in some background on the nature of the disabilities to be accommodated and how current technology can address these needs. Current technology is also described in case studies in Chapters 3 and 4, but the technology is developing rapidly, so the main focus of the book is on current research, which can be expected to be the basis of tomorrow's adaptations.

Writing

This book has an international authorship. Although the editor is British, most of the authors are North American. It was therefore agreed that spelling and grammar conventions followed on the western side of the Atlantic would be followed in the text. Any remaining errors are not the authors' but are due to the editor's lack of fluency in American.

The conventional rules for using capital letters (proper nouns, at the start of sentences, etc.) have been applied. Many new words in computer science are acronyms, and the convention is that the letters of an acronym should all be capitalized. However, if the word formed is pronounceable, there seems no good reason why it should be SHOUTED at the reader merely because of its etymology. Once a word has passed into the language, there no longer seems this urge, so that many people are probably (rightly) unaware of the origin of words like "radar" (<u>ra</u>dio <u>d</u>etection <u>a</u>nd <u>r</u>anging) and "laser" (<u>l</u>ight <u>a</u>mplification by <u>s</u>timulated <u>e</u>mission of <u>r</u>adiation). In this book, therefore, the editor has applied the normal rules of capitalization if an acronym is pronounceable but has used small capitals for trademarked acronyms (e.g. DOS). Only if an acronym is not normally pronounced as a word, but spelled (e.g. HCI) is it capitalized.

---

[1]   This fact was first pointed out to me by Eddis Bevan.

Acknowledgments

The Chi workshop, on which much of this book is based, was organized with the invaluable assistance of Susan Brummel and Gregg Vanderheiden. Bill Buxton provided very helpful comments on a draft of the manuscript.

A.D.N.E.

Contributors

John L. Arnott
Microcomputer Center
Dundee University
Dundee
Scotland
DD1 4HN

Paul Blenkhorn
Department of Computation
University of Manchester Institute
of Science and Technology
PO Box 88
Manchester
England
M60 1QD

Steve A. Brewster
Department of Computing Science,
University of Glasgow
Glasgow
Scotland
G12 8Q

Alistair Y. Cairns
Microcomputer Center
Dundee University
Dundee
Scotland
DD1 4HN

Sherry Perdue Casali
Management Systems Laboratories
Industrial and Systems Engineering
Department
Virginia Tech
Blacksburg VA
USA
24060

Norman Coombs
Department of History
Rochester Institute of Technology
One Lomb Memorial Drive
Rochester NY
USA
14623

John J. Darragh
Department of Computer Science
University of Calgary
Calgary, Alberta
Canada
T2N 1N4

Alistair D. N. Edwards
Department of Computer Science
University of York
York,
England
YO1 5DD

W. Keith Edwards
Multimedia Computing Group
College of Computing
Georgia Institute of Technology
Atlanta GA
USA
30332-0280

Jerome Elkind
Lexia Institute
2040 Tasso Street
Palo Alto CA
USA
94301

Saul Greenberg
Department of Computer Science
University of Calgary
Calgary, Alberta
Canada
T2N 1N4

Peter Gregor
Microcomputer Center
Dundee University
Dundee
Scotland
DD1 4HN

Rex Hancock
KGDO, Room 2022
General Services Administration
18th & F Streets NW
Washington DC
USA
20405

Kate Howey
Husat Research Institute
Loughborough University of
Technology
The Elms, Elm Grove
Loughborough, Leicestershire
England
LE11 1RG

Anne Loomis
1221 Montmorency Drive
San José CA
USA
95118

David Maulsby
Department of Computer Science
University of Calgary
Calgary, Alberta
Canada
T2N 1N4

Elizabeth D. Mynatt
Multimedia Computing Group
College of Computing
Georgia Institute of Technology
Atlanta GA
USA
30332-0280

Alan F. Newell
Microcomputer Center
Dundee University
Dundee
Scotland
DD1 4HN

Randy Pausch
University of Virginia
Thornton Hall
Charlottesville VA
USA
22903

Ian J. Pitt
Department of Computer Science
University of York
York,
England
YO1 5DD

Ian W. Ricketts
Microcomputer Center
Dundee University
Dundee
Scotland
DD1 4HN

Robin Shaw
11483 Hessler Road #1
Cleveland OH
USA
44106

Jeff Shrager
Xerox Parc
3333 Coyote Hill Drive
Palo Alto CA
USA
94304

Robert D. Stevens
Department of Computer Science
University of York
York,
England
YO1 5DD

Gary W. Strong
College of Information Studies
Drexel University
Philadelphia PA
USA
19104

Harold Thimbleby
Department of Computing Science
Middlesex University
Bounds Green Road
London
England
N11 2NQ

Gerhard Weber
Institut für Informatik
Universität Stuttgart
Breitwiesenstrasse 20-22
Stuttgart 80
Germany
D-7000

Ronald D. Williams
University of Virginia
Thornton Hall
Charlottesville VA
USA
22903

Beverly H. Williges
Department of Industrial and
Systems Engineering
302 Whitemore Hall
Virginia Tech
Blacksburg VA
USA
24061-0118

Bob Williges
Department of Industrial and
Systems Engineering
302 Whitemore Hall
Virginia Tech
Blacksburg VA
USA
24061-0118

Ian H. Witten
Department of Computer Science
University of Calgary
Calgary, Alberta
Canada
T2N 1N4

Trademarks

Many of the designations used by manufacturers and sellers to distinguish their products are claimed as trademarks. The editor and authors have made every attempt to supply trademark information about manufacturers and products mentioned in this book. All trademarks are acknowledged and include, but are not limited to:

Apple, Macintosh, Finder and SonicFinder are registered trademarks and HyperCard is a trademark of Apple Computer Inc.

CP/M is a trademark of Digital Research Inc.

Dataglove is a registered trademark of VPL Inc.

Dectalk is a registered trademark of Digital Equipment Corporation.

DragonDictate is a registered trademark of Dragon Systems, Inc.

IBM and Personal System/2 are registered trademarks of International Business Machines Corporation.

Looking Glass is a trademark of Visix Software Inc.

Lotus 1-2-3 is a trademark of Lotus Development Corporation.

Microsoft and MS-DOS are registered trademarks and Windows is a trademark of Microsoft Corporation.

Outspoken is a trademark of Berkeley Systems, Inc.

Pal, PalStar and Speller are trademarks of Lander Software.

Polhemus is a registered trademark of Polhemus Navigation Sciences.

PowerGlove is a trademark of Mattel Toys.

Power Rolls Arrow is a registered trademark of Invacare Corporation.

Private Eye is a trademark of Reflection Technology Inc.

Touch Talker is a registered trademark of the Prentke Romich Company.

Unix is a registered trademark of AT&T.

UnMouse is a trademark of MicroTouch Systems Inc.

Vax is a trademark of Digital Equipment Corporation.

Visual User Environment is a trademark of Hewlett-Packard Corporation.

Wordstar is a trademark of MicroPro International Corporation.

X Window System is a trademark of the Massachusetts Institute of Technology.

Introductions

This section is an introduction to the field, both to the needs of users with disabilities and to the approaches which can be made to meeting those needs. In Chapter 1 Alan Newell sets the theme of the whole book. He has a long history of designing interfaces for users with a wide range of abilities and disabilities, as described in Chapter 5. There is no point in attempting to summarize Chapter 1; it is essential for all readers. Chapter 2 summarizes the current state of the field. The nature of the disabilities addressed is described, as are current interface adaptations. This chapter will be most useful for HCI practitioners who are newly aware of the need to accommodate users with special needs.

1

Extra-ordinary human–computer interaction

Alan F. Newell

HCI and "average users"

The concept of extra-ordinary human–computer interaction highlights the links between two research and development fields – mainstream human–computer interface studies and the design of computer based systems for disabled people. Although they share similar problems, these fields have traditionally been seen to have very little in common. In the great majority of cases, human–computer interface research seems to assume that "the user" will be an ordinary person with average abilities. Researchers often use a single model of the user, with little or no attempt being made to specify the actual characteristics of this user. In some cases, the user population is divided into simple groups such as "novice" and "expert." but the two groups are often seen to be very homogeneous within themselves. At its worst, the human interface to some software applications gives the impression that the designer's model of the user was a 25-year-old male with a doctorate in computer science who is besotted with technology and is more interested in playing with a computer than in completing a useful job of work!

Although the situation is changing, very little HCI research fully takes into account the individual differences among potential users of software and the vast range of abilities of human beings in general. Bespoke tailors are well aware of the "average person" myth (Grandgean, 1982); their customers come in a range of sizes and with a vast range of preferences. The clothing analogy of some software houses would be for a gents' outfitter to stock only suits which would fit a six-foot man with a 42" chest who clearly wanted to be a pop star (a range of 256 different fastenings would be available but the cus-

CLOTHES BY SOFTWARE SUPPLIES P L C

tomer may have great trouble finding out how to specify which one he wanted!) In addition to physical "fit," however, software needs to match the sensory and cognitive abilities of users. A great deal of HCI research is expended in determining the "user's model of the system" but very little in how to cope with the range of sensory and mental abilities of potential users, to say nothing of their varied cultural backgrounds.

Designing systems for those people who exhibit significantly lower than average abilities has traditionally been the remit of rehabilitation engineers. They have developed many computer access systems for disabled people. However, there has been very little communication between this group of human interface designers and those who consider themselves to be in the mainstream of the field. With very few exceptions, they read different books, attend different conferences, and market their designs via different manufacturers, who often operate within very different market structures (e.g. the British National Health Service and private purchasing versus defense procurement and business purchasing). Rehabilitation engineers tend to be committed to their user population, concentrating on their needs without considering the wider ramifications of their work. In contrast, many HCI designers see serving disabled users as a fringe activity of a charitable rather than professional nature. The purpose of this book is to show that these distinctions are false and to build bridges between the communities who work in the two fields. The contributors to the book believe that if such bridges can be built, both fields will benefit enormously.

Although we believe that such links will be mutually beneficial, this book concentrates particularly on benefits which could accrue to mainstream HCI research and development from a consideration of the needs of disabled people.

Lack of interest in the design of systems for disabled people

Addressing the needs of people with disabilities has not been a very prominent part of mainstream HCI research to date. For example, in *HCI '86* and *'87* in the UK there were no papers which were specifically concerned with interfaces for disabled people. In the same years, the American Chi conferences were a little better. Chi '86 did include a panel discussion called "Human Interface Design and the Handicapped User," and Chi '87 had a single session of three papers of applications for disabled users plus two or three other papers on issues relevant to the needs of this population. In subsequent conferences on both sides of the Atlantic, however, attention to the needs of the disabled user has stayed at a very low level.

There is a view that this field addresses only small, unprofitable markets, and this may imply the need for low-cost intellectually and technologically trivial solutions. This can lead to a belief that research in this area contains little or no intellectual challenge. When this is contrasted with the sexy "high-tech" image of leading-edge HCI research, it is not altogether surprising that engineers have not shown great interest in this area of activity.

The reason may, however, have more to do with lack of information than lack of interest. At Interchi '93 I addressed these issues (Newell, 1993), and the delegates' response was very positive. It is thus probable that the reason for apparent lack of interest is a lack of information and awareness of the actual characteristics and requirements of the field. I hope this book will go some way to correct this.

A personal journey

A realization of the value of links between these two fields grew from my own history. I have worked both in mainstream HCI and in the design of systems for disabled people and have discovered from personal experience the parallels between the two fields and the opportunities they present. In the early part of my career, I worked in automatic speech recognition research (Newell, 1968) but then became more interested in problems presented by disabled people. I started by examining the potential of this technology to assist physically disabled people (Newell & Nabavi, 1969), and this led me into developing communication systems for those with speech and hearing impairments (Newell, 1974, 1977) and the development of television subtitling (Newell & Hutt, 1978) and speech transcription systems for deaf people (Downton & Newell, 1979). Both these systems – the subtitling system being used by Independent Television and the transcription system being installed in the British House of Commons to be used by the deaf member of parliament, Jack Ashley (Newell, 1978) – proved successful.

It was significant, however, that the early work which I and others had been doing to transmit "closed" subtitles (i.e. those which could be seen only if the set was specially tuned) predated, and utilized the same technology as, the teletext services which are now provided for users of all abilities. In the same way, the speech transcription system which we developed specifically to enable a deaf person to read what was being said on a screen, formed the basis of a very successful verbatim transcription system which is now being used in many law courts and other reporting situations in the UK (Newell, 1988a). Thus, in contrast to the situation where disabled people have benefited from developments designed for the able-bodied, these were cases of able-bodied people benefiting from developments designed, at least initially, specifically for disabled people. These experiences led me to write two papers, "Communicating by Speech: The Able-Bodied and the Disabled" (1986a), and "Speech Communication Technology – Lessons from the Disabled" (1986b). The response to these papers led me to a more wide-ranging investigation of this idea and to the position paper for the Department of Trade and Industry entitled "A Strategy for Co-ordinated Research into Ordinary and Extra-Ordinary Human–Computer Interaction"

(1988b). (See also Newell, 1985 and Newell & Cairns, 1987, as well as Chapter 5 of this volume.)

In these publications I claimed that coordination of research between these two fields would produce:

- Better HCI design practice, and thus
- better HCI for everyone

as well as

- more research which examines the needs of all human users, and
- a greater market share for those manufacturers of human interfaces and computer systems who accept this message.

In addition, I commented that it is often more difficult to design good human interfaces for extra-ordinary people than for ordinary ones, and made the point that research work in this field is:

- challenging and exciting,

as well as

- worthwhile.

This book tries to justify these claims. It also contains descriptions of a range of research and development projects into systems for disabled people so that human–computer interface engineers can see for themselves practical examples of such techniques and can assess where they can be usefully applied in their own work.

Lessons from a consideration of people with special needs

There is a tendency for system designers to see themselves or their immediate colleagues as archetypes of the system user. A significant number of research studies give the impression that subjects were chosen on the basis of being administratively easy to organize rather than being representative of the true user populations. These faults are understandable: It is very easy to assume that the human race (with the exception of one's enemies) is relatively homogeneous and similar to oneself, and to design systems accordingly.

The HCI research worker, who should know better, can often give the impression that he or she is concerned with a single well-defined group whose only differentiation is on the naive–expert axis (e.g. Potosnak, 1986). If able-bodied engineers are asked to design a system for "the disabled," however, it is very clear to them that the users have characteristics different from their own. In fact this can be such a powerful tendency that it produces an exaggerated view of the differences, which can lead to significant design faults. Domestic equipment designed for disabled people can be so ugly that it is quite inappropriate to locate it within a home, and many communication systems for people without speech seem to have been designed on the assumption that disabled people are always polite, are never angry, and have bowel and food fetishes (Newell, 1984).

Having those with disabilities as a user group highlights the importance of individual differences in users. It is very clear to the design engineers that they need to study the important characteristics of their users before and during the design of their equipment, and that the equipment should be evaluated by representatives of the intended users. In addition, it can often be very difficult for a disabled user, particularly a severely disabled one, to achieve very much despite the provision of very efficient interfaces. In terms of system design, this leads to giving very detailed consideration to the real needs and wants of the user, how they differ from the expectations of the designer, and whether and how these vary among the various potential users of the proposed equipment. Such a design methodology should be standard practice for human–computer interface engineers, but it often seems to be neglected.

Everyone has ordinary and extra-ordinary abilities

There is a basic fallacy in discussing the user population in terms of two groups of people – those with disabilities and those without. First, this conceals the wide range of abilities within both groups. The sign for disabled people is a stick figure in a wheelchair. This is often taken as the model of disability, and it can lead to the belief that the needs of all disabled people can be met simply by providing wheelchair access. This completely ignores all sensory and cognitive disabilities as well as the many physical disabilities which can be more handicapping than being confined to a wheelchair. This classification also implies that disability is a very simple binary division: You are either confined to a wheelchair or you are not. But wheelchair users are a group with as large a range of physical, sensory, and cognitive abilities as other groups. They share only one characteristic – a mobility impairment which can be partially alleviated by the use of a wheelchair.

Common sense and observation show us that every human being has a set of abilities and characteristics, some of which can be described as "ordinary" and some which are very obviously extra-ordinary. A very substantial number of people have visual impairments; many, particularly the elderly, have hearing impairments; some are significantly weaker physically than others; some have less control of their limbs: any single human being has a range of cognitive abilities in processing, memory, and recall of different types of data and in expressive and receptive language capabilities, as well as in having different sexual, cultural, political, and emotional characteristics. It is rare for human interface design to consider these dimensions and the interaction among them, but they can all affect the usefulness of human interfaces to computers.

Extra-ordinary needs are only exaggerated ordinary needs

It is important to note that, in most cases, needs and abilities which society would consider extra-ordinary are not different in quality from ordinary ones; they are simply an exaggeration, a different point on the continuum of human ability. Those who are categorised as disabled simply have some functionalities which differ from the average (often by a fairly arbitrary amount).

This is obvious with physical disability. It is rare for people to have no motor control; some simply have significantly less motor control. This is also the case with cognitive dysfunction. A mentally handicapped person has lower abilities, not no abilities. A person who has aphasia following a stroke cannot remember the names of objects, but most human beings exhibit mild symptoms of this nature, particularly under stress. The myth of there being two distinct and homogeneous groups does not greatly affect those working for disabled people. They are usually well aware that their user group has very wide variations. It can, however, lead to mainstream HCI researchers having too narrow a view of their user population. Shneiderman (1986) commented that "we should be aware of subtle design decisions that make usage more difficult for people with physical and mental difficulties and for individuals from different cultures and not create a situation where the disadvantaged become more disadvantaged." Unfortunately, this is exactly what has happened with the introduction of graphical user interfaces (GUIs), which are usually much less accessible to blind users than orthographic interfaces.

People are handicapped by their environments

There is a continuum between the ordinary and the extra-ordinary, but again the situation is more complex than this statement implies. The capabilities of a human are not static: they change with time – accidents can cause temporary or permanent dysfunction; disease and age produce substantial changes. Also a particular person's capabilities are specified to a substantial degree by the environment within which he or she has to operate. It is often said that disabled people are handicapped by their environments and not by their lack of abilities, but this is true of everyone. Thus, for example,

- smoke or inadequate illumination will produce effects similar to visual impairment,
- noise can have the same effect as deafness,

- mobility impairment can be caused by inhospitable ground,
- extremes of temperature and safety suits can cause tactile insensitivity and motoric dysfunction, and
- fatigue and stress can cause reductions in cognitive abilities.

An extreme case is that of a soldier on the battlefield (King, 1986). He or she can be blinded by smoke, be deafened by gunfire, be mobility impaired by being up to the waist in mud, have poor tactile sensitivity and dexterity because of wearing a chemical warfare suit, and be cognitively impaired because of being scared stiff of being killed – and this is before the soldier is wounded! If one were to measure the effective abilities of a person in such an environment, they would be poor enough over a number of dimensions for him or her to be classified as severely disabled in a more normal environment. The case of the soldier is a particularly clear demonstration of the similarities between an ordinary person in an extra-ordinary environment and an extra-ordinary person in an ordinary environment, but similar parallels exists in a less extreme form in a range of nonmilitary situations.

Bandwidth limitations

A further parallel between the HCI problems of able-bodied and disabled people concerns people who have to operate in high workload environments. Again the military situation is an extreme case of this. The pilot of a combat aircraft may not have sufficient sensory ability to receive all the information which is bombarding him or her from the cockpit instruments and the view from the window. Equally he or she may not have the physical ability (or enough hands) to provide sufficient control signals to the aircraft to cope adequately with the situation. That is, the input and output bandwidths available to him or her, as a very fit human being at the peak of performance are not sufficient for the task he or she is trying to accomplish. And available bandwidth can be further reduced through temporary dysfunction of either the pilot or the instruments or environmental factors, as mentioned earlier (e.g. g forces).

Physically disabled people, who can strike keys only very slowly are inefficient operators of a word processor and cannot perform many tasks effectively because of this speed restriction. Their input bandwidth is much less than is required for the efficient production of a letter. If they are also visually impaired or blind, they may have to use large fonts or a braille display, but these provide a very much lower bandwidth for receiving information than is necessary for efficient use of normal word processing software. Thus the disabled operator of a word processor is in a similar position to the pilot of an aircraft – the differences in the two situations are the amount of bandwidth available and the complexity of the tasks (Peddie, Filz, Cairns, Arnott, & Newell 1990).

Spin-off from research into human interfaces for the disabled – Parallels with medical science

There are thus significant parallels between ordinary and extra-ordinary HCI, but much can also be learned from research paradigms used in the latter field. A significant part of HCI research consists of examining the interaction of the person with the machine in an attempt to understand what is happening. This is often a very complex situation and can provide a very challenging task for researchers. One of the paradigms used by medical science to increase our understanding of the human being is the examination of extreme cases, including cases where there is significant dysfunction. This has provided a great deal of useful information, for example in anatomy and also in the understanding of cognitive processes, where research into aphasia has provided the backbone of knowledge in this field.

The paradigm of learning from extreme cases also has a place in HCI research: An examination of those situations where the human side of the interface is not functioning correctly can be very beneficial in understanding the complex processes involved in many human–computer interactions. Consideration of the needs of extra-ordinary users can be a spur to good interface design. Most ordinary users perform reasonably well with notably suboptimum interfaces, and the effects of poor design become obvious only in situations of fatigue or other extreme conditions. Thus able-bodied users, particularly well-motivated ones, often provide little challenge to the interface designer. In contrast, a disabled user can present very difficult problems which can stimulate the designer to develop new and more effective interfaces .

Where designers have produced novel interfaces, there is evidence that they do not seem to be aware of, and thus do not benefit from, work which is reported in the rehabilitation literature. For example, Pearson and Weisser (1986) reported on the design and assessment of a foot-operated mouse with no reference to the many foot-operated systems which have been used by physically disabled people for many years. Similarly, Jakabossin (1986) described an autocompletion system for text with no reference to the many systems which had predated his work but were designed for disabled people (e.g. Foulds, Baletsa, & Crochetiere, 1975; Heckathorne & Childress, 1983; Swiffin, Pickering, Arnott, & Newell, 1985; Vanderheiden, 1984). Using disabled people to evaluate interfaces can also highlight problems which would not have been noticed with only able-bodied subjects. A simple example of this was reported by Kippenberg (1987) in a study of the use of kitchen equipment by disabled people. Subsequent to ascertaining that users could not open a refrigerator door, it was discovered that even people of average strength could not open the door in the way the designer intended!

Historical examples of knowledge from the study of extremes

Mention has already been made that work on television subtitles and speech transcription systems for the deaf has led to benefits for able-bodied people. There are, however, many other instances where the design of equipment for disabled people has led to substantial improvements in the design of systems for the whole population. A number of interesting examples were reported to me during my survey for the Department of Trade and Industry (Newell, 1988b).

It is well known that Alexander Graham Bell's original research was investigating how to assist deaf people. It is somewhat ironic that his invention of the telephone, which must have benefited from this work, served to increase the social isolation of the deaf. There are also many examples of how technology originally designed specifically to assist disabled people became widely used. Examples of such mass market products include long playing records, multitrack tape recorders, and even the now ubiquitous cassette tape recorder (Sanders, 1987); all of these were designed originally to provide talking books for blind people. Although it is impossible to say whether such an invention would have been made without the impetus from users who clearly could not cope with threading reel-to-reel tapes, it is interesting to note that many experts claimed that they would never be popular, as they would always produce lower audio quality than reel-to-reel systems.

Other products which were originally designed in response to the needs of a group of people with particular disabilities include the carpenter's miter block (McTyre, 1987), the ballpoint pen, remote control on television sets, water beds (Foulds, 1987), the Kurzweil reading machine, and the transmission of control signals for domestic equipment via the mains (Shipley, 1987). It has also been claimed that the first typewriter was invented for a blind countess. Other areas of activity where research focusing on the design of systems for disabled people has had a significant impact include speech pattern presentation (Fourcin, 1987), collision avoidance techniques for robots (Jackson, 1987), head-up displays (Shipley, 1987), and low bit rate television transmission techniques (Downton, 1987). The first reported work on the introduction of emotion into synthetic speech was as part of a research project developing systems for nonspeaking people (Murray, Arnott, & Newell, 1988).

For the future, work on the communication problems of aphasic people and those with severe language disorders (Lessor & Milroy, 1987) have clear implications for human interface research particularly for non-native speakers or high cognitive load and/or high stress environments (Enderby 1987; Steele, 1987). The data from studies of pathological conditions by speech therapists and research into teaching strategies for those with special learning difficulties can tell us a great deal about effective reading and naming strategies, appropriate sentence and dialogue structures, and turn-taking rules which facilitate communication (Alm, Arnott, & Newell, 1989), plus strategies which inhibit and destroy communication ability (Kraat, 1985).

Researchers in communication systems for people without speech have been using symbol systems for many years (McNaughton, 1980; Baker, 1982), and the experience of the use of these systems should provide valuable data and insights into iconic interaction with computers. Research into writing systems for children with specific learning difficulties could be valuable for interfaces for illiterate users, dyslexics, or others with poor literacy skills (Newell & Booth, 1991, Elkind & Shrager, this volume).

The economic case for HCI research for disabled people

This introduction has concentrated on the value to able-bodied people of a consideration of the needs of those with disabilities. However, we should not forget the actual needs of disabled people, nor their economic impact. It should not be necessary to comment that developing equipment for disabled people is a socially worthwhile activity in its own right. The provision of usable equipment can make enormous differences to educational opportunities, quality of life, and employment possibilities for people with disabilities. Information technology can provide for the absolutely basic communication needs of people who cannot write or speak, and, where there is cognitive and language dysfunction, even greater advances are possible from properly researched technology

It is always assumed that disabled people represent a tiny minority, but this is far from true. Depending on the definition, it is estimated that between 10 and 20 percent of the population have significant disabilities, and there are trends which will cause this sector to become more important. Sandhu and Wood (1990) give demographic statistics on disability within the European Union. Demographic trends are leading to there being a higher proportion of elderly people: In 1987 there were 29 million persons over 65, of whom 14 percent were over 80, and this was the fastest growing sector of the population (Selreg, 1987). Both for the elderly and for other age groups, medical science is enabling those with more and more severe dysfunctions to survive, and to survive for longer periods. The notion of quality of life means that society is increasingly expecting medicine to do more than just keep these people alive. Current trends toward care in the community mean that such people will need and benefit from more technological support than would be the case if they were confined to institutions.

Increasingly, and particularly in the USA and the Scandinavian countries, the rights of people with disabilities are being enshrined in legislation (Vanderheiden, 1987a, 1987b), and this is leading to demands for technology to be accessible to everyone. The market is thus demanding interfaces which will cope with extremes of human conditions rather than those which have been acceptable in the past. Market pressure for systems to assist people with disabilities has been recognized in some sectors for many years. Hearing aids were the first massmarket use of many electronic and power source miniaturization techniques (Shipley, 1987), and the talking calculator for blind users was the first domestic product containing a speech synthesizer (Scholfield, 1987). In fact, one of the biggest markets for both speech synthesis and speech recognition systems to date has been as part of systems designed for use by disabled people (Newell, 1991).

Birthrate trends in some parts of the world could lead to a shortage of workers. This, together with the economic and political power of elderly and disabled people, will increase the demand for interfaces which are truly universal in being usable by almost everyone. Thus, not only is there a moral imperative for engineers to consider the needs of a wider range of people than has been the case in the past but there is also a solid commercial motive for producing equipment with a wider application. It is important to set these advances within an appropriate economic framework. Bliss (1987) commented that "rehabilitation engineering is too important to be left to charitable feeling alone, but is worthy of serious investment with expected returns." In discussing the employment potential of disabled people, he calculated that a particular piece of equipment which put a visually impaired person back to work gave a return on investment of 178 percent. Romich (1988) has also commented that markets for alternative communication systems for the speech impaired "have now reached a size that

can support the development of speech technology to serve their special needs."
Other obvious examples of potentially very cost-effective applications include
computer based systems which reduce the need for twenty-four-hour nursing care
of elderly people or the need for one-on-one teaching for children with special
educational needs.

Conclusions

The premises which lie behind this book are that

- most people have a mix of ordinary and extra-ordinary abilities;
- extra-ordinary needs are only exaggerated ordinary needs;
- ordinary people can be handicapped by their environments in the same way as disabled people are;
- taking into account extra-ordinary needs produces better and more widely useful design solutions for everyone; and
- demographic and other trends will increase the need for interfaces which can be operated by people with extra-ordinary abilities.

This book contains examples of interfaces and of interface research focused on
the needs of extra-ordinary people. We hope that this will show that this sort of
work:

- is central to good human–computer interface engineering;
- is scientifically and technically challenging;
- is exciting and worthwhile;
- is of substantial social value; and
- provides expanded and expanding markets for good human–computer interfaces.

We also hope that this book will lead to more human–computer interface engineers becoming interested in the needs of extra-ordinary people. Clearly there is also a need for designers of systems for disabled people to become more aware of mainstream HCI research, and we would encourage them to read and attend conferences in this important and expanding field. Such a coming together will lead to a symbiosis of ideas between mainstream research and the type of research which is reported in this book. In its turn this should produce:

Better interfaces for everyone and

Better design practice – together with

More research effort being concentrated on those people who have special needs.

References

Alm, N., Arnott, J. L., and Newell, A. F. (1989). Pragmatic issues in the design of a conversation prosthesis. *Journal of Medical Engineering and Technology, 13*(1–2): 10–12.

Baker, B. (1982, September). Minspeak. *Byte*: pp. 186–202.

Bliss, J. C. (1987). Rehabilitation technology – Past, present and future. *Proceedings of the 10th Annual Conference of the Rehabilitation Engineering Society of North America (Resna),* ed. R. D. Steele and W. Gerrey. Washington, DC: Resna Press.

Downton, A. C. (1987). Private communication, University of Essex, Colchester.

Downton, A. C., and Newell, A. F. (1979). An assessment of palantype transcription for the deaf. *International Journal of Man-Machine Studies, 11*: 667–680

Enderby, P. (1987). Private communication, Frenchey Hospital, Bristol.

Foulds, R. (1987). Private communication, Tufts University, Boston, MA.

Foulds, R. A., Baletsa, G., and Crochetiere, W. J. (1975). The effectiveness of language redundancy in non-verbal communication. In *Proceedings of the Conference on Devices and Systems for the Disabled* (pp. 82–86). Philadelphia, PA.

Fourcin, A. (1987). Private communication, University College, London.

Grandgean, E. (1982). *Fitting the task to the man*. London: Taylor and Francis.

Heckathorne, C. W., and Childress, D. (1983, June). Applying anticipatory text selection in a writing aid for people with severe motor impairment. *IEEE Micro*, pp. 17–23.

Jackson, R. D. (1987). Private communication, University of Cambridge.

Jakabossin, M. (1986). Autocompletion in full text transaction entry. In *Human Factors in Computer Systems: Proceedings of the ACM Conference Chi '86,* ed. M. Mantei and P. Orbeton (pp. 327–332). New York: ACM Press.

King, R. (1986). Private communication, Royal College of Military Science, Cranfield.

Kippenberg, A. H. M. von. (1987). Private communication, Instituut voor Revalidatie-Vraagstukken (IRV), Hoensbroeck, Netherlands.

Kraat, A. (1985). State of the art report – Communication between aided and natural speakers. *IPCAS Report (International Project on Communication Aids for the Speech Impaired)*. Toronto: Canadian Rehabilitation Council for the Disabled.

Lessor, R., and Milroy, L. (1987). Two frontiers in aphasia therapy. *Bulletin of the College of Speech Therapy*, 420: 1–4.

McNaughton, S. B. (1980). The application of Bliss symbolics. In *Non-speech language communication, analysis and intervention,* ed. R. L. Schiefelbusch (pp. 303–21). Baltimore, MD: University Press.

McTyre, J. H. (1987). Private communication, IBM, Boca Raton, FL.

Murray, I. R., Arnott, J. L., and Newell, A. F. (1988). Hamlet – Simulating emotion in synthetic speech. In *Proceedings of Speech '88: 7th FASE Symposium,* ed. W. A. Ainsworth and J. N. Holmes (pp. 1217–1223). Edinburgh: Institute of Acoustics.

Newell, A. F. (1968). Spectral analysis using a filter bank and PDP8 computer. In *Proceedings of IEE Colloquium, "Some Aspects of Speech Recognition for Man–Machine Communication "* (pp. 6/1–6/4).

Newell, A. F. (1974). The talking brooch: A communication aid. In *Aids for the severely handicapped,* ed. K. Copeland. London: Sector Publishing.

Newell, A. F. (1977). Communication aids for people with impaired speech and hearing. *Electronics and Power*, 23(10): 821–827.

Newell, A. F. (1978, May–June). The palantype transcription unit – Its history and progress to date. *Hearing*, pp. 99–104.

Newell, A. F. (1984). Do we know how to design communication aids? In *Proceedings of the International Conference on Rehabilitation Engineering*, ed. O. Z. Roy and R. Foulds (pp. 345–346). Bethesda, MD: Rehabilitation Engineering Society of North America.

Newell, A. F. (1985). Speech the natural modality for man-machine interaction? In *Proceedings of Interact '84,* ed. B. Shackel (pp. 231–238). Amsterdam: North Holland.

Newell, A. F. (1986a). Communicating via speech: The able-bodied and the disabled. In *Proceedings of the IEE International Conference on Speech Input/Output: Techniques and Applications* (pp. 1–8). IEE Conference Publication 258.

Newell, A. F. (1986b, September). Speech communication technology – Lessons from the disabled. *Electronics and Power* (pp. 661–664).

Newell, A. F. (1988a). An idea to the market place. *Industry and Higher Education*, 2(1): 25–28.

Newell, A. F. (1988b). *A strategy for co-ordinated research into ordinary and extra-ordinary human–computer interaction*. Position paper prepared for the Department of Trade and Industry.

Newell, A. F. (1991). Whither speech systems? In *Advances in speech, hearing and language processing*, ed. W. Ainsworth. London: JAI Press.

Newell, A. F. (1993, May). Chi for everyone. Keynote address, Interchi '93, Amsterdam.

Newell, A. F., and Booth, L. (1991). The use of lexical and spelling aids with dyslexics. In *Computers and literacy skills*, ed. C. Singleton (pp. 35–44). The British Dyslexia Association Computer Resource Center.

Newell, A. F., and Cairns, A. Y. (1987). Human interface studies and the handicapped. In *Proceedings of the British Computer Society Disabled Specialist Group Third Annual Conference*. London: BCS.

Newell, A. F., and Hutt, P. (1978). An optional TV subtitling service using Oracle. In *Proceedings of the International Broadcasting Convention* (pp. 308–311). London.

Newell, A. F., and Nabavi, D. D. (1969). Votem: The voice operated typewriter employing morse code. *Journal of Science Institute 2*(2): 655–657.

Pearson, G., and Weisser, M. (1986). Of moles and men – the design of foot controls for workstations. In *Human factors in computer systems: Proceedings of the ACM conference Chi '86,* ed. M. Mantei and P. Orbeton. New York: ACM Press.

Peddie, H., Filz, G., Cairns, A. Y., Arnott J. L., and Newell, A. F. (1990). Extra-ordinary computer–human operation (ECHO). In *Proceedings of 2nd Joint GAF/RAF/USAF Workshop on Human-Electronic Crew Teamwork "The Human-Electronic Crew: Is the Team Maturing?"* (pp. 5.1–5.8). Ingoldstadt, Germany.

Potosnak, K. (1986). Classifying users: A hard look at controversial issues. In *Human factors in computer systems: Proceedings of the ACM conference Chi '86,* ed. M. Mantei and P. Orbeton (pp. 84–88). New York: ACM Press.

Romich, B. A. (1988). Alternative communication: digital and synthetic speech in perspective in use and in the future. In *Soma: Proceedings of the American Speech–Language–Hearing Association Conference*, Mesa AZ.

Sanders, K. B. (1987). Private communication, Clarke and Smith, UK.

Sandhu, J. S., and Wood, T. (1990). *Demography and market sector analysis of people with special needs in thirteen European countries: A report on telecommunication usability issues.* EEC Race R1088 Tudor Report, Special Needs Research Unit, Newcastle-upon-Tyne Polytechnic.

Scholfield, J. (1987). Private communication, Scholfield Consultants, UK.

Selreg, A. (1987). Editorial. SOMA, *2*(3).

Shipley A. D. C. (1987). Private communication, UK Department of Health.

Shneiderman, B. (1986). 7 ± 2 central issues in HCI. In *Human factors in computer systems: Proceedings of the ACM conference Chi '86,* ed. M. Mantei and P. Orbeton. New York: ACM Press.

Steele, R. (1987). Private communication, Veterans' Administration Research Center, Palo Alto, CA.

Swiffin A. L, Pickering, J. A., Arnott, J. L., and Newell, A. F. (1985). Pal: an effort-efficient portable communication aid and keyboard emulator. In *Proceedings of the 8th Resna Conference,* ed. C. Brubaker (pp. 197–199). Washington, DC: Resna Press.

Vanderheiden G. C. (1984). High-efficiency flexible keyboard input acceleration technique. *Proceedings of the 2nd Annual Conference on Rehabilitation Engineering,* ed. O. Z. Roy and R. Foulds (pp. 353–354). Bethesda, MD: Resna.

Vanderheiden, G. C. (1987a). *Guidelines for the design of computers and information processing systems to increase their access by persons with disabilities.* Trace Center, University of Wisconsin.

Vanderheiden, G. C. (1987b). *White Paper: Access to standard computers, software and systems by persons with disabilities.* Trace Center, University of Wisconsin.

2

Computers and people with disabilities

Alistair D. N. Edwards

Disability

This chapter includes broad descriptions of the sorts of impairment which can be accommodated by adapted information technology. It should be read bearing in mind the caveats presented in the Preface regarding language and labeling. One objective of this chapter is to present a precise, correct, and hence understandable vocabulary, as used in the rest of the book. Another language problem is how to refer to this field. The discipline of *rehabilitation technology* is quite well established and is often broadened to include information technology as applied within the field. However, one should be aware that in some people's minds rehabilitation technology is concerned more with mechanical aids, such prostheses as artificial limbs, and the like.

According to the United Nations Declaration on the Rights of Disabled Persons, "The term 'disabled person' means any person unable to ensure by himself or herself, wholly or partly, the necessities of a normal individual and/or social life, as a result of a deficiency, either congenital or not, in his or her physical or mental capabilities" (UN, 1981). One has to ask to whom does that definition *not* apply; we all have physical and mental limitations – but the point is that some people have impairments of their faculties which severely affect their ability to take part in everyday life, and those people are usually referred to as being *disabled*.

The Americans with Disabilities Act (ADA) is a little more specific: A disability is "a physical or mental impairment which substantially limits one or more major life activities." The authors of the legislation were careful not to create a laundry list of conditions which were defined as being disabilities. There would have been obvious dangers in that approach: The wrong people might be included or excluded, and the Act could have been inflexible and not adaptable to changes in society and technology. Thus, while examples can be given as to what constitutes a "physical or mental impairment," a "substantial limitation," or a "major life activity," these terms can be interpreted in individual cases.

This law goes significantly farther though, in that it encompasses those "having a record of such impairment or being regarded as having such an impairment," "A record of such impairment" includes people who have had impairments in the past, such as back injuries or heart attacks. At the same time, such an existing record might be inaccurate: A person who has erroneously been recorded at some time as having a learning disability, for instance, is likely to be handicapped by that record. "Being regarded as having such an impairment" is also a broadening clause. It recognizes that a person may be limited not by his or her true level of ability but by others' *perceptions* of that level.

The terms "disability" and "handicap" are often used interchangeably, but it is generally useful to make the distinction that handicap refers to the degree to which a disability affects a person's life. As described by Zala Lusibu N'Kanza,

> A handicap is not simply the corollary of a disability, it is also in part imposed by society. Furthermore, the definition of a handicap varies according to a country's culture, traditions and level of development. In a rich country a blind person can, for example, obtain a complete education giving access to a profession, whereas in most developing countries he or she may not have access to education; such a person would be handicapped not only by a disability, he or she would have an additional handicap imposed by the social and economic conditions in his or her country. (UN, 1981)

The International Classification of Impairments, Disabilities and Handicaps (ICIDH) is an attempt to unify the terminology in a manner broadly in line with the definitions already given (World Health Organization, 1980; Martin, Meltzer, & Elliot, 1988). It distinguishes between *impairment, disability* and *handicap.* Impairment is "any loss or abnormality of psychological, physiological or anatomical structure or function." Thus it refers to parts or systems of the body that do not work. Disability is "any restriction or lack (resulting from an impairment) of ability to perform an activity in the manner or within the range considered normal for a human being." So disability refers to the things that people cannot do as a result of an impairment. Finally, a handicap is "a disadvantage for a given individual, resulting from an impairment or disability, that limits or prevents the fulfillment of a role (depending on age, sex and social and cultural factors) for that individual." Here the disability is put into the context of the environment. Martin, Meltzer, and Elliot (1988) illustrate the relationship between these concepts with examples:

Impairment		Disability		Handicap
Vision	⟶	Seeing	⟶	Orientation
Skeletal	⟶	Walking	⟶	Mobility
Cardio-respiratory	⟶	Walking	⟶	Mobility

It is important to be aware that despite projects such as ICIDH, this use of language is by no means universal. One should be aware that an author may use these terms in other (usually less precise) ways.

Use of labels can be unhelpful and negative; there is a temptation to talk of "the disabled" and "the able-bodied" as if they were two distinct and easily identifiable groups (indeed, the UN declaration mentions the concept of the "normal individual" and the ICIDH definition of disability uses the word "normal"), but that is quite unrealistic and can be counter-productive. Nevertheless, there are people for whom special accommodations must be made so that they can access modern information technology; in this sense, they are "extra-ordinary." To be more specific about the sorts of people and the accommodations required so that they may use a computer, see Tables 2.1–7.

As can be seen from the above discussion, although disability is something we talk about freely, on reflection it is very difficult to characterize with any precision. What most attempted definitions have in common is that a person who is classed as disabled has lost some degree of *independence*. In a society we are all dependent to a greater or lesser extent on other people. For instance, most of us rely on other people to grow our food for us, while other people depend on us for the fruits of our labor, whatever they may be. It is people who are dependent on others to perform everyday functions ("the necessities of a normal individual and/or social life," in the UN's definition) who are classed as being disabled. To a very large extent, the objective of the technologies we are discussing is to reduce that dependence, to give control back to the individual – or at least giving the person the opportunity to *choose* to be independent; choices for disabled people are often restricted.

Another argument against the use of language which implies a them-and-us approach to disability is that disability can occur to anyone and indeed *will* occur to most of us. Many disabilities are associated with aging. In the UK, around 5% of people aged 30 are classed as disabled. By age 60 the proportion rises to 30%, and over the age of 80 it is 70% (Eurostat, 1992). Furthermore, with advances in medicine, an increasing number of people are achieving an advanced age. Thus, in the West at least, an increasing proportion of the population in future will be disabled; furthermore, those people will generally have significant disposable income – and votes.

It is impossible to give definitive statistics for the incidence of disability internationally. Just as the terms are difficult to define, countries and cultures vary as to what they consider constitutes a disability. There are also various levels of collection of data. The figures given here should therefore be treated with some caution, especially in making comparisons across countries.

Disability and technology

There is a vast range of impairments which can amount to being disabilities and which require special accommodation to ensure access to information technology. They can be divided broadly into sensory, physical, and cognitive impairments. The definitions are often imprecise and the boundaries blurred; many people have a combination of conditions.

Sometimes the cause of an impairment is obvious (trauma caused by a road accident, for instance), but very often the etiology is not known. This is not a medical text, and the conditions which affect would-be computer users are not described in any detail here. Those requiring further details should consult the references.

A recurring distinction in this book is between the use of computer based technology as *prostheses* to alleviate the handicapping effects of disabilities and the adaptation of human–computer interfaces to make them accessible to users with disabilities for mainstream use in work, education, and leisure. Examples of prosthetic applications include the eye-wink controlled wheelchair presented in Chapter 13. A wheelchair is clearly a prosthesis; it gives mobility to someone who cannot walk. Similarly, the speech prostheses described in Chapters 3 and 5 substitute for speaking abilities. By contrast, the adaptations of computer interfaces for blind people discussed in Chapters 9, 10, and 11 enable such people to use computers for the same sorts of purposes for which their sighted peers would use them: word processing, spreadsheets, and so on.

The requirements of designing a prosthesis and an adaptation are rather different. For an adaptation one side of the interface (that between the adaptation and the application) is fixed. There are certain aspects of that interface which cannot be changed. This is what makes access for blind users to graphical user interfaces (Chapters 9, 10, and 11) so hard: There are some aspects of a GUI which are inherently visual and very difficult to present in a nonvisual manner (Edwards, 1991). This is illustrated, somewhat crudely, in Figure 2.1. Figure 2.1a shows an unadapted application. Its interface (represented by the semicircle) matches the intended user well. (Of course most computer users will agree that in reality the user and interface do not really fit quite as snugly as implied in this picture.) The problem for users with special needs is that they do not fit the standard interface, or, in terms of Figure 2.1c, they have a pointed interface which does not fit the rounded interface to the application.

What is required, therefore, is an intermediate interface or adaptation. On one side it interfaces to the user and on the other to the application, and ideally (as in Figure 2.1d) it should fit well on both sides. In practice such a perfect fit is impossible. So in Figure 2.1e some of the roundness of the original interface remains, making the interface between the adaptation and the user a less than perfect fit (Figures 2.1e and 2.1f), implying that users with special needs will find the interaction more difficult than they might – and more difficult than will users of the standard interface.

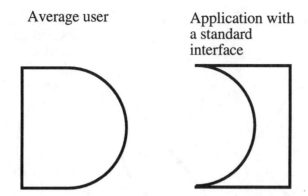

Figure 2.1a. This represents the ideal situation in which the intended user of the application is matched to its interface, as in Figure 2.1b, below.

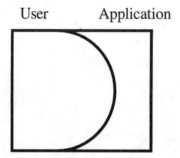

Figure 2.1b. The well matched user and application interface.

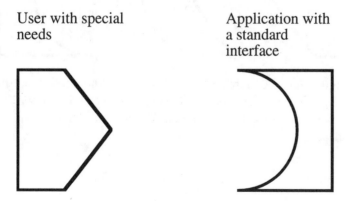

Figure 2.1c. Here there is a mismatch. The user does not "fit" the interface to the application – to the point that it is unusable.

Continued

User with special   Adaptation   Application with
needs   a standard
                                                     interface

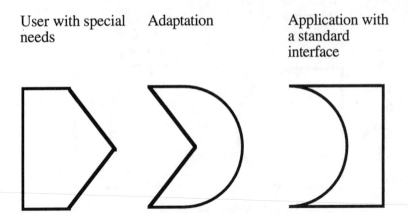

Figure 2.1d. The ideal remediated situation. An adaptation well suited
to the user's interface requirements provides a "better shaped"
interface to the application.

User with special   Adaptation   Application with
needs   a standard
                                                     interface

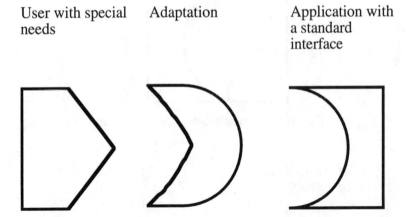

Figure 2.1e. A more realistic situation. Although the interface of the
adaptation is better suited to the user, the match is not perfect, because
some aspects of the original application interface are too difficult to
adapt.

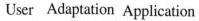

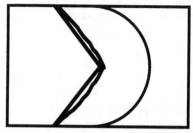

Figure 2.1f. The less-than-perfect match of the adaptation is illustrated by the gap in the fit of the user to the adaptation.

Ideally one adaptation should be available for a range of applications. This makes the best sense economically for the adaptation only need be carried out once, and each user need buy just one version of it. The alternative of building a range of adapted applications (a talking word processor, a talking spreadsheet, *and* a talking database, for instance) represents wasteful duplication.

On the other hand, because a prosthesis is designed to be used only by a person with a particular limitation, it will be designed from the start to match that user. The designer does not inherit constraints from any application (the roundness of the interface in Figure 2.1). Otherwise, to the HCI designer, the problem is much the same – in terms of the diagram, it is to build the pointed straight-edged interface. Therefore many of the techniques and designs discussed in this book are equally applicable to the design of both prostheses and adaptations.

Adaptation: Similarity and difference

As described above, much of the design effort is concerned with adapting existing interfaces. The question is often asked as to why one should adapt an existing interface rather than designing one from scratch with the needs of disabled users in mind. There are three reasons. First, there are simple practicalities: If everybody in the organization uses the same software, their files and data can easily be shared. Although translators do exist, all users know the problems of incompatibility. Secondly, many formats exist because there is such a wide range of applications available. There is a very good reason why we do not use the same (say) word processor: No one has yet built the perfect word processor, the one that all users prefer. It is equally unlikely that someone can write the best word processor for (say) blind users. Hence we cannot think of designing one such program and expecting or forcing all blind people to use it. They have a right to have access to as many programs as possible. Finally, and most important, there is the question of the self-esteem of computer users. People who are labeled as disabled have already been singled out. They do not want to be marked as different from their peers any more than is necessary. As far as is practical, they want to use the same equipment.

Participative design

One point to be stressed throughout this book is that the intended users of any product must be involved at all stages of design and development. All too often designers who are not themselves disabled waste time producing what *they think* clients need, not what they really want. What is the most used mobility aid for blind people? It is the white cane. Many people have produced clever infrared and ultrasonic range-finding devices which are rarely used. Had blind people been involved in the development, those devices would probably never have got off the drawing board.

For a start, many of those clever devices require the user to wear headphones, and any blind tester would have told the developers that putting headphones on cuts them off from sources of information much richer than the simple beeps of an electronic device. Another disadvantage relates to a theme expanded below: People do not like to stand out. A cane is relatively discreet; an electronic device in the hand and headphones on the ears are conspicuous. (It has to be admitted, though, that the advent of the personal stereo may have contributed to making such devices more socially acceptable!) Another advantage of the cane is that it is inexpensive. This means not only that it is cheap to acquire but that there is no great penalty for losing it. A certain amount of swapping at events where visually disabled people are gathered is not unusual.

The point is not to list all the design advantages of the white cane but to make it clear that there are aspects of the technology which are apparent only to its users. Someone who has never used a mobility aid – or at least consulted those who do – would probably never think of most of the properties above.

These sorts of mistake also illustrate the dangers of an attitude which is all too easy to slip into, that of Doing Good. It is impossible for a hearing person to know what it is like to be deaf; and to be a hearing person is equally meaningless to one who is deaf. With an incomplete understanding of what it is like to be disabled, it is all too easy to assume that anything that can be done to alleviate the handicapping effects of an impairment will be gratefully received. This is not the case. To use a new device or adaptation generally implies an *investment* – of time, effort, and usually money. The client will not make that investment unless he or she perceives that it will be worthwhile, that the benefits to be gained will be worth the expenditure. The designer will be able to judge that only if potential clients are involved in the design process.

Sensory disabilities

Given the dominance of screen based visual communication, visual impairment is the most significant sensory impairment in terms of human–computer interaction. An important distinction must be made between blindness and partial sight. A blind person has no useful vision and so must rely on nonvisual forms of communication (i.e. touch or sound).

A partially sighted person has a degree of useful vision, and in general partially sighted people prefer to make maximum use of their sight. Thus their need is for aids which will support the use of residual vision. Sometimes enlargement is the appropriate form of assistance, but this is by no means always so. For instance, some conditions cause a narrowing of the field of vision ("tunnel vision"), in which case enlargement further reduces the amount of viewable information.

Other factors which can be controlled to improve communication for partially sighted people include appropriate lighting, choice of colors, and appropriate screen technology (CRT rather than LCD, for instance). It should be stressed that, in general, nonvisual forms of communication are *not* appropriate. In principle it is possible for partially sighted persons to use an interface intended for blind users, but in fact they are unlikely to want to.

Visual impairment illustrates some important points about disability and its definition. Were it not for the invention of eyeglasses, many more people would be classed as visually disabled. This is an almost ideal example of technology reducing handicap. The solution is so effective, convenient, and inexpensive that it is hardly seen as a prosthetic technology at all. The other interesting point is that glasses are really rather conspicuous but are so common that they are not remarkable and in fact are used by some for cosmetic enhancement.

A blind user must substitute one (or more) of the other senses in order to communicate with the computer, which implies using touch or hearing. The best-known form of tactile communication is braille. Computer generated braille is available in two forms: hard and soft. Hard copy braille is traditional paper based braille produced by a computer rather than by a human operator. Computers have an important role to play here, because the most useful form of braille is *contracted* (several letters may be represented by just one or two braille cells). The rules for translating from letters to contracted braille are complex – just the sort of thing a computer can do efficiently. Hard copy braille is also increasing in importance as more texts become available in machine readable form. Publishers now often have books typeset from computer files, and if those files were made available to braille publishers, then braille editions could be produced at virtually no extra cost.

While translation into contracted braille can be achieved by computer programs, there are still questions about the quality of the braille compared with that produced by people. For instance, a computer translator might contract the word "guidedog" into *guid-ED-OG* rather than the more readable *guide-DOG*.

"Soft" braille provides the reader with something similar to a computer screen for a sighted user – a transient, dynamic display. Such devices are explained in Chapter 9. As described there, most soft braille displays offer a single line of at most 80 characters. This is not truly analogous to the computer screen, which has perhaps 24 × 80 characters. An obvious development would be a braille display of similar dimensions, and many people have wanted to produce one. Unfortunately it is not so simple. Any such "pin matrix" display will be an electromechanical device, which implies several problems: It may be prone to breakdown; it will have to be built to very high tolerances; it will be expensive to manufacture; it is liable to have a very slow refresh rate. At the time of writing, no such device has been produced to surmount those problems. Another form of tactile communication – the Optacon – is also discussed in Chapter 9.

The alternative to tactile communication is the use of hearing. This has long been a viable alternative to print in the form of tape recordings of readers. Unfortunately, the world of blind people has been largely divided for some time into separate camps of braille users and tape users. However (as discussed in Chapter 11), current interfaces can offer the possibility of speech *and* nonspeech sounds combined with braille to give the best of all worlds. Also, the design of speech synthesizers for use by blind people is discussed by Paul Blenkhorn in Chapter 16.

Braille combined with speech synthesis has been used successfully to adapt text-based command line interfaces such as MS-DOS and Unix, but the development of graphical user interfaces has raised new challenges for the interface designer. Some of the current approaches to adapting such interfaces are discussed by Mynatt and Edwards in Chapter 10.

Another important technological development for blind people has been optical character recognition (OCR). As mentioned above, the availability of texts in machine readable form can be very important. However, if a text is available only in print form, then OCR can be used to translate it into an electronic form. The accuracy of recognition is very important. Even a relatively small number of errors can mean that the effort required to correct the document manually makes it impractical. Modern OCR devices do achieve acceptable levels of recognition at a price which is not too high.

Of course, to be used by a blind person the OCR must have an accessible interface. Such interfaces designed for sighted users often use such characteristics as color to highlight parts of the scanned text (such as where the machine is unsure of a character). Clearly such an interface is inappropriate for a blind user. At the same time, it is necessary for the system to be tolerant to the fact that users will generally not be able to orient the input (book or whatever) in a given direction, for they cannot independently ascertain which way up the writing is.

Hearing impairments are rather less of a handicap with respect to computer access – at least with the current design of interfaces. Nevertheless, the needs of users with hearing losses must be borne in mind, particularly with the increasing use of multimodal interactions, including sounds. Interfaces which make use of sounds are very strongly advocated. This is the result of several factors: the availability of the technology; the apparent limitations of traditional interfaces and – not least significant – improvements in adaptability for users with visual disabilities.

This is a good illustration of what might be referred to as the "curb cut" phenomenon: Disadvantaging one group while attempting to empower another. One way or another, Western city planners have become aware of some of the needs of citizens who use wheelchairs and so have built curb cuts into their sidewalks at junctions where wheelchair users may need to cross a road. This has turned out to benefit other people as well – people pushing baby carriages or trolleys of goods. However, what the planners did not anticipate was that curb cuts would handicap other people. For example, guide dogs trained to recognize a curb and stop at it had to be "recalled" and retrained.

So it is that in accommodating one class of extra-ordinary needs, designers must be aware of the possibility of disenfranchising another group. An interface which relies on sound may be more usable by a person with a visual disability but may exclude one with a hearing loss. Current interfaces which use sounds for little more than a beep to signal an error can be adapted relatively easily by supplementing or replacing the beep with a visual signal, such as a flash of the screen.

Information technology can be used in a prosthetic role by people with hearing impairments through an alternative to the telephone. Text terminals, such as the American *Telecommunication Devices for the Deaf* (TDD) and the British *Minicom,* allow pairs of deaf people to communicate using keyboard and screen connected by normal telephone lines. As yet, speech recognition has not been sufficiently developed to facilitate automatic speech-to-text translation that would enable a deaf person to communicate using his or her terminal with a hearing person using his or her normal telephone. Currently a human mediator is needed for such conversations. Exchanges exist through which such links can be made and speech-to-text and text-to-speech translation carried out. This is clearly an area where improvement in speech recognition technology would have a very significant effect: It would allow deaf people to keep their telephone conversations confidential

Physical disabilities

Physical disabilities are relevant to both the adaptive and prosthetic use of information technology. People with impaired manual function may not be able to use conventional input devices such as keyboards and mice, while some people are unable to carry out such everyday operations as walking and may use computer controlled wheelchairs. In practice the two applications are often in-separable. For example, conditions which affect the lower limbs may also impair the upper limbs, so that the wheelchair user may also make use of an adapted word processor in her or her job, for instance.

The most severe form of impairment is the absence of a body part or a body part which is useless – paralyzed. Paralysis may be caused by brain damage or damage to the spinal cord. It often affects one area of the body: *Paraplegia* refers to paralysis of the legs; *tetraplegia* and *quadriplegia* mean paralysis of all four limbs. Paralysis can also affect one side of the body – usually when damage has occurred to (one side of) the brain. Paralysis is not always complete; it may amount to reduction in the movement of the limb or limbs.

The form of paralysis due to spinal cord injury depends on the severity and site of the damage. The higher up the spine the damage, the farther up the body the impairment. Thus tetraplegia can be caused by damage high on the spine, whereas a lower injury may cause paraplegia. The site of the damage is often labeled according to vertebra. The highest vertebrae are the cerebral vertebrae, labelled C2 to C8, counting from the top down. So damage in the low numbers will have the greater effect.

Above C4 the spinal cord controls breathing, and a complete break above that level will cause death. Someone with severe damage at the C4 level might be able to use the chin or a mouthstick to interface with the controls of an electric wheelchair or computer or some form of environmental control. With damage at C5, the person will still need to use special devices and assistance. He or she will be able to eat, wash, comb the hair, and help with the dressing of the upper body. The person may be able to wheel a wheelchair on the flat but will not be able to move from the chair to a toilet independently. Someone with damage at C6 has better function and may be able to drive an adapted car but will still need some assistance with personal care. With damage at C7, the person can transfer from a wheelchair independently and can dress and eat without assistance, and a person with damage at C8 can lead an independent wheelchair based life (see Collier & Longmore, 1989).

Not all conditions which limit physical activity are caused by direct damage to the part of the body concerned. In particular, various forms of brain damage can affect motor control. This is the case in cerebral palsy, for instance, and similarly partial paralysis can be due to disruption of the brain, as in the case of a stroke.

Minor impairment of manual dexterity can be overcome by quite simple adaptations. For instance, some people have tremor of the hands, which means they cannot use a keyboard accurately. They find it impossible to hit one key without touching adjacent keys. For them a simple plastic keyguard may be all that is required. Such a guard fits over the keyboard with holes corresponding to the keys underneath. The user can rest a hand on the guard without activating any keys and then press the desired key through its hole.

Such "hardware" solutions may also be supported by software modifications. Electronic keyboards usually have a repeat function whereby a key held down for longer than a set time *autorepeats*, producing multiple copies of the letter. Users with slow reactions may be unable to lift their fingers off the key within the autorepeat time and so get unwanted multiple letters. This can usually be avoided by adjusting the keyboard software to either switch off the autorepeat feature altogether or lengthen its trigger time. It is also often possible to adjust the sensitivity of the keys to accommodate a user with a particularly light or heavy touch.

Some people have good control of their hands but not of their fingers. If so they may press the keys using sticks held in or strapped to their hands. Other people may not be able to use their hands at all, but some other part of the body over which they have sufficient control may be utilized, often by attaching a stick to that part. A common example is the head; a "unicorn" stick may be strapped to the forehead so that the user can see the keys as they are pressed.

Some people have no part of the body which they can use to access a keyboard, and for them some alternative must be provided. Usually this takes the form of keyboard emulation software controlled by one or more switches. Again, any viable part of the body will be used to operate switches. Hands, feet, head, arms – all might be used. For a tetraplegic person, the limbs are unusable, and a "sip–puff" switch, controlled by sucking and blowing on a tube in the mouth, might be used.

In the simplest setup a single switch will be used. This represents a very low bandwidth communication channel, just one bit at a time being communicated. This leads to very slow communication. Most keyboard emulators allow the user to select input from menus of some kind. Many techniques have been developed to try to speed up the rate of communication through such an interface. Several of these are described in this book (see Chapters 3, 5, and 6).

More high technology solutions have also been attempted. Eye gaze interfaces may be used by people with tetraplegia: A screen cursor follows eye focus. Experiments have been carried out with many different technologies. (Currently one of the most successful detects infrared light bounced off the retina.) There are many problems in using eye gaze. For instance, head movements can often disrupt the mechanism. However, the fact that the technology has been pursued despite the difficulties illustrates an interesting point: The challenge of accommodating a user with severe limitations makes it worthwhile to pursue difficult lines of research and development. Currently eye gaze input may not have sufficient advantages over (say) the mouse for the majority of users to make its development viable for mainstream use – but the work going into this technology for extra-ordinary usage will eventually lead to its becoming a feasible alternative or addition for the majority of users.

Speech input is another example of high technology being developed for users with disabilities that is likely to lead to better speech based interfaces for most users. In Chapter 5 Newell and his colleagues show how the concept of using "spin-off" from research for users with special needs to inform the development of interfaces for other users can be pushed to its limits, to the benefit of both specialized and mainstream research.

An interface between a physically disabled person and a computer can be vital. Not only does it give access to the normal functions of the computer (for work, education, and leisure), but the computer can also be used as a gateway to many prosthetic devices. For instance, the user of an electric wheelchair needs an interface to that technology in order to control movement. (Such an interface which exploits the minimal control provided by eye winks is described in Chapter 13.) Similarly, many environmental devices can be controlled from the computer; one can turn lights on and off, open and close curtains, "pick up" a loudspeaker phone, and so on.

Speech disabilities

The main application of information technology for people with speech impairments is the provision of prostheses – often referred to as augmentative communication. The requirement is for a communication device to replace the missing ability to speak, a means whereby the user inputs what he or she wants to say and communicates it to another person. The output can be in written or spoken form. Some of the simplest devices use an alphanumeric display, such as a strip of paper or an LED display. Devices which produce speech have an obvious attraction as a replacement for natural speech. At the same time, since they rely on synthetic speech, which is as yet not very natural sounding, they are a poor substitute.

The principal requirement of a user of a communication device is to be able to specify and produce speech at a rapid rate. Normal conversation proceeds at a rate of around 150 words per minute, so ideally someone who uses a communicator as his or her voice in a conversation should be able to generate speech at that rate. That is very hard to attain. The problem is made more difficult in that the sorts of conditions which affect speech very often affect other physical functions too. Thus most users of augmentative communication have impaired manual dexterity, making access through conventional keyboards difficult or impossible. This means that many of the techniques and adaptations for people with physical disabilities discussed above are also used in this application. The difference is that the need for high speed of input is much more critical in this case.

An intriguing possibility is speech input for people with speech impairments. This may seem like an odd idea, but the suggestion is that as long as a person can *consistently* produce the same sounds, it does not matter what those sounds are as long as the "listener" has been trained as to their intended meaning. In other words, some speech recognition devices work on the principle of matching sounds to stored templates. The individual user creates the templates; so as long as he or she can consistently produce the same sound, it will match the template and be recognized.

For example, it may be necessary for an application to recognize the command "Open," so the user would first train it to his or her voice by repeating the word several times. From those utterances a template would be formed and stored. The system has no other information about the sound of the word "open." Therefore it would be feasible for the person to actually say another word ("Monday," perhaps) and thereafter "Monday" would evoke the "open" command. More realistically in the case of persons with speech impairments, users would utter the nearest approximation they could manage to "Open," and that would then be recognized. Their only requirement is to utter the word in a manner very similar to when they trained the system.

This implies that this approach is feasible only for people with certain kinds of speech impairment. However, it does open up the interesting possibility that a (trained) machine may be better at recognizing impaired speech than an untrained person. It might even be practical to have an augmentative communicator which uses voice input and produces synthetic speech output – with the synthetic voice being more easily understood than the natural one. The potential of this approach has been demonstrated by Edwards and Blore (1992) and Kay (1992).

Cognitive disabilities

As its name implies, information technology manipulates information. Thus an apparently obvious application would be as a prosthesis for a person who has difficulty in handling information – in other words a person with a cognitive impairment. In practice rather less has been achieved thus far than in the other areas described in this chapter.

Currently this is probably the most hazardous area of language for the unwary or potentially "politically incorrect" writer, presumably because problems of thinking and cognition are still significantly stigmatized. In Britain the concept of "mentally subnormal" has long since been recognized as being far too value laden and the generally accepted term now is "learning difficulty" or "learning disability." "Mentally retarded" is not thought in the UK to be much of an improvement – while in the USA it is usually treated as a precise clinical term. Furthermore, people are assigned to different classes ("mild," "severe," etc.) usually depending on the results of IQ tests (but recognition of the validity of IQ testing is far from being universal). Cognitive impairments include limitation in thinking, memory, language, learning, and perception. Causes include birth defects, head injuries, stroke, diseases, and age related conditions. The figures given below for the United States are taken from Elkind (1990), and those for Europe from Carruthers, Humphreys, & Sandhu (1993).

Whatever the impairments are called, a significant number of people have nonspecific difficulties in thinking and learning which amount to a disability (2.4 million Americans are classed as being "mentally retarded," as are a similar number of Europeans). In the majority of cases the cause is unknown. Some people have language impairments. That is to say, they have difficulty in listening, speaking, reading and/or writing, but they should generally be distinguished from persons with *speech* impairments, as discussed earlier.

The effects of head injuries and strokes can affect cognitive abilities (as well as have physical effects, like partial paralysis). There are approximately 400,000 to 600,000 people in the United States who have had head injuries and approximately 2 million who have had strokes (Elkind, 1990).

Alzheimer's disease leads to progressive intellectual decline, causing confusion and disorientation. As many as 5% of Americans over 65 have the disease; at ages over 80 the proportion rises to 20%. Dementia is a brain disease which results in the progressive loss of mental functions, starting with memory, learning, attention, and judgment deficits. The underlying cause is obstruction of blood flow to the brain. Some forms of dementia are curable; others are not. Again, this disfunction is partially age related. Of people aged over 65, 10% have mild or moderate impairment and 5% have severe dementia. Of those over 85, 35% are affected.

The problems faced by people with cognitive impairments are various but can be loosely categorized in four groups:

- Memory problems include difficulty in retrieving information from short term, long term, or remote memory. Difficulty in recognizing and retrieving information is included in this category.

- Perception problems include difficulty in taking in, attending to, and discriminating sensory information.

- Problem solving impairments include difficulty in recognizing a problem, identifying, choosing, and implementing solutions; and evaluating outcomes.

- Conceptual difficulties include problems in sequencing, generalizing previously learned concepts, comprehension, and skill development.

Since the cognitive loads for different tasks and users vary greatly, design guidelines for reducing cognitive barriers to computer use are quite general. These designs must address the *whole* of the interface. For example, many early programs for people with reading difficulties were inaccessible because the input mechanism – a keyboard – required a higher cognitive level than the task represented in the software. As summarized in the tables below, the Industry/Government Cooperative Initiative on Computer Accessibility recommended the following steps for reducing cognitive barriers:

- simplify language in task instructions;

- provide on-line help;

- make displays simple; and

- use consistent displays, menus, and selection techniques.

Successful implementation of these guidelines is difficult because the determination of what is simple or conceptually beneficial is largely subjective and variable across situations and users. Cress and Goltz (1989) have collected from rehabilitation and education literature a more detailed list of recommendations for improving computer accessibility for people with cognitive impairments.

Guidelines

The document *Considerations in the Design of Computers and Operating Systems to Increase Their Accessibility to Persons with Disabilities* (Scadden & Vanderheiden, 1988) includes a set of tables which summarize very well the requirements of a range of users with different disabilities and possible approaches to meeting them. They are included here (with permission) on pp. 36 ff. to give the reader a very rapid overview of the field. More details about this document and its production in response to legislation appear in Chapter 19.

Lessons

One of the important points illustrated in this chapter is that extra-ordinary users challenge the boundaries of the technology. For example current speech technology – synthesis and recognition – is good enough for many "ordinary" applications but is not sufficiently developed for users who will be more reliant on it. The quality of current synthetic speech is good enough for untrained listeners to understand with little effort. Yet it could not be said to be very natural – and that is important for a person who uses such a voice as his or her main means of communication. One's voice is an important part of one's self-image, and an inappropriate synthesized voice is really not acceptable. Not only should the voice sound human, but it ought also to be possible for the user to choose the sort of voice he or she might expect to have naturally – including its gender and accent.

Speech input has developed to the extent that isolated word recognition is good enough for many applications (including possible use by dyslexic people, as described in Chapter 7), but without continuous speech recognition and automatic speech-to-text translation the technology is not good enough for deaf people to use for telephone communication.

That improvements in technology can occur is illustrated by OCR. Systems available in the 1980s were good enough for many applications, though they were expensive. Now the technology is cheap – *and* sufficiently accurate for blind people to use to read texts.

Table 2.1. *Persons with moderate physical disabilities have difficulty using input devices and controls*

Problem areas	Examples	Needed features or capabilities	Example strategies
P1: Cannot do simultaneous actions such as shift, control, Alt. etc. (e.g. can only use 1 hand or mouthstick)	Individuals with 1 arm, or those who use a mouthstick, cannot use shift/control keys on standard keyboards or use a 2-button mouse	Alternate sequential method for achieving all functions which normally require simultaneous actions	(1) Sticky keys (1-finger option) (2) Keyboard alternative for 2-button mouse
P2: Cannot respond quickly (key repeat and other timed responses)	Individuals with a slower reaction time can have trouble if the key repeat rate is too fast	Ability to slow down or turn off timed response	(1) Key repeat adjustable (start/rate/on–off) (2) Software design rules for 3rd party manufacturers
P3: Cannot use standard mouse or other pointing devices which use fine movement	Individuals with motor problems or paralysis cannot accurately use a mouse or touchpad	Alternate way to move/control mouse or pointing device cursor without fine movement	(1) *Mousekeys* (keyboard control of mouse) (2) Keyboard simulation of touchscreen
P4: Difficulty in handling storage media delicately. Difficulty in reaching drives (disks. CD-roms, etc.)	Individuals with cerebral palsy have difficulty handling fragile media and reaching into drives to remove floppy disks, CDs, etc. Also have trouble reaching built-in drives, especially on floor-mounted computers	Removable media should be easy to insert and remove. It should also not require delicate handling. Drive would preferably have an external mounting option	(1) Electric pushbutton operation (2) Concave buttons (if manual eject) (3) Ejects 1/2" to 3/4" or more (4) External mount drives available (5) Rigid, self-protecting media

Table 2.1 (continued). *Persons with moderate physical disabilities have difficulty using input devices and controls*

Problem areas	Examples	Needed features or capabilities	Example strategies
P5: Trouble operating controls that require manual dexterity or reach	Individuals with limited dexterity (arthritis, cerebral palsy, etc.) are unable to use controls which they cannot reach or which require a twist motion.	Controls and latches needed for operation in easy reach & require minimum dexterity (e.g. stick in mouth. or arthritic hands)	(1) Front mount (controls and drives) (2) No twist motions (3) Pushbutton controls and latches (4) Edge operated (wheel) controls (5) Functions operable from keyboard
P6: Bump wrong keys when typing	Individuals with cerebral palsy, tremor, or weakness have trouble hitting keys accurately without touching adjacent keys.	Delay key acceptance and/or provide for keyguard	(1) Keyguard or keyguard mounting (2) *Slowkeys* utility (with a start-up warning signal!)

Table 2.2. *Some people with severe physical disabilities cannot use standard input devices*

Problem areas	Examples	Needed features or capabilities	Example strategies
SP1: Need to connect special input devices or interfaces (sip-puff, eyegaze, etc.)	Individuals who require an eyegaze or sip-puff controlled input cannot use the standard input devices on the computer and need a way to connect their device in place of the normal input devices (keyboard, mouse, touchscreen) on the various computers they encounter at work/school, etc.	Way to connect alternate input systems (internally and externally). (For access to user owned/controlled computers, internal system hooks or access points can be used. For shared and public use computers, access must be external)	(1) Point in operating system where simulated input can be injected (before first application or system use of input) (2) A callable system utility which when invoked takes data from serial port and creates fake (simulated) keystrokes and other input activity

Table 2.3. *Some people with visual impairments cannot see lettering and symbols on keyboard, equipment, or screen because it is too small or has low contrast*

Problem areas	Examples	Needed features or capabilities	Example strategies
V1: Screen display is too small to see	Individuals with low vision have difficulties reading the screen because the characters and images on the screen are too small	Ways to make screen image larger (up to 16 times)	(1) Video connectors for external displays (2) Zoom enlarge feature or utility
V2: Color blind persons cannot see information presented through some colors	Color blind individuals cannot see text or highlights with some text/background color combinations	Allow user to select the colors or make color information redundant	(1) Colors selectable by user (2) Color redundancy whenever possible (3) Color redundancy design rule for 3rd party manufacturing
V3: Trouble seeing/ reading keys and legends on equip-ment	Individuals with low vision have difficulty seeing keys and reading legends on monitors, printers, etc.	Larger, high contrast characters on keys and controls	(1) Avoid low contrast colors (2) Larger letters on keys and controls (3) Stickers with large letters (and/or colors) (4) Replaceable keycaps with removable clear plastic lids

Table 2.4. *Some people are blind and cannot use standard visually based output and input devices and indicators*

Problem Areas	Examples	Needed features or capabilities	Example strategies
B1: Need electronic access to information displayed on the screen in order to use special non-vision display substitutes	Blind individuals can use a portable voice output access device in place of the computer's standard screen display, except where these devices cannot get access to the contents (information) displayed on the computer's screen	Provide display contents in an electronically accessible, interpretable form. (For access to user owned/controlled computers, internal system hooks can be used. For shared and public use computers, access must be external)	(1) Document access to screen memory (2) Export screen image memory (3) Screen description call/utility (internal) (4) Export description of screen contents
B2: Do not have eye–hand coord-ination required for mouse tasks, touch-screens, etc.	Blind individuals cannot use a mouse because they cannot monitor the mouse cursor's continually changing position as they move	Provide alternative ways to achieve same function without eye-hand coordination whenever possible (e.g. as keyboard commands)	(1) Keyboard access to menus (2) Keyboard access to window functions (3) Keyboard simulation of touchscreen
B3: Cannot tell state of toggle keys/buttons whose state is only indicated visually	Blind individuals have trouble with toggle keys, printer status buttons, etc. which use LEDs to indicate state	Nonvisual status cues or means to determine status nonvisually	(1) Tone feedback for toggle keys (2) Auditory query of status (tones)
B4: Trouble finding/ identifying keys and controls	Blind individuals have difficulty using perfectly flat membrane keyboards, since they cannot find the keys even if they have memorized their position and function. They also have difficulty in locating keys on large keyboards without tactile landmarks	Tactile border to keys (e.g. no flat membrane keyboards without ridges or key dividers). Nonvisual key/control labeling	(1) No perfectly flat membrane keypads (2) Nibs on home keys (3) Tactile map with braille labels (4) Braille stickers on or above keys (5) Tactile labels on or next to keys (6) Voice cuing

Table 2.5. *Some people with hearing disabilities cannot hear auditory output at normal volume levels or at all*

Problem areas	Examples	Needed features or capabilities	Example strategies
H1: Cannot hear auditory warnings or other indications or output (including speech)	Individuals who are deaf cannot hear beeps that indicate errors when typing or issuing commands. They also cannot hear any spoken or other auditory output from the computer or programs. Natural noises (disk drives) used by hearing persons are also not available	Present all auditory information visually as well	(1) Flash with system beep (2) "Hearing Impaired User" or "Feedback Preference" flag in OS (3) Auditory redundancy design rule (4) "Active" lights for disk drives (5) Captioning (open or closed) of any spoken output
H2: Cannot hear sounds at normal volume	Individuals who are hard of hearing have difficulty receiving auditory output at nominal volume levels	Adjustable volume and facilitation of external amplification (useful but not critical if all auditory information is also visual)	(1) Speaker near edge for easy pickup (2) Adjustable volume (with sufficient range) (3) Audio output jack

Table 2.6. *Some people with seizure disorders are sensitive to certain flicker frequencies which can cause them to go into seizure*

Problem areas	Examples	Needed features or capabilities	Example strategies
S1: Screen flicker at certain frequency can cause seizures (even if the person is only near the computer)	People with photosensitive epilepsy may have a seizure if exposed to strong stimuli in the 10–50 Hz range.	Avoid those frequencies	(1) Avoid refresh or flicker rates in the 10–50 Hz range (esp. 15–30 Hz)

Table 2.7. *Some design features or changes would greatly reduce the cost or difficulty third-party manufacturers and agencies encounter in developing special access devices and materials*

Problem areas	Examples	Needed features or capabilities	Example strategies
Ml: Agencies have difficulty preparing manuals in alternate form (disk, braille, speech)	Agencies who support persons with disabilities could provide special manuals in braille, voice or electronic form if they could get the source text for the manuals in electronic form	Provide manuals in electronic form	(1) Text from manuals available in electronic form (2) Information in all figures and graphics presented also (redundantly) in text (3) Special electronic manuals
M2: Need to have speech output from computer for special need programs/ utilities	Programs for blind access and for nonspeaking persons need to have access to a built-in or external speech synthesizer	Provide speech capability built in or ability to attach a synthesizer	(1) Serial port (2) Speech capable sound system
M3: Some alternative input routines require a window which always remains on top	Some special access programs need to use a window that is never hidden from the user, yet is not the "active" window	Provide a window which can always appear and remain on top	(1) Build necessary hooks into operating system
M4: Some alternative input routines require connection of special switches or interfaces	Morse code, scanning, and other special input routines require the ability to connect special sip-puff, eyeblink, etc. switches.	Provide a means for connecting switches and transducers	(1) Assign pins on existing connectors (2) General switch/transducer interface
M5: Software sometimes ignores keystrokes sent faster than it can process them, thus defeating special macros	Word processing programs often throw away excess typeahead backspace characters. This prevents some abbreviation expansion programs from working	Provide way in OS for distinguishing between typed, autorepeat, and macro characters	
M6: Trouble mounting keyguards to keyboards	Disabled individuals who share a computer with others have difficulty attaching and removing their keyguards	Provision in keyboard design to facilitate keyguard mounting	(1) Groove or holes in edge of keyboard (2) Keyguard from manufacturer

Summary

Human–computer interaction is quite a well established discipline. One of the themes of this book is that extra-ordinary interaction is becoming accepted as a branch of the field and this is a good thing. Yet it is still relatively immature and by no means are all the answers known. In this chapter we have attempted to provide some answers, but much of the rest of the book is about formulating better questions.

Acknowledgment

Thanks to Wendy Hall for providing medical information.

References

Apple Computer Inc. (1987). *Apple human interface guidelines: The Apple desktop interface.* Reading, MA: Addison-Wesley.

Carruthers, S., Humphreys, A., and Sandhu, J. (1993). *The market for RT in Europe: A demographic study of need*, in Ballabio, E., Placencia-Porrero, I., and Puig de la Bellacasa, R. (editors), *Rehabilitation Technology: Strategies for the European Union,* Proceedings of the First Tide Congress. Amsterdam: IOS Press.

Collier, J. A. B., and Longmore, J. M. (1989). *Oxford handbook of clinical specialities* (2nd ed.). Oxford: Oxford University Press.

Cress, C. J., and Goltz, C. C. (1989). Cognitive factors affecting accessibility of computers and electronic devices. In *Proceedings of the 12th Annual Resna Conference* (pp. 25–26). Washington, DC: Resna Press.

Edwards, A. D. N. (1991). *Evaluation of Outspoken software for blind users.* Technical Report YCS150. University of York, Department of Computer Science.

Edwards, A. D. N., and Blore, A. (1992). Speech input for persons with speech impairments. In *Computers for handicapped persons,* Proceedings of the 3rd International Conference on Computers for Handicapped Persons, ed. W. Zagler. Vienna: R. Oldenbourg, pp. 120–126.

Elkind, J. (1990). The incidence of disabilities in the United States. *Human Factors, 32*(4): 397–405.

Eurostat (1992). Rapid Reports, *Population and social conditions: Disabled people*, Luxembourg: Eurostat.

Kay, P. (1992). User interface for speech-controlled drawing. In *Proceedings 3rd International Conference on Computers for Handicapped Persons*, ed. W. Zagler. Vienna: Österreichische Computer Gesellschaft, pp. 256–262.

Martin, J., Meltzer, H., and Elliot, D. (1988). *Surveys of disability in Great Britain, Report 1: The prevalence of disability among adults*. Office of Population Censuses and Surveys. London: HMSO.

Scadden, L. A., and Vanderheiden, G. C. (1988). *Considerations in the design of computers and operating systems to increase their accessibility to persons with disabilities.* Working document of the Industry/Government Cooperative Initiative on Computer Accessibility. Trace Center, University of Wisconsin.

UN (1981). The United Nations Declaration on the Rights of Disabled Persons. *Unesco Courier,* no. 1: 6–7.

World Health Organization (1980). *International classification of impairments, disabilities and handicaps.* Geneva: WHO.

Case studies

The first section introduced the current state of the art, and this section continues the theme. The criterion for inclusion of chapters in the second section was that they should describe products which are currently available commercially. The approach is generally candid; the products presented are by no means ideal, and there is plenty of scope for further improvements and developments.

Like several other authors in this book, the writer of Chapter 3 is an established human factors specialist who came to apply his skills and knowledge to the question of interfaces for disabled people through personal contact, in this case with his daughter. He describes an evaluation of the interface to a particular augmentative communication device based on synthetic speech. The chapter also includes consideration of the speech synthesis requirements of an augmentative communication user, which should be contrasted with the requirements of a blind user of synthetic speech as described by Paul Blenkhorn in Chapter 16.

Part of the work described illustrates some of the points made in Chapter 1 regarding the benefits to HCI in general of studying special cases. The communication aid described is based upon the use of small iconlike pictures. To maximize the power and richness of what can be said, each icon must be heavily loaded with (potential) meaning so that it can be used in multiple contexts without the user's forgetting what any of its meanings are. Surely the lessons learned from such a design can be applied to making the icons in any graphical user interface more informative?

Blind people represent a very good example of a lot of aspects of this field. Early developments in personal computer technology led to the emancipation of many blind workers. With the aid of adapted computer systems, it became possible for such people to do jobs from which they were previously excluded. However, subsequent developments in human–computer interfaces – graphical user interfaces – have led to the potential reexclusion of blind workers. *Outspoken,* the adaptation described in Chapter 4, was the first commercial product released to address this problem. As explained in that chapter, Outspoken did not answer all the problems There is still plenty of scope for further research and development, some of which is described in the Research section of this book.

Alan Newell set the theme of the book in Chapter 1. Chapter 5 describes the research work which formed his background and which led to several commercial products. A number of the projects described in that chapter are concerned with increasing the speed and efficiency of the user's input to the system. This is a good example of how a general problem in human–computer interfaces is brought into sharper focus by the limitations of disabled users. Many computer users would like to be able to input information more quickly. For instance, to be able to type into a word processor as quickly as one can think would not only save time but might lead to a much more lucid style of writing. However, for the most part we learn to cope with the inadequacy of the bandwidth and can still type fast enough for most purposes.

When speaking to people, we do communicate at a speed comparable to that at which we think. For someone who cannot speak naturally and therefore uses a computer based prosthesis, there is a genuine need to be able to generate input at much greater speeds than can be attained on a conventional keyboard. The irony is that most such people have disabilities which also affect their manual dexterity, so that their ability to use any kind of keyboard is reduced. There is therefore the double challenge of providing very fast forms of input which can be used by people with limited dexterity. The chapter is not concerned only with physical prostheses, however, but includes an example of use of the computer as a *cognitive* prosthesis – an important and as yet underdeveloped concept.

Chapter 6 explores the application of predictive techniques to the human–computer interface. No computer can predict completely what a user is going to do; if it could, the user would become redundant! However, the more actions the computer can predict, the fewer input operations are required. This has proven to be particularly helpful for people with physical disabilities, for whom any manual input can represent a significant investment of effort and time. This chapter introduces predictive interfaces, discusses their general attributes, and provides examples of several quite different systems. The systems differ substantially from each other in their task domains, intended users, algorithms for generating predictions, and user interfaces.

3

An evaluation of the PRC Touch Talker with Minspeak: Some lessons for speech prosthesis design

Gary W. Strong

Introduction

People with a speech impairment have a variety of options available to use as language surrogates. One of the most common nontechnological solutions is the use of sign language. Unfortunately, signing is understood only by a small fraction of the general population. Computer technology has permitted a variety of approaches to address this problem, and a number of devices are currently sold that assist individuals with a speech impairment. They vary over a spectrum of functionality, price, and usability. This variation is due, in part, to the broad range of needs of the subject population. Some users within the nonspeaking population have, along with an inability to speak, an extreme mobility impairment. Such impairments require that particular attention be given to the adaptability of the device interface for selecting speech. Since adaptation in the realm of computers is often merely a matter of reprogramming, computers can serve as the basis for highly adaptable speech prosthesis devices, and there are a number of special purpose speech-generating computers on the market.

One notable example is the *Touch Talker* from Prentke Romich Company (PRC) of Wooster, Ohio. The Touch Talker has enjoyed wide use among the population of individuals with speech impairments since the mid 1980s. It currently holds about two-thirds of the market for such devices in the United States (Baker, 1991). The Touch Talker's design makes it clear that for many individuals it replaced a paper communication board on which users pointed at sequences of symbols or words in order to communicate. The facilities of a computer, however, are far beyond those of a communication board, and the rapidly developing technology of laptop computers allows designers to further address the communication needs of individuals with speech impairments.

This chapter is a presentation of a case study which draws some conclusions that may help in the design of a new generation of computer-based speech prostheses. As in any case study, the sample is very small – in this instance, one. Therefore the principles suggested must be subjected to a more formal validation.

This limitation notwithstanding, there is a rich body of design data available from people who have had long-term experience with the same user, such as parents of individuals with speech impairments. This rich data can be used to develop principles for the design of new devices that would greatly increase usability by the subject population.

I hope to demonstrate this from my own experiences over 7 years with my own daughter. A danger in presenting such data is that it is personal, anecdotal, and of little use to designers. However, in this case, my 25 years of experience in designing, from electrical engineering projects to information systems, and human–computer interfaces in particular, helps me to avoid these pitfalls, and to present the data and derive a set of design principles that might be used by designers. The main motivation to produce this chapter is the belief that some attention to end users in the design of speech prosthesis devices would dramatically improve the usability of such devices.

Often in the field of human–computer interaction, the focus is on the virtual realities that skilled programmers can bring about for users with impairments. Even in these cases, however, the computer is only a communication channel, not the focal point of the design process. Computers would be largely toys if it were not for the fact that they connect users to information and information management tools in ways that can greatly enhance the quality and efficiency of human work. Specifically, within the field of speech prosthesis devices the communication issues to address are even more dramatic. Computer devices in this area should be transparent to the basic natural language processes of human beings. In order to approach this goal, designers must pay increased attention to the evaluation of current devices by end users (not solely to speech therapists, who may not be familiar with computer technology or with the practice of nonvocal communication in nonclassroom situations). Thus, designers must be aware of the techniques of evaluation available in the field of human–computer interaction, as well as of methodologies for involving end users in the development of computer-based information systems.

The main argument of this chapter is that current speech prostheses are not supported by current technology to the extent that they could be because designers have not paid sufficient attention to end users. My observation suggests that two important issues are often overlooked: Feedback during language production and adaptability of the language. The ability to perceive what one is saying during language production is extremely important yet is easy to overlook unless one closely observes situations where this basic process has been interfered with. Petitto and Marentette (1991) have shown that personal feedback is critical in the development of language, and specifically in sign language. It may be that the importance of feedback continues even after primary language concepts have been acquired. In some cultures (e.g. the Japanese) feedback dependency is carried to an extreme. The meaning of a sentence in Japanese can be edited up to the very end, since the exact meaning (if there is one) is determined in large part by the final ending of the verb at the end of the sentence.

This is presumably the case so that a speaker can adjust the intensity of his or her statement according to the reactions of the listener. The main effect is to give the speaker a chance to edit the sentence even as it is being spoken, resulting is a high level of adaptability of the language. This adaptability is largely missing in speech produced by prostheses whose designs are derived from manual communication boards. This lack of adaptability may cause undue attention to the device itself and to the constraints imposed by its interface, rather than to the message which is intended to be conveyed.[1] Having to think out the entire interaction process in advance before typing it in makes the whole process unwieldy even for natural speakers.

The PRC Touch Talker

The Touch Talker from Prentke Romich Company is a specialized, 5.25 lb (2.38 kg) laptop computer. It is approximately 13" (33 cm) wide by 9" (23 cm) long and stands 3.75" (30 cm) high at the back of its sloping surface. The one I will describe (Figure 3.1) was loaned to my daughter by the state of Pennsylvania in 1986, but it is not substantially different from the majority of those currently in use.[2] It has a physical interface consisting of a 130-key keyboard and a 40-character by 2-line LCD (liquid crystal diode) display, both protected by a fairly transparent plastic keyguard through which keyholes have been cut. The keyguard holes keep the user from pressing on any key other than the intended one. There is also a serial communications port and a serial printer port, each of which consists of an RS232 jack on the side of the device. There are two rotating controls on the side, one to adjust the volume of the synthesized speech and the other for adjusting the intensity of the LCD display. Since the LCD display does not use twisted or supertwisted LCD technology, the angle of viewing and ambient light greatly affect the ability to see the display, requiring the intensity to be controlled to maximize contrast. Since the device is portable, it has internal batteries that after a normal day's use should be charged overnight with an AC adapter plug. Otherwise there is a danger of losing the programmed phrases in the internal battery-operated ram.

The Touch Talker is generally operated by means of the *Minspeak* language, which maps keystroke sequences to previously programmed phrases which are synthesized into speech. Programming of the Touch Talker occurs by means of

---

[1] Consider the phenomenology of tool use and the effect of breakdowns when a tool becomes ineffective with respect to its intended goal and is no longer transparent to the user, as discussed in Winograd and Flores (1986).

[2] A new version of the device has recently been placed on the market and is not included in this evaluation.

an internal proprietary speech synthesis program and by using built-in functions for control. All the keys can be reprogrammed as desired, except for the "on" and "off" keys which are in the upper right corner of the keyboard. The function or meaning of a key is written on a thin plastic overlay that sits between the rigid keyguard and the keys (except for an opening in the plastic corresponding to the LCD display). Most Touch Talker programmers (typically speech therapists or parents) use icons to indicate the meaning of the keys and either draw these on the plastic with indelible pen or use stickers which are sold by the company.

There are two types of overlays in regular use. Switching from one to another is accomplished by lifting up the keyguard, pulling off the unwanted overlay, inserting a new one, and replacing the keyguard. Instructing the computer which one is on the keyboard is accomplished by a special keystroke sequence that does not interfere with normal use. The first overlay is a built-in "fixed overlay" that allows access to all programming functions. Custom, programmable overlays are made by reassigning selected keys from the fixed overlay and by programming key sequences to have phrases stored with them. The device remembers which overlay was in use when it was turned off. The advantage of this is that the custom overlay can be the one recognized by the machine when it is turned on without the user's having to go through any preparatory keystrokes.

The fixed overlay represents each of the device functions on a separate key. These functions include those necessary to generate custom overlays. Certain functions are usually kept on the fixed overlay, such as serial and printer port control and some speech synthesis control. The most important functions, however, are those that control the mode of use of the custom overlay, and many of these are transferred to special keys of the custom overlay so that they can be used by the user as well as by a programmer updating custom overlay phrases. Such functions include keys that allow one, two, or three keys to serve as context keys (automatic keystroke prefixes), keys that allow entry of phonetic spellings (to produce more accurate speech synthesis along with normal spellings for the display), keys that allow selection of keystroke sequences for phrases to be stored, and, most important, keys to represent each letter of the alphabet as well as a few punctuation characters. Additional function keys control the user's ability to type in words (the spell mode) or to select stored phrases by using keystroke sequences (the communication mode).

The Case

The data to be presented here derived from participant observation of my daughter over the period from spring 1986 – when she received her Touch Talker

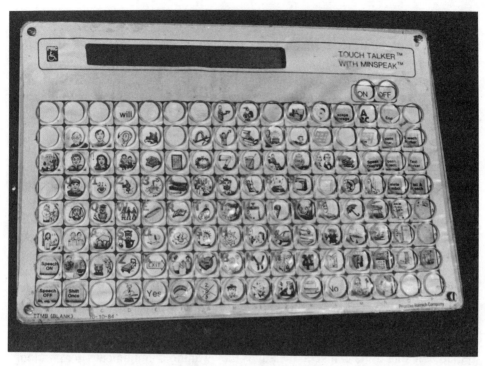

Figure 3.1. View of the Touch Talker.

– to the present (she still uses the device). At the time of writing, my daughter is an 11-year-old with spastic quadriplegia (a generic form of cerebral palsy) with very limited vocalization abilities. She uses the device both at home and at school and recently acquired a printer as a companion to the device. She is able to spell 100 to 200 words in groups of up to 7 or 8 words in length. She can also use the device in its Minspeak mode and is able to remember approximately 50 one- to three-key sequences. She does not use the automatic keystroke prefixes referred to in the preceding paragraph.

Although I have enjoyed limited observation of other Touch Talker users, I know that my daughter is not an unusual user. Her Touch Talker is a loan from the Commonwealth of Pennsylvania Assistive Device Center, which has provided hundreds of such devices to persons with speech impairments throughout the State. I have worked as a parent with three sets of special education teams: one from the Easter Seal Society and two teams from an intermediate unit of a Pennsylvania county. Each team consisted of a teacher, a teacher's aide, a speech therapist, a physical therapist, and an occupational therapist. Parents working with such teams is mandated by federal and Pennsylvania law governing Individualized Educational Programs (IEPs).

Evaluation

In recent years, significant advances have been made in the quality of speech that is synthesized from text. Even so, the artificiality of the synthesized speech often prevents a casual listener from understanding what is said, so that repetition of the phrase is required. Accuracy of synthesizer pronunciation can be increased, however, in difficult cases by using an alternative phonetic spelling. In addition, newer synthesizers allow both male and female speech output.

For any speech synthesis device, there is a latency period between keystrokes and the beginning of speech output. This can be considerable for longer phrases in older devices, greatly interfering with the flow of communication. For example, in the spelling mode on the device I am familiar with, it takes approximately 1.75 sec after the key press before the device starts to make the letter sound. In the communication mode, it takes over 2 sec for the synthesizer output to start after a word is selected from a single key press. For multiple word phrases, like "How are you today?" it can take up to 4 sec from the pressing of the key to the beginning of the synthesized output. Since most phrases are stored under multiple keystrokes, one should also take into account in calculating the full latency period the time it takes to enter the entire sequence. The key search and press time may vary substantially with the user's disability. It seems remarkable that users can keep messages they want to communicate in mind long enough so that when a listener responds the users still remember to what they are responding.

The secondary output device of the Touch Talker is the LCD text display. This display can be used by the listener to confirm what he or she has heard. A severe disadvantage of some LCD displays is that they cannot easily be seen at all angles of view and may be obscured by their plexiglass display covering, which regularly becomes dirty or scratched. This is even more of a problem for the user than for the listener, since the user needs the display to confirm the message he or she is composing. Editing of the display is possible. One technique is to retrieve a message which is close to what the user wants to say and then edit it to be more apt in a particular situation. Thus, the ability to see the display is critical. With the display adjusted so that the user can see it adequately, it is sometimes not visible to the listener, unless the listener is standing directly behind the user's head.

Many nonspeakers, particularly those who have cerebral palsy, drool. Hence it is of critical importance in the physical design of the system that the overlays on the keys are plastic and drool-resistant, because the user often leans over the device in order to see the LCD display (see, for example, Figure 3.2). Even though the overlays are plastic, after a number of months of use by a drooling user the writing on the overlay will degenerate, even if it has been done in permanent ink. The use of permanent markings also means the writing cannot be altered without creating a new overlay.

Figure 3.2. The Touch Talker in use with the user leaning over to see the display.

The Touch Talker is similar to a laptop computer in size and weight, so it is manageable by either wheelchair users or walking users. However, it is not designed to be carried by a user in a walking frame, since both hands will be on the walker (see Figure 3.3). In addition, the device must be laid upon a surface before it can be used. Although the device has internal batteries which make it portable, those batteries are heavy and liable to be dislodged by physical shock. Therefore, carrying the device around is often discouraged.

A major issue in evaluating the Touch Talker is the user's reactions to Minspeak. Strictly speaking, Minspeak is not a language but essentially an index system for retrieving text by means of mapping sequences of keystrokes to stored phrases. Since each key can have any icon or character written on the overlay on top of it, Minspeak is essentially a translator from symbol sequence to phrase. For example, pressing a key with "?" on it, followed by a key with a picture of a man on it, might result in the retrieval of the sentence "Where is he?," whereas "?" plus a woman might retrieve "Where is she?" The inventor of Minspeak, Bruce Baker, can demonstrate how, with some simple paradigms, one can model

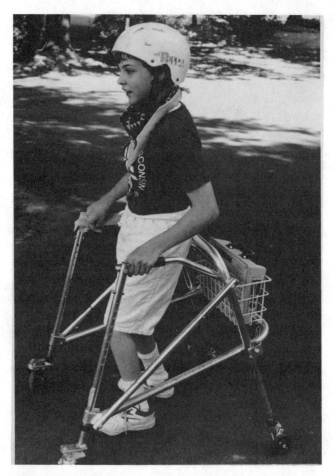

Figure 3.3. Carrying the Touch Talker while using the walker.

a large number of language constructs with a few keystrokes on a relatively few keys (Baker, 1982, 1988; Baker, Schwartz & Conti, unpublished). The difficulty remains that the user must remember what each key can stand for, and so it is incumbent upon the programmer to choose highly evocative icons that can serve a multitude of purposes.

Even though there are only 128 programmable keys on the Touch Talker, Minspeak key sequences may be of any length as long as no sequence is the prefix of any other sequence. Hence the only length limitation on sequences is the memory of the user – there is no browsing mechanism by which users can see what is available. (The newest version of the Touch Talker addresses this problem with lights on the keys indicating what keys are available next among all programmed sequences.) It has been a constant problem in our case that whenever a key sequence unintentionally includes as a prefix any shorter sequence, the shorter sequence is no longer available. For instance, if the shorter sequence, say "?" + man, is typed in but is in fact a prefix to a longer one, such as "?" + man + car, the device sits waiting for the completion of the longer sequence rather than producing the shorter one, and the user cannot always remember what the longer sequence was.

There is a lot of flexibility in the design of the particular symbol-sequence-to-phrase translation table for a particular user. For example, one could have one or more symbols serve as a context marker, within which keystroke suffixes determine the retrieved phrase to synthesize. This was a method of organization that was suggested for my daughter's use. It is not clear whether this method is easy to learn and use or whether or not it models basic language processing skills (which the nonspeaking user may have even if he or she cannot speak). This method of context marking is no longer the standard practice (Baker, 1991). Now one acquires one of the existing application programs that consist of a customized vocabulary of 2,000 to 4,000 words indexable by one to three keystrokes each, and the keys are covered with "consciously ambiguous" (*ibid.*) multivocal icons that can provide a variety of different associations using a variety of different techniques ranging from index to sign (or icon) to symbol (Peirce, 1958). Therefore, the strategy is no longer sentence based but word based, where a user now can gain an additional level of flexibility in combining keystrokes into a desired target sentence. Approximately 50 to 70% of the systems now being sold were supplied with such an application installed.

This development of Minspeak over the years has been in the direction of trying to enhance the recovery of as large a portion of language as possible (Baker, 1991). In this progression, it has increased the flexibility by which keystroke sequences may be mapped to language sequences. It seems, however, that the one basic feature of natural language, its phrase structure, is still missing. In other words, sequences of symbols cannot be used as units within other sequences unless the specific keystroke sequences are programmed that way, which may involve a great deal of effort on the part of the programmer if all combinations are to be obtained. (Whether or not specific applications have this capability is unknown; they were not available for evaluation.) My daughter user constantly wanted to combine symbols into new combinations that did not have a stored phrase associated with them. Baker has developed ways to code the grammatical structure of English, such as identifying modals, verb tenses, and negation, so that the efficiency of language can be exploited rather than its being a straight memorization process. These techniques too were not available for evaluation.

One of the most significant observations I made was that there was a constant effort on my daughter's part to try slight variations on given keystroke sequences. In part, these may have been due to an inability to remember the exact keystrokes and sequence necessary for a desired phrase. On the other hand, there was a clear effort to recombine keystrokes to get at additional phrases. For example, once she had learned the phrase "The teacher is at school," she tried to produce a similar phrase with different subjects, such as "Daddy," "Mommy," and other known people. If these had not been anticipated by the programmer, the device would not respond. Thus, for situations where there is an error in entering the proper keystroke, the device should be able to find the closest match and reproduce its stored text. While this type of function would be easy to program into a computer, it does not exist in the Touch Talker.

If there were some intelligence built into the matching program that used other programmed phrases as prototypical schemata, it is possible that enough flexibility could be programmed into some future device to allow it to approximate a phrase-structured grammar (Strong, 1992). The limitation that one symbol sequence cannot be a prefix of another can also surely be solved by such an intelligent pattern matching device. On the other hand, if each word were to be programmed by a set of keystrokes and the user were able to remember which keystrokes indexed the desired new word in a sentence, he or she could just make the proper substitution in what may be a very long sequence of keystrokes.

Conclusions

A speech prosthesis can fundamentally improve the quality of life of nonvocal users. It allows the person to communicate in the presence of nonsigners and others, such as family members, who may vary in their signing abilities. And for the user with a mobility impairment such that the person cannot sign, the advantages are obvious. This is not to say that a speech device is all that is necessary. There are often times when a user needs to augment communication with signing. The typical device is too large to carry all the time and may be too slow for emergency communications. Also, for certain subjects who use walking frames, the portability of the devices is not sufficient. In spite of these restrictions, I believe no nonspeaker should be deprived of the use of a speech prosthesis device, even of the quality I have investigated.

Within current technology, there is much that could be done to improve the quality of speech prostheses. Almost all improvements are related to the issue of feedback in language production. The following principles for speech prosthesis design are derived from my own experiences:

1. A textual display is essential for feedback during the process of selecting input for the device. Therefore, attention should be paid to the angle of view of the user and the lighting conditions under which the device will be used.

2. Processing time from the end of a keystroke to textual display and speech output must be kept as short as possible, and no longer than 1 sec under any circumstances.

3. Greater attention needs to be paid to icon design in order to create icons which are generic and extensible. Much has been learned in the field of

human–computer interaction regarding icon designs that would greatly benefit the speech prosthesis user.

4. Computers are capable at matching patterns, and so speech prostheses should operate to find the closest match whenever the user fails to type in an exact sequence. This flexibility may allow the keystroke language to more closely approximate a phrase-structured grammar and solve the limitation that one symbol sequence cannot be a prefix of another.

5. The physical device must be rugged and portable so that it can be carried around by a child, implying occasional abusive treatment, especially from a frustrated nonspeaker.

6. Since the device is a computer, it ought to be easily backed up onto a secondary storage medium in a format consistent with some computer standard.

7. The software should give some response to any sequence of keystrokes without requiring that the programmer enter them all. The device should never produce nothing as output to any given input.

These speech prosthesis design principles have been derived from observation of a single user over a long period of time. They have validity as end user input to the design process, which is badly needed in devices such as these. It is past the time to pay attention to disabled end users in the same way that conventional information systems design pays attention to users, and for the same reason – end users are the only ones who know best what they need.

References

Baker, B. R. (1982). Minspeak. *Byte*, *7* (9): 186–202.

Baker, B. R. (1988). The Touch Talker: Organization of the Icons. *Communication Outlook, 10*(2): 8–12.

Baker, B. R. (1991). Personal communication, Semantic Compaction, Inc.

Baker, B. R., Schwartz, P. J., and Conti, R. V. (unpublished). Minspeak models and semantic relationships.

Peirce, C. S. (1958). Values in a universe of chance. In *Selected writings,* ed. P. P. Wiener (pp. 391–396). New York: Doubleday.

Petitto, L. A., and Marentette, P. F. (1991). Babbling in the manual mode: Evidence for the ontogeny of language. *Science, 251*: 1493–1496.

Strong, G. W. (1992). *A usability evaluation of the PRC Touch Talker with Minspeak,* presented at the ISAAC '92 Conference (International Society for Augmentative and Alternative Communication), abstract in *Augmentative and Alternative Communication,* 8 (2), p. 170.

Winograd, T., and Flores, F. (1986). *Understanding computers and cognition – A new foundation for design.* Norwood, NJ: Ablex.

4

Outspoken software for blind users

Alistair D. N. Edwards

Introduction

Throughout the development of human–computer interfaces one aspect has remained quite constant: Communication from the computer to the user has been visual. This would seem to put people with visual disabilities at a disadvantage, but in fact the parallel development of speech synthesis has meant that this is not necessarily true.

A clear distinction has to be made between the majority of visually disabled people, who have some useful vision and are therefore *partially sighted,* and those who are blind; their needs are very different. Partially sighted people need aids which enable them to make the most of their residual vision: spectacles, magnifiers, special lighting, and so on.

The advent of computers has been a positive development for many visually disabled people. With suitable adaptations, many computers and applications have been made accessible to such people, so that, as Scadden (1984) pointed out, many visually disabled people have attained a degree of equality in job opportunities in areas involving the use of information technology, such as word processing. Screen enlargement, synthetic speech screen readers, and "soft" braille displays all work well with text based computer interfaces (e.g. Unix and MS-DOS).

However, problems have arisen with the advent of more visually complex user interfaces, alternatively known as GUIs (graphical user interfaces) or wimps (window, icon, mouse, and pull-down menus). No longer is the interaction based solely on text (typed on a keyboard and displayed on a screen); there are graphical items on the screen at which the user must point, usually by way of a mouse pointing device.

The Apple Macintosh was the first microcomputer to make this style of interaction available in the mass market, but since its release in 1984 the concept has become so popular that it is an option on most modern computers and is the only means of access to many. The implications of this for blind people were summed up by Bowe thus: "When Drexel University required every freshman to buy a Macintosh. . . it was sending a message that 'No blind person need apply here.'" (1987, p. 54).

Outspoken is a commercially available piece of software which attempts to answer this problem by making Macintosh software accessible to blind users through the use of synthetic speech. Outspoken is unique in that it was the first commercially available GUI adaptation and in attempting to make accessible a machine which had previously been barred to blind users. Technically it is excellent, in that its authors had to find ways of gleaning information from the system which was never meant to be accessed by software (since it relates only to the visual appearance of the interface) and rendering it in an auditory form. However, their success in making the interface accessible was not complete, because the problem they set themselves was just too difficult.

There have been a number of other attempts to adapt GUIs for blind users. *Slimware Windows Bridge*[1] is notable among these in that it is an adaptation for Microsoft Windows, the most common GUI on PC platforms. Berkeley Systems, the manufacturer of Outspoken, is also developing toolboxes with which developers will be able to build their own speech based interfaces to Macintoshes and Windows. IBM's Screen Reader has been extended to accommodate its PS/2 Presentation Manager GUI (Schwerdtfeger, 1991). One other attempt to adapt GUIs in general and Windows in particular is the *Guib* project, funded by the European *Tide* initiative (Petrie, Strothotte, Weber, & Deconick, 1993; Weber, 1992, and Chapter 9, this volume). Although a research project, this is intended to lead to a commercial product and is interesting in that it involves experiments with some novel multimedia interactions.

Inevitably this report highlights the shortcomings of Outspoken. For the most part, the deficiencies are caused by the fact that the interface which its authors attempted to adapt was inherently too visually oriented. Some of the problems are common to most GUI implementations, and some of them are specific to the interface on the Macintosh and its implementation.

The tone of this evaluation may seem to be very negative. So it should be stated at the outset that Outspoken is a very significant development. It has enabled some blind people to use some Macintosh software, whereas previously none of it was accessible (except a word processor, *Soundtrack* – see below). Yet the more important, and potentially the very significant, contribution of Outspoken will be that it has highlighted why adapting interfaces is so difficult and where the pitfalls lie. All designers of interfaces should take heed so that future interfaces will not be so difficult to adapt.

Soundtrack, the other piece of Macintosh software which is accessible to blind users, was developed at the University of York. It represents a very different

---

[1] Syntha-Voice Computers Inc, 125 Gailmont Drive, Hamilton, Ontario, Canada, L8K 4B8.

approach to the problem. Edwards and Pitt (1990) is a short comparison of the two pieces of software, and more details of Soundtrack can be found in Edwards (1989a and 1989b).

This chapter will make most sense to anyone who has used Outspoken on a Macintosh. For those who have not done so, the next section provides a brief overview of its operation. (For a more complete description, one should consult the user manual supplied with the software.) Anyone who has not used the Macintosh (or any computer with a similar interface) at all may have further difficulty in following some of the descriptions. No operational description is provided for such readers, because it is too difficult to describe. In many senses this difficulty is the essence of the difficulty of designing Outspoken.

Operation of Outspoken

There are two fundamental problems in adapting a GUI. One is how to present the visual information on the screen, and the second is how to help users to navigate the cursor. In Outspoken the former is achieved mainly through the use of synthetic speech (though some nonspeech sounds are used as well), and the latter is achieved by use of a keypad.

The cursor is normally controlled by way of a mouse, so that movements of the mouse are reflected by movements of the cursor on the screen. However, guiding a mouse through auditory feedback is an inherently difficult task (see Pitt & Edwards, 1991), and the designers of Outspoken have chosen to sidestep this by replacing the mouse with keypad controls. The basic layout of the keypad as interpreted by Outspoken is shown in Figure 4.1. The cursor is controlled principally by four keys (shaded in the figure) which move it up, down, left, and right. As the cursor crosses an area of the screen, its contents are read out. That is to say text is read; graphical items are named or described ("icon," "system folder," etc.). The item currently under the cursor can be selected by pressing the SELECT key.

The cursor can be moved to particular areas of the screen through other keys. For instance, the MENU key moves the cursor directly to the menu bar. The user can then move the cursor along the bar (using RIGHT) to the appropriate menu (their names are read as it moves), which is then pulled down by pressing DRAG/RELEASE. To move the cursor into a particular window, the user presses the WINDOW key. This causes a special menu to appear on the screen (this is not related to any of the menus in the menu bar) which contains the names of all the windows currently on the screen (i.e. open), plus another entry for Desktop, which is the mechanism for moving out of any window and onto the desktop (to interact with disk icons or the Wastebasket, for instance).

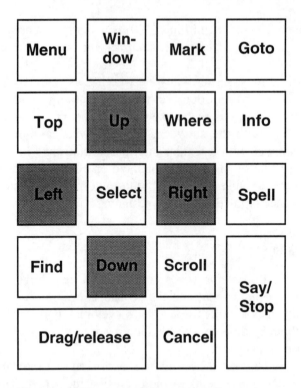

Figure 4.1. The keypad as used by Outspoken.

Operation of Outspoken can be illustrated by way of an example involving typical interactions. The example involves a user who wishes to use a word processor in order to insert a new paragraph in a text document. The new paragraph is to be inserted following one already in the document which the user knows contains the word "Tuesday." For the purposes of this commentary the user is assumed to be female.

The user must first launch the word processor application and open the document to be edited. This can be achieved on the Macintosh by opening the document, which causes the application which created it to be automatically launched. Assuming the screen is as shown in Figure 4.2 and the document is the one called "Text," the user must first move the cursor into the window called Documents. To do this she presses the WINDOW key. This pops up the Window menu, which can be searched with the UP and DOWN keys until Documents is located. That is then selected with the SELECT key. The cursor will normally be located at the top of the window (but not always – see below), and the user can then locate the Word Processor icon, using the cursor keys. The DOWN key generally does not simply move the cursor down but makes it scan along the current horizontal level and then move down. So if the user now presses DOWN, the top level of the window (including its title, "Documents") is described.

Eventually the cursor will reach the level of the Word Processor icon. Pressing DOWN now causes Outspoken to "describe" the contents of the Documents window in Figure 4.2 thus: "Icon, word processor. Document, text. Folder, manilla." The cursor would now be at the end of that "line" (to the right of "Manilla"), and the user would use the LEFT key to get the cursor back to the Text icon. She can now launch that application by double clicking on the SELECT button.

The word processor will be launched with the first page of the document "Text" visible in the window. There is a Find command in the word processor's Edit menu. Outspoken does allow the user to access commands in menus via the cursor (see below), but Macintosh applications also have *keyboard equivalents* for the most commonly used commands. These are specified using a modifier key. This is very similar to the control key on other keyboards, but is called the Command key, and is marked by the special symbol ⌘.

The command ⌘-*f* is typed to evoke the Find command. This opens a dialogue window through which the user will specify the word to be found. When the dialogue opens, Outspoken announces, "Dialogue." The user types the target word, "Tuesday" – which is spelt out letter by letter by Outspoken – and then presses the RETURN key on the main keyboard. The first occurrence of the word is highlighted in the document window. However, the Find dialogue is essentially another window, and it has become the active one. To examine the occurrence of the word in the document, the user must first make its window the active one and move the cursor to the selected word. The user must again use the Windows menu to move the cursor out of the Find dialogue and back into the document window. She must now move the cursor to the target word, which implies finding it within that window. This is accomplished by pressing the FIND key on the keypad and then entering the target word, "Tuesday," again (terminated by a RETURN). Now the text surrounding that word can be explored using the cursor keys.

Suppose the user decides that this is not the required occurrence of the word. She must search for it again. Pressing ⌘-*f* reopens the Find dialogue. This has retained "Tuesday" as the target word, so it does not need to be typed again, and the user merely enters RETURN. Again the document window has to be reactivated (through the WINDOW key and menu) and the word found in the window. Outspoken's Find command also retains the previous target, so to locate the word on the current screen, the user simply types FIND RETURN. She might decide to explore the paragraph further this time. Pressing UP causes the current line, up to the selection, to be spoken. Pressing it twice again causes Outspoken to read the preceding two lines. The user now decides to hear those lines in the right order and presses DOWN three times.

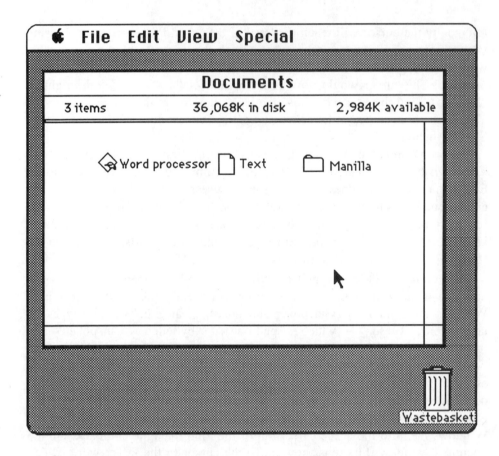

Figure 4.2. A typical Macintosh screen, which could be accessed through Outspoken.

Having decided that this is the paragraph preceding the point at which a new paragraph should be inserted, the user searches for its end. She can listen to each line, using the DOWN command as before. She does not have to listen to every word. Once she has heard enough of one line, pressing DOWN will interrupt the current speech and start the next line immediately. Having located the appropriate position, she must select that point by pressing SELECT. She then types in the new paragraph. When she types slowly, each word is spoken; if she increases her speed, speech stops.

Having entered the paragraph, the user proofreads it. She uses the UP and DOWN commands as before. Having located a line in which she suspects there is an error of an extra letter, she uses RIGHT to move along word by word to the erroneous one. When she presses SPELL, that word will be spelt out. To delete the extraneous letter, it must first be selected, so the user holds down the SHIFT key and presses RIGHT, which moves the cursor letter by letter. The simplest way to delete the extra letter is to move the cursor to the right of it, press SELECT, and then press the DELETE key on the main keyboard. Nothing is spoken when DELETE is pressed, but the user can check that she has deleted correctly by pressing SPELL again.

To quit the word processor, there is a keyboard equivalent available (⌘-*q*). First, through a dialogue, it will find out whether the user wishes to save the document to disk. It poses the question "Do you want to save file?" and offers three options (called buttons), YES, NO, and CANCEL. Again Macintosh software has a convention which allows one to use the keyboard. The default button in a dialogue (which in this case is *Yes*) is executed if the user presses RETURN. However, let us suppose that this time the user decides she has not made all the changes she wants and so wishes to abort the quit command. She must move to the dialogue and locate the *Cancel* button. The cursor will have been moved into the dialogue automatically, so that pressing DOWN makes Outspoken read out "Do you want to save file?" Pressing it again makes it read "Button, yes. Button, no. Button, cancel." The user can home in on *Cancel* using the cursor keys and then execute it with the SELECT key.

One of the attractions of word processing on computers such as the Macintosh is that it offers a variety of typefaces, sizes, and styles. Suppose the user decides to change the typeface of the whole of this document. First the whole document must be selected. There is a keyboard equivalent to do this, ⌘-*a*. To choose the new typeface, she must use a menu. She presses the MENU key. This moves the cursor to the left end of the menu bar. There is always a special menu in that position, marked by an apple symbol, so Outspoken says, "Menu apple." Pressing RIGHT moves the cursor along the menu bar, and Outspoken reads out the menu titles thereon. The one required is called Font. Once that is located, the user presses SELECT. This causes the menu to be pulled down, revealing a list of the available fonts. The user moves down that list and hears the names of the typefaces. When the user hears the one she wants, she presses SELECT again. This will have the desired effect of changing the typeface in the document. Now the user does quit the word processor, as outlined above, except that this time she selects OK from the "Do you want to save file?" dialogue (probably by simply pressing RETURN).

Suppose the user changes her mind completely about the alterations and now wants to discard the document. On the Macintosh the only way to remove a file is to drag its icon onto a special Wastebasket icon. To do this, the user must first locate the document icon, as before. Having moved the cursor to the icon, she presses DRAG/RELEASE to select it and prepare it to be dragged to the Wastebasket. Always at the bottom of the Window menu is a special entry, Desktop. This refers to the screen area which is the background to all the windows. The user selects Desktop and presses RIGHT. This moves the cursor to the Wastebasket, which is signaled by Outspoken's saying "Wastebasket," and it drags the file icon with it, so that by pressing DRAG/RELEASE once more the icon is "dropped" into the Wastebasket and hence its file removed.

Although Outspoken uses mostly speech, it does also make use of other simple sounds. A particular beep signals "no more," such as at the edges of the screen and the bottom of a menu. Text documents on the Macintosh usually display a flashing selection marker, and in Outspoken this is represented as a clicking sound. Various other beeps are used to signal various other factors. There is a sound associated with dragging; as long as an item is selected for dragging, that sound is heard. Other sounds depends somewhat on how the user has set up Outspoken for her own use

This brief description should help the reader follow my discussion. It by no means covers all of the facilities of Outspoken, which is quite powerful and flexible. This is supported by the fact that the keypad is effectively not as simple as Figure 4.1 would suggest. The keys can be used in combination with modifier keys, such as OPTION and SHIFT, giving the user a wide range of facilities and control. Full details are available in the Outspoken documentation.

Problems inherent in adapting GUIs

The main difficulties in using Outspoken are caused by the fact that there are aspects of the interaction which are part of the visual interface – and the way that interface is implemented – which just do not lend themselves to presentation in speech.

Although a computer screen is a two-dimensional surface, a GUI (such as the Macintosh's) effectively has three dimensions, since items on the screen are allowed to overlap. A sighted user can cope with the implicit third dimension by applying the same sort of perceptual tricks as are employed in looking at a picture. For instance, anyone looking at a picture of someone standing behind a counter does not assume that the person has no legs.[1] Similarly, someone may have two windows on the Macintosh screen but with only part of one visible behind the other. The viewer will be able to separate the two conceptually, and make assumptions about the portion of the window which is invisible. On the basis of these assumptions and knowledge of the real world (which has been modeled by the designer of the interface), users will be able to manipulate the windows in three dimensions, so that they can, for instance, pull one window from the bottom of a pile to the top.

---

[1]   That is not to say that a blind person would necessarily not appreciate visual phenomena such as occlusion. Studies such as Kennedy (1980) suggest that they can. This just makes the designer's job even harder; there are few assumptions which can be made about blind people's perception – and a sparse, inconclusive psychology literature to draw on.

System Folder

Figure 4.3. An icon which might have to be "pronounced" by Outspoken.

The designers of Outspoken have coped well with this problem. The cursor is constrained to moving within the currently selected screen item. So, for instance, if the cursor is at the right edge of a window, moving it right does not move it out of that window (and possibly into another window beneath the current one). It is a constraint on the Macintosh interface that only one window can be active at any time, and the way the Outspoken user activates any given window is through the special Windows menu. (See the section below, on Window/Menu confusions).

The third spatial dimension of the screen is thus transformed into menu selection, something the Outspoken user can perform quite easily. To a large extent, therefore, the three-dimensional nature of the screen is irrelevant. This is also true when dealing with the Macintosh pull-down menus. In the visual interface, there is always a row of menu titles at the top of the screen. Pointing at a menu title and pressing the mouse button causes the menu to appear beneath its title. It will always overlap whatever was on the screen below the menu title. This is not at all apparent to the Outspoken user, and it does not matter. The corresponding sequence of actions for the Outspoken user is as described earlier, through the MENU and cursor keys. The fact that when the menu was pulled down it overlapped some other item (usually a window) on the screen is irrelevant; that item is inaccessible in the current mode anyway.

Part of the problem arises from the fact that there are many dimensions to a graphical display on screen. Quite apart from the obvious two (or three) spatial dimensions, there are pictorial properties which are hard to translate into auditory form, and particularly into speech. For instance, Figure 4.3 shows a detail from a window which might be shown on the screen. The icon represents the special System folder. Outspoken recognizes this icon and announces it as "System folder." However, once the icon is located, if the Outspoken user moves the cursor downwards the text below the icon will be spoken, so it repeats, "System folder." Outspoken does attempt to make a distinction between the two by varying the intonation between the two uses of the phrase, but the speech synthesizer used (Macintalk) is not flexible enough to make the difference noticeable (though adjusting the speech parameters can make the voices more distinctive). Hence, to most blind users, there is no means of distinguishing the two, while there is a very clear distinction to a sighted user.

Other problems are caused by the assumption effectively built into Outspoken that the screen layout is a grid on which the only directions to move are orthogonal – up, down, left, and right – and that the natural scanning strategy is top left to bottom right. This works well if the content of the screen being examined is a document, which inherently has that structure, in that documents are usually read from left to right and top to bottom, but is not as well suited to other screen items, as described below. Even within a document, additional confusion can be caused by the way up and down are interpreted. As described in the earlier example, in most situations pressing DOWN does not simply move the cursor down. Instead it acts on the cursor more like a carriage return on a typewriter or word processor. In other words, normally when the user presses DOWN the cursor scans to the right, reading out the items it moves over, and then moves down one level and skips back to the left edge. This corresponds to the way a user might read text on the screen or scan the icons in a window.

Confusion can occur when the current screen item does not have the linear structure of a piece of text. For instance, a dialogue window, such as that shown in Figure 4.4, does not have such a structure. A file icon, the filename "abstract," a scroll control, a disk icon, and the name of the disk all appear on the same horizontal level. So if a user scans the list of filenames (by pressing DOWN), that line would be spoken as "File, abstract. Scroll up. Hard disc. SE30." Although the latter three items clearly have no relationship to the file in the visual presentation, they are read out together, so that the blind user infers some connection between them.

Problems caused by the implementation of the interface

To make a complete nonvisual interface to a GUI it is necessary to build an *off screen model* (OSM) of the screen (Schwerdtfeger, 1991). That is a data structure which embodies all the information displayed by the interface. The quality of the OSM depends on the level at which the adaptation can intercept the data used by

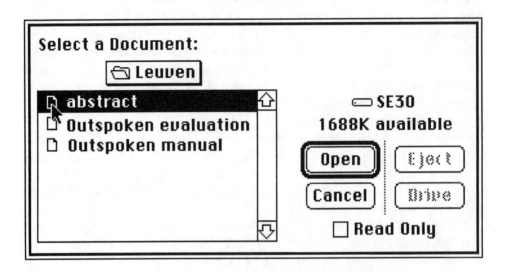

Figure 4.4. A dialogue which might be scanned by Outspoken.

the visual display. At the lowest level, it may rely on a simple bitmap of the visual screen. In such a case, the adaptation must embody a vast amount of information to infer the meaning of items within the bitmap. This is essentially a very difficult problem similar to that of optical character recognition – but even more difficult since graphical objects must be recognized as well as characters. This approach has been attempted but with limited success in the Tide *Visa* project (Harness, Pugh, Sherkat, & Whitrow, 1993). At the other extreme the adaptation would have access to a high level description of the information content of the screen, which it could render in any appropriate form – visual or nonvisual. This might be possible in future, if user interface management systems (UIMS) are developed which succeed in separating applications and their interfaces (Pfaff & ten Hagen, 1985).

For the present, however, there is no clear separation and adaptation designers have to extract what information they can – which implies a level somewhere between these two extremes. This is the challenge which confronted the designers of Outspoken. One of their problems was that it was not possible to implement the principle that every action should have a perceivable effect. Events happen on screen which are signaled only visually that Outspoken has no means of recognizing and communicating aurally. For instance, if the user selects a word in a word processor, the word is displayed in reverse video, but Outspoken does not indicate to the user what the selection is – because it has no means of accessing the internal data structures which contain this information.

Similarly, one of the helpful features of menus in the Macintosh is that entries are disabled when they are not available. For instance, it is not possible to close a file when no file is open. Whereas on a conventional system the user would get an error message if he or she tried to close a nonexistent file, on the Macintosh he or she cannot execute that command at all – and hence avoids getting (possibly incomprehensible) error messages. The fact that a menu entry is not enabled is signaled by its being displayed in a dimmed typeface (as the "Close" command is in Figure 4.5). Unfortunately, Outspoken does not give any indication of dimmed items. For instance, in scanning the file menu in Figure 4.5, "Close" would be read in the same voice as all the other entries. Selecting it would cause nothing to happen – not even an error message to inform the user that the close had failed. Again, this occurs because Outspoken cannot access the relevant internal data structures.

A considerable number of user errors occur because of the fact that information which is available to the sighted user is not available to the Outspoken user. Often the information amounts to informing the users that they are in a *mode*, a phenomenon discussed further in "Analysis," below. The implementers of Outspoken have done an impressive job of extracting as much information as possible about the screen contents from the data structures maintained by the system. Nevertheless, it seems that there is some information which is not accessible, making the interface less than perfect for users.

Figure 4.5. A menu which has been pulled down by the user pressing the DRAG/RELEASE key once. Notice that "Close" is displayed in gray type, signifying that it is not currently an available command.

A major problem with speech in general is its slowness, and this is even more true of synthetic speech. Outspoken attempts to alleviate this by cutting short unnecessary speech. Unless the user waits to hear all the current speech, any action he or she performs (such as moving the cursor) will interrupt the speech. So, for instance, if the user were going down the list of files as shown in the window in Figure 4.4, he or she might recognize the filename "Outspoken evaluation" on hearing just the first syllable or two and would not have to wait for the rest, but could immediately press DOWN again. Of course that could cause confusion if the user had forgotten that there were in fact two files in that folder, "Outspoken evaluation" and "Outspoken manual." Similarly, when a user types text (say, into a word processor), the typing may be echoed. However, because the speech cannot keep up with a dextrous typist, it is effectively silenced once the user gets up to a certain speed. However, given the limited consistency of manual skills, the typing rate is likely to fluctuate, which causes some words to be spoken and others not; indeed, if the user pauses in the middle of a word, the incomplete word typed so far may be spoken. Obviously these phenomena can cause confusion.

One practical implementation problem related to typing speeds is that Outspoken slows down the Macintosh so much that a fast typist can input so fast that the software cannot keep up and characters are lost. This is another consequence of the way in which Outspoken had to be implemented – very much as an add-on adaptation.

Another source of confusion to the Outspoken user is the fact that the cursor can move unpredictably. For instance, on activating a window, the user cannot expect the cursor to be in any given position in that window. Normally it will be in the top left corner, but this is not always the case.

Shortcomings in the design of Outspoken

As described above, most of the shortcomings of Outspoken are caused by factors over which its designers had little or no control. There are, however, one or two design decisions they made which were perhaps ill advised.

The Macintosh interface is designed around the desktop metaphor, whereby the screen operates as if it is a desk, which may be covered with windows, much as a real desk may be covered with sheets of paper. Thus the screen around the windows is known as the Desktop (or *underneath* the windows, if one thinks in terms of three dimensions). The Outspoken user has the option of locating the cursor in any one of the windows or on the Desktop, and this choice is made through the Windows menu. There is a further discussion below of aspects of the Windows menu, but one design decision which is open to question is that the Desktop appears in it. This implies to the user that the Desktop is another window – or at least is in some way equivalent to a window, which is not true.

This is an example of a very common phenomenon in using Outspoken: To a sighted Macintosh user the Desktop is clearly not a window, and confusion between them is impossible, but to the Outspoken user the concepts are much less clear and hence prone to being confusing if presented in an ambiguous manner. An alternative mechanism would have been to assign one of the keypad keys causing the mouse to move to the Desktop (just as the MENU key moves the mouse to the menus). Obviously this would have meant reassigning or eliminating one of the key commands, which is presumably why the designers chose the mechanism they did, but the modification would have been much more consistent and easier to work with.

As mentioned, files are deleted from the Macintosh Desktop by dragging their icon on top of a Wastebasket icon (Figure 4.6). Once a file has been put in the wastebasket in this way, the icon changes to a bulging one, as shown in Figure 4.7. The analogy with a wastebasket is maintained in that as long as it is bulging, the user can have a change of mind about discarding a file and take it back out of the wastebasket again. However, the bin is periodically emptied (at the explicit request of the user, via a menu command), so that once the icon has reverted to the form in Figure 4.6, discarded files are no longer recoverable.

There is no limit to the number of files which can be discarded at any time. In other words, dragging a file icon over to a bulging wastebasket has the effect desired, no matter how full the basket is. However, this is not the impression that the Outspoken user gets. The normal (Figure 4.6) wastebasket is described by Outspoken as "Trash," and the bulging (Figure 4.7) one is described as "Trash full." To say a bin is full implies that it must be emptied before anything further can be put in it, and users may think that they have to empty it before they can put any more files in it. It would be more accurate to suggest that the bin is not empty, rather than that it is full.

Wastebasket

Figure 4.6. An "empty" wastebasket icon.

Wastebasket

Figure 4.7. The bulging wastebasket icon, which signifies that there are (recoverable) files in it.

Where overlapping windows are present, the Windows menu sometimes does not work properly, and although the user selects a window from it, that window is not brought to the top, and the user cannot access it. It seems likely that this bug is due to problems in accessing the system information, and it may be that there was nothing the Outspoken programmers could do about it.

Interface inconsistencies

One major contribution of Outspoken is that it serves as a means of highlighting inconsistencies in the interface. Design is always a matter of compromise. Consistency is an important feature of any interface, but sometimes it has to be traded off against other factors. Indeed, it has been argued that consistency it practically unattainable (Grudin, 1989). In general, the Macintosh interface has a very high degree of consistency, as encouraged by Apple's interface guidelines (Apple Computer, 1987), but there are examples where there are inconsistencies, and some of these are even more apparent when the interface is accessed through Outspoken.

Inconsistencies might not be noticed or might be considered of minor importance when the user has visual feedback as to what is happening, but they cause great confusion when accessed through an auditory interface. For example, many actions are invoked by the user's simply selecting an item. For others the user must first select the item and then do something else, such as press the ENTER key. To the user of the visual interface, there is no apparent inconsistency, because in the latter case there will be reminders on the screen. For instance, Figure 4.4 shows a dialogue from which the file selection must be confirmed either by selecting the *Open* button (which is emboldened) or by pressing the ENTER key. Should the sighted user forget how the dialogue works and not confirm the selection, the dialogue will not go away; indeed, it will remain on the screen with the buttons serving the purpose of reminding the user or prompting him or her as to the correct action. An Outspoken user who forgets to confirm the selection will get no indication that nothing has happened or any reminder of what should be done next.

Another example is that one of the interface guidelines states that there must always be a File menu available on the screen. Furthermore, one of the entries in that menu must be *Open*. This rule ensures a degree of consistency, but the manner in which the *Open* command is used may be inconsistent. In particular, at the top level of interaction, the Finder, the user can open a file by selecting it with the mouse and then selecting *Open* from the file menu. However, within applications, the usual style of interaction is for the user to select the *Open* command first and then specify which file to open. This lack of consistency does not appear to cause sighted users any real problems but does confuse Outspoken users. This inconsistency is a glaring violation of Apple's own interface guidelines: "The general form of user actions is noun-then-verb, or 'Hey, you – do this'" (Apple Computer, 1987, p. 4).

Menu/window confusions

A window is an inherently visual concept. After all, a real-world window is something you *look* through. Furthermore, the way windows are presented in computer interfaces and accessed through Outspoken is potentially very confusing to a blind user. The menu is a simpler concept, and the design of Outspoken encourages the user to deal with windows as if they were more like menus, but therein lies another source of confusion as to the difference between a menu and a window.

There may be a large number of windows open on a screen at any time, and they may well overlap. The Macintosh user specifies which window he or she wishes to interact with by pointing to it and pressing the mouse button. This brings that menu to the top of any overlapping ones and allows the user to interact with its contents. The same operation is achieved in Outspoken through an additional menu, one which is not part of the standard visual interface. Pressing the MENU key causes a menu to appear on the screen containing the names of all the currently open windows (plus a special entry for Desktop). The user just needs to press DOWN to locate the required window; pressing SELECT will bring that window to the top and move the cursor to it.

The contents of a window may be almost anything: a document, a picture, a set of icons. The most general case is probably a window displaying the files in a folder. Those files may be represented as a set of icons (as in Figure 4.8) or as a list of names and attributes (as in Figure 4.9). Icons are difficult to handle through Outspoken, for reasons already described, and because they can be placed anywhere within the window, not necessarily in the grid pattern favored by Outspoken. It is therefore generally easier for the Outspoken user to use the name-list format. The format can be further simplified by reshaping the window to hide a lot of the extraneous information, as in Figure 4.10. This format is similar to a menu, and the Outspoken user moves down the names to the required one and then selects it.

The descriptions above illustrate some of the problems of using Outspoken. The Windows menu is a necessary addition to the interface which gets round the very difficult problem of dealing with objects which can overlap on the screen. However, it is somewhat anomalous in that it is a menu but one which cannot be accessed through the normal menu procedure (i.e. using the MENU key). Furthermore, interaction with this menu is unlike interaction with the other menus. The user does not press the DRAG/RELEASE key before pressing DOWN and can select the required window using either SELECT or DRAG/RELEASE.

Again it is easier for the blind user to use a window layout which resembles a menu, but it may be that this does add to the confusion as to the distinction between menus and windows. Once again, this is a confusion which would never occur to the sighted user, because the two look completely different; through Outspoken they appear to be very much the same.

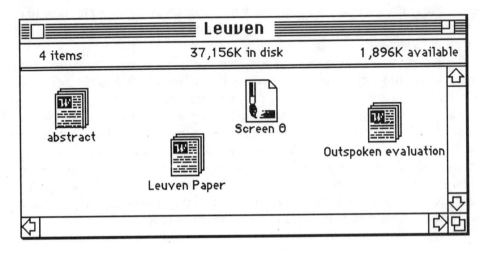

Figure 4.8. A Macintosh window displaying files represented as icons.

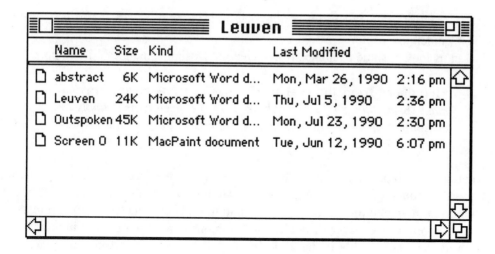

Figure 4.9. The same files as in the window in Figure 4.8, but now given a different representation.

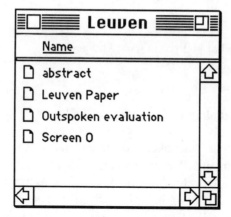

Figure 4.10. By reshaping the window shown in Figure 4.9, it can be made easier to use.

Analysis

The interfaces to any Macintosh application should conform to the Apple interface guidelines (Apple Computer, 1987). Though generally a good and effective set of guidelines for visual interfaces, many of the problems of designing and using Outspoken can be traced back to and analyzed in terms of those guidelines.

Let us look at some examples from "General Design Principles" (ibid., pp. 3–9):

> **Metaphors from the real world.** *Use concrete metaphors and make them plain, so that users have a set of expectations to apply to computer environments. Whenever appropriate, use audio and visual effects that support the metaphor.*

That appears to be equally applicable to an auditory interface; it even mentions the use of sound. The problem is that the extent to which the metaphors can be supported in an auditory form is limited, and to embody a metaphor in a purely auditory form is even more difficult. The commonest metaphor used in interfaces such as the Macintosh's is the desktop, and what does a desktop sound like? Gaver (1989) has succeeded in adding an auditory component to many of the Desktop items, but not in a way which would make the interface accessible without the visual component.

> **See-and-point.** [One of two basic assumptions is] *that users can see. . .*
>
> **WYSIWYG** (what you see is what you get).

Need one say more?

> **Feedback and dialogue.** *Keep the user informed.*

One of the problems that Outspoken's designers had was that it was not possible to implement this principle. Events happen on screen which are signaled only visually, and Outspoken has no means of recognizing that signal and communicating it aurally. For instance, if the user selects a word in a word processor, the word is displayed in reverse video, but there is no means of communicating the identity of the selection to the Outspoken user.

> **Aesthetic integrity.** . . . *Different "things" look different on the screen.*

As discussed above, Outspoken does not succeed in making different things *sound* different. This results from the limitations of synthetic speech, and of the speech synthesizer used in this case and from the fact that nonspeech audio was not used more extensively.

There is a need to reformulate interface guidelines (in general, and the Apple guidelines specifically) in media independent terms. For instance, the last statement above might become "Different 'things' are presented differently." Clearly some guidelines will be difficult to reformulate; (this subject will probably be the basis of a separate paper). For instance, how does one present "what you see is what you get" in nonvisual terms?

Modality and modeless interaction have become something of a *cause célèbre* in the field of human–computer interaction. There are different ideas as to what modes are, but they generally amount to the idea that an interface can have different states and that the effect that a user input will have varies according to the current state of the system. The commonest example is found in some word processors, which operate in two modes, Insert Mode and Command Mode. When the word processor is in Insert Mode, anything the user types on the keyboard goes into the document. However, when the word processor is in Command Mode, keypresses are interpreted as commands. That means that the effect of pressing a particular key depends on the current mode. For instance, the command to quit the program may be the letter Q. In Command Mode, pressing Q will cause the program to terminate, whereas in Insert Mode, pressing Q will insert that letter in the document.

Modal software is often presented as a Bad Thing because many errors can occur if the user loses track of the mode. For instance, a user may want to insert the word "Quebec" in a document and, thinking the program is in Insert Mode, start typing it, but in fact the program is in Command Mode and interprets the first letter of the word as a command and so terminates. Clearly such errors are annoying and there is evidence that they are frequent (Monk, 1986; Tesler, 1981). However, Tesler may have gone too far in making a T-shirt emblazoned with the slogan "Don't mode me in," because modes are an inevitable and necessary aspect of many interactions (see Thimbleby, 1990, chap. 11).

To some extent, the effects which can be ascribed to modality depend on the definition of the term you choose. Tesler's attitude can be justified in terms of the prescriptive definition he proposes: "A mode of an interactive computer system is a state of the user interface that lasts for a period of time, is not associated with any particular object, and has no role other than to place an interpretation on operator input." (Tesler, quoted in Smith, Irby, Kimball, Verplank, & Harslem, 1982, p. 276).

Many of the difficulties of using Outspoken are associated with the Macintosh interface's having a modal nature. For instance, input expected from users is different depending on whether they are interacting with a menu or a window. According to Tesler's definition, this is not truly a question of modality, because the different "modes" are associated with different objects. What is missing for users of Outspoken is any confirmation that they are interacting with a particular object. When a sighted user moves the cursor from a window to a menu, there is a clear visual representation of the different context – the menu looks different from the window. To the blind user they sound the same. The user remembers that the cursor is in a menu *and* remembers the (slightly) different rules that apply to interacting with menus. Outspoken does signal one mode aurally: As

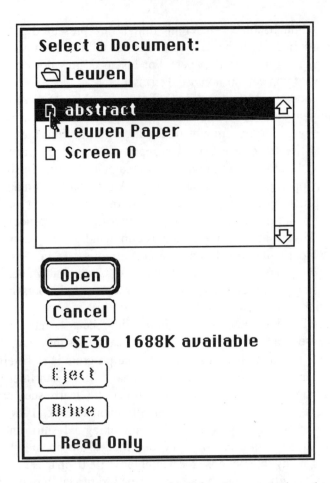

Figure 4.11. A dialogue which has been redesigned to make it more compatible with Outspoken.

long as the user is dragging an icon, there is a low buzz. Greater use could be made of continuous (but transient) sounds to signal the occurrence of a modes. Indeed, it seems likely that much greater use could be made of continuous background sounds to signal the current state of the system (Brewster, Wright, & Edwards, 1994).

Improving on it

There is some scope for customizing software to be more compatible with Outspoken, using facilities available on the Macintosh. The screen items (menus, dialogues, etc.) used by a given application are stored as *resources* in a special section of the application's file. A special editor is available which allows users to modify such resources.[1] Using this facility, it is fairly simple (for a sighted person) to reformat the dialogue shown in Figure 4.4 to that in Figure 4.11. By rearranging nonrelated items vertically, the user avoids their being announced together. For instance, with the redesigned dialogue the speech "File, abstract. Scroll up. Hard disc. SE30." would not occur – although the user would still hear "File, abstract. Scroll up."

Modifying the software in this manner means that the blind user will still have access to "standard" applications. A step further would be to develop software specifically intended for use with Outspoken. Although this defeats one of the objectives of Outspoken – to be a generalized adaptation – it is probably the best hope for making Outspoken and the Macintosh genuinely useful to blind people. Of course there is no reason why software thus developed should not be equally usable by sighted people through the standard visual interface. The exercise of designing software from this point of view could be a valuable one in teaching how software ought to be written to make it more easily adaptable.

Compatibility

The Outspoken user manual acknowledges some commercial applications with which Outspoken cannot be used because of software incompatibilities. Chief among these is HyperCard, a very popular piece of Macintosh software. Additionally, however, there is a whole range of software which is inherently so visual that it would make no sense to attempt to use Outspoken – all drawing programs, for instance.

Another keyboard incompatibility is with Apple's Macintosh Programmer's Workshop (MPW). Although this is intended mainly as an interface for programmers developing software on the Macintosh, it can be used to access most of the machine's facilities, not just software development tools. As a text based interface (somewhat similar to the Unix shell) it might be rather easier to use than the standard graphical interface for the Outspoken user. However, whereas most Macintosh software treats the RETURN key (on the main keyboard) and the ENTER key (on the keypad) as equivalent, MPW interprets them differently, and the ENTER key is effectively not available (Outspoken uses it for SAY/STOP).

During the evaluation of Outspoken a problem occurred which cannot be positively attributed to Outspoken but is worth mentioning as its effects were serious. A Macintosh running Outspoken was left unattended for some time. The (public domain) screensaver *Darkness* was installed on the system, and it self-activated as normal after due delay. On return to the machine, Outspoken was no

---

[1] The original motivation for allowing this facility was to make it easy to convert software for use in different countries. Menu entries can be converted into French, for instance, without having to rebuild the whole application.

longer speaking, and all interactions with the system had become exceedingly slow (several seconds to pull down a menu). On attempting to alleviate the situation by shutting down and rebooting, I found that the System file had become severely corrupted. It would seem that some interaction between Outspoken and Darkness was to blame, but it is difficult to pin down the exact responsibility, and experimenting in order to get more information seems unwise.

Conclusions

Outspoken is a worthy attempt to address a very difficult problem. Unfortunately, that problem was just too complex for it to succeed completely: The availability of Outspoken will not persuade large numbers of blind people to buy Macintoshes. Nevertheless, the development of Outspoken will prove to be very significant, as it has highlighted exactly what is difficult about adapting software with a graphical user interface. Hopefully software designers will benefit from those lessons and make programs which are both usable by the able-bodied majority and easily adaptable to make them accessible to users with disabilities.

Postscript

This report was written on the basis of the experience of a very small number of users of Outspoken. A much broader and more complete evaluation would be achieved if the experience of other users were pooled. Any Outspoken users who would be interested in contributing to such a broader review are urged to contact me.

Acknowledgments

This chapter was based on the experience of two blind users of Outspoken, Alistair Williamson and Chris Bartlett, without whom it would have been impossible to write it. Thanks also to Janet Finlay and Ian Pitt for reading a draft of the chapter, and providing some very useful comments on it.

References

Apple Computer Inc. (1987). *Apple human interface guidelines: The Apple Desktop interface.* Reading MA: Addison-Wesley.

Bowe, F. (1987). Making computers accessible to disabled people. *Technology Review*, *90*(1): 52–59.

Brewster, S. A., Wright, P. C., and Edwards, A. D. N., (1994). *The design and evaluation of an auditory-enhanced scrollbar.* In *Human factors in computing systems: Celebrating interdependence,* Proceedings of Chi'94, ed. B. Abelson, S. Dumais, and J Olson. Reading, MA: Addison-Wesley, pp. 173–179.

Edwards, A. D. N. (1989a). *S*oundtrack: An auditory interface for blind users. *Human–Computer Interaction, 4*(1): 45–66.

Edwards, A. D. N. (1989b). *Soundtrack 2 user manual,* Technical Report YCS120. University of York, Department of Computer Science.

Edwards, A. D. N., and Pitt, I. J. (1990). *Adapting the Macintosh and other graphical user interfaces for blind users.* Proceedings of 6th International Workshop on Computer Applications for the Visually Handicapped, Leuven, Belgium, the proceedings are published as a special edition of *Infovisie Magazine*, 4(3).

Gaver, W. W. (1989). The SonicFinder: An interface that uses auditory icons. *Human–Computer Interaction, 4*(1): 67–94.

Grudin, J. (1989). The case against user interface consistency. *Communications of the ACM, 32*(10): 1164–1173.

Harness, S., Pugh, K., Sherkat, N., and Whitrow, R. (1993). Fast icon and character recognition for universal access to wimp interfaces for the blind and partially sighted, In *Rehabilitation technology: Strategies for the European Union*, ed. E. Ballabio, I. Placencia-Porreo, and R. Puig de la Bellacasa. Amsterdam: IOS Press, pp. 19–23.

Kennedy, J. M., (1980). *Blind people recognizing and making haptic pictures.* In *The perception of pictures*, Volume 2, ed. M. A. Hagen. New York: Academic Press, pp. 263–303.

Monk, A. F. (1986). Mode errors: A user-centred analysis and some preventative measures using keyboard-contingent sound. *International Journal of Man–Machine Studies, 24*:313–327.

Petrie, H., Strothotte, T., Weber, G., and Decononick, F. (1993). The design and evaluation of rehabilitative computer technology for blind people: The need for a multi-disciplinary approach. In *Rehabilitation technology: Strategies for the European Union*, ed. E. Ballabio, I. Placencia-Porreo, and R. Puig de la Bellacasa. Amsterdam: IOS Press, pp. 220–224.

Pfaff, G., and ten Hagen P. J. W (eds.) (1985). *Seeheim workshop on user interface management systems.* Berlin: Springer-Verlag.

Pitt, I. J., and Edwards, A. D. N. (1991). *Navigating the interface by sound for blind users*. In D. Diaper and N. Hammond (eds.), *People and Computers VI*, Proceedings of the HCI'91 Conference, Cambridge University Press, pp. 373–383.

Scadden, L. A. (1984, November). Blindness in the information age: Equality or irony? *Journal of Visual Impairment and Blindness*, pp. 394–400.

Schwerdtfeger, R. S. (1991, December). Making the GUI talk. *Byte*, pp. 118–128.

Smith, D. C., Irby, C., Kimball, R., Verplank, B., and Harslem, E. (1982, April). Designing the Star user interface. *Byte*, pp. 242–282.

Tesler, L. (1981, August). The Smalltalk environment. *Byte*, pp. 90–147.

Thimbleby, H. (1990). *User interface design,* New York: ACM Press.
Weber, G. (1992). Adapting graphical interaction objects for blind users by
    integrating braille and speech. In *Computers for handicapped persons,*
    Proceedings of the Third International Conference on Computers for
    Handicapped Persons, ed. W. Zagler. Vienna: R. Oldenbourg, pp. 546–555.

Manufacturer

Outspoken is manufactured by Berkeley Systems Inc., 1700 Shattuck Avenue,
Berkeley, CA 94709.

5

Intelligent systems for speech and language impaired people: A portfolio of research

Alan F. Newell, John L. Arnott, Alistair Y. Cairns, Ian W. Ricketts, and Peter Gregor

Communication systems for people with speech and language impairments

The capability of complex communication with others is the major characteristic which separates human beings from the rest of the animal kingdom. We use speech to make bonds between us and our fellow human beings, and without these bonds life can be a very isolated existence. Communication dysfunction is a seriously debilitating disability. Communicating even the simplest message to another person, however, is a very complicated act. In order to be understood, we have to obey very elaborate and often little-understood rules. Our communication has to use correct vocabulary, it has to be syntactically and semantically correct, and it must be congruent with the rules of politeness of our particular culture. If the communication is spoken, we must use correct pronunciation, and speak with an appropriate intonation pattern and emotional tone. We must obey the laws of discourse and pragmatics (e.g. "turn taking" – when to say something, and how to indicate you intend to start speaking and have finished). Our speech must be accompanied by the appropriate eye contact, body language, and gestures. Violation of any one of the rules governing these behaviors may mean that the communication is significantly misunderstood.

The types of communication dysfunction are many and varied. Obviously those who are illiterate cannot communicate by writing, and this may be caused by physical difficulties, insufficient or poor education, or special learning difficulties of the individual. Physical disability may mean that a person is unable to speak. Congenital brain dysfunction or brain injury caused by a stroke or other trauma, however, can cause much more complex problems with language. For example, people may know what they want to say but cannot produce the words or cannot produce grammatically correct sentences. Others may use correct words and syntax, but the semantics of their sentences is totally wrong. Some do not understand the rules of discourse. Some have intact language abilities in the written but not in the spoken form.

Communication impairment thus covers a very wide range of problems, and so it is not easy to provide an efficient and effective prosthesis for people with communication dysfunction. Even the relatively simple problem of providing an effective speech output device for a person with intact language skills who simply cannot speak has yet to be solved. Nondisabled people usually speak at between 150 and 200 words per minute (news readers are trained to speak at 180 w.p.m.), whereas a competent typist can produce only 60 to 80 w.p.m., and a person with additional physical disabilities may be able to type at only 5 to 10 w.p.m. Thus, if a keyboard is simply connected to a speech synthesizer, there is a very large difference between normal speech rates and the rate at which a person could talk using such a system. In addition, in order to control a conversation, a speaker has to be able to say something immediately after the previous speaker has ceased talking and also be able to interrupt other speakers. A gap of a few tenths of a second may mean that the opportunity is lost. If it takes several seconds for nonspeaking people to create their replies, this will severely limit their contributions to conversations. If a person has cognitive difficulties which mean that he or she finds it difficult to formulate the appropriate words, the situation becomes even worse.

The cartoon is a caricature of this situation. Before the non-speaking person has had time to reply to the simple greeting, the other person in the conversation has become bored and moved on. A simple but ineffective solution to this problem is to store in a computer all the phrases which the nonspeaking person may wish to articulate. The storage of a very large number of phrases poses no problem to the system designer, but such systems are ineffective for two major reasons: (1) They do not allow for the unexpected and (2) even if the situation is expected, the user is often unable to remember whether a particular phrase is stored in the system and, if it is, how to access it. (One early aid could store 999 phrases, and each had a numeric code, but users were able to remember only a handful of such access codes.)

Thus we need to tackle the problems of increasing the speed at which unique statements can be made by the nonspeaking person and of providing easy access methods to a large database of recorded information. In terms of the rationale of this book, it should be noted that both these problems are generic human interface problems – speed of input and navigation within large database systems. Nonspeaking users of alternative communication systems (such as a keyboard and a speech synthesizer) have a problem similar to the person in certain very high workload environments who may not, for example, be able to prevent an aeroplane's crashing or a power station's becoming critical because he or she cannot push enough switches or turn on or off the appropriate circuits in the time available before the situation becomes catastrophic. Even highly trained operators could not be expected to learn a list of numeric codes associated with a very complex series of operations. The person with cognitive dysfunction also has some similarities to an operator is no longer able to think coherently about a problem because of the high stress level.

A portfolio of research into augmentative and alternative communication systems

At Dundee University we have an integrated set of projects which is tackling these problems. Figure 5.1 shows these projects and how they are related to each other. One of them, the *Echo* (Extra-Ordinary Computer–Human Operation) project, is specifically concerned with the relationship between systems designed for disabled people and human–computer systems used by able-bodied people, particularly those who are in high workload situations.

We have taken as our design goal the concept of an integrated communication system for a person without speech, and we have divided the communication needs of such a person into three major types:

(a) unique conversation,

(b) formulaic conversation, and

(c) reusable conversation.

We have projects which are tackling these three areas of need. Many of them use the concept of prediction to assist the users, but the different projects utilize different levels and styles of prediction. The project which is considering the problems of producing unique conversation is based on a predictive text entry system which works at the level of the word. Although originally designed for nonspeaking people, this system has been found to be very widely useful amongst a wide range of clients with both physical and intellectual problems with writing as well as people without speech.

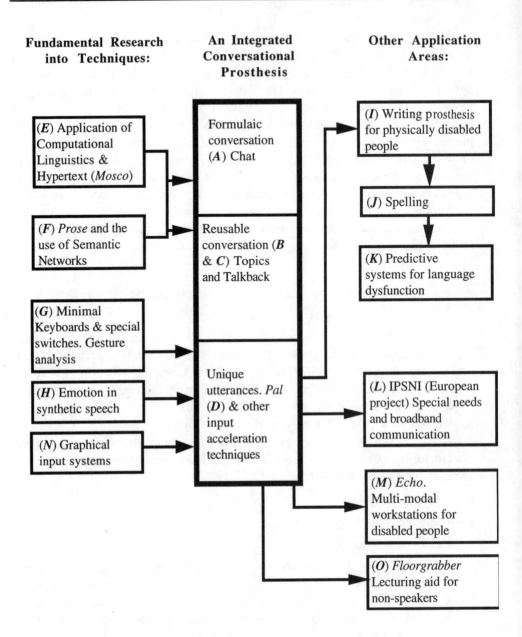

Figure 5.1. Research into an integrated communication system for disabled people at the Microcomputer Centre, Dundee University.

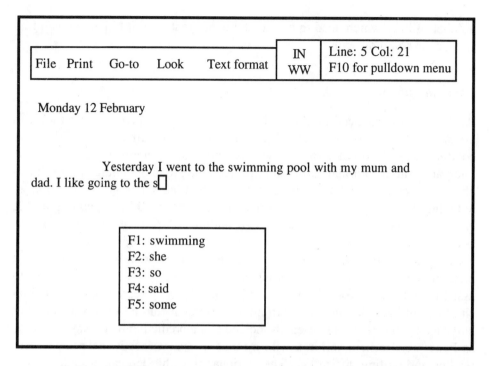

Figure 5.2. Pal as a window on the screen of the word processor.

Unique conversation and an aid for writing and spelling

Pal (Predictive Adaptive Lexicon) was developed to assist physically disabled people to increase the rate at which they can input unique text. Figure 5.2 shows Pal being used in conjunction with *PalStar,* a word processor which was also developed in the Microcomputer Centre specifically for children. Pal works by producing a list of five words based on the last letter or group of letters typed in by the user. If one of these predictions is correct, the user can select it using a single key. If none of the words is correct, the user simply types the next letter of the word, and Pal produces a revised list of predictions based on the new prefix. Words which are not in Pal's dictionary have to be typed in full by the user. These are then captured by the program and will be used in future predictions. In this way Pal can become personalized, since it automatically adapts to the user's own vocabulary. This significantly increases the probability of the correct word being predicted: Pal predicts the current user's most recent frequently used words that begin with the typed-in prefix. It is also possible to use Pal with different dictionaries for individual subjects or writing styles. Pal works with a wide variety of word processing and other software packages. The reduction in the number of keys which need to be pressed is of great benefit to people who find using a keyboard difficult.

Pal in the classroom

Pal has been introduced into the school environment to investigate how it can assist children who experience speaking or writing difficulties. Trials are conducted in close collaboration with schools, and wherever possible Pal is integrated into the normal curriculum. Initially the group of children targeted had physical problems. Pal was found to be of great assistance to these children, reducing the keystrokes needed to create text by up to 60%. Depending on the type of disability, this increased speed and/or reduced fatigue. After a few sessions, however, it became obvious that many of these children also had classic learning difficulties with spelling and language. They soon became aware that prediction could assist their own specific problems and used Pal's predictions to assist them to spell words correctly. Subsequently the research was targeted on children with a wide range of learning difficulties including dyslexia and other language dysfunction. The research showed that a predictive writing system such as Pal is able to help children with a range of special needs including severe reading and writing difficulties. The dictionaries within Pal can be individually designed for each child (in some cases containing a very small number of carefully selected words, and in others over 5,000 words). They also automatically adapt as the users' vocabularies expand and change. This has ensured that Pal is flexible enough to adapt as each child develops and progresses through using the program. Pal has assisted :

- children with physical disabilities, who can produce work much faster;
- children with spelling problems, who use the predictions to help their spelling; and
- children with very limited language skills, by developing their written language, boosting their confidence, and giving them a sense of achievement.

Pal has proved to be very successful in the school environment, and current developments include modifications suggested by children's use of the program.

Using syntax and context to improve predictions

Pal is currently being extended to include a sentence parsing component, which will cause syntactically plausible words to be predicted before implausible words. This will be tested on individuals with language problems, some of whom are nonspeakers. It is hoped that syntactically based prediction will encourage the use of correct words and word order, and the inclusion of small but important words such as "the" and "is," which are often omitted by individuals with language problems. In addition, the syntactically based prediction will be tried by people with a physical disability but no language problem in order to see whether they prefer it and to measure the saving of keystrokes and time.

Pal will continue to learn vocabulary from its users but will not learn syntax, thus preventing Pal from learning bad grammar from its users! Statistics on frequency of use of each of the grammar rules are, however, kept, and thus the predictions will adapt to a particular user's style and knowledge of grammar. As in the original Pal, short phrases can be stored in the syntactic Pal's dictionary. We hope that it will be useful to combine the use of phrases with syntactic prediction in exercises designed to build sentence construction skills.

Spelling

Further work is centered on the development of *Speller*, a system which works with Pal and is designed specifically with poor spellers in mind. There are a number of commercially available spelling correctors designed for the mistakes made by all typists. These systems are inappropriate for the needs of poor spellers and people with dyslexic-type problems. Originally Speller was intended to remove incorrect spellings from Pal dictionaries, but as spelling problems took on greater importance within the project, the program was extended to be useful for a wider range of text production tasks. The program scans through a previously produced text file searching for spelling errors. When one is encountered, the program produces a list of suggested corrections based on lexical and phonetic analyses.

Speller has been tested against commercially available spelling correctors, using a large sample of misspellings produced by the children being studied by the project group. It performed significantly better than the other programs examined in the tests, which failed to find the intended correction for misspellings up to eight times as often as Speller. Speller is now being evaluated in schools, and initial responses from teachers and children have been very positive. In the future we intend to integrate the Pal and Speller programs to provide an interactive spelling correction system within the Pal+PalStar word processing package. Pal, PalStar, and Speller are commercially available packages.[1]

---

[1] Pal and PalStar are trademarks of the predictive text entry system and an associated word processor marketed by Lander Software Ltd., 74 Victoria Crescent Road, Glasgow, Scotland, G12 9JN.

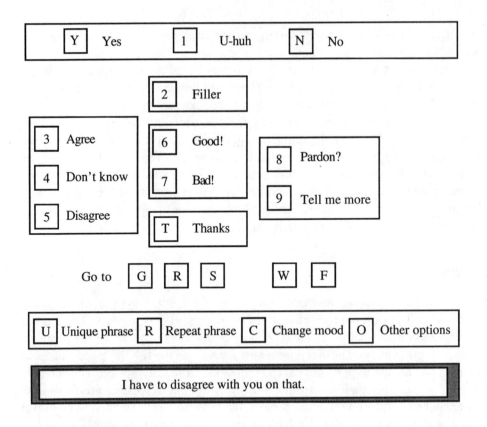

Figure 5.3. Chat discussion stage control screen.

Formulaic conversation – Chat and Topic

Pal can be used to assist people without speech to utter unique sentences. A large amount of conversation, however, is formulaic but very important for creating social bonds. This social conversation is highly predictable, and the choice of words is much less important than in such situations as giving instructions. *Chat* and *Topic* are designed to facilitate such conversations. They are based on computer models of human conversational patterns.

Using ideas and techniques from discourse and conversation analysis, we aim to predict appropriate conversational moves and be correct often enough to make a significant difference to the speed and effectiveness of the user's conversation. The current version of Chat models the opening and closing stages of a conversation and allows for small talk and for feedback to the other speaker. Chat also supports a variety of moods and styles of speech. The control screens for Chat are shown in Figures 5.3 and 5.4.

A prototype of Chat has been used successfully by a number of nonspeaking people, and initial evaluations confirm that such a system can be a valuable aid in social communication. Another prototype, Topic, demonstrates the use of a database to store and retrieve conversational material. Current research is exploring ways to help users navigate through such systems and to offer them predicted conversational items. We are also examining appropriate structures for the storage and retrieval of conversational data. Currently hypertext is being

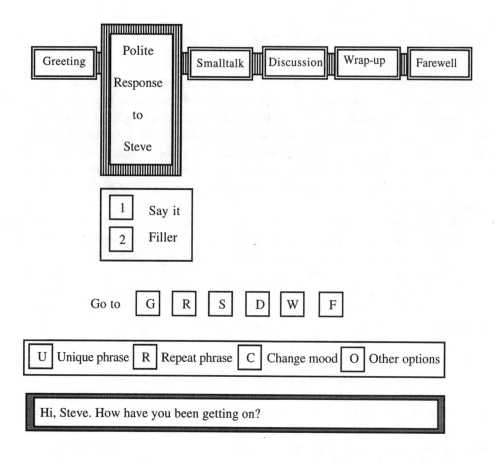

Figure 5.4. Chat control screen for opening and closing a conversation.

examined as such a structure, with a graphical interface to aid navigation. This work is being done in partnership with a nonspeaking young man who recently conducted a lecture tour of North America using this system to describe his experiences as a nonspeaking person.

Reusable conversation

In between unique utterances and purely formulaic conversational moves lies a vast range of conversation which essentially consists of repeating things one has said in the past. A great deal more of our conversation than we would like to think has been uttered by us in some form in the past. In the case of the user of a computer based communication aid, there would be no problem in storing everything he or she has ever said; the problem would be retrieving a particular message when the operator thought it was appropriate to reuse it.

TalksBack, a knowledge-based communication system

TalksBack is a communication system which uses personal knowledge to predict appropriate utterances. The intention is to take advantage of the knowledge we use in some of our more predictable conversations with regular partners and in stereotyped social situations. The system is designed as a "shell" structure into which individual users can enter their own information about (a) themselves, (b) conversation partners, (c) conversation topics, (d) social situations, and (e) speech acts. This information is then used by the system to navigate through a database of stored utterances to select a prediction for the user to speak through a speech synthesizer.

TalksBack operates in either *conversation* mode or *knowledge input* mode. In conversation mode, the user sets the scene by selecting the subject, partner, speech act, and, if relevant, situation. The system then uses its database to select a possible utterance, which the user can command the system to "speak" or "reject and continue the search." If nothing suitable is found, then a new utterance can be added. For example, with subject set to *children*, person set to *Christine*, and speech act set to *question*, the system might suggest "How is Terry getting on at school?" (Terry is Christine's son.)

In knowledge input mode, the user can enter information about subject, person (including the user), speech act, and social situation; this becomes part of the system's database. New speech utterances can be added in preparation for a conversation. TalksBack is being developed in collaboration with two nonspeaking users who have acquired language disorders. The system is written in Prolog and runs on the Macintosh SE and portable. The screen layout is very simple and has proved to be usable in practice by our clients who have significant receptive language problems.

Mosco – A modular social communicator

The goal of the Mosco system is also to enable those with speaking difficulties to take part in everyday conversations. It works by generating a set of phrases, given the input of an initial word or phrase. The user can then select one of these with a single keystroke or mouse button click and have the system speak it through a standard speech synthesizer.

Mosco is designed so that the phrases it generates are socially appropriate. If a phrase is spoken, hearers will recognize it as a sensible follow-on from what has already been said. This means that, where the user wishes, he or she can easily maintain the level of his or her conversational contribution with little effort. Mosco is a modular system. It contains a central phrase generating component and a number of different user environments which range from Makaton-based icons to an on-screen word processor. For users who have relatively high language skills, the on-screen word processor environment offers, in addition to phrase generation, a combination of (a) a form of word prediction based upon single character input, (b) retention and retrieval of blocks of text of paragraph length or longer, and (c) a pseudo-Chat form of social function generation (greeting, farewell, etc.).

Prose – Predictive retrieval of story extracts

The Prose project concerns the development of a predictive storage and retrieval system for conversational narratives such as stories and story extracts. Retrieval of such conversational narratives will enable nonspeaking people to relate experiences, stories, and so on – a communication activity which up to now has been impossible for these people. A prototype system has been developed which will have enough semantic information to retrieve stored narratives for the user without his or her having to do the equivalent of a database search while trying to hold a conversation. The prediction of narrative texts and assisted searches for requested texts will require minimal input from the user.

The intention is to take much of the cognitive load from the user, leaving him or her freer to get on with the conversation. Once the desired narrative has been located, the system assists the user to tell the story. Instead of outputting the narrative in its entirety, the user is able to navigate through the text at will. Story beginnings, story interruptions, and story endings are provided automatically when choosing and exiting text narrative modes. Pilot trials of a prototype version of Prose are indicating the benefit of having access to narratives within a communication device in real situations.

Hamlet – Adding emotion to synthetic speech

The quality of speech synthesizers has improved dramatically over the last few years, but all still speak with an unemotional voice. The *Hamlet* system (Helpful Automated Machine for Language and Emotional Talk), designed for speech impaired users, produces synthetic speech which includes emotional characteristics based on a commercial speech synthesizer.

Hamlet uses a rulebase of emotional speech effects which has been assembled after investigation of human emotional speech. The current system can imitate six emotions: happiness, sadness, anger, fear, grief, and disgust, and is being expanded to simulate a much wider range of emotions. To operate Hamlet, one types a phrase into the system, and at the press of a key it speaks the phrase with any of the above six emotions in its voice. The emotion rulebase alters the synthesizer's voice as well as the duration and pitch of the phrase to imitate the emotion required. A range of male, female, and children's voices is available, and the characteristics of the voices can be altered as required.

The aim of the Hamlet project is to enhance the quality of the speech available to a disabled user and to complement the other communication aids which are under development at the Microcomputer Centre. Hamlet will be of benefit to disabled people who speak using a synthesizer, which previously had only robotic male voices. Continuing development is aimed at improving the realism of the Hamlet voices and increasing the range of emotions which can be simulated by the system.

The system runs on an industry standard IBM microcomputer and uses a *Dectalk* speech synthesizer. The Dectalk is one of the best commercially available speech synthesizers and offers many features, including the ability to impersonate voices and to sing.

Computer interpretation of gestures made by people with severe disabilities

Some nonspeaking people have such severe physical disabilities that they are unable to use a standard keyboard and even have great difficulty in operating a simple switch. (A number of such clients will experience severe muscle spasm if they try to hit a switch.) We believe that gesture is a viable alternative to conventional input techniques for people with severe physical impairments and that it provides a number of advantages. We are thus developing a computerized gesture recognition system. The system will provide an alternative input to computer based systems for communication aids, but an identical system could be used for such other tasks as text production and controlling the user's environment (e.g. lights, heating, call buttons).

Gesture data from arm movements has been collected from a number of disabled subjects ranging from 2 to 30 years old, using a commercially available position monitoring system. This data has been analyzed with the aim of developing gesture recognition techniques which will automatically recognize the intentional movements made by subjects and ignore such unintentional movements as tremor and spasms. Signal processing and pattern recognition techniques are being investigated, and the best algorithms will be used in a prototype gesture recognizer. This will be used with communication systems developed in the Microcomputer Centre.

Broadband communication systems and people with special needs

The European nations are investing heavily in telecommunications technologies in preparation for a modern information society where computers and communications are integrated. This offers disabled people, as well as the able-bodied, great opportunities, but only if disabled people have access to computer equipment and the information it can provide. Thus early in the design stage of equipment, hardware and software designers should incorporate ideas from people working in the field of computers and disabilities. An example would be to build in predictive software of the type described above. This would help disabled people but would offer much to able-bodied users as well – the designs would be better for everyone.

The IPSNI project (Integration of People with Special Needs into Integrated Broadband Communications) aims to define for designers exactly what a future communications terminal should be able to do to accommodate the needs of disabled people. It draws on the expertise of research and telecommunications organizations in seven European countries who are pooling their knowledge on computers and disability. The project has produced a survey of the state of the art in technology for the disabled, has developed a functional model of a communications terminal of the future, and is currently specifying the functions such a terminal should include. The terminal model will be able to handle still and moving pictures, speech and sound, and a variety of data (text or graphics). The final stage will be to implement the model and to develop demonstrations to show designers what can be achieved by incorporating facilities for disabled users into their designs.

Extra-ordinary computer–human operation (Echo)

The Echo project follows the principles which lie behind this book. The aim is to develop an accessible office workstation for disabled users. This includes investigating the various types of input and output devices which are currently available for use by a disabled user and incorporating a selection of these in a workstation application. Input devices which are being used in this project include special switches (e.g. operated by the head or the foot), an eye gaze monitor, an arm position monitor, a dataglove which measures positions of the fingers, and speech recognition and synthesis systems.

Intention inferencing and prediction will also be implemented in the system to improve the interaction between the disabled user and the application. The system will also include design features highlighted by the IPSNI project. This research is being carried out in collaboration with an avionics company, which is involved with the human–computer interaction problems faced by pilots in modern aircraft, so that there will be shared ideas and resources. The prototype high-quality computer based workstation will incorporate all of the features above, and thus increase the facilities available to disabled users and the efficiency and effectiveness with which they can work in an office environment. Relevant ideas from this prototype will be transferred to the avionics company's research program which is investigating computer assistance to pilots, and also to other high workload and safety critical applications.

Conclusions

The problem of designing an effective communication prosthesis for people with speech and language problems is formidable. This chapter describes some research projects at Dundee University which are investigating various aspects of the problem. The long-term aim is to produce a prosthesis in which the various ideas being examined will be integrated to form a system which will cope with all aspects of communication. Such a system will be configurable for different groups of users and users with different disabilities. Although parts of our research have been successfully implemented in realistic situations, we have scarcely scratched the surface of this problem, and there is much more important and exciting research to be conducted in this area.

This chapter has concentrated on the work being done in Dundee University. Other centers throughout the world are also working in this field, and the reader's attention is drawn in particular to the work at the du Pont Institute of the University of Delaware[1] and the IRV in the Netherlands.[2] Their work, and that of others in the field, is published mainly in the proceedings of Resna,[3] in *Augmentative and Alternative Communication,*[4] and in *Augmentative Com-*

---

[1]   Dr. R. Foulds, Director, Applied Science and Engineering Laboratories, University of Delaware/A. I. du Pont Institute, PO Box 269, Wilmington DE 19899.

[2]   Dr. M. Soede, Institute for Rehabilitation Research, Zandbergsweg 111, 6432 CC Hoensbroek, The Netherlands.

[3]   Published by Resna Press, Washington DC 20036.

[4]   The journal of ISAAC (the International Society of Augmentative and Alternative Communication), published by Decker Periodicals, Inc., 1 James Street South, P.O. Box 620, L.C.D.1, Hamilton, Ontario, Canada L8N 3K7.

munication News. [1] An excellent review of the research questions which are being asked in this field can be found in *Augmentative and Alternative Communication in the Next Decade.* [2]

Bibliography

Communication systems for people with speech and language impairments
Alm, N. (1991). Future possibilities for technology in the workplace. In *Proceedings of the World Congress on Technology* (pp. 46–48). Washington DC.

Arnott, J. L. (1990). The communication prosthesis: A problem of human–computer integration. In *Proceedings of the European Conference on the Advancement of Rehabilitation Technology (ECART)* (pp. 3.1.1–3.1.5). Maastricht, The Netherlands.

Brophy-Arnott, M. B., Newell, A. F., Arnott, J. L., and Condie, D. (1992). A survey of the communication impaired population of Tayside. *European Journal of Disorders of Communication, 27*(2): 159–173.

Newell, A. F. (1990). Using models of human interaction for rate enhancement. In *Proceedings of the Visions Conference: Augmentative and Alternative Communication in the Next Decade*, ed. B. Mineo (pp. 49–51). Wilmington DE: Applied Science and Engineering Laboratories, University of Delaware and A. I. du Pont Institute.

Newell, A. F. (1991). Assisting interaction with technology – research and practice. *British Journal of Disorders of Communications, 26*(1): 1–10.

Newell, A. F. (1992). Today's dreams – tomorrow's reality. *AAC Augmentative and Alternative Communication 8*(2).

A portfolio of research into augmentative and alternative communication systems
Newell, A. F., Arnott, J. L., and Alm, N. (1990). Developments towards an integrated prosthesis for the non-vocal. In *Proceedings of the 13th Annual Conference of the Rehabilitation Engineers Society of North America (Resna)*, ed. J. J. Presperin (pp. 97–98). Washington, DC: Resna Press.

---

[1]　Edited by Sarah Blackstone and published by Augmentative Communication Inc., 1 Surf Way, Suite 215, Monterey, CA 93940.

[2]　Edited by B. Mineo and published by Applied Science and Engineering Laboratories, A. I du Pont Institute, PO Box 269, Wilmington, DE 19899.

Unique conversation and an aid for writing and spelling
Newell, A. F. (1989). PAL and CHAT: Human interfaces for extraordinary situations. In *Computing technologies, new directions and applications,* ed. P. Salenieks (pp. 103–127). Chichester: Ellis Horwood.
Waller, A., Beattie W., and Newell, A. F. (1991, January). The computer is mightier than the sword. *Speech Therapy in Practice,* pp. 18–20.

Pal in the classroom
Booth, L., Beattie, W., and Newell, A. F. (1990). I know what you mean, *Special Children, 41*: 26–27.
Newell, A. F., Arnott, J. L., Booth, L., Beattie, W., Brophy, B., and Ricketts, I. W. (1992). The effect of the PAL word prediction system on the quality and quantity of text generation. *AAC Augmentative and Alternative Communication. 8*(4): 304–311.
Newell, A. F., Booth, L., Arnott, J. L., and Beattie, W. (1992). Increasing literacy levels through the use of linguistic prediction. *Child Language Teaching and Therapy 8*(2): 138–187.
Newell, A. F., Booth, L., and Beattie, W. (1991). Predictive text entry with PAL and children with learning difficulties. *British Journal of Educational Technology, 22*(1): 23–40.

Using syntax and context to improve predictions
Morris, C., Newell, A. F., Booth, L. and Arnott, J. L. (1991). Syntax PAL – A system to improve the syntax of those with language dysfunction. In *Technology for the nineties: Proceedings of the 14th Annual Conference of the Rehabilitation Engineers Society of North America (Resna)*, ed. J. J. Presperin (pp. 105–106). Washington, DC: Resna Press.

Spelling
Newell, A. F., and Booth, L. (1991). The use of lexical and spelling aids with dyslexics. In *Computers and literacy skills.* ed. C. Singleton (pp. 35–44). The British Dyslexia Association Computer Resource Centre, University of Hull, UK.
Wright, A. G., Beattie, W., Booth, L., Ricketts, I. W., and Arnott, J. L. (1992). An integrated predictive word processing and spelling correction system. In *Proceedings of the 15th Annual Conference of the Rehabilitation Engineers Society of North America (Resna).* ed. J. J. Presperin (pp. 369–370). Washington, DC: Resna Press.
Wright, A. G., and Newell, A. F. (1991). Computer help for poor spellers. *British Journal of Educational Technology, 22*(2): 146–148.
Wright, A. G., Newell, A. F., and Ricketts, I. W. (1991). Speller: An alternative spelling correction system. In *Technology for the nineties: Proceedings of*

the 14th Annual Conference of the Rehabilitation Engineers Society of North America (Resna) ed. J. J. Presperin (pp. 103–104). Washington, DC: Resna Press.

Formulaic conversation – Chat and Topic
Alm, N., Arnott, J. L., and Newell, A. F. (1989). Database design for storing and accessing personal conversational material. In *Technology for the next decade: Proceedings of the 12th Annual Conference of the Rehabilitation Engineers Society of North America (Resna)* (pp. 147–148). Washington, DC: Resna Press.
Alm, N., Arnott, J. L., and Newell, A. F. (1989). Discourse analysis and pragmatics in the design of a conversation prosthesis. *Journal of Medical Engineering and Technology, 13*(1/2): 10–12.
Alm, N., Arnott, J. L., and Newell, A. F. (1990). Hypertext as a host for an augmentative communication system. In *Proceedings of the European Conference on the Advancement of Rehabilitation Technology (ECART)* (pp. 14.4.1–14.4.2). Maastricht, The Netherlands.
Alm, N., Arnott, J. L., and Newell, A. F. (1992). Evaluation of a text-based communication system for increasing conversational participation and control. In *Proceedings of the 15th Annual Conference of the Rehabilitation Engineers Society of North America (Resna)*. Washington, DC: Resna Press.
Alm, N., Newell, A. F., and Arnott, J. L. (1989). Revolutionary communication system to aid nonspeakers. *Speech Therapy in Practice, 4*(7): vii–viii.
Newell, A. F. (1989). PAL and CHAT: Human interfaces for extraordinary situations. In *Computing technologies, new directions and applications*, ed. P. Salenieks (pp. 103–127). Chichester: Ellis Horwood.
Newell, A. F., Alm, N., and Arnott, J. L. (1991). The use of models of human communication patterns within a prosthesis for nonspeaking people. *Bulletin of the Institute of Maths and Its Applications, 27*(12): 225–231.

Reusable conversation
TalksBack: A knowledge-based communication system
Broumley, L., Arnott, J. L., Cairns, A. Y., and Newell, A. F. (1990). TalksBack: An application of AI techniques to a communication prosthesis for the nonspeaking. In *Proceedings of the European AI Conference* (pp. 117–119). Stockholm, Sweden.
Broumley, L., Cairns, A. Y., and Arnott, J. L. (1990). A case study in applying artificial intelligence in a personalised communication aid. In *Proceedings of the European Conference on the Advancement of Rehabilitation Technology (ECART)* (pp. 14.1.1–14.1.2). Maastricht, The Netherlands.

Mosco: A modular social communicator

McKinlay, A. (1991). Using a social approach in the development of a communication aid to achieve perceived communicative competence. In *Technology for the nineties: Proceedings of the 14th Annual Conference of the Rehabilitation Engineers Society of North America (Resna)*, ed. J. J. Presperin (pp. 204–206). Washington, DC: Resna Press.

Prose: Predictive retrieval of story extracts

Waller, A., Alm, N., and Newell, A. F. (1990). Aided communication using semantically linked text modules. In *Capitalizing on technology: Proceedings of the 13th Annual Conference of the Rehabilitation Engineers Society of North America (Resna)* (pp. 177–178). Washington DC: Resna Press.

Waller, A., Broumley, L., Newell, A. F., and Alm, N. (1991). Predictive retrieval of conversational narratives in an augmentative communication system. In *Technology for the nineties, Proceedings of the 14th Annual Conference of the Rehabilitation Engineers Society of North America (Resna)*, ed. J. J. Presperin (pp. 107–108). Washington, DC: Resna Press.

Hamlet: Adding emotion to synthetic speech

Murray, I. R., and Arnott, J. L. (1990). Evaluation of a synthetic speech system which simulates vocal emotion by rule. *Proceedings of the Institute of Acoustics, 12*(10): 117–123.

Murray, I. R., Arnott, J. L., Alm, N., and Newell, A. F. (1991). A communication system for the disabled with emotional synthetic speech produced by rule. In *Proceedings of Eurospeech '91: 2nd European Conference on Speech Communication and Technology* (pp. 311–314). Genova, Italy.

Murray, I. R., Arnott, J. L., Alm, N., and Newell, A. F. (1991). Emotional synthetic speech in an integrated communication prosthesis. In *Technology for the nineties: Proceedings of the 14th Annual Conference of the Rehabilitation Engineers Society of North America (Resna)*, ed. J. J. Presperin (pp. 311–313). Washington, DC: Resna Press.

Broadband communication systems and people with special needs

McKinlay, A., and Newell, A. F. (1991). Dialogue structures in computer-mediated communication. In *Integration of People with Special Needs into Integrated Broadband Communication, Pre-proceedings of the 2nd Venaco Conference*, Acquafreda di Maratea, Italy.

Woodburn, R., Procter, R., Arnott, J. L., and Newell, A. F. (1991). A study of conversational turn-taking in a communication aid for the disabled. In *People and computers VI, Proceedings of the HCI '91 Conference*. ed. D. Diaper and N. Hammond (pp. 359–371). Cambridge University Press.

Extra-ordinary computer–human operation (Echo)

Cairns, A. Y., Peddie, H., Filz, G., Arnott, J. L., and Newell, A. F. (1990). ECHO: A multimodal workstation for ordinary and extra-ordinary human–computer interaction. In *Digest of the IEE Colloquium, "Multimedia: The Future of User Interface"* (pp. 6/1–6/3). London.

Newell, A. F., Arnott, J. L., and Cairns, A. Y. (1991–92, Winter). Ordinary and extra-ordinary HCI. *Usability Now, 6*: 4–5.

Peddie, H., Filz, G., Cairns, A. Y., Arnott J. L., and Newell, A. F. (1990). Extra-ordinary computer human operation (ECHO). *Proceedings of 2nd Joint GAF/RAF/USAF Workshop on Human–Electronic Crew Teamwork :"The Human–Electronic Crew: Is the Team Maturing?"* Ingoldstadt, Germany.

6

Predictive interfaces: What will they think of next?

Saul Greenberg, John J. Darragh, David Maulsby, and Ian H. Witten

Introduction

Typical dialogues with interactive computer systems contain a great deal of repetition. Frequently used actions (commands, menu items) and objects (file names, mail addresses, icons) are invariably a very small subset of the plethora of options that are available to the user. Furthermore, action sequences such as drawing a picture or using a calculator are inherently repetitive. Even free text is redundant, because of the statistical nature of language. While repeating what was just done is a minor nuisance to the average computer user, it may be challenging for the physically disabled person, who finds every keystroke or mouse selection demanding.

System designers have taken several measures to reduce repetition, including use of terse commands, abbreviation processors, command completion facilities, and macro recorders, but these often meet with resistance from their intended audience. Brief commands are cryptic, hard to remember, and easily mixed up; abbreviation mechanisms are complex to use and take time to learn and set up; command completion is useful only when the possibilities are known in advance; and macros take time to construct and do not easily permit variables or conditionals within a specified sequence. In most cases, users must anticipate their future system usage and divert themselves from the task at hand to create the model explicitly.

Suppose the system could automatically form a model that adapts to what the person is currently doing. An underlying assumption is that what has been done before will most likely be done again. Such a model could be constructed in several ways.

- The system automatically builds it by capturing previous actions. It then predicts the entries the person is about to make, based upon the previous interactions.

- The user teaches the system with explicit instructions. Once the system is taught how to do a task, it will try to do it in the user's stead.

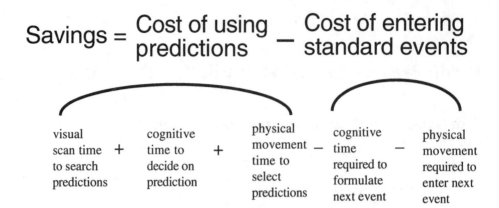

Figure 6.1. The potential savings of a predictive system, showing cognitive–physical trade-offs.

• The user provides the system with examples of the task. As specific problems and their solutions are demonstrated, the system automatically structures them into a model that applies to the more general task.

Obviously, these schemes are unlikely to predict correctly all the time, for then you could walk away and leave the computer to do your work! Given an imperfect predictor, it is essential to ensure that erroneous predictions are easy for the user to ignore while correct ones are easy to accept. This implies a *cognitive/physical trade-off*. The decrease in the number of keystrokes and mouse selections that results from a successful prediction must be weighed against the time a person takes to search visually for the prediction, decide if it is appropriate, and physically select it (Figure 6.1). If the cognitive load of choosing a prediction is high and the mechanical benefits modest, an able-bodied person will find the predictive system of little benefit. The payoff may be much greater for someone with a physical disability. This is essentially a function of the "bandwidth limitation" problem mentioned by Newell in Chapter 1 and Edwards in Chapter 11.

Suppose that in a particular situation the system has generated several (perhaps erroneous) predictions. These can be presented to the user in many different ways; the best method depends on the type of task and the actual predictions made. A conservative approach is to provide users with a list of predictions from which to choose. This reduces the user's job to a recognition and selection process and takes advantage of the fact that the user is the best judge of a prediction's suitability. The disadvantage is that a decision must be made on every prediction. A second approach is for the system to go ahead and perform the predicted actions while the user monitors correctness, interrupting and guiding the system only when erroneous predictions are performed. A third approach is for the interface to rearrange the presentation to make more likely actions easier to take. Here predictions are presented within the language of the standard interface; no additional interface artifacts are required.

Over the last decade we have investigated a variety of predictive systems for use by a broad spectrum of computer users, ranging from physically disabled to able-bodied to graphically gifted individuals. We have been particularly concerned with several issues.

- What is an appropriate model of user activity?
- How much domain knowledge of the user's task is needed?
- What are practical predictive algorithms, and how good are their predictions?
- How can we minimize both cognitive and physical load when using predictive systems?
- What characteristics do predictive interfaces need in order to integrate smoothly with technical and interface aspects of the system?
- How can the system best be implemented on today's (and tomorrow's!) computers?

We have implemented several interesting predictive systems, ranging from one in actual use around the world to more experimental "proof of concept" systems. The systems differ substantially from each other in their task domain, intended users, algorithm for generating predictions, and user interface. While some systems were designed explicitly for users with special needs, others were not. However, we believe that all computer users are "handicapped" in one way or another (see Chapter 14), and that predictive systems should be viewed as a prosthesis that could fit both general and special needs.

This chapter introduces five quite different predictive systems (Table 6.1) and discusses the general attributes and usefulness of each. The *Reactive Keyboard* is a device that predicts free text and operating system commands based upon the text or commands entered so far. *Adaptive Menus* automatically reconfigures menu hierarchies by moving frequently selected items closer to the top. *Workbench* is a command line processor that allows people to organize and reuse their on-line activities easily. The *Autoprogramming Calculator* looks over your shoulder while you perform a repetitive calculation on a simulated calculator and tries to predict future key presses. Finally *Metamouse* is an example of a system likely to be of utility to able-bodied people as well as those with motor impairments. Metamouse is a drawing program which learns from your inputs and predicts your future actions. Reducing the number of inputs makes drawing tasks less tedious for dexterous users and more efficient for those with limited manual dexterity.

Table 6.1. *Summary of five predictive interfaces.*

System	Goal	Dialogue style supported	Predictive model	Usability
Reactive Keyboard • RK-button in MS-DOS, Unix • RK-pointer in Macintosh	Text entry for disabled people	• Command line interactions in MS-DOS & Unix, free text in Unix • Free text in point-and-click environment	Variable-length predictive models (also known as PPM – prediction by partial matching)	RK-Unix, a front end to the Unix Shell, used by many disabled people (and some able-bodied ones); comments from users encouraging
Adaptive Menus	Early demonstration of viable and testable self-adaptive interface	Ordered hierarchical menu navigation through a very large ordered name space	Menu items assigned probabilities; menu hierarchy recursively split into equal probability ranges	Controlled study showed improved performance by subjects using these
Workbench • Reuse facility • Organization facility	• Treat computer activities as tools that can be easily reused • Allow user to organize tools into a personal workbench	Command line interactions in point-and-click environment	• Design of reuse facility based on empirical study of how people repeat their activities on computers • Organization tool based on concept of situated history	• Reuse sub-system has measurably better predictions offered than current history systems • Benefits seen, but effective use tempered by several usability issues
Auto-programming Calculator	Early demonstration of the power of predictive interfaces	Specialized keypad; emulation of simple calculator	Fixed-length predictive models	Works well, but no user studies done
Metamouse	Automate repetitive editing tasks by teaching an agent	Click-and-drag graphical drawing	Explanation based learning by analyzing actions to infer constraints	Questionnaire indicated system's behavior understandable; usability study now in progress

The Reactive Keyboard

Background

The Reactive Keyboard is a program that accelerates typewritten communication with a computer system by predicting what the user is going to type next (Darragh & Witten, 1991; Darragh & Witten, 1992; Darragh, Witten, & James, 1990). Obviously, predictions are not always correct, but they are correct often enough to support a useful communication aid. Predictions are created adaptively, based on what the user has already typed in this session or in previous ones. Thus the interface conforms to whatever kind of text is being entered: English, French, Pascal, operating system commands, and so on.

The Reactive Keyboard is quite general and can be used for a variety of purposes. In some ways, it is similar to the Pal (Predictive Adaptive Lexicon) system described in Chapter 5. It is unlikely to help a skilled typist – except perhaps when entering documents such as legal contracts that contain a preponderance of standard boilerplate paragraphs. However, moderate typists will find that it assists with the highly structured text commonly found in interactive dialogues and formatted data entry, and novice and reluctant typists (including children) will appreciate the help it gives in free-text entry situations. Within its uniform adaptive mechanism it subsumes numerous features provided by interactive interfaces, such as short versions of command names, command and filename completion, user-definable abbreviations for words and phrases, menus of common operations, and brief command files. Being menu based, it can also be used to replace a physical keyboard in click-and-drag interfaces that also require some text entry. Finally, and most important, it has already found application as a user interface for physically disabled people who find a regular keyboard difficult to use.

Predictions are generated from a model of previously entered text. The modeling technique was developed for the purpose of text compression and in fact forms the core of one of the most effective known compression methods (first described by Cleary & Witten, 1984; see Bell, Cleary, & Witten, 1990, for a recent survey of the field). It builds large tree-structured models of characters in context, and for prediction these models are consulted for matches to the current context. To render it suitable for use in a communication aid, two issues had to be addressed. First, whereas in text compression the adaptive prediction mechanism feeds an encoder that generates a bit-stream representing the message, for interactive use it had to be equipped with a human interface that allows predictions to be displayed and selected. Second, a number of problems concerned with resource consumption – both adaptation/retrieval time and storage space – had to be solved to make the mechanism practical for use in an interactive personal computer environment.

Description

Several versions of the Reactive Keyboard exist. In the standard terminal/keyboard based versions, collectively called *RK-button*, predictions appear in reverse video after the cursor location, and users can accept predictions with a single keystroke or reject them by typing over them. In the window based versions, called *RK-pointer*, an ordered list of predictions appears in a separate window. Users select all or part of a prediction by pointing to the desired text. Thus the ideas in the Reactive Keyboard can be tailored to handle two different types of hardware and interface methods: typing and mouse pointing. Other hardware devices, if required, could probably be incorporated with modest effort (see Chapter 17).

An interaction with Unix using RK-button is shown in Figure 6.2a. The predicted characters are written in reverse video on the screen and represented in the figure with enclosing rectangles. Control characters are preceded by ^, and ^J is the end-of-line character. The column on the right shows the keys actually struck by the user. Figure 6.2b gives the meaning of a few of the control keys; in fact, many more line-editing features are provided.[1] Although not illustrated in the figure, the system is set up so that typing non-control characters simply overwrites the predictions; thus one may use the keyboard in the ordinary way without even looking at the screen.

Figure 6.2a shows the entry of five command lines. Within each of the five groups preceded by the $ (the system prompt), each line overwrote its predecessor on the screen. Consider the first group. After the first prediction, "mail^J," the user struck ^N to show the next one. This prediction, "cd news^J," replaced the previous prediction on the screen. The user accepted the first word of it, "cd," using the ^W command, moved to the next prediction, and accepted it in its entirety. The only thing remaining on the screen at this point was "cd rk/papers/ieee.computer." Following this, the next three commands were predicted in their entirety, while the last one required four keystrokes. The screen contents at the end of the dialogue are shown in Figure 6.2c.

In summary, five command lines comprising a total of 138 characters were entered using 11 strokes on just three function keys – an average of 2.2 keystrokes to enter each command line, or 12.5 predicted characters per keystroke. This is fairly typical for command-line dialogues with Unix. A scaled-down version of RK-button designed for MS-DOS computers achieves similar savings.

---

[1] The choice of control characters used originates from a PCD Maltron one-handed keyboard; while it may seem unsystematic, these functions are invariably bound to function keys on the terminal for convenience.

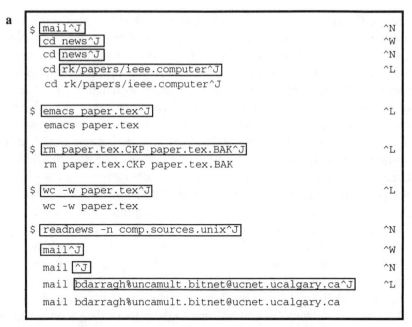

a

```
$ mail^J                                            ^N
  cd news^J                                         ^W
  cd news^J                                         ^N
  cd rk/papers/ieee.computer^J                      ^L
  cd rk/papers/ieee.computer^J

$ emacs paper.tex^J                                 ^L
  emacs paper.tex

$ rm paper.tex.CKP paper.tex.BAK^J                  ^L
  rm paper.tex.CKP paper.tex.BAK

$ wc -w paper.tex^J                                 ^L
  wc -w paper.tex

$ readnews -n comp.sources.unix^J                   ^N
  mail^J                                            ^W
  mail ^J                                           ^N
  mail bdarragh%uncamult.bitnet@ucnet.ucalgary.ca^J ^L
  mail bdarragh%uncamult.bitnet@ucnet.ucalgary.ca
```

b

Key	*Description*
^C (= control-C)	Accept the next predicted character
^W	Accept the next predicted word
^L	Accept the whole predicted line
^N	Show the next alternative prediction
^P	Show the previous alternative prediction

c

```
$  cd rk/papers/ieee.computer
$  emacs paper.tex
$  rm paper.tex.CKP paper.tex.BAK
$  wc -w paper.tex
$  mail bdarragh%uncamult.bitnet@ucnet.ucalgary.ca
```

Figure 6.2. Using RK-button, the Unix version of the Reactive Keyboard.
    (a) Dialogue with Unix.
    (b) Some commands.
    (c) Screen contents at the end of the dialogue.

Whereas RK-button has proven most useful in enhancing the command interface to the Unix and MS-DOS operating systems, RK-pointer is designed for entering free text and runs on the Apple Macintosh computer. Full use is made of the mouse/window environment to give users convenient control over both display and acceptance of predictions – no physical keyboard is required. It is embedded within a simple text editor. Figure 6.3a shows a typical view of the screen. The standard editor window appears at the top and contains the text being created. A cursor marks the place where new text will appear. The window below gives predictions from which the user can select the next characters of text. On the left is the *visual context*, the characters that precede the cursor in the text window. On the right is a menu of predictions which are offered as suggestions of how the context might continue. The user enters text by choosing one of these and clicking at a particular point within it. Characters up to that point are inserted into the upper window, and both context and predictions in the lower one are updated accordingly – the context moves on, and the predictions change completely. At any time the user may enter characters from the keyboard, and both context and predictions are updated as if they were selected with the mouse; thus one can use the keyboard in the normal way until useful predictions appear.

Figure 6.3b shows RK-pointer in use. The entry of several words of text is illustrated as a sequence of five screen images. (For presentation purposes, the windows are rather small and are placed side by side. In practice, all the action takes place in a single pair of windows that are considerably larger than those in Figure 6.3b.) First, the words "Reactive Keyboard " are entered. The initial two letters are taken from "Research," and to the right of the second snapshot can be seen the updated context and new predictions. At this point "active Keyboard " is entered with a single mouse click, and fresh predictions appear. Again two words – "primed with " – are entered together. The fourth image shows the effect of moving the cursor back into the context part of the prediction window: Now the last few characters of context ("with ") are highlighted and, when the mouse is clicked, deleted from the text buffer (and, of course, from the context too). The remaining illustration shows the word "from " being entered. The final result is that four words are entered in just five selections from a four-item menu, including one selection that was needed to delete an erroneously chosen word.

While it is perhaps easiest to envisage the situation where text is being entered at the end of the text window, as in Figure 6.3a, the system works equally well when the cursor is in the middle of the text buffer. Predictions are conditioned on the context preceding the cursor, and accepting a prediction inserts new characters at the cursor position.

The line termination character is shown by the carriage return icon, and in the examples predictions end when this character is encountered – the system makes no guesses about how the next line will begin. For some kinds of text, it is appropriate to predict past the end of the line. Such things are controlled by the "Options" item in the menu bar at the top of the screen, which, when clicked, reveals a preferences dialogue.

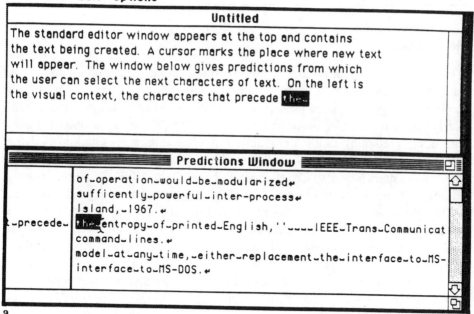

File Edit Options

Untitled

The standard editor window appears at the top and contains the text being created. A cursor marks the place where new text will appear. The window below gives predictions from which the user can select the next characters of text. On the left is the visual context, the characters that precede the␣

Predictions Window

␣precede␣

of␣operation␣would␣be␣modularized↵
sufficently␣powerful␣inter-process↵
Island,␣1967.↵
the␣entropy-of-printed␣English,''␣␣␣␣IEEE␣Trans␣Communicat
command␣lines.↵
model␣at␣any␣time,␣either␣replacement␣the␣interface␣to␣MS-
interface␣to␣MS-DOS.↵

a

File Edit Options

Untitled		Predictions Window
This text has been generated with the R␣	␣with␣the↵	Shannon␣␣shannon R␣search␣and␣upd J.G.␣Cleary␣and␣ Likely␣continuat i
This text has been generated with the Reactive␣Keyboard␣	ith␣the↵Re	search␣and␣updat i active␣keyboard␣ turn''␣can␣be␣con habilitations␣are
This text has been generated with the Reactive Keyboard primed␣with␣	␣Keyboard␣	This␣text␣has␣bee primed␣with␣the␣p communication␣aid to␣generated␣with
This text has been generated with the Reactive Keyboard primed with	med␣with␣	the↵ a␣standard␣commun both␣the␣predicti your␣program,␣the
This text has been generated with the Reactive Keyboard primed from␣	rd␣primed␣	from␣a␣very␣large with␣the↵ correct␣and␣desti to␣the␣model␣is␣s

b

Figure 6.3. Using RK-pointer, the Macintosh version of the Reactive Keyboard.

Mechanism

The ability to guess or predict future text relies on the statistical redundancy of language. Shannon (1951) estimated that English is about 75% redundant and noted that, in general, good prediction does not require knowledge of more than a fairly small number of preceding letters of text. While for a native speaker success in predicting English gradually improves with increasing knowledge of the past, it does not improve substantially beyond knowledge of eight to ten preceding letters (see also Cover & King, 1978; Suen, 1979). The predictions in Figures 6.2 and 6.3 were generated using at most seven letters to predict the next.

The Reactive Keyboard works by suggesting on the basis of preceding inputs what the user might want to select next, exploiting stored information about past selections to predict future ones. Likely continuations are identified by locating a *prediction context* of recent selections in a large memory of previously encountered element sequences. In other words, predictions are made on the basis of the present situation, represented by short-term memory, and past experience, represented by long-term memory (Figure 6.4). The model is continually updated and adjusts itself automatically to the individual user's linguistic idiosyncrasies. The prompting display changes after each selection to present a new menu of predicted elements. A four-phase cycle of user selection, memory update, look up, and display update continues for the duration of a message composition session.

An adaptive model could be based on any of the levels of redundancy present in natural language, ranging from orthographic through syntactic, semantic, and even pragmatic (Pickering & Stevens, 1984). However, models become increasingly hard to generate and utilize at the higher levels, so the Reactive Keyboard uses a simple lexical model that is based on n-grams – consecutive sequences of n characters of text – where n is termed the "order" of the model. These, together with associated occurrence frequencies, are gleaned from representative text samples and from the user's input. The basic idea of prediction is to use the first $n - 1$ letters – the prediction context – to predict the nth). The model's predictive power depends on how accurately its experience matches the user's current communication needs, and on the number and length of stored sequences.

An important innovation in the Reactive Keyboard is that likely continuations for the current context are sought on a longest-match basis. If no elements in memory match the full prediction context, the context is truncated until a match can be found. This proves extremely effective, because it is capable of predicting from more complete lower-order models if less complete higher-order models lack instances of the current context. All lower-order models are implicit in the highest-order model, so no extra storage is required. Such models have been found to be extremely effective for text compression (Bell, Cleary, & Witten, 1990; Cleary & Witten, 1984).

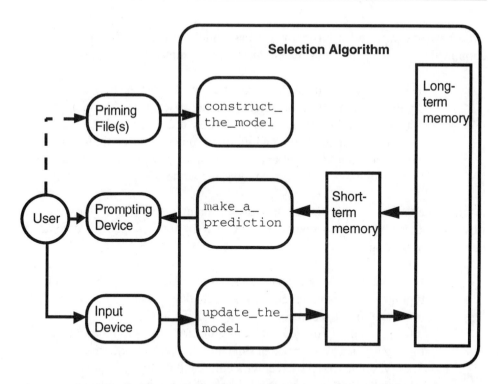

Figure 6.4. Overview of the Reactive Keyboard system.

By far the most important factor affecting the quality of predictions is the text used to prime the model. Finding truly representative text is difficult, and the statistical characteristics of seemingly similar samples can vary greatly (Gibler, 1981; Kucera & Francis, 1967). This implies that the text used for priming must be carefully selected to be as representative as possible of what the user wants to generate. The Reactive Keyboard derives its model in three ways, using a combination of automatic and explicit modeling techniques. As shown in Figure 6.4, priming occurs (a) automatically from a default (or user specified) startup file, (b) automatically from current user inputs, and (c) explicitly from any text file the user chooses to add into the model.

Experience

The predictive terminal emulator of Figure 6.2 has been in use for some time by two physically disabled students at the University of Calgary as their standard command interface to Unix. Their combined daily experience amounts to approximately eight years. One types with a single partially paralyzed hand and uses the system for entering commands and electronic mail. He estimates that over a two-year period it has provided assistance on over 30,000 host system commands, averaging 10 predicted characters per command, and writes:

> The Reactive Keyboard has dramatically changed the way I use computers. I now use much longer, more descriptive, file names than I otherwise would have without its reliable recall and typing assistance. I also rely completely on RK-button to remember such things as electronic mail addresses and long complex command-line sequences. Life on-line would just not be the same without it.

The other user has a progressive neuromuscular disorder and is extremely slow and otherwise unable to write. He uses RK-button as a general command interface and writing aid.

> I find the Reactive Keyboard to be an extremely beneficial tool for typing. Since I have severe neurological damage in my hands, it seems to cut the time I spend coding manyfold. To illustrate this, I need only inform you how I mailed John this letter. All that was required was my typing "`ma,`" after which time it predicted "`il darragh^J.`" So, I was able to type and enter a command normally requiring thirteen keystrokes in but three! This saves much time since it is rather difficult for me to access some keys on the board. It must be remembered that both my hands and fingers move slowly and inaccurately.

The system has recently been released on the Usenet network, and the following unsolicited comment is typical of those received:

> I have cerebral palsy, so my typing is a little bit impaired. I am very impressed with your program. It seems to be ideal for significantly speeding up my typing in the shell while I am programming. I like it a lot, and it saves me a lot of time. I am very glad to have it available to me. The other people that I have showed it to are also very impressed.

The Unix version of RK-button has been tried, tested, and improved with the experiences of people who use it every day. As with any tool that saves people effort, using RK-button has become a matter of course for many users. The occasional experience of using systems that are not equipped with it drives home forcefully how helpful it is.

The IBM PC version of RK-button presents a similar interface to MS-DOS. However, it was completed more recently and is not yet as widely used as the Unix version. RK-pointer on the Macintosh is also relatively new and was designed more as a demonstration program than as a fully integrated application; consequently there is little user experience to report. This version would probably be more useful if it were reimplemented as a desk accessory and could be used with arbitrary Macintosh applications.

All three versions of the Reactive Keyboard are available free of charge. These systems are provided in source form so that they can be modified to suit different people's requirements. Users are encouraged to make and distribute as many copies as they wish. Recipients are encouraged to report any modifications they make so that others will be able to benefit.[1]

Adaptive menus

Background

Hierarchical menus, where users reach an item of choice by navigating through a large tree, are the standard interface for many interactive systems. Although "hot keys" and other methods can speed access to particular items in the tree, their usefulness is limited to menu hierarchies where a few items are consistently chosen over and over again. When a user's choice of items in a hierarchy varies over time and over situations, alternative strategies must be used for accelerating item selection.

It is possible to devise interactive menu-based interfaces that dynamically reconfigure a menu hierarchy so that high-frequency items are treated preferentially, at the expense of low-frequency ones. Adaptive Menus provide an attractive way of reducing the average number of choices a user must make to select an item without adding further paraphernalia to the user interface (Greenberg, 1984; Greenberg & Witten, 1985; Witten, Cleary, & Greenberg, 1984; Witten, Greenberg, & Cleary, 1983).

Description

Consider a computerized telephone directory of names presented through a menu hierarchy. Normally the hierarchy would be constructed by splitting the name space into equal units to provide a tree with a balanced number of leaves at every point. Such menus are "frozen," and the user must always navigate the same path to reach a friend's phone number, regardless of the number of times that same call has been made.

---

[1] Up-to-date versions are available electronically via "anonymous ftp" from "cpsc.ucalgary.ca" (Internet 136.159.2.1) or by writing to the authors at the University of Calgary (E-mail darragh@cpsc.ucalgary.ca).

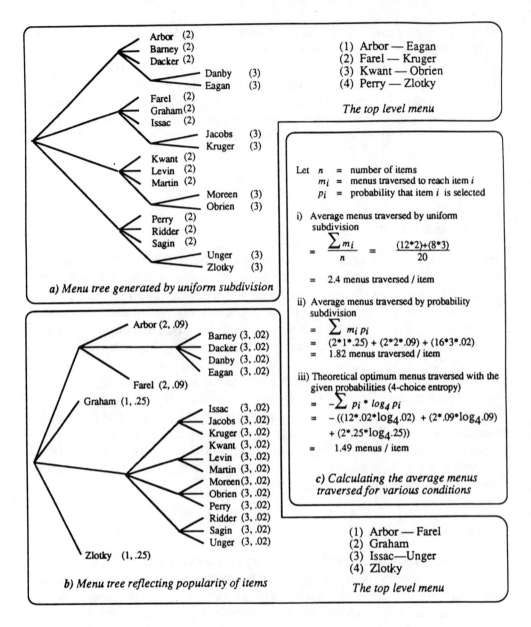

Figure 6.5. Menu trees generated by uniform and probability subdivision.

However, the access frequencies of names, combined with their recency of selection, defines a probability distribution which reflects the "popularity" of the names selected. Instead of selecting regions at each stage to contain approximately equal numbers of names, it is possible to divide the probability distribution into approximately equal portions. As the program is used, the act of selection will alter the distribution and thereby increase the probability of the names selected. Thus the user will be directed more quickly to entries which have been selected already – especially if they have been selected often and recently – than to those which have not. The key point is that the assigning of probabilities is dynamic; the hierarchy presented adapts to the user's evolving (and ever changing) usage over time.

Figures 6.5a and 6.5b depict two menu hierarchies for a very small dictionary with 20 name entries (left side of box) and their corresponding top-level menu (right side of box). Figure 6.5c calculates the average number of menus traversed per selection. In Figure 6.5a, the hierarchy was obtained by subdividing the name space as equally as possible at each stage, with a menu size of four. The number following each name shows how many menu pages have to be scanned before that name can be found. Figure 6.5b shows a similar hierarchy that now reflects a particular frequency distribution (the second number following the name shows the item's probability of selection). Popular names appear immediately on the first-level menu. Less popular ones are accessed on the second-level menu, and the remainder are relegated to the third level. In this particular case, the average number of menus traversed is less with probability subdivision (Figure 6.5c, point ii) than with uniform subdivision (point i), although this improvement is not as much as is theoretically possible (point iii).

Mechanism

Two factors are critical to the performance of Adaptive Menus: how probabilities are updated over the name space as items are retrieved, and how the probability space is split into a hierarchy that minimizes the average number of transitions to names.

The algorithm for updating probabilities as items are selected is shown in Table 6.2. It is based on several heuristics derived from a study of telephone usage statistics (Greenberg, 1984). First, we ensure that first-time access to entries is not noticeably longer than in a nonpersonalized system. We do this by deciding in advance the maximum number of selections that can be tolerated for worst case access to new items as compared to the uniform distribution. This is implemented as a weight $\mu > 1$ that indicates the maximum multiplicative increase in menus traversed. Second, when a new "friend" is accessed, we immediately increase the probability associated with the friend on the assumption that she or he is now much more likely to be selected again. Third, the probability associated with friends who are not accessed decays slowly (the constant α), thus making room for new or more popular friends. It is the decay factor that builds in a way of balancing frequency and recency. Whereas low decay will see frequently chosen items migrate up the tree, a high decay rate gives more room to recently chosen items. Finally, when a friend is accessed, we

Table 6.2. *Retrieval and update algorithms for assigning probabilities*

Let N be the total number of people on the list and F be the total number of friends. Keep a list of pointers to friends, f, who have already been accessed, together with a weight $\omega(f)$ for each in the range [0,1]. The update algorithm will ensure that the weights sum to 1 over all friends. The parameter α is a measure of how quickly friendships fade away and should be slightly less than 1; the closer α is to 1, the slower friendships will fade. The constant μ, with $\mu > 1$, determines the maximum number of menus traversed that can be tolerated for names that are not treated preferentially (the new or infrequently chosen items). The closer μ is to 1, the closer the number of menus traversed to these names will be to that provided by the uniform distribution.

Retrieval

If F = 0, probability for each name is $\dfrac{1}{N}$

otherwise,

if friend, probability is $\dfrac{1}{N\mu} + \omega(f)\left(1 - \dfrac{N}{N\mu}\right)$

else probability is $\dfrac{1}{N\mu}$

Update

If a new friend has been made, put on the friend list and update F. Then

initialize the friend's weight to $\dfrac{1}{F}$

decrease all other weights by $\dfrac{1}{F(F-1)}$

If an old friend f has been accessed again,

$\omega(f) \leftarrow \alpha\omega(f) + 1 - \alpha$
$\omega(g) \leftarrow \alpha\omega(g)$ for all other friends $g \neq f$

In either case, check if any $\omega(f) \leq \dfrac{1}{N}$; if so

delete f from the friend, decrementing F

increase weights of other friends g by $\dfrac{1}{F}\omega(f)$

increase the probability associated with him or her to reinforce his or her popularity. The full algorithm is explained in Greenberg (1984) and in Witten, Greenberg, and Cleary (1983).

Given a probability distribution, it is surprisingly difficult to construct a menu hierarchy that minimizes the average number of selections required to find a name. Despite the apparent simplicity of this problem, optimal menu construction is possible only through exhaustive search over all menu trees, an approach that is infeasible for all but the smallest problems (Witten, Cleary, & Greenberg, 1984). Fortunately, the simple processes of iteratively splitting the probability distribution at each stage into regions whose probabilities are as similar as possible achieves good (but not optimal) performance in practice. For example, if seven menu items are allowed per page, we would divide the entire probability distribution into seven equal parts. We would then recursively subdivide each portion of the distribution until only leaves are left.

The implementation of the iterative splitting algorithm introduces the interesting side effect that popular names appear at the splitting boundaries. The advantage is that during presentation of the menus, popular names frequently occur as a range delimiter in menus high in the hierarchy, making the user's search process easier. An example is shown in Figure 6.5b, where a user may be searching for Farel. As Farel appears as a range delimiter on the first-level menu, the user's task of deciding which range (and corresponding subtree) must be navigated is made far simpler.

Experience

With Adaptive Menus, previous actions are almost always resubmitted in fewer keystrokes, as the path through the hierarchy is shorter. Also, since no extra detail is added to the interface presentation, there is no need to learn a new subsystem, and screen use is minimized. The trade-off is that since paths change dynamically, memory cannot be used to bypass the search process. Users must now search the menus for their entries all the time, even for those accessed frequently. However, this is not a problem in practice.

Human factors experiments using able-bodied subjects were performed to compare Adaptive Menus with their nonadaptive counterparts (Greenberg & Witten 1985). Subjects simulated one month of telephone usage in a one-hour session, where names were retrieved from the menu for each simulated call. The average time taken to "dial" a number was reduced by an average of 35% when Adaptive Menus were used. In addition, as subjects did not have to descend deep into the tree (the place where most errors occur), the average number of errors decreased by 60%. When one considers the high penalty of errors in real-life applications – users going down incorrect branches not only lose time but also suffer the risk of getting lost in the hierarchy – then the significance of reducing errors becomes apparent. Also encouraging is that subjects preferred Adaptive Menus to the nonadaptive ones, mostly because of the generally shorter search paths and the frequent appearances of popular names as range delimiters.

Workbench

Background

Top-level interfaces to general purpose computing environments are designed to help people pursue a wide and varying range of tasks by providing them with a rich set of tools and materials. In a command based system, for example, one invokes an action by typing simple commands and arguments, although some modern systems augment or replace this primitive dialogue style with menus, forms, natural language, graphics, and so on (see Witten & Greenberg, 1985, for a discussion of interface styles).

Users repeat activities that they have previously submitted to their computers surprisingly frequently (Greenberg & Witten, 1988b). Yet reformulating the original activity can be both difficult and tedious, especially for someone with a physical impairment. Mental contexts must be re-created for complex activities, command syntax or search paths must be remembered, input lines retyped, icons found, directories and files opened, and so on. There are two ways to make it easier to reformulate old activities. One is through *reuse*: predicting those activities that are likely to be repeated and placing them ready to hand. The other is through *organization*: allowing people to arrange their command sets in a manner that fits their task. Both facilities have been designed into a system called *Workbench* (Greenberg, 1988).

Description

Workbench is a graphical window-based front end to the Unix command line interpreter. Using the metaphor of a handyman's workbench, it provides both a list that predicts future submissions from old ones and a way for users to structure and store submissions for later use. Its major visual components are detailed below and illustrated in Figure 6.6, which shows one paned window and two pop-up windows.

The *work surface* is a terminal emulator running the standard Unix command line interpreter (the bottom pane in Figure 6.6). This is the main working area of Workbench, and users can submit command lines by typing them directly.

The *reuse facility* is the list from which the user can select, edit, and insert into the work surface an old command line entry (middle pane in Figure 6.6). It implements a policy of temporal recency, where the last few user submissions are considered good candidates for reuse. This is commonly known as a *history list*. Items are also presented in a "fish eye" view, where the font size of the text is matched to its probability of selection. Furthermore, every history item has a pop-up menu attached to it which is itself a history list of all the arguments previously used with the command. The figure shows the pop-up menu for the "cd" command.

Through the *tool cache* (mid-right pane), a user can type in or copy items from the reuse area to any one of the six editable fields. These entries remain available for reuse until they are changed by the user. Beyond this, the tool cache is the same as the reuse facility. Selecting an item inserts it into the work surface for execution. Pop-up menus of previous arguments are associated with each item.

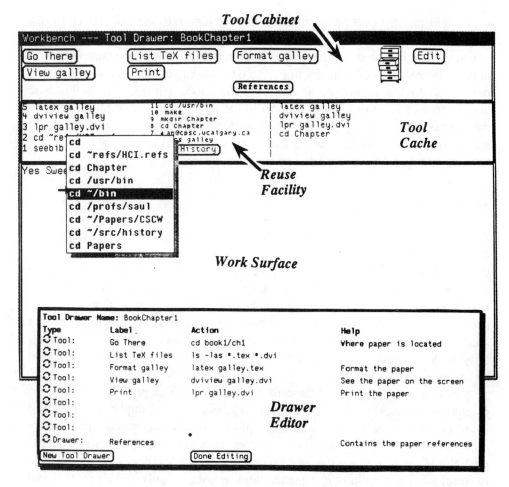

Figure 6.6. Workbench in use, showing the main Workbench window and two pop-up windows.

Finally, the *tool cabinet* allows users to organize their environment by placing their "tools" (Unix command lines) into "drawers" (collections of tools). Tools and drawers are presented as buttons labeled with distinctive text fonts (top pane in Figure 6.6). A tool has three components:

- a Unix command that will be executed when the button is pressed,
- an optional text label for the button, and
- an optional help string that appears when the pop-up menu is raised.

Choosing a drawer opens it and makes its tools available in the tool cabinet pane. Selecting the cabinet icon on the top right of this pane allows the user to access a history list of drawers visited. What distinguishes the tool cabinet from a conventional menu or panel is that a drawer and its contents are user defined. When the edit button is selected, an editable representation of the current drawer appears (lowest pop-up window in Figure 6.6). Users are then free to type in the definition of a tool or to copy an already well-formed expression from the reuse area or tool cache into a drawer. Items in the reuse area are not only excellent candidates for becoming more permanent tools, but are easy for a person to gather into a task specific drawer. Users are also invited to document their new tools by adding a descriptive label and help message.

Mechanism

An empirical study motivated the design of Workbench and in particular its reuse facility (Greenberg, 1988; Greenberg & Witten, 1988a, 1988b). An analysis of the interaction records of 168 Unix users revealed that 75% of a user's online activities are repeated submissions. However, finding and selecting items for reuse can sometimes be more work than entering them afresh, particularly if it is necessary to search a complete list of previous entries. To be practical, a reuse facility must choose a small set of previous submissions as predictions and offer only these to the user. The difficulty, of course, lies in choosing good predictions.

A further study contrasted the effectiveness of various predictive strategies: recency, frequency, partial pattern matching, treatment of duplicate items, and using commands as hierarchical entry points to past arguments. The results indicated that the temporal recency of previous submissions is a reasonable predictor of the next one – the user's recently submitted activities are the likeliest to be repeated, particularly if duplicate items are shown only in their most recent positions on the list.[1] The recency policy is cognitively attractive, because users generally remember what they have just entered and can predict what the system will offer them. Predictive power is further increased when items are used as hierarchical entry points to past arguments (implemented as the pop-up menu in Figure 6.6).

Using the strategies above, a list of ten entries successfully predicts 55% of all user activity, with a potential keystroke saving of around 6 characters per selected prediction, or 3.3 characters over all submissions (including new ones). An optimal reuse facility could predict at most 75% of all activities (the percentage of repeated submissions), which results in savings of 4.4 characters over every reused and new submission. Thus the predictions offered by our

---

[1] In contrast, frequency ordering and presenting duplicates in their order of first appearance are quite poor predictive strategies.

method (55%, 3.3 characters) make up roughly 75% of the theoretical maximum saving (75%, 4.4 characters).

The design of the tool cache and tool cabinet is supported by the idea that plans are derived from *situated action* – the necessarily ad hoc responses to the contingencies of particular situations (Suchman, 1987). In Workbench, the elements of a plan are the tools contained in a drawer. By drawing on the reuse facility as a primary source of tried and tested candidates for new tools (something we call *situated history*), a person can rapidly create, annotate, and modify his or her personal workspace so that it accurately reflects the task at hand. Placing a tool in a drawer is just a matter of dragging it in from the reuse facility – there is little disruption to the user's task.

Workbench is implemented as a stand-alone process that can interoperate with any application. It maintains a communication port, and applications are invited to send any tokens that should be displayed on the reuse facility. While this requires each application to have limited knowledge about Workbench (how to establish communications and the protocol of sending tokens), the applications do not control or need to know anything about its internal behavior. At the same time, Workbench allows any application to connect to it and does not need any syntactic or semantic information about the tokens it receives.

Experience

Workbench was constructed in Suntools, a window system that has now been eclipsed by the newer X Window standard. As a result, we have limited user experience with it. However, several colleagues who used Suntools enjoyed having Workbench available, although their enthusiasm was tempered by the usability issues outlined below.

First, difficulties arose because Workbench is a bolt-on front end to a single application. Ideally, all applications in a user's environment would cooperate with Workbench, each being responsible for collecting, massaging, and passing on relevant user input for display. However, this is difficult to achieve in a Unix environment, because the source code of every application would have to be altered. Even if source code were available, the task of modifying just a few key applications would be daunting. The result was that Workbench worked only with the Unix command line interpreter. It was particularly frustrating to have the reuse facility turn off just because one had entered a different application (a text editor, for example). An integrated system incorporating reuse primitives in every application would have to be designed at the operating system level.

Second, some cognitive and physical trade-offs come into play. On the cognitive side, the user must still decide what items to select from the display and undergo the process of constructing and maintaining the Workbench organization. In practice, users gain considerable benefit from having situated and well-formed actions available in the reuse facility. History items are selected for reuse and collected in drawers. Still, some modification is usually required to verify and generalize the action, and the entire process could be simplified (see Greenberg, 1988, for further discussion of the design issues). We also found that it takes a conscious effort to switch from performing a task to using predictions, and users must do the extra work of moving from the keyboard to the mouse, selecting items, and, if necessary, navigating drawers. But once the switch was done, users expressed pleasure in being able to perform their actions simply and economically by making Workbench selections.

The Autoprogramming Calculator

Background

When tasks are a sequence of activities, they constitute a procedure that can be specified by the user giving one or more examples of the sequence. The goal of programming by example (Myers, 1986) is to allow sequences and more complex constructs to be communicated concretely, without the user's resorting to abstract specifications of control and data structure (in a programming language, for example).

The simplest kind of programming by example is verbatim playback of a sequence. The user performs an example of the required procedure, and the system remembers it for later repetition. For example, the use of "start remembering," "stop remembering," and "do it" commands enable a text editor to store and play back macros of editing sequences (Stallman, 1987; Unipress, 1986). Except for these special commands, the macro sequence is completely specified by normal editing operations. With a little more effort, such sequences can be named, filed for later use, and even edited (if presented in a human-readable form). A practical difficulty with having a special mode – remembering mode – for recording a sequence is that frequently one has already started the sequence before deciding to record it and so must retrace one's steps and begin again.

The ability to generalize these simple macros could extend their power enormously. Ideally, programming-by-example strategies should allow inclusion of standard programming concepts – variables, conditionals, iteration, and so on – either by inference from a number of sample sequences or through explicit elaboration of an example by the user. While completely automating the general programming process is impossible, it can be done in simple enough situations. Using a calculator (rather than a programming language) sidesteps some of the more difficult problems of automatic programming, for the calculator is suited to simple jobs.

Many programming actions, such as those performed on a simple calculator, are quite repetitive. A long function must be continually reentered even though only a few arguments (the variables) will differ. Whereas advanced calculators (and computers) could be programmed to do a mathematically repetitive task, this may be beyond the skill of particular calculator users.

Instead, the Autoprogramming Calculator looks over your shoulder while you perform a repetitive calculation where the calculator would try to predict the next key pressed (Bell, Cleary, & Witten, 1990; Darragh & Witten, 1992; Witten, 1981). The idea is that if a computer is shown the steps to perform a task a number of times, it can automate the process by building a model – a program – of the sequence of steps. Entries and operations that are the same each time are considered constants and will be predicted. Any that cannot be predicted correspond to "input" that the system must get from the user. The different input data provided each time will often cause the task to be executed in different ways, adding new paths to the model. Once the model is good enough, it can predict the next step at all times and be left to run its "program" all by itself. Thus the calculator will behave exactly as though it had been explicitly programmed for the task at hand, waiting for the user to enter a number and simulating the appropriate sequence of keypresses to come up with the answer.

Description

The Autoprogramming Calculator, modeled after a simple Casio calculator, was built in the early 1980s to demonstrate the power of predictive interfaces. It constructs an adaptive model of the sequence of keys the user presses. If the task is repetitive (like computing a simple function for various argument values), the modeler will soon catch on to the sequence and begin to activate the keys itself. Inevitably the prediction will sometimes be wrong, and an "undo" key allows the user to correct errors.

Figure 6.7 gives some examples of this "self-programming" calculator. The first sequence in Figure 6.7a shows the evaluation of xe^{1-x} for a range of values of $x = 0.1, 0.2, 0.3$, and 0.4. The keys pressed by the operator are in normal type; those predicted by the system are shaded. From halfway through the second iteration onwards, the device behaves as though it had been explicitly programmed for the job. It waits for the user to enter a number and displays the answer. It takes slightly longer for the constant 1 to be predicted than the preceding operators because numbers in a sequence are more likely to change than operators. Therefore the system requires an additional confirmation before venturing to predict a number.

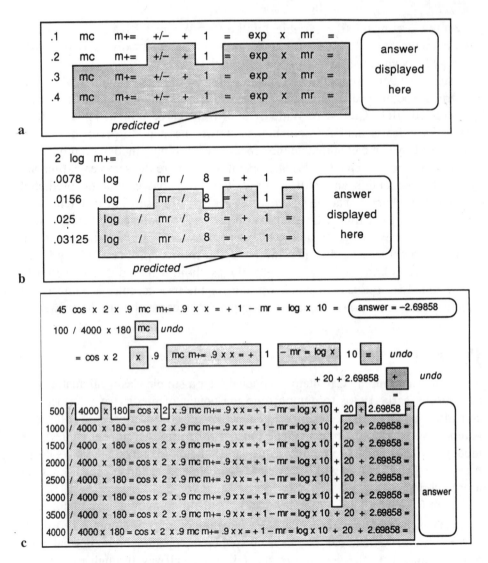

Figure 6.7. Example of operating the Autoprogramming Calculator for various values of *x*.

Figure 6.7b shows the evaluation of

$$1 + \frac{\log x}{8 \log 2}$$

for various values of *x*. The first line stores the constant "log 2" in memory. More complicated is the evaluation of

$$20 + 10 \log \left[1 + a^2 - 2a \cos \frac{180x}{4000} \right]$$
$$- 10 \log \left[1 + a^2 - 2a \cos 45 \right]$$

for $a = 0.9$ (Figure 6.7c). Since the calculator possesses only one memory location, it is expedient to compute the last subexpression first and jot down the result. The result of this calculation (2.69858) has to be keyed only twice before the system picks it up as predictable. Some interference occurs between this initial task and the main repeated calculation, for three suggestions had to be "undone" by the user. The negative effect of one of these undo's continues right up till near the end of the interaction. This means that the penultimate plus sign on each line has to be keyed by the user several times to counter the system's reluctance to predict it.

Mechanism

The Autoprogramming Calculator uses a fixed length (length-k) predictive model, which is a limited-context state machine created from the set of k-tuples that occur in the input string (the input sequence) being modeled. Context models effectively split an input sequence into overlapping substrings of length k, where $k - 1$ is the context length. The first $k - 1$ characters of each substring predict its last character. The sequence of k-tuples that occurs in a particular string fully characterizes the string.[1]

When a new input symbol appears, a k-tuple is created with the new symbol at its end. Given an existing state model formed from previous input symbols, the tuple must now be incorporated into it. If that k-tuple has never occurred before, a new state is added to the model and labeled with the new symbol, with an appropriate transition leading to it. (A transition out of the state will be generated when the next symbol is processed.) If the k-tuple has occurred before, it uniquely determines a state of the model. However, it may call for a new transition to be created into that state. If so, it will be necessary to reevaluate the model by expanding it around the state and by adding the new transition. The model must then be reduced to ensure that extraneous sequences are excluded. A complete description of this process is found in Bell, Cleary, and Witten (1990, chap. 7).

---

[1] Length-k modeling is a more general but fixed length form of the variable-length modelling technique used in the Reactive Keyboard. Another difference is that the calculator uses a confidence parameter to forestall prediction of numbers, where numbers require more evidence than operators (Darragh, in press).

Experience

The Autoprogramming Calculator was built as a research tool and has not been released for general use. Still, the experience of designing and building the calculator laid the foundations for the Reactive Keyboard, and several lessons have been learned that can be applied to programming by example in general.

First, there is a fine line between "teaching" the system and "providing examples" to it. As Figure 6.7c illustrates, a user must be conscious of how a problem should be broken down in order for the system to learn it, and must minimize variation between examples by presenting sequences consistently. The user must also show all steps to the system; performing some calculations in one's head may represent a mental leap that the system cannot bridge (Witten, MacDonald, Maulsby, & Heise, 1992).

Second, the interface presented to the user is critical for a system's success. It is important for the user to understand what predictions the system has made and for the system to present the predictions in the language of the interface. For example, the calculator would ideally show the formula learnt so far and indicate where the input token accepted from the user would be applied. Also important is the need to minimize the work required of the user. The Autoprogramming Calculator, for example, aggressively predicts an input sequence. When predictions are correct, the user just enters whatever arguments are required. When incorrect, the user undoes the prediction and corrects it.

If programming by example proves successful, all users will benefit. The dreary reentry of repetitive program sequences will be reduced to having the user supply only the critical arguments. Also, the cognitive effort of a user's mentally forming and reforming each example task will decrease as the system learns and takes over the task.

Metamouse

Background

Metamouse is an "instructible" interface that predicts repeated actions in graphical editing tasks (Maulsby, Witten, & Kittlitz, 1989). Creating and reformatting structured drawings involves not only repetition but input precision at the pixel level. Such tasks are tiresome and error prone because they require many repeated and highly accurate movements. For users who have some neuromuscular or visual difficulty, editing a drawing by direct manipulation is exhausting toil, if it can be done at all. Metamouse helps the user by learning iterative procedures from single demonstrations and by inferring precise constraints from approximate actions. The cost of automation is a little extra intellectual effort, since the user must focus Metamouse on relevant spatial relations while editing. Although teaching the computer requires more thought, the user – particularly the physically disabled person – is rewarded by being relieved of tedious work: A tiresome task becomes easy, and the next-to-impossible becomes feasible.

Most commercial drawing programs support very limited kinds of graphical constraint, such as a grid for placing points and commands for aligning objects. Systems like *Gargoyle* (Bier & Stone, 1986) have general capabilities but complex interfaces. Metamouse was designed to do three things with a very simple interface: infer primitive (system defined) constraints from single actions; enable the user to invent more complex constraints as construction procedures; and match action sequences in order to predict loops and branches. Owing to its use of domain-specific knowledge in generalizing a situation, the predictive interfaces Metamouse most resembles are Witten's Autoprogramming Calculator, *Tels* (Witten & Mo, 1993), and *Eager* (Cypher, 1991).

Description

Metamouse was designed for programming by demonstration (Myers, 1988). The user teaches an agent a task by performing it, now and then issuing simple instructions to focus attention and correct mistaken inferences. The agent's persona is Basil, a nearsighted turtle who follows the user step by step and highlights graphical constraints it judges important. "Constraint" in this system means a point of contact between two objects. Thus, to show Basil some spatial relation, the user might have to construct a sequence of touch constraints by drawing one or more objects connecting the related ones.

Figure 6.8 illustrates a session with Basil in which the user's task is to align a set of boxes to an input guideline, while keeping each box at the same vertical coordinate; the final result is shown in Figure 6.8i. The user creates a guideline (step a), then selects and drags the first box to it (b, c); the black tack indicates a touch constraint Basil has inferred. When the user picks the second box (d), Basil matches this with step b and predicts a repetition. She drags the second and third boxes to achieve the same touch constraint (f, g). The user's only input for these actions is to click "OK" to approve them. When Basil fails to find another box, he terminates the loop and asks the user to take over (h). The user removes the guideline and tells Basil to save the procedure under the name "align to guide."

Basil uses three learning strategies. The first employs domain knowledge to "explain" individual actions. Since Basil knows about touch constraints but not other spatial relations, the user has to draw a line to express alignment in terms of touch (step a). An action not resulting in touch constraints, such as drawing the guideline itself, is assumed to be governed by a potential input or constant. The second strategy uses multiple examples to select hypotheses consistent with them. For instance, when predicting an action whose location may be constant or input, Basil performs it using the same location user demonstrated (proposing a constant) but invites the user to alter it (checking for input). The third strategy is

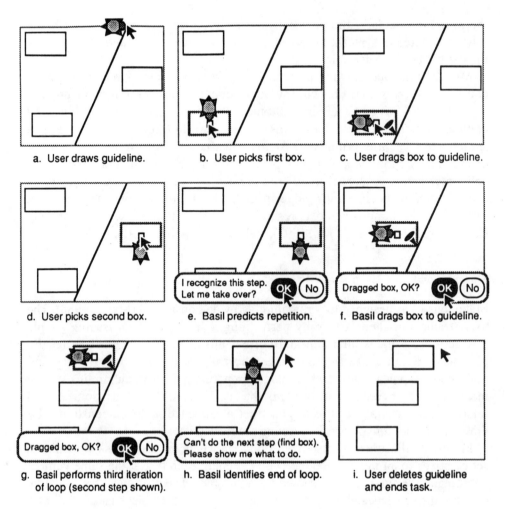

Figure 6.8. Using Basil to align a set of boxes.

to get direct instructions from the user. The system highlights inferred constraints and predicts actions step by step: the user can reject these inferences, causing Basil to try an alternative. The current implementation does not afford all three strategies for all aspects of a task.

Mechanism

Focusing inference on graphical constructions rather than general spatial relations was believed to be a viable approach because people find it natural to express constraints procedurally – they envisage spatial relations with imaginary lines and motions and convey them by gestures. Van Sommers (1984) found in studies of drawing on paper that people typically orient new components of a drawing to old ones according to touch.

The problem tackled by Metamouse is to predict, from examples, the constraints on selecting and positioning primitive two-dimensional geometrical objects. In both cases, the only example features considered are:

- the object type (line, box) and pre-defined parts (edges, vertices, centers);
- whether the target object is a specific individual or a member of a set;
- the general direction of search over a set of objects (up, down, left, right);
- touch relationships between parts of objects.

For each new action, the system substitutes variables for objects and identifies constraints on position. Constraints are chosen by explanation-based generalization (deJong and Mooney, 1986), using a weak theory of 15 rules. If the action's constraints match those of some previous step, Basil predicts that step's successor. A task is represented as a set of production rules.

The following subsections describe the kinds of inference the system makes and the instructions by which a user can modify them. The examples are taken from Figure 6.8.

Object selectors

When the user selects the first box (step b), Basil infers a variable to stand for it and a selector function to set the variable:

$$BoxVar1 := find\text{-}novel\text{-}object(prevBindings = nil, typeBox, pathDownward).$$

When predicting, this selector will choose the next box farther down that has not been assigned to *BoxVar1* already. The *find-novel-object* selector permits iterating once over a set of objects, processing them in the order of their occurrence along an axis. The other selector, *use-value-of(X)*, picks the object currently assigned to some variable *X*. The current implementation does not let the user modify Basil's choice of selector.

Directions

One parameter of *find-novel-object* is the direction of search, *pathDownward*, inferred from the dominant axis in Basil's path of motion. The system provides multiple-example and choice strategies for modifying this inference. In the alignment task, the second example given by the user (step e) does not match the predicted path, hence it is generalized to "any direction." If the user had instead disagreed with the inference that Basil should move downward, he or she could have clicked on his shell to rotate him (for instance, to upward).

Constraints

Basil applies a set of rules to rate the significance of touches observed after each action; the top ranked are selected as constraints. The significance of a touch depends on two factors: the extent to which it was – or could have been – affected by the action and the degrees of freedom that remain when positioning Basil after achieving the touch with the given graphical operator. The most significant touches are those caused by the action and leaving the fewest degrees of freedom. For instance, when the user drags the box to the guideline (step c), Basil notes that the box's lower right corner touches the line. This touch is caused by the move and is therefore highly significant in that respect. It involves two objects already known to Basil, so there is no freedom in the choice of object. It involves a vertex and a line segment, so there is one degree of freedom in the actual position. Since no other touches are observed, Basil selects this one as a constraint and marks it with a black "tack" (white tacks are used to indicate irrelevant touches that would not be enforced when predicting). If the user disagrees with Basil's inference, he or she can click on the tack to toggle it.

When the user dragged the box, he or she kept it at nearly the same vertical coordinate; Basil infers that this value should be held constant when selecting the destination point on the guideline. Two alternative inferences are that the destination should be the nearest point or a point selected by the user. The current implementation does not let the user give explicit instructions about selecting a particular solution, but the user could construct a horizontal or nearest point (perpendicular) constraint.

Flow control

Predictions are made by consulting a set of production rules of the form

$$\text{if } context = [action]^* \rightarrow prediction = action.$$

The difference between Metamouse's context model and those used in the Reactive Keyboard and the Autoprogramming Calculator is that its rules have variable context lengths and are tested in length order. Thus, each context is as general (i.e. short) as possible, yet the model as a whole is deterministic (i.e. no two rules fire in the same context). This approach is intended to maximize the number of predictions made yet distinguish states as determined by events arbitrarily far back in history.

Rules are checked in the order specific to general, that is, from longest to shortest context. A rule fires if it meets two conditions: (a) its context of k previous consecutive actions matches the k most recent actions in history; (b) its prediction is performable, in the sense that its constraints can be satisfied. After a rule has fired, the predicted action is appended to history, and the rule set is consulted again. If no rule fires, the user performs the next action, N, which Basil analyzes and matches with generalized steps already stored. If no match is found, Basil stores N as a new type of action. Whether matched or not, a new rule that predicts N is created. If N was performed because some rule R predicted a nonperformable action, then the new rule is *[R-fails]* $\rightarrow$ N. This happened, for instance, at (h) in Figure 6.8. Otherwise, the new rule is initialized as *[M]* $\rightarrow$ N, where M is the immediately preceding action in history. If N was performed because the user had rejected the prediction made by rule R, the system tries to specialize R by extending its context backwards through history, such that it would not have fired on this occasion. If no specialization covers all previous successful firings of R, then the new rule for N is specialized instead, such that it covers no previous instance of R.

Experience

We did a small, quasi-controlled user study to learn whether people could put Basil to effective use in practice and to identify shortcomings in its design and implementation (Maulsby, Witten, Kittlitz, & Franceschin, 1992). We tested the system on three computer science students and four nonprogrammers. All subjects were given the same single page instruction sheet and performed the same six tasks several times, with and without Basil's assistance. Four of the tasks required graphical constructions to express alignment or distance, and one (sorting boxes by height) required either an explicit setting of Basil's direction or the use of a movable construction (such as a sweeping line) to select boxes in order.

All subjects, programmers and nonprogrammers alike, benefited from Basil's predictive ability in the two tasks where no constructions were required. The three programmers and three of the nonprogrammers successfully used simple constructions to teach Basil two different ways of aligning boxes. The one user who did not benefit from prediction in these cases did not use constructions during any of the tasks. The study showed that when users employ appropriate constructions, Basil is able to help them by making appropriate predictions. The users, especially the nonprogrammers, were able to explain most of Basil's behavior to themselves (including bad predictions or failures to predict) after just a few minutes' experience.

Of greater research interest, however, are the problems users encountered. The following paragraphs outline the major difficulties and their causes.

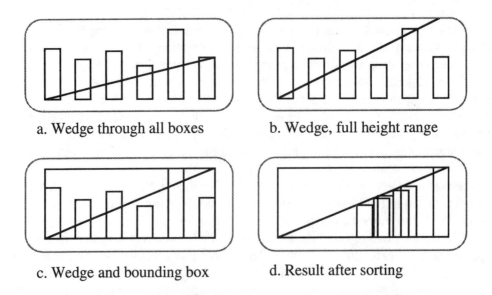

a. Wedge through all boxes   b. Wedge, full height range

c. Wedge and bounding box   d. Result after sorting

Figure 6.9. Tools attempted in sorting by height.

Constructions

We found that users readily invented "static," declarative constructions for spatial relations but had no insight into using "dynamic," procedural ones like a sweeping line. Figure 6.9 illustrates one nonprogrammer's experiments with a static tool for ranking boxes by height. His tool is based on a "wedge," an oblique line that maps height order onto horizontal order. The first attempt (Figure 6.9a) is a mistake, because the line does not map the entire range of heights. The second version (Figure 6.9b) would work but for the inadequacy of Basil's selector functions (see below). Blaming himself for the failure, the user adds a bounding box (Figure 6.9c), which he believes will show Basil that all the rectangles are to be processed, regardless of whether they touch the wedge initially, and also ensures that boxes are moved strictly horizontally, since they must touch the bottom of the bounding box. Figure 6.9d shows the result he obtained (without predictions from Basil).

Touch metaphor

Users immediately understood Basil's bias towards touch and focused their attention on that characteristic. They rightly did not expect Basil to infer intrinsic properties like object height. All were puzzled when asked to teach him how to sort by height, because they believed they were supposed to find some way of expressing height in terms of touch. Several said they would prefer a more direct way of instructing Basil with commands.

Selectors

Users who did not initially decompose tasks in a way compatible with Basil's object selector functions did not learn to do so. In particular, if a task could be done either as a single loop or multiple loops with simpler bodies, most users chose the latter; but Basil cannot predict multiple loops over the same objects. Only one user, a nonprogrammer, tried using a single loop after observing that Basil predicted only the first of multiple loops.

The limited choice of selector functions also prevented some constructions from working as users expected. For instance, the wedge tool in Figure 6.9 initially touches several of the boxes, generating a distinct variable for each one; Basil cannot form a loop when observing the user select these, because the variables cannot be coalesced.

Further work

Based on this user study, we conclude that Metamouse needs two additional selector functions and the ability to alter the choice of selector based on multiple examples. One selector iterates over a set of objects that touch a given object; the other iterates over the binding history of a variable. The multiple examples strategy involves comparing rejected or nonperformable predictions with the user's action: If substituting other selector functions for those in the prediction results in a match with the user's action, that substitution is made (if it covers previous instances of the predicted step), or a new rule with that substitution is stored (if not).

The rules for inferring constraints and directions worked well enough (with respect to the drawing tasks studied here) so that we have no data regarding the use of direct instruction (such as clicking on tacks or rotating Basil). The production rule learning algorithm proved successful in distinguishing special contexts such as the first and last iterations of a loop and in suppressing erroneous steps (by lengthening their context such that they are never predicted again). Further testing of these aspects of the system will be warranted once the improvements mentioned above have been made.

In conclusion, Metamouse is a predictive interface that uses background knowledge to abstract features for pattern matching; we have found that this improves the quality of Basil's predictions. The system's metaphor, based on teaching a touch-sensitive turtle and using graphical objects to express spatial relations, is (on the whole) easily grasped by users. Its notion of sets of objects is computationally inadequate to model the way people really do repetitive editing.

The combined use of generalization from examples and direct user instruction has yet to be tested in user studies.

What will they think of next?

The five interfaces described in this chapter and summarized in Table 6.1 illustrate how predictive interfaces can help to reduce the input required not only from physically disabled people, for whom data entry may be mechanically taxing, but from able-bodied users as well. Although the systems have a common theme, they are quite different from each other in three important respects:

- their reliance on application-related background knowledge and syntactic analysis;
- their ability to generalize past input for reuse in predictions; and
- their implementation of mixed-initiative interfaces where the system and user share control over the formation and use of the underlying predictive model.

The Autoprogramming Calculator distinguishes numbers (which can be variables) from operators (which cannot). Workbench distinguishes the first token of a command line from the remainder. The Reactive Keyboard and Adaptive Menus are completely general, have no a priori knowledge, and perform no syntactic analysis.

The ability to generalize history depends on syntax analysis and is enhanced by background knowledge. The Autoprogramming Calculator selectively predicts subsequences of a calculation interleaved with user inputs. Workbench, the Reactive Keyboard, and Adaptive Menus do no generalization.

Most of our predictive systems have separate interfaces which provide the user with a means of controlling, accepting, and rejecting predictions. Adaptive Menus is the exception. The Reactive Keyboard lets the user browse among potential predictions and has a statistically optimized presentation scheme. The user can easily augment or modify the model and its predictions by choosing different text files to prime it. Similarly, Workbench users can save (and edit) their interaction records in separate files and use any one to prime predictions. Workbench provides an array of mechanisms for organizing history, including storage metaphors under which the user can build his or her own task model. The Autoprogramming Calculator's only extra interface option is the "undo" command. The Reactive Keyboard requires that the user explicitly accept a prediction or implicitly reject it by performing an alternative action.

We have learnt several lessons from the design and implementation of these systems and from studying how people use them. First, powerful predictors can be built that can be applied to a variety of task domains. The best example is the Reactive Keyboard. Because its predictive power is based on principles of adaptive text compression, it can be applied to any text domain. We have used it for composing free text, for writing programs, for supplementing the Unix and MS-DOS command based interfaces, and – through the Autoprogramming Calculator – for formulating mathematical expressions. Furthermore, any advances in text compression algorithms can be applied directly to increase the accuracy of the Reactive Keyboard's predictions. The algorithm behind Adaptive Menus can configure any ordered name space. Workbench is capable of becoming a front end to any command based interface, regardless of whether commands are typed or selected through menus.

Second, predictive systems work well in practice and, if well designed, are easy to use. The Reactive Keyboard has proven its usefulness to disabled people – its users find it indispensable. Users of Workbench appreciate the support it provides. The controlled experiment on Adaptive Menus indicates that user performance is enhanced by the assistance that it gives. We believe that these systems have illustrated the viability of predictive interfaces.

Third, predictive systems can be implemented today using existing technology. All the systems described here have been built on conventional computers, and all perform well in real time.

Finally, whether or not users accept a predictive system will depend on their individual needs. Because of the cognitive/physical trade-off, using the predictions may be more work for some people than just continuing without them. Of course, the greater the need, the greater the motivation to learn and use these systems. A predictive interface that is a curiosity to the able-bodied may be a beneficial – indeed, indispensable – tool for a person who is physically disabled.

The adaptive predictive techniques we have described could easily be made widely available to disabled people. The mechanisms of Adaptive Menus and the Autoprogramming Calculator are suitable for integration into existing applications. Moreover, it is feasible to use predictive techniques such as the Reactive Keyboard and Workbench in conjunction with current systems without the necessity to integrate them into particular applications.

What will they think of next? We would like to see a series of modules that allow users to access these techniques, both integrated within individual application programs and in the form of add-on "system extensions" (as in Macintosh System 7). For example, the Reactive Keyboard could be integrated into the command shell in systems like Unix or MS-DOS as a switchable option for all users. A Macintosh desk accessory could combine the adaptive predictive technique of the Reactive Keyboard with a conventional augmentative communication aid for entering single letters – this would be usable with any Macintosh application. We see no reason why pocket calculators and spreadsheet programs should not routinely embody predictive techniques. A personalized phonebook system, with autodial capability and local telephone directories available on CD-rom, could use Adaptive Menus as its basic interface. Perhaps more futuristically, a full implementation of Workbench could provide users with easy opportunities to create individually crafted tool sets for any application.

Acknowledgments

This research has been supported by the Natural Sciences and Engineering Council of Canada, Esso Resources Limited, Apple Corporation, and the Alberta Heritage Foundation for Medical Research. Amongst many people who have helped us with various aspects of this work, we would like to acknowledge in particular the enthusiastic support of David Hill.

References

Bell, T., Cleary, J. G., and Witten, I. H. (1990). *Text compression.* Advanced Reference Series in Computer Science. Englewood Cliffs, NJ: Prentice-Hall.

Bier, E. A. and Stone, M. C. (1986). Snap-dragging. *Computer Graphics 20*(4): 233–240.

Cleary, J. G., and Witten, I. H. (1984). Data compression using adaptive coding and partial string matching. *IEEE Transactions on Communications, 32*(4): 396–402.

Cover, T. M., and King, R. C. (1978). A convergent gambling estimate of the entropy of English. *IEEE Transactions on Information Theory, 24*(4): 413–421.

Cypher, A. (1991). EAGER: Programming repetitive tasks by example. In *Reaching through technology: Proceedings of ACM CHI' 91 Conference on Human Factors in Computing Systems*, ed. S. P. Robertson, G. M. Olson, and J. S. Olson. (pp. 33–40). New York: ACM Press.

Darragh, J. J., and Witten, I. H. (1991). Adaptive predictive text generation and the reactive keyboard. *Interacting with Computers, 3*(1): 27–50.

Darragh, J. J., and Witten, I. H. (1992). *The reactive keyboard.* Cambridge Series on Human–Computer Interaction. Cambridge: Cambridge University Press.

Darragh, J. J., Witten, I. H., and James, M. (1990). The reactive keyboard: A predictive typing aid. *IEEE Computer, 23*(11): 41–49.

deJong, G., and Mooney, R. (1986). Explanation-based learning: An alternative view. *Machine Learning, 1*: 145–176.

Gibler, C. D. (1981). *Linguistic and human performance considerations in the design of an anticipatory communication aid.* Unpublished PhD thesis, Northwestern University.

Greenberg, S. (1984). *User modeling in interactive computer systems.* MSc thesis, Department of Computer Science, University of Calgary, Calgary. Research Report 85/193/6.

Greenberg, S. (1988). *Tool use, reuse and organization in command-driven interfaces.* PhD thesis, Department of Computer Science, University of Calgary. Research Report 88/336/48.

Greenberg, S., and Witten, I. H. (1985). Adaptive personalized interfaces – A question of viability. *Behavior and Information Technology, 4*(1): 31–45.

Greenberg, S., and Witten, I. H. (1988a). Directing the user interface: How people use command-based systems. In *Proceedings of the IFAC 3rd Man–Machine Systems Conference*, Oulou, Finland.

Greenberg, S., and Witten, I. H. (1988b). How users repeat their actions on computers: Principles for design of history mechanisms. In *Human factors in computing systems,* Proceedings of the ACM CHI'88 Conference on Human Factors in Computing Systems, ed. E. Soloway, D. Frye, and S. B. Sheppard (pp. 171–178). New York: ACM Press.

Kucera, H., and Francis, W. N. (1967). *Computational analysis of present-day American English.* Providence RI: Brown University Press.

Maulsby, M., Witten, I., and Kittlitz, K. (1989). Metamouse: Specifying graphical procedures by example. *Computer Graphics, 23*(3):127–136.

Maulsby, D. L., Witten, I. H., Kittlitz, K. A., and Franceschin, V. G. (1992). Inferring graphical procedures: The compleat Metamouse. *Human Computer Interaction, 7*(1): 47–90

Myers, B. A. (1986). Visual programming. programming by example, and program visualization: a taxonomy. *In Human Factors in Computer Systems: Proceedings of the ACM conference Chi'86,* ed. M. Mantei and P. Orbeton (pp. 59–66).

Myers, B. A. (1988). *Creating user interfaces by demonstration.* San Diego, CA: Academic Press.

Pickering, J. A., and Stevens, G. C. (1984). The physically handicapped and work-related computing: Towards interface intelligence. In *Proceedings of the Second International Conference on Rehabilitation Engineering* (pp. 126–127). Ottawa, Ontario, Canada.

Shannon, C. E. (1951). Prediction and the entropy of printed English. *Bell System Technical Journal, 30*(1): 50–64.

Stallman, R. (1987). *GNU Emacs manual.* Cambridge MA: Free Software Foundation.

Suchman, L. A. (1987). *Plans and situated actions: The problem of human–machine communication.* Cambridge: Cambridge University Press.

Suen, C. Y. (1979). *N*-gram statistics for natural language understanding and text processing. *IEEE Transactions on Pattern Analysis and Machine Intelligence, 1*(2): 164–172.

Unipress (1986). *UniPress Emacs screen editor: User's guide.* Edison NJ: Unipress Software Inc.

van Sommers, P. (1984). *Drawing and cognition.* Cambridge: Cambridge University Press.

Witten, I. H. (1981). Programming by example for the casual user: A case study. In *Proceedings of the Canadian Man–Computer Communication Conference* (pp. 105–113). Waterloo, Ontario.

Witten, I. H., Cleary, J., and Greenberg, S. (1984). On frequency-based menu-splitting algorithms. *International Journal of Man–Machine Studies, 21*(2): 135–148.

Witten, I. H., and Greenberg, S. (1985). User interfaces for office systems. In *Oxford Surveys in Information Technology*, ed. P. Zorkoczy (Vol. 2, pp. 69–104). Oxford: Oxford University Press.

Witten, I. H., Greenberg, S., and Cleary, J. (1983). Personalizable directories: A case study in automatic user modelling. In *Proceedings of Graphics Interface '83* (pp. 183–190). Canadian Man-Computer Communications Society.

Witten, I. H., MacDonald, B. A., Maulsby, D. L., and Heise, R. (1992). Programming by example: The human face of AI. *AI and Society* 6:166–185.

Witten, I. H., and Mo, D. H. (1993). Tels. In *Watch what I do: Programming by demonstration,* ed. A. Cypher. Cambridge, MA: MIT Press.

Research

The description of current products in the last section illustrates that there is plenty of scope for improvement in the interfaces for disabled users. What is lacking is knowledge of how to achieve such improvements. The focus of this book is forward looking, and hence this section presents some of the most important research work in the field.

There have been a number of attempts to build a foundation for HCI research based on models of the user. This approach has the advantage of giving designers a "theoretical" basis for their work. One of the problems, though, is that models are often of limited applicability; people are too diverse for their behavior to be adequately captured by a single model. Quite small deviations from the perceived norm may not be included, and gross deviations (to the extent of being labeled as "disabilities") are generally far outside the scope of the model. However, Chapter 7 describes work which is significant in representing a move toward the application of models to disabled users. The *goms* model is a commonly used one. Elkind and Shrager show how it can be successfully applied to the modeling of the interaction between a person with dyslexia and alternative interfaces to writing tools.

The *Candy* project (Communication Assistance to Negate Disabilities in Youth) seeks to provide a real-time speech synthesizer for disabled individuals, particularly nonvocal children with cerebral palsy. Existing speech synthesizers convert user input into discrete linguistic or phonetic symbols which are converted into sound. Complicated sentences must be created by concatenating lower level symbols, precluding real-time conversational speech. The authors of Chapter 8 have developed an articulator based speech synthesizer which simulates the motion of the human tongue and produces the corresponding speech sounds in real time. The synthesizer is driven by two continuous input signals, and nondisabled users can produce real-time speech with a joystick. Disabled users will drive the synthesizer via passive tracking of their body movements. Magnetic trackers attached to the user report their location, and tailoring software allows each user to move the tracker in an optimal orientation and range. The user motion is then converted into the two continuous signals that drive the speech synthesizer. In this way it is hoped to allow each child to compensate for an inoperative vocal tract by using a better set of muscles to operate a simulated vocal tract. The motion mapping software may also have future potential as a physical therapy aid.

The tactile system of writing known as braille is an old communication mode, having been developed by Louis Braille in the nineteenth century. It was the principal medium for independent textual communication for blind people for many years. More recently there have appeared the alternatives of audio recordings of people reading texts and, latterly, speech-based computers (see Chapters 16 and 11). The advent of computers has also led to the possibility of greater flexibility in the use of braille, as is reported in Chapter 9.

Currently within the community of blind people there is something of a schism between those who prefer to use speech and those who favor braille. This is not the place to rehearse the arguments on either side, but in reality neither is a panacea. To a large extent the power of information technology is that it allows information to be transformed into many different forms, so that there is now the possibility of displaying the same information in speech or braille or both.

The chapter details some of the technical details of how the output to a visual display has to be intercepted in order to render it in another form (in this case braille; similar techniques must be used for speech based screen readers). In terms of the future development of user interface architectures, perhaps one of the most important lessons to be learned from such examples is that output should not be so closely tied to visual display. If designers of interfaces are more aware of the requirement for nonvisual display of information, they will be able to build in a more abstract treatment of output such that it can be rendered in different forms and so avoid the awkward post hoc adaptation techniques as described here.

Some novel HCI design problems are also referred to in Chapter 9. There are "routing" problems attendant on coordinating the user's point of interest on the screen and the point currently active within the program. Also "review mode" access can be very powerful but correspondingly complex. Some of these problems might bear consideration by experienced HCI designers who have not hitherto worked with nonvisual interfaces.

The work described in Chapter 10 is significant from several points of view. First, it concerns the development of an interaction metaphor specifically designed to be accessible to blind users. The particular metaphor – the Room – is one which is being researched for use in visual interfaces, but if it can be designed from the start with a multimedia realization (rooms that you can see and hear and even possibly *feel*), it will surely be accessible to a much wider range of users. After all, blind people operate successfully in real rooms every day.

Another important aspect of this project is that it is being supported by an important institution, the National Aeronautics and Space Administration (Nasa). Nasa is involved for very simple, pragmatic reasons; it employs a significant number of blind people and foresees the possibility that those employees will be excluded from certain work areas unless it can make the newer interfaces accessible to them. Thus the project is specifically concerned with accessibility of the standard X Windows interface.

Multimedia is something of a buzzword. It has come to refer to little more than interactive video, but there is a wholly different potential use of multiple communications media in information technology, where the different media are used *within the interaction*. (Some writers have started to use the term "multimodal" to distinguish this from multimedia.) There are many interfaces in which use of multiple forms of communication is appropriate; one is interfaces for people with disabilities, particularly sensory disabilities. Chapter 11 describes some work which has been done exploring some of the less well understood media and how they might be used in combination.

Part of the motivation behind the work described in this book lies in the idea that the unusual challenges presented by computer users' disabilities will generate novel solutions. The concept of a "cognitive prosthesis" is mentioned in more than one chapter and is an idea yet to be picked up by mainstream HCI workers. Chapter 12 introduces a similarly new idea, that of "surrogate electronic traveler." This is based on the idea that an important human resource is information and that in some cases it is difficult to move the human to the place where information is required, and may make more sense to move the information. In some senses this is not a new idea; is that not what the letter and the telephone call do? However, we all know that those channels of communication are impoverished; people often remark that there is no substitute for face-to-face communication. The premise of this project is that modern information technology means that there is possibly a substitute.

The chapter is written from a unique perspective. Bob and Beverly Williges have been active and well respected human factors researchers for a substantial period. However, when Bob himself became disabled as the result of a car accident, they began to apply their skills to that area of human factors research. Bob has limited use of his arms and uses a wheelchair. He has vast experience of the difficulties of physical travel for someone in his position. The degree of handicap he experiences (and the potential benefit of surrogate travel) is well illustrated by the fact that he generally carries a copy of federal regulations with him when flying so that he can demonstrate to airline staff that legally his wheelchair takes priority in the use of luggage space over their own garment bags.

Chapter 13 describes a prosthetic use of information technology. Perhaps the most challenging problem for any interface designer is to provide some form of rich broadband communication for a user who has minimal bodily control. That task is faced by the authors of this chapter. Their clients include people whose only reliable voluntary movement is of the eyes. This may be the only channel of communication through which they can hope to have any control over their environment. In particular, they wish to control their own locomotion in an electric wheelchair. The same interface is likely to be used for most – if not all – of their communication.

The chapter describes a prosthetic application controlling a wheelchair. A physical impairment which prevents a person from walking and necessitates his or her using an electric wheelchair may also affect the ability to control the chair. Whereas most wheelchairs are controlled by a simple joystick, some people do not have sufficient manual dexterity to use one.

As described in Chapter 11, a basic problem is that of the bandwidth of communication in a simple interface. Users with severe physical limitations may only be able to press a . As described earlier, a single switch represents a very low rate of communication. One way around this is to add more switches. For users with severe limitations on bodily control, the problem then becomes one of maximizing the number of switches they can access. This chapter describes an approach whereby the simple winking of the eyes is interpreted as commands to the wheelchair. In some senses this is the ultimate challenge to the HCI designer – to design an interface to a complex machine to which the user has a minimal level of input. Yet to succeed may mean that the user will attain a life-enhancing degree of independence.

7

Modeling and analysis of dyslexic writing using speech and other modalities

Jerome Elkind and Jeff Shrager

Introduction

In Chapter 5 Newell et al. discuss communication and conversation aids for people with speech and language impairments. They review the problems that these people have producing natural sounding speech at acceptable rates and with low response latency, and they discuss a number of computer based prostheses to assist them. In this chapter we focus on the specific problem that people with dyslexia have in communicating through the written medium, and we analyze in detail the performance obtained from several ways of using computers to support writing. The objective is to present a general methodology for analyzing compensatory aids designed to help people with disabilities, to show how this methodology can be used to understand how writing speed is affected by the characteristics of the compensatory aids, in particular a speech recognition system, and to suggest ways in which the speech recognition system could be redesigned to improve performance.

Many designers of complex devices believe that better psychological and physiological models will lead to better design (e.g. Sheridan & Ferrell, 1974; Card, Moran, & Newell, 1983; Elkind, Card, Hochberg, & Huey, 1990; Rouse, 1991). This view has led to a fruitful interaction between these human sciences and design that goes by the name "human factors." Human factors research has influenced the design of many systems, and designers themselves often engage in human factors observation or thought experiments.

What psychology can offer design, beyond what designers can gather on their own, is a set of models that are rigorously grounded and relatively general. Unfortunately, rigor and generality are accomplished through experimental controls and statistical analysis and thus at the expense of richness and detail. The resulting models, paradoxically, describe the normal case even if there is not even a single exemplar of that case. Individual differences dissolve into variance from the mean, or worse, are considered outside of the scope of the model. Thus the capabilities of people with impairments lie outside of general models almost by definition, and the handicaps they experience are exacerbated by norm-based human factors designs.

One practical remedy for this state of affairs is to design systems in accordance with models that specify dimensions and ranges rather than particular values. For instance, one can imagine an automobile dashboard whose illumination color is adjustable to accommodate various sorts of color blindness. Such flexibility is not usually so straightforward to implement, and most human impairments do not lie along such simple dimensions. Moreover, the extreme case, even on simple dimensions, is often qualitatively different from the other ranges; it is a significant oversimplification, for example, to equate deafness with lesser hearing impairments.

A general model nonetheless has heuristic value as long as we are willing to modify it in significant ways when it fails to describe a specific person's condition adequately – thus bending the model to the person rather than the person to the model. The resulting new model can then usefully be studied to produce design proposals that are likely to address the specific needs of persons with impairments.

In this chapter we apply this method in the case of computer supported composition by dyslexic individuals. Dyslexia is a complex class of cognitive/ linguistic impairments, principally of the ability to process written language. It is important to keep in mind that each dyslexic person has specific impairments from this complex class and must be understood individually. Assistive devices and remediation programs must be adjusted for individual differences.

We examine how dyslexia affects the writing process and how to improve the performance of dyslexics in computer supported writing and other text related tasks. We have studied transcription by dyslexic and nondyslexic persons in several settings: writing longhand without computer assistance, using a computer text editor, using a speech recognition prosthesis, and dictating to a typist. Here we develop a model of transcription activity and use the model to isolate points of difficulty for a dyslexic person. This analysis enables us to see clearly why the speech recognition prosthesis is less effective than expected in compensating for the dyslexic person's disability. Finally, from these analyses and from observations of the collaborative setting in which the writer is working with a human typist, we produce several suggestions to improve the effectiveness of speech recognition as a prosthesis for dyslexic writing.

Dyslexia

Dyslexia affects a large number of people. Exactly how large is difficult to pin down (Elkind, 1990). U.S. census data indicate that about 5% of public school students are enrolled in special education programs for the learning disabled, a disabilities category that includes dyslexia (U.S. Department of Commerce, 1987, 1989). Since not all students with learning disabilities are enrolled in these programs, the fraction of students with this condition is probably higher. Speier and O'Connell (1990) cite data from the National Institutes of Health showing that 10% to 15% of the population have learning disabilities. Other data suggests that it is of the order of 7.5% of the population (Gaddes, 1985). Of these, somewhere between 60% (Gaddes, 1985) and 80% (Speier & O'Connell, 1990) would be considered dyslexic. Thus more than 10 million people, and perhaps as many as 20 to 30 million people, in the USA have this disability. Dyslexia can be a serious handicap that often blocks intelligent people from education and employment. Learning disability and dyslexia are associated with a large fraction of school dropouts and juvenile delinquents (Speier & O'Connell, 1990).

Dyslexia is a language disorder, particularly a disorder of written language. Dyslexics are slow to develop fluency in reading and writing and to automate the processes involved in these skills. Many dyslexics never become fluent, and their reading and writing remain inaccurate, slow, and limited in vocabulary. Dyslexics have difficulty associating the written form of language with its oral form. Their ability to decode words, to spell, and to recall letter sequences of words and even images of individual letters is frequently poor. Their sight recognition of words is limited. As a result, their reading requires conscious effort, is error prone, and is associated with poor comprehension.

Writing, because it is generative, is even more severely affected. The demands of spelling associated with writing – retrieving the correct sequence of letters in words or computing them from phonological rules – impose a substantial cognitive load that often interferes with the demands of organizing and expressing ideas in well formed sentences and paragraphs. Dyslexics often have difficulty in choosing correct prepositions and word endings and suffixes, and in verb–subject agreement. They omit words from sentences and telescope ideas so that thoughts are incomplete and conjunctives and transitions are missing. These difficulties, coupled with their meager writing vocabulary, leads to written work that is a poor reflection of their intellectual abilities. Sometimes these difficulties spill over to oral language, but usually written language is more severely affected. Dyslexics therefore are usually better able to express their thoughts orally. The use of a speech recognition prosthesis would thus seem to be an attractive method for increasing their fluency in composition.

Dyslexia results from deficits in language processing, memory, perception, and discrimination occurring either separately or in many different combinations (Doehring, Trites, Patel, & Fiedorwicz, 1981; Levine, 1987). The language processing system may have difficulty appreciating the phonetic elements of language or the morphology of language (e.g. prefixes, suffixes). It may have trouble associating words with meanings. There may be weakness in visual–aural associative memory, in sequential memory (grasping and retrieving sequences of letters, words, sounds), difficulty in storing and retrieving linguistically encoded data, difficulty in retrieving motor sequences for letter or word production. Working memory deficits may make it difficult to recall the beginning of a word or sentence while reading the end of it or to retain the components of a sentence or word while carrying out higher level processing. Sensory memory limitations often make it difficult for a dyslexic to capture visual or aural sequences. Recent results suggest that at least some dyslexics may have a dysfunction in the fast response path (magnocellular system) of the auditory and visual perceptual systems (Livingstone, Rosen, Drislane, & Galaburda, 1991). This complex of deficits affects writing as well as reading because the limitations make it difficult for a dyslexic writer to retrieve or compute the spelling of words, to use correct forms of words, and to find appropriate words to use.

Comparative performance

Our empirical and analytic methodology is deployed in two phases. In the first phase we observe dyslexic and nondyslexic individuals in typical writing activities. (We will use the name K for the dyslexic subject of the studies reported here, and S for the nondyslexic subject.) K is a 23-year-old male college sophomore. His reading is slow, and he has difficulty decoding and remembering written forms of words. He has great difficulty with spelling, limited immediate recall spelling vocabulary, difficulty in generating correct sentence syntax, and some word retrieval difficulty. He is very slow in producing written material. He is taking two-thirds of a normal course load at school and relies extensively on taped books for reading and on dictation for writing. The nondyslexic subject, S, is a 25-year-old female graduate student who has excellent reading and writing skills and speed.

We investigated three kinds of activities:

1. transcription, in which the individual has to copy a document;

2. performance on a battery of diagnostic tests; and

3. composition of an essay describing a picture.

Four output methods were studied:

1. longhand writing;

2. into a computer word processor (Microsoft Word running on a Macintosh SE computer);

3. dictating to a computer based speech recognizer (*DragonDictate*);[1] and

---

[1] DragonDictate™ is a product of Dragon Systems Inc., Newton MA. We used version 1.0 of the DragonDictate software. It had a 30,000-word vocabulary that adapted to the user's speech patterns and vocabulary as it was being used. It is not a continuous speech recognizer but requires words to be separated by a brief pause. The user must check that each word is recognized correctly. The recognizer appends its first-choice word to the line of text shown on the computer screen and then posts a short ordered list of other candidate words on the screen. The user can select a word from this list by saying, for example, "Choose 3." If the word spoken is not on the list, the user can

Table 7.1. *Typical rates for producing text by a dyslexic and nondyslexic in three activities using four methods for capturing text*

Activity	Method			
	Writing (words/min)	Typing (words/min)	Speech recognizer (words/min)	Collaborative transcription[a] (words/min)
Transcription				
Dyslexic	12	12	9	69
Nondyslexic	27	47	NA	155
Diagnostic test (simple sentences)				
Dyslexic	14	10	7	58
Nondyslexic	25	35	NA	68
Essays				
Dyslexic		5	6	29
Nondyslexic		33	NA	49

[a] Excludes typing time.

4.   collaborative transcription, where the writer dictates to a human transcriber who types into the word processor.

Each activity was videotaped. From analysis of the videotapes we obtained measures of overall performance that enable us to compare the several activities and methods. Table 7.1 shows the text production rates of the two subjects in the three activities using the four output methods. First consider the performance of K, the dyslexic subject, in the transcription task. Handwriting, typing, and the speech recognizer gave roughly equivalent text generation rates, a slow 9–12 words/minute. For this individual, the speech recognizer was not faster than writing or typing; in fact it was a bit slower, for reasons we discuss below. However, when dictating to a human transcriber, the subject was able to perform at a rate of 69 words/minute, six to eight times faster than with the other methods. This is approximately the oral reading rate for this subject. In computing the rate for dictating to a human transcriber, we subtracted from the total task completion time the amount of time the subject spent waiting for the typist to complete the typing of previously dictated material. Thus, the rate shown in Table 7.1 for the collaborative transcription output method is the rate that would have been achieved if the typist had been infinitely fast.

Subject S, the nondyslexic, had good typing skills (47 words/minute) and was almost two times faster typing than writing by hand (27 words/minute). When

type it in. If the word is in the system's vocabulary, it will usually appear on the list after a few letters have been typed, and it can be selected by a "Choose" command. If it is not in the vocabulary, it must be typed in full.

dictating to a human transcriber, S could produce text at a rate of 155 words/minute (after subtracting time spent waiting for the typist to complete previously dictated text), more than three times faster than typing. S was two to four times faster than K, depending upon the method.

The diagnostic test included in Table 7.1 required the subject to look at sketches of simple scenes (for example, a boy holding a baseball bat and looking anxiously at a broken house window) and then rapidly to write short sentences describing the scenes.[1] This is an example of a very simple composition task. In this activity the subject did not have to read text sentences as in the transcription task, but instead had to examine the sketch and generate a descriptive sentence. For K, the text production rates in this diagnostic test were similar to those for transcription (± 20%). Collaborative transcription remained six to eight times faster than the other output methods. For S, text production rates for this task were slower than for transcription. The decrease is especially large for collaborative transcription; text production rates declined by more than a factor of two from 155 words/minute to 68 words/minute. For S, this simple composition task apparently took more time than reading, whereas for K it took about the same time. K and S had roughly equivalent rates when dictating, whereas with the other methods K was slower by a factor of two to four.

In the essay composition activity the subjects looked at a sketch of a more complex scene (for example, a group of people walking and playing on a city street on a windy day) and were asked to write an essay of two to three paragraphs describing the scene.[2] This is a more demanding composition activity, and it is not surprising to see the word rates for K decline substantially. His word production rates were about half those obtained in the other activities. Typing and speech recognizer rates were only 5–6 words/minute. Collaborative transcription was reduced to 29 words/minute, although it was still five to six times faster than the other methods. Working collaboratively with a human transcriber is clearly a much more effective way for K to write than any of the other methods.

Rates for S also declined, but by smaller amounts. There was a small reduction in typing rate to 33 words/minute and a greater reduction in dictation rate to 49 words/minute. Thus S does not gain not much advantage by working collaboratively with a human transcriber. Her typing speed is about as fast as her ability to compose text.

It is important to note the difference in word production rates between the dyslexic and the nondyslexic. When K had to generate typewritten text, his rate

---

[1] Test material was taken from the Writing Fluency component of the.Woodcock Johnson Tests of Achievement (WJ-R) (Woodcock & Johnson, 1989).

[2] Test material was taken from the PIAT-R test of written expression (Markwardt, 1989).

was one third to one sixth that of S, depending upon the task. When dictating to a human transcriber, his rates were more competitive, from almost equal to about one half of S's rate. Clearly he is at a substantial disadvantage compared with his nondyslexic peers in school or in work activities that require the production of written material unless he can dictate. A computer based writing prosthesis that would allow him to use speech in a way that mimics his interaction with a human transcriber would be of enormous value.

The DragonDictate system did not provide him this facility. One reason is that the DragonDictate requires considerable attention to control, error detection, and error correction functions. Another reason may be that K was not really expert in the use of the DragonDictate. Although he had about 20 hours of use of the system prior to these tests and was reasonably proficient with it, more experience would probably have led to greater facility and better strategies for control and error handling. Although the DragonDictate was not faster than typing or writing, K reported lower cognitive stress when using it, since it eliminated most of the cognitive load associated with spelling.

Flow models of language interaction with computers

In the second phase of analysis we produced detailed activity flow models of the interaction between computers and dyslexic and nondyslexic persons in performing the transcription tasks. These models identify the processes that take time in the activity. Individual processes might involve the person (whether in cognitive or physical action), the computer, some other aspect of the environment (e.g. the document being transcribed), or relationships between these.

We think of these models as part of the overall writing activity as studied by Hayes and Flower (1980). Figure 7.1 is an extension of the model postulated by Hayes and Flower. Their model, derived from detailed analysis of protocols obtained from subjects performing writing assignments, consists of three major processes: *planning* the composition, *translating* the material developed under the plans into written sentences, and *reviewing* the written text to improve its quality. These processes operate in a context defined by the writing assignment and the writer's experience.

The Hayes and Flower model – and most other studies of writing – assumes an unimpaired writer. The model does not dwell on the processes for producing and capturing text in written form or for reading existing text. For most people, once a sentence is formulated, text production is a highly automated process; for the dyslexic it requires conscious and often great effort. To account for the difficulty associated with these activities, we have added to the original Hayes and Flower model components concerned with the production and capture of text. The *text production* process converts the words of the sentences to be written into characters (that is, generates the spellings and produces the keystrokes or character forms). The *text capture* process is the system (e.g. word processor, speech recognizer, or human transcriber) used to capture these characters and display them as text sentences.

In our studies we modeled the writing activity as a transcription activity in which the text to be entered is externally given. This simplification retains many of the aspects of the activity that are affected by K's dyslexia. The *translating* process in the Hayes and Flower model is replaced with a preordained text that the person must first read, encode, and store and then use to produce text for display on a computer screen or on paper. Transcription exercises memory, word recognition, lexical access, syntactic skill, spelling, and motor activation. It does not, however, exercise the generating, organizing, goal-setting, or translating processes of the composition task. Although performance in these is likely also to be handicapped by dyslexia, they are much more complicated to study and model and are left for future studies.

The models we construct are from the *goms* family introduced by Card, Moran, and Newell (1983). Goms models are derived from a Model Human Processor (MHP) that is defined by processors, memories, and principles of operation governing these. There are three processors: perceptual, cognitive, and motor which may work concurrently, subject to some data flow limitations. Each processor has a characteristic cycle time and other properties that are described by Card et al. Associated with the perceptual processor is a sensory memory for visual and auditory images. The cognitive processor operates in conjunction with working memory and uses information previously stored in long-term memory.

Goms models are based on a cognitive structure of the user consisting of (1) the user's *G*oals, (2) the basic *O*perations that the user can perform to achieve the goals, (3) *M*ethods or combinations of the basic operations, and (4) *S*election rules for choosing among alternative methods. The basic goms structure can be realized with different types of control structures, and operations can be defined at various levels of aggregation to match the grain of the data that are available and the purposes for which the model is being used. We represent behavior by a flow graph rather than by a program and use operators that are at a fairly high level of aggregation.

In our flow graph models, each observed or inferred process is represented by a rectangular box. Shown beneath each box are durations, rates, ranges of such measures, and other parameters of the process, such as chunks of working memory consumed. Directional lines connecting the processes indicate the *observed* or *inferred* flow of the activity. (This is not all the *possible* flow of the activity, which might be from any process to any other process.) The video recordings provided a detailed record of each subject's performance, from which we estimated the durations and other properties of most of the processes represented in the models. Where direct observation of process parameters was not possible, we inferred the durations from related experiments or from recourse to the literature.

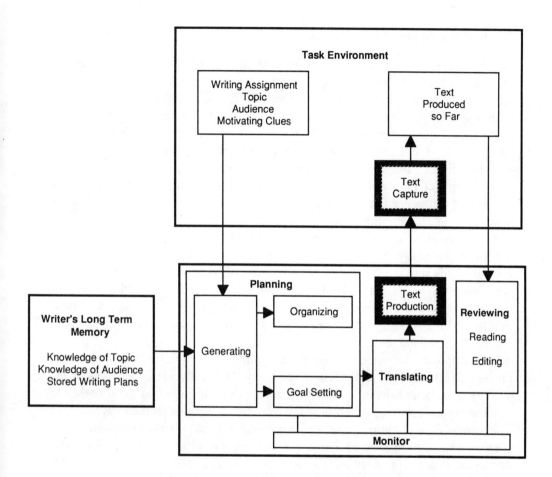

Figure 7.1. The Hayes and Flower model for the writing process, with the addition of text production and capture processes (highlighted).

The flow models enable us to estimate path times for both observed and unobserved routes through the model. From these data we are able to estimate worst case and best case rates for the writing methods and devices used. From the worst case analyses we can identify bottlenecks. This leads us to propose designs that relieve the bottlenecks. The models can then be used in the opposite direction. We restructure the model in accordance with the proposed design and reestimate the parameters of the new model. Redoing the best and worst case analyses then enables us to compare the observed activity with the way that that activity might develop in the new setting, utilizing the new design. We must be careful in carrying out this analysis to be sure that we do not introduce new bottlenecks in the designs.

Method of estimating parameters

Parameters of the models were obtained in one of three ways: by direct measurement from the videotapes, by borrowing from the literature, or by interpolation between observations and borrowed values. Because we are dealing with a special population, we obviously preferred direct measurement, but this was sometimes not possible. When we were forced to rely on other work, we carefully chose what to borrow and borrowed only as a fallback. When it was possible both to measure and borrow parameter values, we tried to compare them. Conflict between measured and borrowed parameters may point up interesting differences between dyslexics and nondyslexics, and we note these in the following discussion.[1]

Our method of direct measurement involved three steps. First, we selected a part of the video in which there was continuous action of the sort that we deemed typical of this activity. Next, we carefully transcribed the observable action into a state diagram. From this diagram we could read off the times at which most of the overt actions (e.g. key strokes and head movements) take place and their durations. Finally, simple computations lead from these data to an average value for the desired parameter.

It is important to realize a significant limitation of this process and of the present effort more generally. There are many potentially important steps of the activity that are not distinguishable by our method. If there was good reason to assume more steps than we observed, we could use various mathematical means to estimate their durations, but we rarely encountered situations in which this seemed necessary in order to obtain a model that was satisfactory for our present purposes. Where this need is felt most strongly is in the case of such mental processes as spelling and in such visual activity as searching for one's place.

The reader probably shares some dissatisfaction with the authors in these cases, as the models seem to compress very complex activities into rectangular boxes. This diagrammatic representation elides a great deal of information, such as what the internal and external representations of information are, how they are translated one to another, where and how internal information is stored, and how branching decisions are made. Much of cognitive psychology is, of course, concerned with unpacking these boxes, and there is certainly literature that we could go to on this point. However, in accordance with our earlier hesitation to rely upon "mean-valued" science to provide useful data on exceptional cases, we choose to rely upon our own data to give outward constraint to these composed complexes and then work back from there at our own pace.

---

[1] In the model diagrams we indicate the source of a parameter. Values with no notation were directly measured. Values with a lowercase letter superscript were borrowed from another source. (The sources are displayed in the table legend.) Underlined values were interpolated.

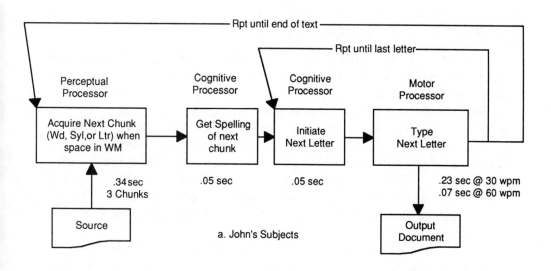

a. John's Subjects

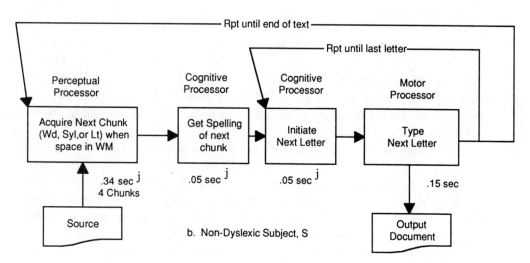

b. Non-Dyslexic Subject, S

Figure 7.2. Model of expert transcription typing in flow chart form adapted from John's (1988) program structure model. Upper flow model (a) has the parameters used by John to represent the performance of her subject. Lower flow model (b) has the parameters for our nondyslexic subject S. S's typing rate computed from the model is 48 words/minute. The observed rate was 47 words/minute. Parameters with superscript j were borrowed from John (1988). Others were obtained from measurements made on video recordings.

Models for transcription typing

The first model, depicted in Figure 7.2a, is adapted from John's (1988) study of skilled touch typing. Chunks consisting of words, syllables, or letters are extracted from the source document (three chunks at a time in 0.34 second); the spelling of a chunk is obtained, unless is it a letter (0.05 second); there is a letter initiation operator (0.05 second); and then the letter is typed. For a slow typist (30 words/minute) the last step takes 0.23 second; for a fast typist (60 words/minute) it takes only 0.07 second. Loop transitions then take the person back either to get new chunks from the source document or to initiate the next letter. John's model allows parallel operation by the perceptual, cognitive, and motor processors, so, for example, a new chunk can be acquired while characters are being typed.

This model is a good representation of transcription typing by our nondyslexic subject, S (Figure 7.2b). To model her performance we borrowed the chunk acquisition, spelling, and letter initiation times from John's model and used the observed letter typing time of 0.15 second. We also observed from handwriting transcription experiments with S that she appeared to acquire four chunks (mostly words) at a time rather than the three used by John. When we employ these parameters in the model, we compute a typing rate of 48 words/minute (assuming text acquisition and typing to be concurrent), which compares with an observed rate excluding errors of 50 words/minute and a rate including errors from Table 7.1 of 47 words/minute.

We next turn to a slightly more complicated model of dyslexic transcription, "sight" (looking at the keyboard) typing (Figure 7.3). The main structural difference between this model and the model adapted from John (above) is the inclusion of a head movement operator (0.44 second to look over to the source document and back to the keyboard). As for differences in duration (and capacity), we see that K acquired one chunk with each look at the source and that acquisition took 1.1 seconds (time to reacquire position in text is included here), whereas John calculated three chunks in 0.34 second for nondyslexic typists. We inferred from John's model that the cognitive processor time to get the spelling of the next chunk was 0.05 second. Finally, the type-letter operator was observed to be 0.5 second for K versus 0.07 to 0.23 second for John's nondyslexic subjects and 0.15 second for S.

The word rate computed from the model was 10 words/minute (about 1 second/character), compared with the observed rate of 12 words/minute (Table 7.1). The combination of head movement time, the long times to acquire text and type the next letter, and the fact that only one chunk is acquired at a time all contribute to K's slow typing rate. The limited number of chunks that are acquired, a major impediment to increasing speed, reflects either working memory impairment of this subject or the fact that working memory is required for the type-letter operation (it is not automated).

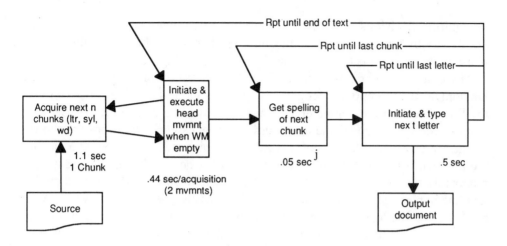

Figure 7.3. Flow model of transcription typing by dyslexic subject, K, who used the sight typing method that required head movements between source document and keyboard. Parameters with superscript j were borrowed from John (1988). Other parameters were obtained from measurements on video recordings.

Loop time for 1-letter chunk = 2.0 sec/letter; word rate = 5.9 words/min

Loop time for 1-syllable (3-letter)chunk = 1.0 sec/letter; word rate = 12 words/min

Loop time for 1-word chunk = 0.8 sec/letter; word rate = 14.7 words/min

Word rate computed from model = 10 words/min

Observed word rate = 12 words/min

Models for speech recognition

The speech recognition experiments were carried out with the DragonDictate system operating on a 33 MHz 80486 PC-compatible computer. It is a trainable, word-at-a-time speech recognition device for simple transcription input to a text editor and other applications software. The system has a 30,000-word active vocabulary. The user wears a headset with one earphone and a microphone. In a training session the DragonDictate software asks the user to speak a training vocabulary that includes the special words used in editing (described below). After this the user can enter and edit arbitrary text using only the speech recognizer, however, he or she needs to pause briefly between each word. The system adapts to the user's speech patterns and to the user's vocabulary during use. Adaptation is accomplished by requiring the user to confirm or correct the recognition decisions made by the system and to enter new words into the vocabulary by typing them after they have been spoken. This allows the system to associate a speech pattern with the new word.

The process of text entry goes as follows. The user speaks a word which the DragonDictate attempts to recognize. It appends its best guess for that word to the line of text on the computer screen. If it is the intended word, the user can simply proceed and speak the next word. Other guesses for the word are shown on the screen in an ordered short list called a choice menu. If the word added to the text line is not correct and the correct word is on the choice menu (say, the number 4), the user can say, "choose four," and that word will be entered on the text line in place of the erroneous word. Alternatively, the user can say, "Scratch that" (one of the learned command phrases) to cause the erroneous word to be removed and can repeat the word in the hope that it will be recognized correctly the second time. If the correct word is not on the choice menu, the user can start typing the word. If the word is in the system's vocabulary, the first few letters will usually cause the appropriate word to appear on the choice menu. If the word is not in the vocabulary, the user must type it completely and press the enter key or give the command "OK" to cause it to be appended. (There is also an editing mode, which we will not try to describe here, as it is not relevant to the present discussion, is complex, and was hard for K to use.)

Parameter estimation

Figure 7.4 is a partial model of K's use of the DragonDictate. The reason this model is only partial is that there are pathways that K took only once, or a very few times, or which were so long and tortuous that we have simply removed them from consideration in our analyses (e.g. editing). Also, this model represents K's final level of performance in our data, skipping over the training phase (of which the very different structure presumably has little bearing on use). More important, this model does not represent the use of the device that one might come to as an expert – but, as we shall see, this will also have little bearing on our analyses.

The uppermost part of the model is the speaking loop, analogous to the typing loop in the other models. The initiate-and-speak-syllable operation required 0.2 second per syllable. This version of the DragonDictate software required about 0.42 second to recognize and append a word to the text line and 0.22 second to put up the choice menu. Note that this model includes a read-and-check-recognized-word operation (0.27 second), which was unnecessary in the other models. Usually K acquired only one chunk (a single word) when looking at the source text. Sometimes, if the text consisted of short, easy-to-pronounce words, he might acquire two chunks (also words). We observed that after confirming that the first word was correct (read-and-check operation) there was a latency of 0.5 second before the second word was spoken. We have identified this latency

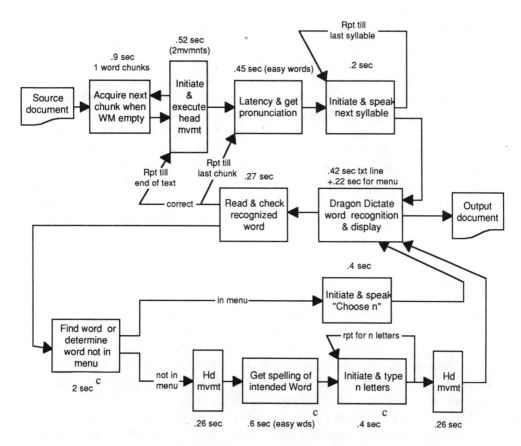

Figure 7.4. Partial flow model of K's use of the DragonDictate speech recognizer for transcription. Parameters with superscript c were obtained from an experiment in essay composition performed with K at approximately the same time as this transcription experiment. Other parameters were obtained from the transcription video recordings.

Loop time for 2 syllables/word if correct recognition of word = 3.0 sec/word; 20 words/min

Loop time if "choose *n*" required = 6 sec/word; 10 words/min

Loop time if typing 2 letters required and then "choose *n*" = 11 sec; 6 words/min

Overall rate from loop times = 13 words/min

Actual transcription rate = 9 words/min

with the get-pronunciation operator shown in Figure 7.4. We attribute this rather long latency to the care K was taking in trying to pronounce words correctly and consistently and in making sure that there was a gap between words.

The lower part of the figure represents the "choose *n*" and type-letter error recovery paths. We observed the menu search time to be about 2 seconds. The other operators involved in these paths and their times are shown in the figure. It should be pointed out that there was great variability in the time to type words or even the first few letters of a word. If the word was easy, so that its spelling was well known and easily retrievable by K, it would take about 0.6 second to get the spelling and 0.4 second to type each character. Since K is not a touch typist, he had to make a head movement from the screen to the keyboard in order to type. If the word was difficult and he had to obtain the spelling from phonological and lexical rules or from repeated reference to the source, successful transcription of the word could take a long time and involve several traverses of the typing-read-and-recognize loop. We observed an occasion when he spent almost 30 seconds on one word.

Loop times

These models enable us to compute loop times – the average time it takes the person to cycle through various pathways in the model. From loop times one can easily compute rates in terms of words/minute that are meaningful to the individual user and useful in comparisons. If the model is of high fidelity, then we can use such times to find best and worst case paths and thus to compare expected performances under different conditions.

Three loops are shown in Figure 7.4. The main loop at the top of the figure is for words that are recognized correctly; it takes about 3 seconds/word (assuming a word of two syllables) to read the word, speak it, wait for it to be recognized and posted on the display, and to read and check the correctness of the displayed word. This corresponds to a rate of 20 words/minute. The second loop, shown in the middle of the figure, is for cases of a word that is incorrectly recognized but appears on the choice menu. This path takes about 6 seconds/word (10 words/minute); the additional time goes to finding the word in the choice menu, speaking "choose *n*," waiting for the word to appear in the text line, and checking it. The third loop, at the bottom of the figure, is for cases where the word is incorrectly recognized, does not appear in the choice menu, and must be typed. For the case in which two letters are typed and then a "choose *n*" loop is traversed, the loop time is about 11 seconds/word (6 words/minute). We observed that the main loop was taken for about 67% of the words and each other loop for about 16% of words. This gives a composite performance of 13 words/minute compared with the observed performance (Table 7.1) of 9 words/minute. The difference between model and actual performance can be attributed to the time taken to correct dictation (as opposed to recognition) errors or to deal with complex words that are not included in the model.

Model of collaborative transcription with human transcriber

Table 7.1 showed that when K was working in collaboration with a human transcriber he was able to achieve rates of 69 words/minute (after subtracting time spent waiting for the typist). Figure 7.5 shows the flow model for this method of transcription. The initiate-and-speak-syllable operation was observed to take 0.2 second. We used John's value for the cognitive processor time of 0.05 second for the get-pronunciation time. We observed from K's speaking patterns that he acquired text in one-word, two-word, or three-word chunks with about equal probability. We could not observe the chunk acquisition time directly and used a value of 0.7 second that is an interpolation between John's value for acquisition time (0.34 second) and the acquisition time (1.1 seconds) observed in the typing transcription experiments (Figure 7.3) and that gives good agreement with the observed rate. The word rate predicted by the model is 68 words/minute versus an observed rate of 69 words/minute.

Possible design improvements in speech recognition prostheses

The method of comparative modeling enables us to answer the question of why the speech recognition prosthesis is not as useful as expected for K's online writing. Furthermore, it enables us to suggest design changes that will improve performance for users with characteristics similar to those of our dyslexic subject. Performance with the speech recognition prosthesis was observed to be 9 words/minute versus 69 words/minute when working collaboratively with the hypothetical infinitely fast typist. The comparison between the two models is 13 words/minute for speech recognition versus 68 words/minute for collaborative transcription. Even the rate for correctly recognized words (the fast loop in the operation of the speech recognition device, is only 20 words/minute.) The two incorrect-recognition loops lead to significant decrements in the performance, down to 13 words/minute. Finally, errors made by the user and difficult words (not in the model) further reduce performance.

Clearly the collaborative setting is an easier and more natural environment for K. The cognitive demands associated with the actual production of text, with device control, and with error management are less than with DragonDictate. Can we look to the collaborative setting for guidance on how the DragonDictate system might be modified to give faster word production rates?

Adjust recognition speed

There are several major differences between the collaborative and the DragonDictate settings. The data presented for collaborative transcription assumed that typing takes zero time, whereas it takes 0.42 second for DragonDictate to recognize a word and enter it on the text line. To put the

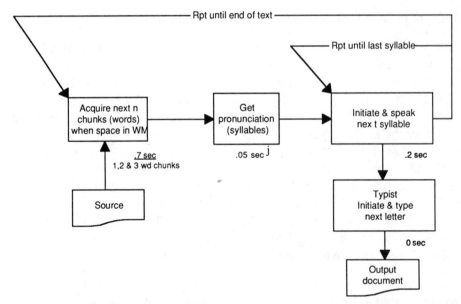

Figure 7.5. Flow model of collaborative transcription in which K dictated text to a human transcriber. Time K spent waiting for typist to finish previously dictated material has been subtracted from total time. This is equivalent to assuming that typing a character takes 0 seconds. Parameter with superscript j was borrowed from John (1988). The underlined parameter (time to acquire next chunk) was interpolated as described in text.
Loop time for 1-word chunks = 1.15 sec/word; 52 words/min
Loop time for 2-word chunks = 0.8 sec/word; 75 words/min
Loop time for 3-word chunks = 0.68 sec/word; 88 words/min
Overall rate of text production from model = 68 words/min; observed rate = 69 words/min

comparison on an equivalent basis, we should examine the case in which recognition is instantaneous, so that the recognized word appears on the text line with no delay. If we make this assumption and set the word-recognition-and-display operator to zero, the word rate for the correct-recognition loop increases to 24 words/minute. When the error loops are included, the rate becomes 15 words/minute, still substantially below the collaborative rate of 68 words/minute.

Auditory notification of uncertain words

DragonDictate requires that each word be verified visually. This takes time for verification and requires head movement after every word to examine the computer display for correctness. There is no need for visual checking or for head movement in the collaborative setting, because the typist simply types on when there is no uncertainty and gives *signals* to indicate confusion, mishearing, or spelling difficulties, thereby leaving the reader's attention for the most part uninterrupted. The recognizer might give a similar kind of feedback. For example, an acknowledgment sound (perhaps the sound of keystrokes) might be used to indicate recognition that has a high probability of being correct. When there is less confidence that the word is correct, the recognizer might read the word back to the user with a questioning intonation and wait for an "OK" command. When there is even more uncertainty, the recognizer might signal with a "Huh?" If this kind of feedback were given by the DragonDictate, the user would not have to check words that have a high probability of being correct, and the head movement time of 0.52 second/word and the read-and-check operation (0.27 second) would not be necessary. In addition, the get-pronunciation latency would probably be reduced, because speech rhythm would be less often interrupted by the need to attend to other tasks. We will assume that it is reduced to 0.2 second, about halfway to the value of 0.05 second used by John. Finally, the acquisition time would probably be reduced, because the reader would not lose his or her place in the source text and have to relocate it. We might assume that the acquisition time under these circumstances would be the same as when dictating to a human typist, where a value of 0.7 second gave a good fit to the data (see Figure 7.5).

Revised flow diagram

We have redrawn the flow model for the DragonDictate to reflect these changes (Figure 7.6). Note that the correct-word loop is much simpler and shorter. These changes would increase the correct-word rate to 43 words/minute, a value that is reasonably close to the 68 words/minute obtained from the model for collaborative transcription. However, the aural feedback generates the need for a correction loop to confirm an uncertain recognition with an "OK." We assume that confirmation will take 0.4 second, the time observed for speaking two syllables. When the user receives the signal indicating an incorrect recognition, he or she must make a head movement (0.26 second) to the display to see if the word is in the choice menu. We assume that incorrect recognitions occur with the same probability as before (16% requiring "choose *n*" and 16% requiring typing) and that half of the correct recognitions (34%) are certain, requiring no action on the part of the user, and half (34%) require a confirming "OK." We do not have a better basis for estimating the probability of traversing these loops. Given these assumptions, the overall rate computed from the model is 19 words/minute.

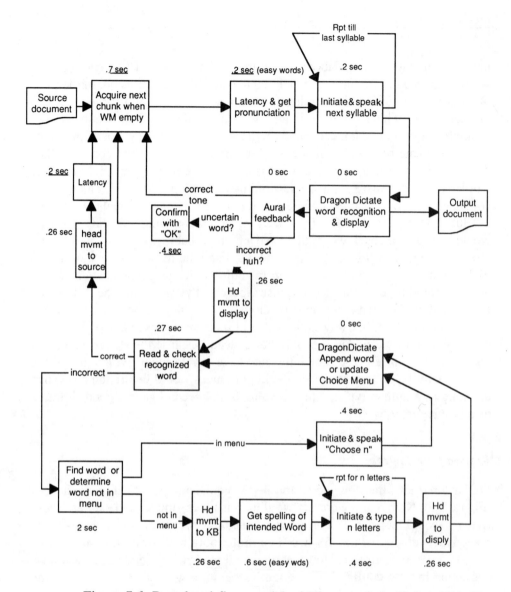

Figure 7.6. Postulated flow model of K's use of the DragonDictate speech recognizer that has instantaneous recognition and is redesigned to use aural feedback to indicate the level of uncertainty in the recognition of words. Parameters are mostly drawn from Figure 7.4. Underlined parameters are interpolated as described in the text.

Loop time for correct recognition = 1.3 sec/word; 43 words/min

Loop time for uncertain correct recognition = 1.7 sec; 35 words/min

Loop time if "choose *n*" required (no check of recognition of "choose *n*") = 4.7 sec/word; 13 words/min

Loop time if typing 2 letters required and then choose *n* = 8.9 sec; 7 words/min

Overall rate from loop times = 19 words/min assuming correct signal 34%; uncertain word 34%; choose *n* 16%; typing 16%

Further increases in word rate would require acquisition of multiple chunks (words), which is certainly possible, but we have no basis for determining whether it will happen, given the requirement for pausing between words and for paying some attention to signals indicating errors. In any case, we have moved well beyond our actual experimental data, and further extrapolation seems unwarranted.

Error rates

It should be noted that although we have drawn designs to improve the primary correct-word loop, we have done nothing yet to improve the error loops. Left unchanged, they limit the overall performance to 19 words/minute. To increase the overall rate substantially, it is necessary either to decrease the fraction of words that are incorrectly recognized or to decrease the time to handle these errors. Error rates should decline with additional training of the system to the user's voice patterns and vocabulary. A reduction of error rate by half from 32% to 16% would cause the overall transcription rate to increase to 26 words/minute. We do not have data for estimating how long it would take to achieve these levels, but representations by Dragon Systems suggest that they are achievable by nondyslexic speakers.

Correcting errors

As we have seen, error handling has a major effect on overall performance. We have two suggestions for improvements in this area. The first is to process errors on a sentence basis so that the user can dictate an entire sentence without shifting attention back and forth from the writing task to the correction task. The measures derived from the spoken words of the entire sentence would need to be buffered. Upon completion of the sentence, the choice menu for the uncertain words would be displayed, and the user could proceed to make the required "choose n" or "type letter" corrections in a second pass through the sentence. The primary advantage of this method is that it will allow the user to dictate a complete thought before being interrupted and thereby speed up the dictation process. It might also result in less time being spent on each error, but further experimentation would be required to confirm this.

A second type of error situation, not represented in the model but mentioned in the discussion, is the problem in correcting errors in words that the user finds difficult to spell. We observed situations in the essay composition experiment in which DragonDictate could not recognize the spoken word and the subject could not spell it. K sometimes spent an extraordinary amount of time, often several minutes, trying to find some way of getting the correct word either by persevering in his attempts to spell it or by speaking similar-sounding words that the system might recognize correctly and that he could modify to the desired word. At times this consumed 20% to 40% of the total time required to capture the text. An escape from this kind of deadlock is needed. A recorder mode in which the speech for these words is recorded for later resolution, or a syllable mode in which the user speaks the phonetic components of the word that are then recognized and resolved later, are possible approaches. There is a significant opportunity for performance improvement if this situation is handled more effectively.

Conclusions

Dyslexia is a relatively common condition that can produce to significant disability. Dyslexics can be especially handicapped by the influence of human factors models that aim to describe a generally nondyslexic population. We sought to remedy this situation by developing detailed models of a particular dyslexic person in computer supported writing and by using these models in the analysis and design of systems.

In studying dyslexic and nondyslexic individuals in a variety of computer aided transcription settings, we found that a speech recognition prosthesis did not compare well in terms of word production rates with collaborative writing, nor was it very easy to use. It did, however, compare reasonably well with typing and handwriting, and the fact that it eliminated most of the burden of spelling was seen as a significant benefit.

Guided by a general model of the writing process, we produced detailed models to describe these situations. The models helped us to understand the bottlenecks in computer aided writing that lead from dyslexia to significant handicaps. Three types of bottlenecks account for most of the performance degradation:

1. operations in which the subject had to confront his areas of impairment, such as spelling words, required excessive times to complete;

2. dealing with errors in the operation of the speech recognition computer system used to support writing, such as correcting errors in recognition of spoken text or command words, accounted for a large fraction of the total time spent doing the primary writing task;

3. the cognitive load of controlling the speech recognition system, whose considerable complexity is depicted by the multi-path flow diagrams shown earlier in the chapter, interfered with performance of the primary writing task.

These three types of bottlenecks are likely to be very important to the performance of all computer-based systems designed to assist people with disabilities. It is important that computer aids be designed to minimize their effects.

The detailed models developed here illustrate a general method for determining where and how computer-based aids should be redesigned so that good performance is achieved and performance bottlenecks are avoided. Analysis of the model of speech recognition transcription enabled us to propose several ways in which the speech recognition system might be modified to give better support to people with dyslexia. The collaborative setting, where the differences in performance are not so great, provided insights about what kinds of design changes would be most effective. These changes include various modes of audible feedback to reduce the time spent in visually checking words that are correctly recognized, changes in the general dynamic of interaction so that errors can be dealt with on a sentence-by-sentence instead of word-by-word basis, and a novel means of correction that uses syllabic input for difficult words. These changes should reduce cognitive load on the writer and thus enable him or her to allocate more attention to the primary task of composition, a task that dyslexics find difficult in any form. Finally, we were able to use the models to estimate the improvement in speech production rates and error frequency that should result from the proposed changes.

The method of detailed observation and modeling and especially of the analysis of natural successful settings is general enough to be used with individuals with widely different capabilities and in a large range of situations. We have shown, moreover, that it can provide a rational basis for individualizing system design. Broad application of this method to different persons with different capabilities and in a variety of settings will make available a large collection of relatively specific models. A library of such models may aid both system designers and therapists concerned with prescribing devices to assist dyslexics in bridging the gap between individuals and their goals.

Acknowledgments

The authors would like to thank Stuart Card for his contributions to planning the experimental studies and developing the models presented in this paper and Becky Agin and Jeannine Pinto for their helpful comments about earlier drafts of this chapter.

References

Card, S. K., Moran, T. P., and Newell, A. (1983). *The psychology of human–computer interaction*. Hillsdale, NJ : Erlbaum.

Doehring, D. G., Trites, R. L., Patel, P. G., and Fiedorwicz, C. A. M. (1981). *Reading disabilities*. New York: Academic Press.

Elkind, J. I. (1990). The incidence of disabilities in the United States. *Human Factors*, *32*: 397–405.

Elkind, J. I., Card, S. K., Hochberg, J., and Huey, B. M. (1990). *Human performance models for computer-aided engineering.* San Diego: Academic Press.

Hayes, J. J., and Flower, L. S. (1980). Identifying the organization of writing processes. In *Cognitive processes in writing,* ed. L. W. Gregg and E. R. Steinberg (pp. 3–30). Hillsdale, NJ: Erlbaum.

John, B. E. (1988). *Contributions to engineering models of human–computer interaction.* unpublished PhD dissertation, Department of Psychology, Carnegie Mellon University.

Gaddes, W. H. (1985). *Learning disabilities and brain function.* New York: Springer Verlag.

Levine, M. (1987). *Developmental variation and learning disorders.* Cambridge, MA: Educators Publishing Services.

Livingstone, M. S., Rosen, G. D., Drislane, F. W., and Galaburda, A. M. (1991). Physiological and anatomical evidence for a magnocellular defect in developmental dyslexia. *Proceedings of the National Academy of Sciences, 88:* 7943–7947.

Markwardt, F. C., Jr. (1989). *Peabody Individual Achievement Test – Revised.* Circle Pines, MN: American Guidance Service.

Rouse, W. B. (1991). *Design for success.* New York,: Wiley.

Sheridan, T. B., and Ferrell, W. R. (1974). *Man–machine systems: Information, control and decision models of human performance.* Cambridge, MA: MIT Press.

Speier, C., and O'Connell, M. (1990, April 16). California Assembly Bill no. 3040, Sacramento CA: California State Legislature.

U.S. Department of Commerce. (1987). Table 214 in Statistical *abstract of the United States: 1987* (107th ed.). Washington, DC: Government Printing Office.

U.S. Department of Commerce. (1989). Tables 221 and 235 in *Statistical abstract of the United States: 1989* (109th ed.) . Washington, DC: Government Printing Office.

Woodcock, R. W., and Johnson, M. B. (1989). *Woodcock–Johnson Tests of Achievement.* Allen, TX: DLM Teaching Resources.

8

Giving Candy to children: User-tailored gesture input driving an articulator-based speech synthesizer

Randy Pausch and Ronald D. Williams

Introduction

The *Candy* project (Communication Assistance to Negate Disabilities in Youth) combines computer scientists, electrical engineers, speech pathologists, pediatricians, and occupational therapists. Our ten-year goal is to create a speech synthesizer for disabled individuals. We are currently in our third year of the project and have produced a set of interim results in both our speech synthesizer and gesture-based input. Our initial target population is children with cerebral palsy (CP), of whom there are approximately 400,000 in the United States alone (Connolly, 1990). When adults are included in the count, the number of Americans affected by CP is approximately 700,000 (United Cerebral Palsy Association, 1985). Persons with other disabilities, such as strokes and Alzheimer's disease, may also eventually benefit from our system.

CP can be broadly defined as brain damage that impairs motor control. Persons with CP are not necessarily mentally retarded, but they do exhibit wide variation in physical abilities. A significant portion of the CP population is communicative but nonverbal – although the desire to communicate is present, speech is prohibited by damage to the part of the brain that controls the vocal tract. Most of these individuals do not have enough coordination for handwriting or typing. Although primitive electronic communication aids exist, most are variations on picture boards, where the user points or looks at a two-dimensional array of pictures to convey a thought such as "hungry" or "tired," and this symbol is transmitted to a traditional text-to-speech synthesizer.

We have developed a speech synthesizer which is articulator based. We simulate the position of physical articulators, such as the tongue, and synthesize the sound that would be made by air passing through the vocal tract with real articulators in those positions. Surprisingly, understandable speech can be produced by moving the tongue and holding other articulators in fixed positions. Our current synthesizer models the positions of the base and tip of the tongue as input signals and then synthesizes the sound produced by that configuration of the tongue. We have implemented a prototype which synthesizes monotone speech from two analog signals representing tongue position, and we can produce limited speech in real time using a joystick.

Our target population cannot use standard input devices to drive the synthesizer. Any approach using physical input devices would require the construction of individual hardware, which is prohibitively expensive. Also, children with CP are often weak, making control of any physical device tiring. As users tire, their efficiency with a particular device decreases, and several devices may be needed to accommodate various stages of fatigue. We avoid physical input devices by using magnetic trackers which report body motion. The only physical effort required of the user is movement of his or her body; those motions are converted by software into continuous control signals for the speech synthesizer. This tailoring software allows us to create interfaces based on the user's individual abilities and will make it possible for those interfaces to adapt as the user tires.

Existing gesture recognition and speech synthesis systems are based on symbols. For example, several systems have attempted to synthesize speech using the deaf alphabet and/or a subset of American Sign Language as user input (Dramer, 1989; Loomis, Poizner, Bellugi, Blakemore, & Hollerbach, 1983). These systems attempt to understand or interpret gestures and are commonly referred to as gesture recognition systems. Our approach is to map continuous data from one or more sensors to a set of continuous device control signals with no intermediate symbols. This should make it possible to produce fluid, real-time speech synthesis with smooth transitions from sound to sound.

An articulator-based model of speech

Existing augmentative communication devices convert symbols into synthetic speech through some form of text-to-speech synthesis. When the symbols represent very small linguistic units, such as sounds or single words, the user has greater conversational flexibility but must transfer many symbols across the human to machine interface. When the symbols represent larger linguistic units, the user enjoys significantly reduced demands from the interface at the cost of conversational flexibility. Both extremes and all intermediate compromises currently offered are frustratingly slow, with communication rates at least an order of magnitude slower than that of normal conversations.

The articulators in the human vocal tract exhibit many degrees of freedom, and the coordinated motion of these articulators produces fluid conversational speech. Human speech is produced as the composition of continuous sounds. The character of these sounds at each instant in time is determined to a significant extent by the instantaneous configuration of the articulators in the vocal tract.

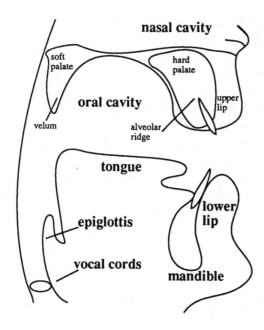

Figure 8.1. The human vocal tract.

The fact that the articulator motion is concerted is fortunate, because it effectively reduces the number of parameters specifying the state of the vocal tract, providing hope that a control signal with severely limited degrees of freedom can be used to drive a continuous speech synthesizer.

Conversational speech synthesis is inhibited by the transfer of symbols across the user interface. While the mental production of speech may be principally a symbolic process, the generation of speech sounds in the vocal tract is physical and continuous. Of course, control of the human vocal tract involves complex coordination. Our hypothesis is that if speaking persons can control their complex vocal tracts at conversational rates, then many nonspeaking individuals should be able to control a simplified simulated vocal tract to synthesize speech at conversational rates. We expect that users may require a long time to control this unique speech prosthesis, as the learning process can best be compared to the steps required for vocal individuals to learn to speak. One benefit of this approach is that children equipped with the speech prosthesis would be able to acquire speech using the normal developmental process. Existing speech synthesis methods require the children first to learn a symbolic language and then learn to drive the speech synthesizer with it.

Our articulator-driven speech synthesizer produces sounds using the positions and motions of implied articulators in a simulated vocal tract. This form of speech synthesis has been discussed previously in the literature (Coker, 1973; Haggard, 1979; Henke, 1967). Our new limitation is that disabled individuals must be able to produce the articular control parameters in real time. Articulator-driven synthesis is unnecessary and constraining in the text to speech environment, but this approach is directly analogous to the mechanisms of speech production used for normal human conversational speech. A brief review of human physical speech production will be helpful in understanding the articulator-driven synthesis approach.

The physical process of speech production can be divided into three parts. First, air is forced through the vocal cords to produce either a voiced or unvoiced glottal excitation. Next, airflow is modified by a series of structures that constitute the vocal tract. Finally, the modified flow is radiated through the lips and nostrils. The articulators used to produce speech are shown in Figure 8.1. To change a sound, the articulators are moved from one position to another in continuous motions which give speech its continuous, fluid quality. The tongue is the most important articulator. The jaw, lips, and velum are less important for shaping the speech spectrum (Zemlin, 1968).

Simplifying and implementing the model

The constraints of the application suggest that we should base our system on a physical model of speech that includes glottal excitation and vocal tract adjustments caused by the articulators. Some simplifying assumptions are made to achieve a minimal system capable of being driven in real time by a human user through a limited interface. The complexity of this interface must be limited because of the speed with which the user can operate the interface.

Our current model focuses only on the tongue. Since the tongue acts as a continuous modifier of speech sounds, its motion can be modeled as a set of analog signals. These signals represent the control of specific muscles in the vocal tract that move the tongue to its proper configuration for a specified sound. Physically, the tongue can be simplified to a movement of its tip and base. This tip and base movement can be viewed as an orthogonal two-dimensional signal where motion along one axis represents the tip and motion along the other axis represents the base. In this way, the tongue tip and base can be described independently by holding one dimension constant, or together by varying the position along both axes. The tongue's base and tip position can be mapped onto a two-dimensional grid, as seen in Figure 8.2. As the tongue is moved from one position to another, the grid location is used to calculate the coefficients for use by the speech synthesizer.

This technique, combined with an interpolation scheme, overcomes the

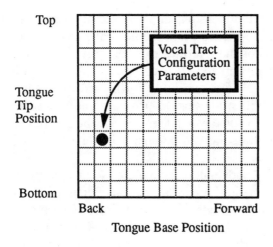

Figure 8.2. Two-dimensional tongue position grid.

transition problem that all discrete-unit synthesizers must address. As an example, consider synthesis based upon the generation of discrete phonetic units for discrete periods of time. The word "same" might be synthesized by concatenating the /s/, /!EY!/, and /m/ units. Between these units transients can occur that make the speech sound unnatural (Childers, Wu, & Hicks, 1987). The simplified articulator-driven system requires a time trajectory between any two sounds. This trajectory will have synthesis data along its path so the transitions are continuous, with interpolation being used to smooth them.

The current implementation can be used to produce crude monotone speech by using a joystick to navigate the tongue position grid (Girson & Williams, 1990). The joystick is a temporary testing device, as the target population does not have the dexterity to control a standard joystick. Early attempts to build interfaces for the synthesizer focused on building analog input devices, such as levers to be placed against the cheek or arm. A number of novel analog devices were devised, including air sacs to detect force and throat microphones that detect the low throat "growl" that some subjects could produce. The intention was to combine two such one-dimensional input devices to provide the analog signals needed for the grid. The difficulty of building effective hardware interfaces, combined with the effects of user fatigue, created major difficulties with this approach.

Passive tracking

When interfaces based on physical devices are problematic, an alternative approach is to track the user's body motions passively. Our general approach is to track user motions in three dimensions and create custom projections to the two-dimensional tongue grid for each user. The most obvious advantage of this approach is that we can tailor the interface to each individual's best range of physical motion. Another advantage is that no strength is required to move a physical switch. For the CP community, a further advantage is that less coordination is required. (With a physical interface, the user must first contact the device and then move it in some way.) The final advantage is that a software interface based on motion tracking can be adapted over time to account for improvement and/or fatigue.

One alternative to tracking body motion is to track eye motion. Eye tracking is not appropriate for our application for several reasons. First, using eye tracking for the speech synthesizer makes it impossible to maintain eye contact or receive visual stimulation while speaking. Second, many disabled users are poor candidates for eye tracking because they tend to move their heads.

Gesture recognition has a long history in many contexts, but most research has focused on converting continuous body motion into discrete tokens. Two-dimensional gesture recognition has been used for printed lettering, cursive handwriting, proofreaders' symbols, and shorthand notation. In all cases, the approach is to convert the continuous motion of a stylus into a discrete token as input to a language-driven computation or process. Recognition of three-dimensional gestures has also been attempted, but again the main emphasis has been on converting the body motions into discrete symbols that are interpreted as commands to the system (Bolt, 1980; Buxton, Fiumes, Hill, Lees, & Woo, 1983). Systems have attempted to recognize static gestures for the deaf alphabet and motions for a subset of American Sign Language. All of these approaches are based on converting three-dimensional signals into a discrete stream of tokens.

Existing work on mapping gesture into continuous control signals is extremely application dependent. For example, advanced military systems exist that map pilot head motion into weapon trajectories. The pilot's face shield contains targeting crosshairs, and as the pilot's helmet moves rigidly with his head, the system computes the angle of gaze (Furness, 1988). More detailed tracking is performed in three-dimensional drawing or sculpting applications (Schmandt, 1983) and in virtual reality systems, where sensors attached to gloves (Foley, 1987) provide three-dimensional signals that are mapped into motions in synthetic worlds shown on traditional or head-mounted displays. These systems perform mappings from position and orientation information, but the mappings are significantly less complicated than those we propose.

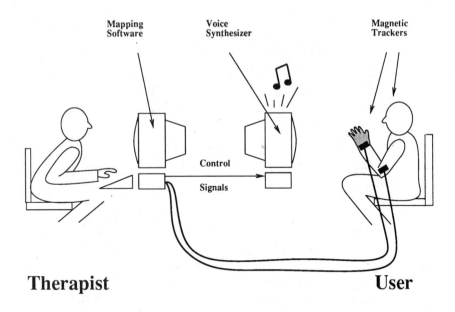

Figure 8.3. The experimental setup

The experimental setup

Our experimental setup is shown in Figure 8.3. One or two Polhemus magnetic trackers[1] are attached to the subject at locations determined by a therapist. If only one tracker is used, the mapping problem reduces to mapping a six-dimensional signal (*x, y, z*, azimuth, elevation, roll) into a two-dimensional signal. There are two possible ways in which two trackers will be used. In the first case, they both generate independent data, and the problem becomes a mapping from twelve dimensions to two dimensions. A second use of dual trackers is to use one as a base for the other. For example, if we are measuring head motion relative to the neck and the subject tends to rock or raise the torso, we may attach the second tracker to the neck and use it as a base to compute the relative motion of the first tracker.

The signals from the trackers are sent via a high speed serial connection to the mapping processor. This station displays mapping visualization and interactive controls for the therapist performing the tailoring. The mapping processor produces one or two continuous signals that are sent to the application processor. The application processor is responsible for providing the visual and/or auditory

---

[1] Polhemus Tracker, MacDonnell-Douglas Electronics Corporation, P.O. Box 560, Hercules Drive, Colchester, VT 05446 (phone (802) 655-3159).

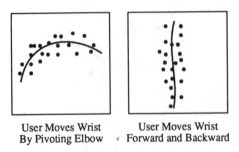

User Moves Wrist   User Moves Wrist
By Pivoting Elbow   Forward and Backward

Figure 8.4. Target curves.

feedback that will guide the user's actions while he or she using the gesture interface. Because the speech synthesizer is a complicated interface to master, we are currently using simpler one- and two-dimensional graphical applications with our disabled users. We currently use one processor, an IBM-compatible PC, for both the mapping and graphical feedback. One of our initial design goals was that our system should run on low-end hardware, since cost is a major concern for the disabled community.

Mapping motion from three to two dimensions

Mapping consists of two basic phases. The *collection* phase determines the comfortable and preferred motions for the user. The *control* phase performs real-time mapping of user motion based on a mapping function created from the data obtained during the collection phase. Although the mappings we create are biomechanically comfortable for each user, there is no reason to expect that they will be easily teachable by the therapist. As the candidate mapping is being used, users notice the results of their motions and experiment to discover the nature of the mapping, rather than having it taught to them by the therapist. Although they will make motions with the intent of changing the device's state, we want them thinking about the device state, not how to make their motions mapped properly. We note that this may not be immediately apparent from the specific examples used in this paper; these examples were chosen because their mappings are easily displayed geometrically.

Our current mapping approaches are based on target curves and target surfaces. We first describe a simple mapping for our current implementation, which provides users with the ability to control a device requiring one continuous input parameter. In this example the device is a vertical slider on a graphical display. During the collection phase, the user is instructed to move the tracker in any manner that is comfortable while we collect position data from the sensors. During this time the user receives no visual or auditory feedback from the system. After roughly 30 to 60 seconds, the data is analyzed to determine a curve

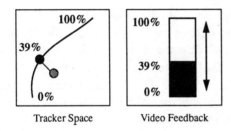

Tracker Space   Video Feedback

Figure 8.5. Tracker space to device space.

in three-dimensional space through which the user would be able to navigate the tracker comfortably.

In order to facilitate the visualization of static diagrams in this proposal, assume that the user had a tracker attached to a wrist and was told to keep his or her hand on a horizontal table during the measurement. This effectively constrains the motion to two dimensions. Based on the on-screen display of this raw data, the therapist creates a piecewise linear curve though the data corresponding to a dominant path of motion made by the user during the control phase. This is done by invoking a heuristic, by manually specifying the curve, or by a combination of both. Figure 8.4 shows two typical target curves and the data used to form them. The first user pivoted the wrist around his elbow, and the second moved the wrist forward and backward.

The user never sees the display of the target curves, although the therapist may attempt to explain the mapping to the user. Because the target curve is composed

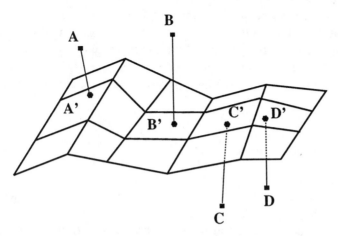

Figure 8.6. Mapping to a target surface.

of comfortable motions, the therapist can often let the user discover the mapping. While observing the user actions during the control phase, the therapist may dynamically alter the target curve using the interactive display. The mapping software may also dynamically display alternative target curves created from continuing to observe the user's motions. The therapist may also specify a nonlinear mapping from position along the target curve to the values of the device signal. By entering explicit scaling points on the two graphs, the therapist may adjust the distance along various parts of the curve that the user must move to cause a unit of motion in the device space.

During the control phase the user moves the tracker along the target curve, and we generate a linear control signal. One end of the curve indicates no signal and the other end indicates 100% of the signal. Intermediate positions along the target curve indicate intermediate signal values, and the signal generates video feedback. The user is not expected to move the tracker precisely along the curve; we map tracker data to the nearest point on the target curve, as shown in Figure 8.5.

Although the previous example hypothesized limiting the user's motions to a table surface, target curves reside in three space. The tailoring tools display the raw tracker data as a green three-dimensional point *cloud* with a red target curve running through the cloud. Dynamic markers show the tracker positions in real time during the control phase. The therapist can dynamically rotate his or her view of the target curve and tracker positions and dynamically adjust the target curve as the system runs.

For some users, it may be possible to use two trackers and two independent target curves to create the two signals needed for the synthesizer. We expect a more common technique will involve the creation of a piecewise planar target surface. During the control phase, each user point is mapped to the closest point on the target surface, as shown in Figure 8.6.

The target surface is decomposed into a grid of planar sections that is then mapped into the grid for the two-dimensional device signal, as shown in Figure 8.7. The therapist can once again specify a nonlinear mapping by stretching the planar patches to alter the transformation to the device signal. As with target curves, we view target surface creation as a joint task for the therapist and the tailoring software.

Creating the target curve

In experiments we have run, humans are very adept at immediately sketching appropriate target curves for two-dimensional data. In three dimensions it becomes more labor intensive to produce the target curve. We have developed greedy heuristics that start at the densest portion of the cloud and produce basically acceptable curves that a therapist can easily alter.

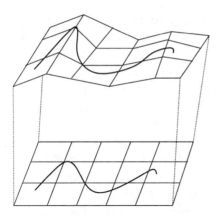

Figure 8.7. From surface to two signals.

For clouds where the heuristic's response is not good enough, we have implemented several genetic algorithms that operate by keeping a population of potential solutions and perform geometric "mating" of them in an attempt to produce better "offspring." Both the heuristic and genetic algorithms measure the success of their solutions by a weighted function with two components. The first component is the sum of the distance from each point in the cloud to the nearest point on the curve. The second component is the smoothness of the curve.

The previous examples all showed mappings based on positional information from the sensors. We expect some of our mappings to be less geometrically obvious. We are initially concentrating on target curves and surfaces that can be visualized by the therapist. We have created a low-cost virtual reality–type head-mounted display using Private Eye displays (Becker, 1990) and a Powerglove which will eventually allow therapists to manipulate target surfaces easily (Pausch, 1991). Later target curves and surfaces will be in spaces not easily visualized; in those cases, we will create the mapping entirely in software.

Often the tracker motion is not best interpreted in an absolute coordinate system. For example, some sample subjects have had good control of head motion relative to the torso but tend to stand up or rock their bodies while concentrating on a task. In these cases, tracking head motion alone would be useless. Instead we will attach one tracker to the torso and treat it as a moving base. The second tracker data will be interpreted relative to the first, and the therapist's display will present clouds and target curves and surfaces as if the user's torso were stationary. We expect that many of our mappings will occur in these anatomically based coordinate systems. We do not expect to create a complex software model of biomechanical motion; that would be beyond the scope of our efforts.

Although we cannot completely predict the advanced mappings we will construct, we can hypothesize several mapping strategies that may be useful. For some users, it may be more appropriate to examine derivative rather than positional information. Another aspect we expect with advanced mappings will be the scaling of time as the control signals are sent to the application. Many disabled users have reduced speed of motion, and it may be appropriate to detect motion over a period of time and then time compress the signals being sent to the application. To keep the mapping and application synchronized, during some time intervals no signal will be sent to the application. This is appropriate for the speech synthesizer, where we would encapsulate a spoken phrase at slower than real time and then compress it before sending it to the synthesizer.

Our approach creates comfortable mappings for each user, but the targets are somewhat abstract. We are currently experimenting with physical guides to focus the user's motions. Our standard example is to instruct the user to run a hand over a teddy bear whose stomach has been specified as the target surface. In this way, we can quickly turn any existing physical object into an input device. The limiting factor is that the user must have a comfortable range of motion over the surface of the object (Pausch & Williams, 1990).

In order to adapt for fatigue over time, our initial plan is to continue to add all user tracking points to the cumulative cloud as the user controls the device. As the cloud shifts, we will make our heuristics and genetic algorithms adjust the mapping in real time. The genetic algorithms are more appropriate for this task than the heuristic, which runs in a batch mode to determine a single solution. In situations where fatigue becomes a dominant concern, the therapist may choose to use a different attachment point or elect to purge the current cloud and begin with only the new motions in order to speed up adaptation.

Another potential use for the motion mapping software is as a physical therapy tool. When children use our system, they become tightly coupled with the action in our on-screen displays, behaving like video arcade game players. We hypothesize that if we were to stretch the target curve or surface during a session, a child would have to increase his or her range of motion in order to continue to perform well in the game. This places the child in a tightly coupled, self-motivating feedback loop and may provide substantial advances over the current methods of physical therapy.

Conclusions

Able-bodied users can currently produce a variety of sentences in real time driving the articulator-based speech synthesizer with a joystick. This requires a great deal of practice, but that is commensurate with our original goals. An active research area is finding grid layouts for speech sounds which are not direct mappings of tongue motion but provide a more usable grid. A major challenge is reducing the number of cases where one must travel through an undesirable sound in order to produce a sequence composed of sounds on opposite sides of that location. We are currently experimenting with both grid layout and "skipping" techniques, where rapid movement over a portion of the tongue grid allows one to avoid producing sound during the transition.

The user motion tracking software currently allows CP children to play a simplified pong video game where paddle motion is controlled by motion along a one-dimensional, user-specific target curve. We are currently performing clinical trials to measure the speed and accuracy of our CP children in order to evaluate their ability eventually to drive the synthesizer (Pausch, Vogtle, & Conway, 1992). In parallel, we are developing software to perform mappings using two-dimensional target curves and are exploring the possibility of using the mapping software as a tool for physical therapy.

Acknowledgment

This chapter is closely based on a paper published in *Communications of the ACM, 35*(5): pp. 58–68 (1992) and is reproduced here with permission.

References

Becker, A. (1990, March). Design case study: Private Eye. *Information Display*.

Bolt, R. (1980). "Put-that-there": Voice and gesture at the graphics interface. *Computer Graphics, 14*(3): 262–270.

Buxton, W., Fiume, E., Hill, R., Lee, A., and Woo, C. (1983). Continuous hand-gesture driven input. In *Proceedings of Graphics Interface '83* (pp. 191–195).

Childers, D. G., Wu, K., and Hicks, D. M. (1987). Factors in voice quality: Acoustic features related to gender, In *Proceedings of the IEEE International Conference on Acoustics, Speech and Signal Processing* (pp. 293–296). New York, NY.

Coker, C. H. (1973). Synthesis by rule from articulatory parameters. In *Speech synthesis*, ed. J. L. Flanagan and L. R. Rabiner (pp. 396–399). Stroudsburg, PA: Hutchinson and Ross.

Connolly, C. (1990). *Compensating for cerebral palsy: A tailorable mapping from voluntary movement to synthetic speech in real time*, Unpublished MSc thesis, University of Virginia Department of Electrical Engineering.

Dramer, J. (1989). The Talking Glove in action. *Communications of the ACM, 32*(4): 515.

Foley, J. D. (1987, October). Interfaces for advanced computing. *Scientific American*, pp. 127–135.

Furness, T. A. (1988). *Super Cockpit: Virtual crew systems*. Armstrong Aerospace Medical Research Laboratory.

Girson, A., and Williams, R. (1990). Articulator-based synthesis for conversational speech, In *International Conference on Acoustics, Speech, and Signal Processing*.

Haggard, M. (1979). Experience and perspectives in articulatory synthesis. *Frontiers of speech communication research*, pp. 259–274, London, UK.

Henke, W. L. (1967). Preliminaries to speech synthesis based upon an articulatory model. In *Proceedings of the IEEE Conference on Speech Communication and Processing* (pp. 170–182). New York.

Loomis, J., Poizner, H., Bellugi, U., Blakemore, A., and Hollerbach, J. (1983). Computer graphic modeling of American Sign Language. *Computer Graphics 17*(3):105–114.

Pausch, R. (1991). Virtual reality on five dollars a day. In *Reaching through Technology: Proceedings of the ACM Conference Chi '91*, ed. S. P. Robertson, G. M. Olson, and J. S. Olson, New York: ACM Press. (pp. 265–270).

Pausch, R., Vogtle, L., and Conway, M. (1992). One-dimensional motion tailoring for the disabled: A user study. In *Human Factors in Computer Systems: Proceedings of the ACM Conference Chi '92*, New York: ACM Press.

Pausch, R., and Williams, R. D. (1990). Tailor: Creating custom user interfaces based on gesture, In *UIST '90: Proceedings of the Annual ACM SIGGRAPH Symposium on User Interface Software and Technology*, pp. 58–67.

Schmandt, C. (1983). Spatial input/display correspondence in a stereoscopic computer graphic work station. *Computer Graphics ,17*(3): 253–261.

United Cerebral Palsy Association. (1985). *What everyone should know about cerebral palsy.* United Cerebral Palsy Association of Westchester County, Inc.

Zemlin, W. R. (1968). *Speech and hearing science.* Englewood Cliffs, NJ: Prentice-Hall.

9

Reading and pointing – New interaction methods for braille displays

Gerhard Weber

Braille codes

Conventional braille, as invented by Louis Braille (1809–1852), is based upon *cells* consisting of six dots in a 2 × 3 matrix. The standard distance between two dots within a braille cell is between 0.10 and 0.11 inches (2.6–3 mm). Since each of the six dots can be either present or not, that implies that there are $2^6 = 64$ unique characters representable. That means that, using a simple one-to-one mapping, all the letters, numbers and punctuation symbols can be represented (*Grade I* braille). However, there are two problems with having such a restricted character set. First, braille is bulky, since each cell is many times larger than a printed letter. To reduce the number of cells required to represent a piece of text, it is advantageous to use codes which allow more than one letter to be represented by a single cell – known as *contracted* or *Grade II* braille. The second problem is that it is often necessary to be able to represent special characters, such as mathematical symbols. Thus the original braille code has changed several times during this century, to the extent that the U.S. Library of Congress recently published a source book enumerating the languages for which braille codes are available (Unesco, 1990).

For example, a German student attending a school for blind students learns braille Grades I and II in German, English, and French. Furthermore, special braille codes, such as German braille shorthand or codes for math and chemistry or a notation for music, may be taught, depending on the level of education and the interests of the student. These six-dot braille codes use special "escape characters" to enlarge the representation. One approach to increasing the representation of braille is to use eight dots. Figure 9.1 illustrates six- and eight-dot braille.

With the advent of computers, it was quickly understood that the computer is the ideal medium for written communication between blind and sighted people. Given an appropriate braille display attached to a computer terminal, any piece of text can be presented either in visible print or in braille. Traditionally, blind people have used six-dot braille. However, the larger character set used by

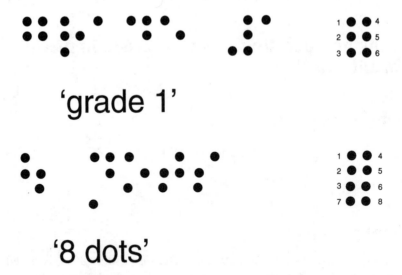

'grade 1'

'8 dots'

Figure 9.1. Examples for six-dot and eight-dot braille with the dot numbering scheme.

computers cannot be rendered on a one-to-one character-to-cell mapping if six dots are used. Specialized six-dot computer braille codes have been developed, as have eight-dot codes.

Programmers quickly made effective use of this technology (Hahn, 1976). A difference between computer oriented braille codes used in Europe and North America is the way digits are treated; the digit n in Europe is coded by the nth letter of the alphabet with dot 6 added (for example, c = dots 1 and 4, 3 = dots 1, 4, and 6) while in North America the nth character is shifted down one row in the matrix to represent digit n (c = dots 1 and 4, 3 = dots 2 and 5); see Figure 9.2. The consequences of such incompatibilities are even greater with the introduction of new eight-dot codes. Eight-dot braille raises several design issues, including:

- every uncontracted six-dot braille code should be included;
- mathematical notation should be readable by both blind and sighted people (see Schweikhardt, 1987);
- only minor modification of existing standards should be necessary, and
- graphical characters should retain their original shape.

The range of print characters used is always increasing. For example, the advent of desktop publishing has led people to expect access to a wide range of

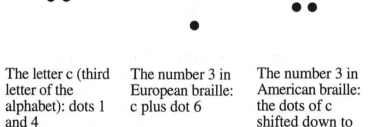

The letter c (third letter of the alphabet): dots 1 and 4

The number 3 in European braille: c plus dot 6

The number 3 in American braille: the dots of c shifted down to dots 2 and 5

Figure 9.2. The different representations of digits in European and American braille.

typefaces. Hence there is little chance of arriving at a universal eight-dot braille code. Therefore manufacturers of braille displays have gone over to giving their customers the freedom to redefine their braille codes individually (through more or less painful procedures).

Today transcription into braille is done by commercially available software; nevertheless, as yet the automatic transfer of documents stored in different braille codes is rare (see Weber, 1986). For some languages like English it is even possible to back translate from braille into print on the basis of some simple rules. Back translation is necessary, for example, if text which has been input in contracted braille is to be spoken by a speech synthesizer.

Braille display technology

Just as computer terminals have developed from paper based teletypewriters to cathode ray screens, so braille has moved from being available only in the form of embossed paper to paperless refreshable displays. Paper is still used for off-line hard copy but not for interactive access. Paperless braille is realized with different technologies. A number of different technologies have been applied:

- polyvinyldifluoride (PVDF);

- plastic, driven by bulbs;

- plastic, driven by tiny electromotors;

- piezoceramic;

- electromagnetic;

- spring loaded electromagnetic; and

- piezoelectric.

Such displays are generally described as "soft" (as opposed to paper hard copy), "refreshable," or "transitory." PVDF is a kind of plastic material that changes its length when a voltage (around 60 V) is applied to it (Legsieffer, 1985).

Only the *Optacon* (Bliss, Katcher, Rogers, & Shepard, 1970) is based on piezoceramic technology. The Optacon is also not typical in the way a tactile impression is produced. The user reads with a finger from a pad of vibrating pins, each pin vibrating with a variable frequency. Another difference is that the pins reproduce the shape of the printed character, not a braille cell, although some experiments (Duerre & Schmidt-Lademann, 1983) have shown that it is possible to read braille on the Optacon by means of passive reading (see below). The advantage of this technology is that it is possible to have a very small distance between pins. However, many blind users find this method of reading fatiguing over a period of hours.

Figure 9.3 shows the components of a single spring-loaded electromechanical braille pin. The casing contains the pin, a spring, and a coil around a tiny iron rod. The spring forces the pin to move upwards. It therefore becomes a raised braille dot. If the iron rod is magnetized by the coil by induction, it pulls the pin (approximately 40 mm long) downwards. The pin is no longer raised.

Production of braille displays is organized around the concept of braille modules which are displays for a single braille character. Manufacture must be carried out to a very high level of precision, the size of the components and the tolerances on them being so small. Hence the cost of manufacture is very high. By way of comparison, a few braille modules can be as expensive as a single phoneme chip of the kind used in speech synthesizers. Speech synthesizers have the advantage that they have a wide range of applications other than for blind people and hence are produced in large quantities for a larger market.

In the USA and increasingly in Europe piezoelectric displays are used – and are even more expensive. A piezocrystal is mounted on a substratum. If a certain voltage is applied, it flexes like a bimetal. As practically no electrical power is consumed, this is the ideal technology for battery based operation. The transition between being flexed and unflexed is very reliable and cannot be suppressed by a finger. Piezoelectric braille displays are much quicker in their response time (vibration is possible) and much quieter than electromechanical operation, but each pin (and its casing) is longer than the casing of an electromagnetically attenuated pin.

Real and virtual braille displays

What is the appropriate number of braille modules in a braille display? There is still no definite answer to this question from theoretical or empirical investigations, as different configurations of braille modules allow different methods of reading. To distinguish the different ways of reading on braille displays, we use these definitions:

1. The finger's *reading region* is the part of the skin in contact with a surface.
2. Reading is referred to as being *active* when the finger's reading region is changed with a movement of the hand smaller than the width of the reading region. *Passive* reading involves no hand motion.

Active reading (Weber, 1989) is intimately related to active touch (Gibson, 1962), which involves additional nervous receptors, thus providing more and richer sensations (Gordon, 1978) than passive touch.

Examples: active or passive reading?

Example 1. *Braille Mate* is a portable device from Telesensory Inc.[1] It displays a braille based notetaking device with a single braille module. The reader places a finger on the display, and the device presents the text in a slow but continuous movement by changing the character shown on the module.

Example 2. The *Optacon II* (also from Telesensory Inc.) can display a single braille character. The display is updated as the reader's second hand moves a pointing device (typically a mouse).

Example 3. The *Braille Mouse,* by DeWulf (see DeWulf, 1990, also Anbary & Mardiks, 1982), has two six-dot braille modules mounted on a carriage. The mechanical construction allows the carriage to slide freely horizontally and vertically in a 25 × 80 matrix. A new position is reached by moving the carriage (keeping the reading finger or fingers in the same position on the cells) and then two new characters are retrieved from a refresh memory and displayed (see Figure 9.4).

---

[1] Telesensory Inc., PO Box 7455, Mountain View, CA 94039-7455.

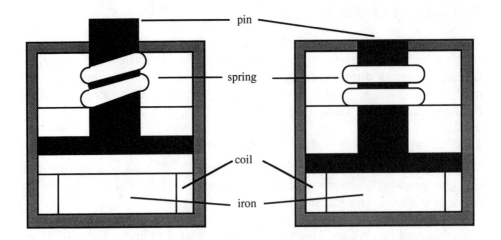

Figure 9.3. A single spring-loaded electromagnetic braille pin.

All of these devices are read by passive reading: The finger's reading region on Braille Mate and Optacon does not move, and therefore no active exploration is possible. Similarly the braille modules on the Braille Mouse are not updated for movements smaller than the width of the finger.

On the basis of these examples we define a *virtual braille* display as a braille display allowing exploration of the display by means of a pointing device. Only the reading region of a finger is updated, and those areas of the display that are not touched are not present. There is no virtual braille display known that allows active reading in that the same finger that reads braille also explores the display.

There are several examples of virtual displays.

- The *Braille Mouse* as implemented by H. Garner of Nasa (Karshmer, Myler, & Davis, 1985). This is a true mouse with a single six-dot braille module built into it.

- The *tactile mouse* and the *virtual tactile tablet,* by G. Vanderheiden. One braille module is used with a specially designed carriage incorporating a specially designed mouse.

- The *slot machine,* by D. Gilden (1990). A carriage with a single line of 80 braille modules can slide vertically between 25 positions which can be detected through tactile feedback. Extensive testing showed that interaction is faster than with a fixed line of braille modules.

Because of the reduced sensation in passive reading, these displays are still under investigation and are not commercially available. Braille displays implement every possible display position. An array of braille modules allows active reading. There are a great variety of braille modules available. Figure 9.5

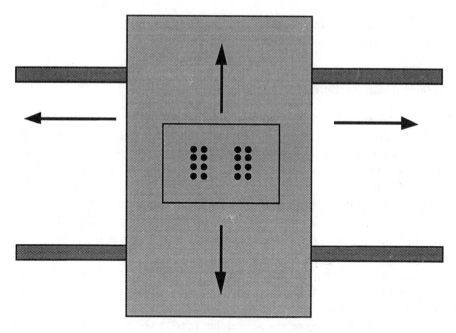

Figure 9.4. Design of DeWulf's Braille Mouse.

shows a modern braille display with a single line of 80 eight-dot braille modules, additional braille modules for status messages, keys for exploration, and sensors for routing input. Also below in Figure 9.7 a braille display is shown with two lines of braille modules, one aligned horizontally and the other vertically. The largest braille display currently available is the *Pin-Matrix Device* manufactured by Metec,[1] which is capable of showing 12 lines with 40 braille characters each in a 3×5 matrix. All pins are equidistant and are set or reset independently, and the device can mix graphical information and textual information (Schweikhardt, 1984).

More recently a few braille displays have been produced which emulate terminals without any connection to a microcomputer. Most displays are directly connected to a board in an IBM PC or compatible computer. There are two approaches: software based and hardware based.

Both approaches are based on the fact that the part of the computer's memory storing the image that is shown on the monitor is copied periodically into a private memory associated with the braille display. The size of this memory is the same as the size of the refresh memory of the screen. The user explores the private memory either with a separate keyboard or – after having switched from interacting with the application to review mode – with the computer's keyboard.

[1] Metec, Gutenburg Strasse 65A, D-7000 Stuttgart, Germany.

In review mode the application itself is put into background. The use of review mode is further described in the following section.

Characterizing interaction

Working with an application program is an interaction between the user and the computer. The dialogue can be initiated by the computer (through pop-up menus, for instance) or by the user (as in a command language). Each style of interaction needs to be adapted for a blind user. Since a user driven type of dialogue can be obtained by analyzing the user's input, this causes only a few conceptual problems. However, if the application puts some information (such as an error message, menu, or status message) anywhere on the screen in an asynchronous manner, then an output device has to inform the user, even if he or she is currently typing or reading something else.

The design of input and output devices is a technological issue which is discussed further in the following two sections. However, a number of definitions are in order here.

Dialogue focus is the place on the screen that needs to be perceived in order to perform the desired interaction with the computer. It is the place a sighted user would look at to proceed with the interaction. Thus the dialogue focus is some portion of the current screen display.

In a visual screen based interface the focus is usually centered on the screen cursor, which marks the point on the screen at which the next interaction (such as typing on the keyboard) will have any effect. However, there are times when the user must make a large-scale jump to move the dialogue focus to a point some distance from the current focus and thus to separate it (temporarily at least) from the cursor. This would occur, for instance, in word processing if the user finished inputting a document and decided to go back to proofread the current section. In this example the user must be able to read parts of the document (establishing temporary new dialogue foci) in order to locate the start of the section, where a new dialogue focus may be established by moving the cursor there.

Broadly the same is true in a braille display, except that, given the fact that a braille display can show only part of the screen contents (usually no more than a single line), user control of the dialogue focus is more critical. Also, given the need to be able to browse it is not always appropriate to identify the focus with the cursor.

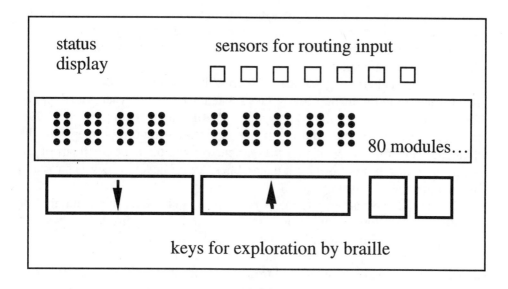

Figure 9.5. Elements of an eight-dot braille display.

In a dialogue controlled by the computer the dialogue focus is determined largely by the application program. In a dialogue controlled by the user, the dialogue focus is determined by the user's input. Hardware based adaptations try to find the dialogue focus by continuously monitoring the screen cursor and the attributes of all characters. The focus varies – often very quickly – and can become much larger than the area the braille display can show. It is in such situations that the blind user has to take steps in the interaction to widen the dialogue focus.

If the dialogue focus is at a point not currently displayed, the user has to explore the screen manually until he or she finds it. This extra step is called *review mode* in software based adaptations. In hardware based adaptations there is no requirement for such an extra mode as the interaction takes place through a separate keyboard.

Tracking is the means by which blind users can determine, follow, and display the dialogue focus.[1] Usually the dialogue focus includes the area where feedback for the next input operation will be given (the next dialogue focus). But sometimes (for instance in review mode) the user is allowed to leave one dialogue focus to move to another which is possibly completely separate from the original one.

---

[1] This is also applicable to screen enlargement devices for people with low vision.

Routing is a facility which allows the unification of the application's dialogue focus and the dialogue focus as specified by the user. In other words, while in review mode the user establishes a new focus and, in order to continue, moves the cursor to the same point.

"Tracking" and "routing" are general terms that need to be specialized for the two elements predominantly used to let sighted users know where the dialogue focus is: the *cursor* and the *mouse pointer*.[1] An example from graphical user interfaces better explains routing. If one equates the mouse pointer with the dialogue focus for reviewing and the text cursor with the dialogue focus of the application, then routing is what a mouse click does: The text cursor is moved to the mouse pointer's position.

The size of the dialogue focus is between one character and a number of braille modules. Some applications use the cursor as built into the hardware of the display unit. This cursor is commonly called the hardware cursor, and its properties (especially position) can be determined very accurately. So-called *soft* cursors are not easily distinguished from simple attributes of text. A soft cursor might be an attribute (like inverse or underlined type) given to an option in a menu. Some interaction methods even allow extension of this spot (e.g. showing the selected text in inverse when selecting a block of text). The soft cursor is then described by the changes the user has achieved. Cursor tracking was described above in examples of software based adaptations.

Cursor routing.[2] The example above of routing in graphical user interfaces is not applicable if there is no mouse, as in most text based interfaces. Nevertheless, the dialogue focus during review is somewhere other than the dialogue focus of the application, and *cursor routing* is the method by which the two foci are united. It is possible that the cursor cannot be routed to every place on the screen. Even in full-screen text editors it is, for example, not possible to place the cursor on status information. Routing is usually performed by emulating the keystrokes for cursor movements. Routing cannot be performed correctly if the application uses keystrokes in an unforeseen manner.

Mouse tracking. The shape of the mouse pointer is often altered by the system according to its current position in order to signal its current mode. Hence special

---

[1] Conventional vocabulary can lead to some ambiguity. In mouse based interfaces the mouse controls a visible pointer on the screen, which is often referred to as the *cursor*. However, text based interfaces incorporate a marker at the point at which the next piece of typing will be inserted which is also known as the *cursor*. (This is generally controllable by a set of *cursor keys*.) Furthermore, when running a text based application (such as a word processor) on a mouse based system, both "cursors" will be present. It is therefore much clearer to refer to the indicator controlled by the mouse as the *mouse pointer*.

[2] Routing has an equivalent in some screen review packages for speech output and is beyond the scope of this chapter, but see Chapter 16 of this volume.

care has to be taken to give feedback for such changes if the dialogue focus is the mouse pointer itself. For this change an appropriate feedback has to be generated.

Mouse routing is an interaction method for blind users which is applicable only in textual environments, since mouse based interaction methods in graphical user interfaces have not been adapted for blind users (apart from the experiments reported in Chapter 11). In a text based user interface the mouse pointer always covers one character, preferably showing its original shape but marking it in some other way, such as changing its color. The mouse pointer can generally be moved to any place on the screen. Likewise the dialogue focus during review can be anywhere on the screen. If cursor routing is performed (through a second pointing device or function keys), the mouse pointer is automatically moved to where the review takes place. Thus no interaction with the mouse takes place, which speeds up the interaction.

Technicalities of adapting the output

A number of programs are available which are designed to work with braille displays, but more often software is used which adapts the output of existing screen based applications to work with the braille display.

Three examples of software based adaptations will show the strategies involved with this kind of extension of the user interface. The operating system CP/M sends all output to the screen by calling an appropriate system call. This is realized by a jump table in ram consisting of addresses for where the code is stored. An adaptation initially has to replace the pointer to the standard output routine by a pointer to its own output routine and store the pointer to the original routine. The new routine makes a copy of the character that has to be displayed, calls the old routine, and then sends the character also to the braille display. Additional steps have to be taken to enable a review mode, but (for example) Wordstar (for CP/M) can be adapted successfully on the basis of this technique.

The MS-DOS operating system is more complex than CP/M but was derived from it. Instead of using a jump table, (some) applications realize by calling interrupt routine 10H (INT 10H) (for more details on the IBM PC, see Norton & Wilton, 1985). This approach will not work with all applications, because some of them directly access the refresh memory for screen output, so no filtering is easily installable. However, all applications use one of the functions of INT 10H: that which sets the cursor position.

To filter all output operations, the following approach can be used to adapt DOS output. Install a filter in INT 10H (the pointer is a double word at location 0:4*10H). When this filter is called, call the old output routine (the old INT 10H) first. After the old routine is finished, retrieve the position of the cursor. The dialogue focus is considered to be the line which the cursor is on. Knowing the position of the cursor allows the adaptation program to inspect the refresh memory at this character cell and also the surrounding line. If the display has 80

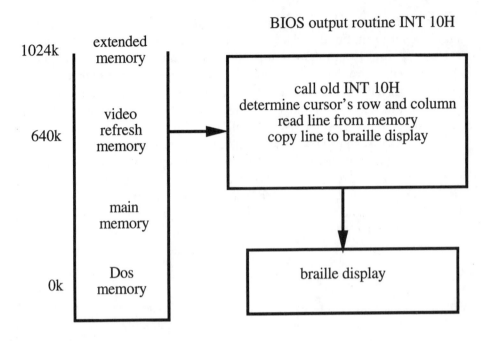

Figure 9.6. Filtering output and duplicating it.

braille modules, copy the line containing the cursor from refresh memory to the braille display (see Figure 9.6).

Implementation of a review mode requires the installation of a *pop-up* procedure (see Stevens, 1987). The pop-up procedure is called if a specified keystroke occurs. The procedure receives all subsequent keystrokes until an exit command is received, whereupon the procedure terminates, review mode is left, and control returns to the application. In review mode the user can move line by line upwards or downwards. Lines can be selected by jumping to predefined marks or even by using a separate pointing device. A wide variety of review features have been implemented by different manufacturers, leading to problems in learning the various complex interfaces.

As explained above, the dialogue focus is considered to be always around the cursor. For every cursor movement, an update of the braille display is generated. This approach can cause problems, as too many of these updates can be generated, but improvements can be made. Most users expect the dialogue focus to be where the cursor ends up after an input operation (a keypress). An update of the braille display should be performed only after a key has been pressed. Such a facility can be implemented by filtering input instead of output operations. In

DOS, INT 16H and INT 9H are used primarily for input from the keyboard, and INT 33H for mouse input. [1]

Input

Input devices for blind users are as important as output devices. As the speed of active reading cannot be improved much more than with today's quickly refreshing piezoelectric braille modules, typing on a keyboard has become the bottleneck in interaction. The problem is not only typing but also the movement of the hand between the display and the keyboard. This is very time consuming, as the user has to find out where the fingers should be placed. In response to the wishes of users, manufacturers have made improvements in the layout of the keypads for controlling the display. This is one design factor which distinguishes different braille devices, externally at least.

Besides the standard *qwerty* keyboard, most large braille displays can also be connected with a special braille keyboard for eight-dot braille input. A braille keyboard is better for input of contracted braille, but the regular keyboard is necessary if a sighted person is to be able to use the computer.

Routing is a unique feature that has no direct equivalent in visual interaction. Associated with each braille module is a button control called a *routing key* or *routing sensor*. Routing is generally implemented by the user's exploring the braille display to find the critical braille cell and then issuing a command via a routing sensor associated with that cell to move the cursor to the position of the cell. A number of examples of routing input are found in different braille displays. They are distinguished by the place, the method of activation, and the technology used for the sensors. (See, for example, Figure 9.7.) The sensing unit can be a key or a touch-sensitive sensor. Current touch-sensitive sensors work optically (the finger covers the sensor) or magnetically (the finger wears a coil and via induction allows its presence to be determined).

A completely different approach to routing is the *taso* (tactile–acoustic screen orientation), a concept of Frank Audiodata. A long vertical slider allows the user to select any line to be shown on the braille display. The user is assisted in navigation by acoustical feedback on the location of the slider.

---

[1] As INT 9H and INT 33H are generating external events for DOS, a software based adaptation needs to take special care with such events, as these are typically found only in a multitasking environment.

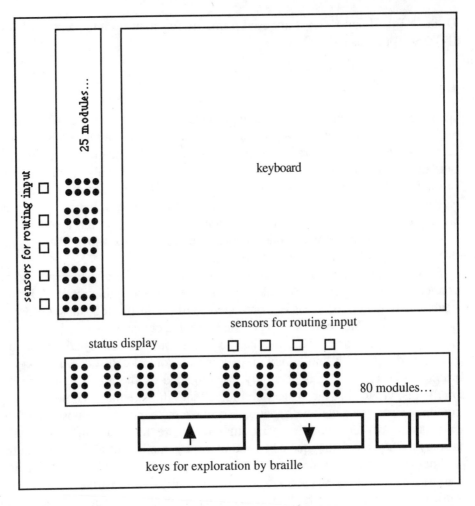

Figure 9.7. A two-line braille display with routing keys.

Braille and speech

The following description of a study undertaken by Hill and Gries (1988) does not deal specifically with braille displays but indicates that pointing devices are of use for speech output.

Touch 'n Talk is an experimental apparatus with a keyboard, never commercially marketed. It uses a graphics tablet for input, and output is produced via a speech synthesizer. The tablet is modified so that horizontal and vertical guidelines can be touched while one is pointing with the stylus. Horizontal guidelines allow control of the speech output. Vertical guidelines introduce additional functionality and replicate function keys. Hill and Gries show that the user takes into account information about the spatial layout as experienced when moving the stylus. Speed of interaction is improved.

Braille and speech for output combined with all the input devices described above can improve accessibility to user interfaces. A study has been undertaken at the University of Stuttgart in close cooperation with the company Papenmeier to get feedback from blind users for such an approach. This is based on the development of *Grabra*, an adaptation of Microsoft *Word* 5.0 for DOS.

Word is a standard word processor well known to many blind people. Word also marks a change in user interfaces of word processors in that it provides support for mouse input, allows preview of the text layout, and has a graphics mode to show different typefaces.[1] Of course it is not the only product with these features and was only chosen to demonstrate our approach.

A blind user can use Word, since all of the word processing facilities are accessible through keyboard based interaction. Nonetheless, it marks a change in the design of user interfaces towards the graphical (see Stephanidis, Savidis, Chomatas, Spyridou, & Sfyrakis, 1991). It does include graphical features intended to improve the efficiency of the dialogue bit which are not accessible to blind users. Grabra gives access to the graphics mode of Word and implements cursor tracking, mouse tracking, and mouse routing.

The screen dump in Figure 9.8 shows the German version of Word, but all the graphical elements are recognizable regardless of the language of the text. The following explanation tries to reconstruct how the user arrived at this point and points out the various changes in the dialogue focus.

The cursor is in the fourth line of the text on the character *t*. There is always only one text cursor. If the user has opened more than one frame, then only the active frame owns the cursor.

The user is working in the menu. Cursor tracking has to recognize that there are two spots on the screen with attributes of a soft cursor. The cursor in the menu is of higher priority, hence the dialogue focus is in line 22.

Actually the user has already changed the dialogue focus. The mouse has been used to scroll through the document. With the menu still accessible, Word allows the user to scroll through the document via the mouse. When the mouse is moved, the dialogue focus follows the line containing the mouse pointer. When the mouse pointer reaches any word shown on the screen, this word is spoken. Of course, it can be impossible for the synthesizer to keep up. So, for instance, if the mouse is moved quickly between words and the synthesizer is still speaking one word as the mouse pointer reaches the next, then only a single high-pitched beep is heard from the PC's loudspeaker, and the new word is suppressed. Thereby good feedback for mouse movements is established without cutting words.

---

[1] Strictly speaking, Word 5.0 cannot be said to be a "what you see is what you get" (*wysiwyg*) editor.

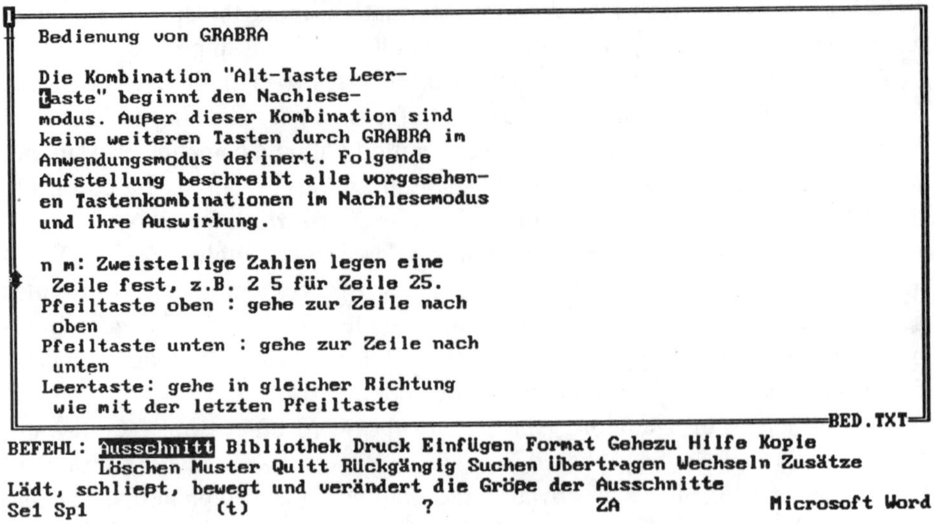

```
Bedienung von GRABRA

Die Kombination "Alt-Taste Leer-
taste" beginnt den Nachlese-
modus. Außer dieser Kombination sind
keine weiteren Tasten durch GRABRA im
Anwendungsmodus definert. Folgende
Aufstellung beschreibt alle vorgesehen-
en Tastenkombinationen im Nachlesemodus
und ihre Auswirkung.

n m: Zweistellige Zahlen legen eine
  Zeile fest, z.B. 2 5 für Zeile 25.
Pfeiltaste oben : gehe zur Zeile nach
  oben
Pfeiltaste unten : gehe zur Zeile nach
  unten
Leertaste: gehe in gleicher Richtung
  wie mit der letzten Pfeiltaste
                                      BED.TXT
BEFEHL: Ausschnitt Bibliothek Druck Einfügen Format Gehezu Hilfe Kopie
        Löschen Muster Quitt Rückgängig Suchen Übertragen Wechseln Zusätze
Lädt, schließt, bewegt und verändert die Größe der Ausschnitte
Sel Sp1        (t)              ?              ZA        Microsoft Word
```

Figure 9.8. Snapshot of Word 5.0 with graphical elements.

When the mouse pointer reaches the border of the frame, its shape changes to a vertical double arrow. This is signaled by a sentence saying that scrolling is now possible. If the user is already scrolling, then this sentence is not repeated, and a low-pitched sound is heard to give feedback for the scroll operation.

During all these mouse operations, the dialogue focus is around the mouse pointer. The braille display follows it and shows a character with all eight dots raised that corresponds to the position of the mouse pointer.

Conclusions

Braille is a long-established medium of textual communication for blind people. The advent of information technology has created new possibilities for its use. It can allow access to texts which are available in machine readable form (which might not be available in braille already), and it provides a means of adapting computer interfaces to make them accessible to blind people – those who can read braille, at least. This chapter has described in some detail how the contents of a textual display can be captured and rendered in braille on a volatile display. The point made in several other chapters can be reiterated here – that if computer system designers were more aware of the needs of extra-ordinary users, adaptation to their needs could be achieved much more easily without resort to the programming tricks described herein. Furthermore, experience has shown that attempting to replace the visual channel with tactile communication alone is likely to be impractical and that it is likely that a combination of braille and speech will be necessary if access to graphical user interfaces is to be provided.

Acknowledgments

Grabra was implemented only because Professor Dr. R. Gunzenhäuser and Mr. J. Bornschein helped get all the necessary computational resources together. Mr. D. Kochanek programmed the first version of the pattern matcher in Grabra and Mr. M. Recker programmed the current version.

References

Anbary, Y., and Mardiks, E. (1982). A computer terminal with a single cell braille display. In *Uses of computers in aiding the disabled*, ed. J. Raviv (pp. 367–376). Amsterdam: Elsevier Science.

Bliss, J. C., Katcher, M. H., Rogers, C. H., and Shepard, R. D. (1970). Optical-to-tactile image conversion for the blind. *IEEE Transactions on Man–Machine Systems ,11*(1): 58–65.

DeWulf, L.(1990). A new device for computer screen display in braille. In *Techniques and Devices for the Blind.* ed. P. L. Emiliani. London: Royal National Institute for the Blind (pp. 78–81).

Duerre, K. P., and Schmidt-Lademann, F-P. (1983). Interactive computer interfaces for the blind – How the blind can interact with the computer using a mouse, In *Proceedings of the IEEE Computer Society Workshop on Computers in the Education and Employment of the Handicapped* (pp. 89–96) Los Alamitos, CA: IEEE Computer Society Press.

Gibson, J. J. (1962). Observations on active touch. *Psychological Review, 69*(6): 477–491.

Gilden, D. (1990). Braille computer screens: A new perspective. In *Computers for Handicapped Persons: Proceedings of the 2nd International Conference* ed. A. Tjoa, R. Wagner, and W. Zagler (pp. 101–112). Oldenbourg: München, Germany.

Gordon, G. (Ed.). (1978). *Active touch*. Oxford: Pergamon.

Hahn, E. (1976). A computer terminal with braille display (in German), *Horus, Marburger Beiträge zum Blind-Sehen 2*: 10–11.

Hill, R. D., and Gries, C. (1988). Substitution for a restricted visual Channel in multimodal computer-human dialogue. *IEEE Transactions on Systems, Man and Cybernetics , 8*(2): 285–403.

Karshmer, A., Myler, H., and Davis, R. (1985). *An inexpensive and portable talking–tactile terminal for the visually handicapped*. Technical report. Computing Research Laboratory, New Mexico State University.

Legsieffer, H. (1985). Polyvinyldifluoride as electromechanical attenuator for tactile sensations [in German]. *Acoustica, 58:* 196–206.

Norton, P., and Wilton, R. (1985). *The new Peter Norton programmer's guide to the IBM PC and PS/2*. Redmond, WA: Microsoft Press.

Schweikhardt, W. (1984). Representing videotext pages to the blind. In *Proceedings of the Third Annual Workshop on Computers and the Handicapped*, (pp. 23–29). Los Alamitos, CA: IEEE Computer Society Press.

Schweikhardt, W. (1987). *Stuttgart 8-dot math notation* [in German]. Technical report. Stuttgart: Institut für Informatik, Universität Stuttgart.

Stephanidis, C., Savidis, A., Chomatas, G., Spyridou, N., and Sfyrakis M. (1991). *Access to graphical user interfaces by blind people*. London: Royal National Institute for the Blind.

Stevens, A. (1987). *Memory resident utilities, screen I/O and programming techniques*. Portland, OR: MIS Press.

Unesco (1990). *World braille usage*. Washington DC: Library of Congress.

Weber, G. (1986). Data transfer between different devices for text storage [in German]. *Proceedings of the 5th International Workshop on Computerized Applications for the Blind*, ed. J. M. Ebersold, T. Schwyter, and A. Slaby (pp. 305–311). Eichstätt: Katholische Universität Eichstätt.

Weber, G. (1989). Reading and pointing – Modes of interaction for blind users. In *Information Processing '89*, ed. G. X. Ritter (pp. 535–540). Amsterdam: Elsevier Science.

10

Metaphors for nonvisual computing

Elizabeth D. Mynatt and W. Keith Edwards

Introduction

Many of the systems in this book exemplify negotiating a technological barrier in order to provide access to a computer or other device. The necessity of providing access of any kind to existing devices has often outweighed the desire to design systems specifically for a small, although important, group of users. For example, computer access has been almost completely driven by the goal of overcoming more and more technological barriers. Currently a significant problem in computer access is providing access to graphical user interfaces (GUIs) for computer users who are blind (Boyd, Boyd, & Vanderheiden, 1990; Buxton, 1986).

The technical problem is capturing the information that is being sent to a bit mapped display. The design problem is creating a nonvisual interface which provides the same power as a GUI. Modern computing environments generally employ GUIs to provide an intuitive abstraction to operating system concepts and actions. This discussion focuses on the design of a nonvisual computing environment that will provide the same intuitive power that graphical computing environments currently offer.

Our target system is called *Audio Rooms*. The purpose of this system is to provide the same level of functionality as visually oriented computing environments such as the Macintosh *Finder* or Visix's *Looking Glass*. Audio Rooms is one part of the Mercator Environment being developed at the Georgia Institute of Technology. The environment as a whole will provide access to standard X Window applications, while Audio Rooms will provide an intuitive interface for working on a Unix workstation.

Many of the ideas presented in this chapter can be applied to the design of other systems. We will spend a great deal of time describing the steps in our design process and the different strategies employed in our design, namely innovative uses of nonspeech audio. It is our hope that these ideas can be applied to the design of systems other than Audio Rooms.

Our first step will be an analysis of the requirements for an intuitive computing environment. To accomplish this task, we will examine GUIs and the power they bring to computer interfaces. We will also describe the features necessary in a computing environment.

Next we will discuss our design methodology, namely the use of metaphors to create an interface that is easy to understand and enjoyable to use. Then we will discuss possible metaphors for a nonvisual computing environment. We will then target our chosen metaphor, Audio Rooms, and evaluate its characteristics. Following the analysis of the Audio Rooms metaphor, we will describe the most powerful strategies that we will use to implement our system. These strategies revolve around the use of speech and nonspeech audio. The remainder of the chapter will provide a brief description of other components in the Mercator environment.

GUIs and computing environments

The power of GUIs

Computers have traditionally been capable of presenting only textual and numeric data to users. Users reciprocated by specifying commands and data to computers in the form of text and numbers, which were usually typed into a keyboard. This method by which users interacted with their computers was adequate at best.

More recently, advances in computer power and display screen technology have brought about a revolution in methods of human–computer interaction for a large portion of the user population. The advent of so-called graphical user interfaces has usually been well received. In this section we will examine some of the defining characteristics of GUIs and explore some of the traits that make them useful to the sighted population. This examination will motivate our design of a powerful interface for users with visual impairments. Figure 10.1 illustrates a typical GUI.

As implemented today, most GUIs have several characteristics in common:

- The screen is divided into (possibly overlapping) regions called *windows*. These windows group related information together.

- An on-screen cursor (or mouse pointer) is used to select and manipulate items on the display. This cursor is controlled by a pointing device, usually a mouse.

- Small pictographs, called *icons*, represent objects in the user's environment which may be manipulated by the user.

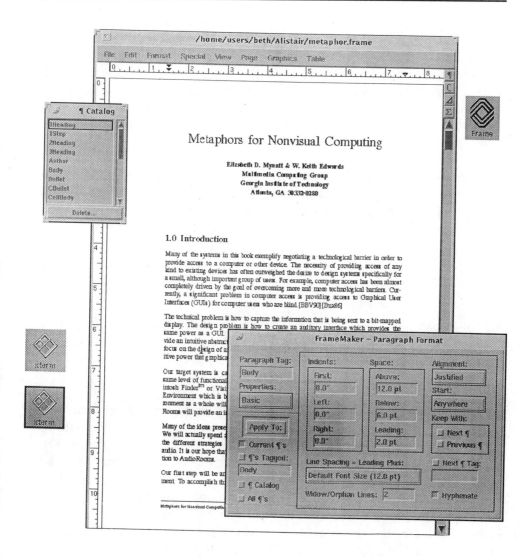

Figure 10.1. A typical graphical user interface (GUI).

Such a system is quite powerful for sighted users for a number of reasons. Perhaps most important, there is a direct correlation between the objects and actions which the GUI supports and the user's mental model of what is taking place in the computer system. Such a system is often called a direct manipulation interface, since to effect changes in the computer's state the user simply manipulates the on-screen objects to achieve the desired result. Contrast this to textual interfaces, in which there are often arbitrary mappings between commands, command syntax, and results. Direct manipulation interfaces are usually intuitive and easy to learn because they provide abstractions which are easy for users to grasp. For example, in a direct manipulation system, users may copy a file by dragging an icon which "looks" like a file to its destination folder. Contrast this to a textual interface, in which one may accomplish the same task via a command line such as 'cp mydoc.tex ~keith/tex/docs.' Of course the syntax for the command line interface may vary widely from system to system.

In addition to direct manipulation, GUIs provide several other important benefits:

- They allow the user to see and work with different pieces of information at one time. Since windows group related information, it is easy for users to lay out their workspaces in a way that provides good access to all needed information.

- An interface to multitasking is easily supported on most GUI based systems. Each window provides a separate input/output point of control for each process which is running in the system. Processes continue running, and users attend to the windows they choose.

- The graphical images used in GUIs lend themselves to the implementation of interface metaphors. The graphics support the metaphor by providing a natural mapping between metaphor and on-screen representation of the metaphor.

Unfortunately, a portion of the community concerned about access to computers for people who are blind has spent its time hoping that GUIs would go out of style, or trying to regulate against the use of GUIs (Vanderheiden, 1989). We feel that it would be beneficial if this community would understand the underlying traits of GUIs that make them powerful and then demand that interfaces as elegant and powerful as GUIs be made available to it as well.

GUIs are not powerful because they use windows, mice, and icons per se. Rather it is the underlying benefits of access to multiple information sources, direct manipulation, access to multitasking, and intuitive metaphors which provide the power. The GUI itself is just a single manifestation (perhaps one of many possible manifestations) of an interface which provides these benefits.

Graphical computing environments

In a typical GUI based computer system there are several components which make up the user's computing "world." First, there are the various applications which use graphical user interfaces. These applications are typically visual in nature and make use of on-screen graphical mechanisms (such as buttons and scroll bars) to control the application.

Second, there is the environment which provides support for performing computer system functions not related to a particular application. Such an environment provides an abstraction for the basic objects in the computer system, such as data files, directories, and so forth, and the basic computer operations, such as copying and deleting. Basically, the environment consists of everything outside the applications.

We can describe a computing environment more succinctly by listing its functions:

- Provide file system and file-system-related operations, specifically copying, deleting, renaming, and linking.

- Provide mechanisms for starting, stopping, and switching between applications.

- Provide various systems services, such as printing.

It is important to draw the distinction between graphical applications and graphical environments because, while the two may seem superficially (or visually) similar, they provide different functionality. In fact, providing access to graphical applications may have fundamentally different goals from providing access to graphical environments. In this chapter we will deal primarily with graphical environments.

The Apple Macintosh provides a popular graphical environment, Finder, an abstraction for executing computer operating system functions. Copying a file may be accomplished by selecting an icon representing the file and then choosing the "copy" operation from a menu of file operations. Deleting a file may be accomplished by dragging the icon representing the file into a trash can icon.

The abstraction employed by the Macintosh is often called a desktop metaphor because the screen layout and supported operations are supposedly reminiscent of a desk. However, the metaphor might be more appropriately termed the *office* metaphor. Although the Macintosh-style graphical environment is based on the desktop metaphor, other graphical environments need not be. One metaphor which is gaining credence in human–computer interface research laboratories is the so-called Rooms metaphor. We will discuss the Rooms metaphor at length later in this chapter.

It should be the goal of an environment to provide easy access to the basic operating system functionality of a computer while maintaining a level of abstraction which makes the system easy to use. Metaphor is commonly employed to make the system intuitive for new users and to provide common means of using functionality across the entire system.

Design by metaphor

We mentioned the concept of interface metaphors in the preceding section, but what exactly is an interface metaphor? How do you use metaphors in designing an interface, and how do you evaluate an interface metaphor? Strictly speaking, an interface metaphor is "designed interface actions, procedures, and concepts that exploit specific knowledge that users have of other domains" (Carroll, Mack, & Kellogg, 1988). The purpose of the metaphor is to give the user instantaneous knowledge about how to interact with the interface. For example, word processing applications exploit the knowledge associated with typewriters by making use of such concepts as margins, spacing, and typing in general. Spreadsheet applications such as Lotus 1-2-3 are designed to look like common ledger sheets. And desktop computing environments such as the Macintosh Finder contain elements of typical office environments such as filing cabinets, copying machines, and trash cans.

Designing computer interfaces with metaphors is a powerful technique, but it is not as simple as it may seem. Interface metaphors allow the user to make assumptions about how a computer application or environment will behave, but the designer must try to avoid allowing the user to make incorrect assumptions. The classic example is the Macintosh trash can, as implemented in early versions of the system. Once I was working with a colleague to put together a presentation for an upcoming conference. We were using some software on the Macintosh to create our slides. We stored our presentation on our floppy so we could take it with us to the conference. My colleague then dragged the icon for the floppy disk to the Macintosh trash can. I gasped in horror, wondering why my colleague had suddenly decided to delete all of our hard work. Then the floppy disk was ejected from the disk drive. My colleague smiled and explained that you could drag a floppy disk to the trash can to *eject* the disk. I was not amused.

Acknowledging that this example is somewhat trivial, the point is that interface metaphors should be examined carefully before implementation. Getner defines several characteristics of metaphors that can be evaluated (Carroll, Mack, & Kellogg, 1988): base specificity (how well a metaphor is known), clarity, richness, abstractness, systematicity, exhaustiveness, transparency, and scope. Typically, there are at least two steps to designing with metaphors. After a metaphor has been targeted, the designer should enumerate all the possible concepts and actions associated with that metaphor. Then the designer should compare the metaphor's concepts and actions with the concepts and actions enforced by the computer application. The designer must be convinced that the items which do not match are within the bounds of acceptable behavior. Three types of mismatch are possible. First, the interface metaphor may contain concepts and actions that are not supported by the computer application. This mismatch will lead to the user's trying to perform actions that lead to failure. Second, the computer application may support actions that are not present in the metaphor. These actions will be difficult for the user to learn and remember. Third, the computer application may behave in ways which directly conflict with what the metaphor predicts. This type of mismatch is the worst, since it will cause the user to mistrust the metaphor as a whole (ibid.).

The second step to designing with metaphors is user testing. No number of paper designs will predict all the things users will try to do with a computer application. User testing is an absolute requirement (ibid.). User testing will always uncover mismatches that were not discovered during paper evaluations. There are many other aspects of evaluating a metaphor, for example determining whether users even like and understand the metaphor.

Metaphors for nonvisual computing environments

Attempts to provide access to computer software and data for those with visual impairments are almost as old as computers themselves. In the old days of simple textual displays there was an obvious and fairly straightforward method of providing access: Text on the screen was sent to a speech synthesis device. This approach worked (and continues to work) acceptably well for those systems and applications which are text based (see Chapter 16).

In the arena of providing access to graphical systems, however, the attempted solutions have been less successful. Most of these systems try to perform basically the same mapping that was done earlier for the textual systems; that is, take the information displayed on the screen and map it into some sort of audio and speech output (Boyd, Boyd, & Vanderheiden, 1991; Fox, 1991; Kane & Yuschik, 1987; Vanderheiden, 1989).

In some systems of this type, visually impaired users use a mouse to manipulate an on-screen cursor. As the cursor passes over objects on the screen, the objects speak their names. This approach is relatively straightforward, yet it is naive. One can easily enumerate several problems with this approach:

- Occluded windows cannot be directly accessed.

- The mouse is a relative pointing device which gives no indication of the absolute location of the on-screen cursor.

- A visually impaired user may not notice or may be confused by subtle changes to the screen.

The flaw in this approach is that it forces a visually impaired user to try to understand an application interface in terms of its visual presentation. A graphical interface is designed to be processed by the visual system. Simply adding auditory cues to a graphical presentation does not generally create a suitable or equally powerful auditory presentation.

Another approach is to organize simply the application windows which are present on the screen into a list or menu. Then users can traverse the list (usually through keyboard interaction) until they select the application they want to work with. Both of these approaches basically do away with all the cognitive benefits which GUIs provide: simultaneously available multiple information sources, direct manipulation of objects, and a rich metaphor to aid in building a mental model of the computing environment. The problem with these approaches is that they simply attempt to retrofit the graphical desktop metaphor with audio information.

We believe that systems designers should take a step back in the interface design process and make use of another metaphor more suited to nonvisual interfaces. We have identified an interface metaphor which we believe is more suitable for a nonvisual implementation. This metaphor, *Rooms*, has already been implemented in graphical systems (Card & Henderson, 1987), and it seems to provide benefits. We intend to explore a nonvisual implementation of Rooms, called Audio Rooms. We believe that the Rooms metaphor is well suited to the needs of our target community.

In the Rooms metaphor, each room serves as a container for grouping some related applications or data. Users may place objects in these rooms according to their own preferences. In Rooms, each object represents an executable application, some data or text file, or a doorway which leads to another room. Users manipulate objects in rooms by first selecting them and then choosing an operation to perform on the selected object. The operations available for an object depend on the type of object. For example, doorways can be traversed; files may be copied, deleted, or renamed. Applications may be started or stopped.

These simple ideas form the core of the Rooms metaphor. Rooms provides mental devices which support cognitive organization of information at a higher level than the desktop metaphor.

Audio Rooms

A good starting point

The concept of Rooms was first developed by the Xerox Palo Alto Research Center (Parc) (Henderson & Card, 1986). The notion arose out of evaluations of the work habits of people using GUI based systems. Observers noticed that people tended to group windows based on functionality. In general, transitions would be made between groups of windows during a session with the computer.

In the Parc system, which is graphical in nature, Rooms provides higher-level organizational entities into which application windows are grouped. Each group of windows is said to exist in a virtual room; the contents of the room are the windows in the group associated with the room. There are connections ("doorways") between rooms through which users may transit from one room to another. These connections approximate the transitions which users make during a typical work session (ibid.).

Following the initial Xerox Parc Rooms implementation, implementations on top of several different GUIs have been developed. The metaphor of traveling through a network of rooms into which users have grouped windows has been shown to be a powerful organizational device. Rooms-like systems are just now beginning to become available for commercial systems (Hewlett-Packard's *Visual User Environment*, for example).

In their current graphical implementations, Rooms systems provide a higher level of conceptual organization than simple windows. Windows serve to group information related to a single application or task; rooms serve to group applications into related sets. It is our belief, however, that the Rooms metaphor has additional benefits which can help create a powerful nonvisual interface for visually disabled users.

Audio Rooms would, of course, provide the same cognitive organizational benefits Rooms provides to sighted users. In addition, there are several characteristics of Audio Rooms which we believe make the system especially attractive to users with visual disabilities. First, the metaphor is well understood by all users. Additionally, sight impaired people must, of necessity, have a well developed sense of space and good spatial memory in order to navigate around their own familiar surroundings, such as their living areas. Also, the Rooms metaphor is especially rich. The objects and operations of the metaphor should map particularly well into an audio based interface, as we shall see in the next section.

Characteristics and extents of the metaphor

Let us catalog some of the characteristics that come to mind when we think of real rooms. First, rooms have certain physical qualities; they have size and shape and occupy some volume of space. Rooms may have windows, doors, and closets. Additionally rooms have certain visual and auditory characteristics. A certain room may have a particular type of floor covering or wallpaper and may present certain acoustical properties. Rooms usually contain objects which the occupants of the room are free to manipulate (move, activate, and so on). These objects are usually placed in a room in some three-dimensional layout according to the preferences of the occupants or owner of the room. Furthermore, we can usually expect object permanence within a room. That is, when we leave an object in a room we can expect it to be there and in the same position the next time we return.

How do we navigate among real rooms? All rooms have doors which usually lead to other rooms. Hallways may serve to connect rooms, and they themselves may have contents as a room might. The layout of rooms is static and has a "flat" organization; that is, we do not usually think of rooms as containing other rooms.

People can be in only one room at a time, although there can be more than one person in a room. A person may be able to hear events which occur in other rooms nearby. People are free to move objects from room to room. Most rooms have a name associated with them and are intended to signal some specific purpose (a kitchen is for food preparation). Rooms have a general configuration consisting of the contents of the room and the placement of those contents.

Table 10.1 summarizes these characteristics in five categories: "Physical" for physical characteristics, "Objects" for the characteristics of objects within a room, "Navigation" for how rooms are connected, "People" for the characteristics associated with people in rooms, and the obligatory "Other" category for those characteristics that do not fit in the earlier categories yet do not form an identifiable grouping. Each characteristic is labeled as a quality of a room, an attribute associated with a room, or an action possible in a room or group of rooms. Qualities determine the general behavior or rules predicted by the metaphor. Attributes are elements predicted by the metaphor, usually physical objects, and actions are simply actions that the metaphor predicts that a user should be able to perform.

By enumerating the well known characteristics of rooms we hope we can develop a nongraphical implementation of the Rooms metaphor which will provide the same power and elegance to nonsighted users that the graphical Rooms implementations provide to sighted users. Which individual room characteristics will be useful to us? As we shall see, some characteristics will map easily and sensibly to our proposed environment; others will not. It may be necessary to "jump outside the metaphor" to include some characteristics in the interface which are not a part of real rooms.

Many characteristics of rooms map well to a computer interface, which leads us to believe that the Rooms metaphor is a good one. A metaphor which did not exhibit a significant set of attributes which carried over to the interface would likely be a poor choice. For example, from the physical category, our Audio Rooms will have closets which can be used to store objects that are not needed on an everyday basis. We will also keep the size attribute associated with our rooms. Unlike real rooms, however, our rooms will change their size to indicate the number of objects in the room. Although this dynamic sizing is not exhibited in real rooms, we feel that it is a valuable trait which will enhance the usability of the interface. (We will examine "trait misses" in more detail below.)

Each room may contain objects, and each object in a room has a certain absolute location within the room. The objects in a room may be manipulated by the users of the system, and, as in real rooms, the objects display general object permanence. The placement of objects within a room is left to the personal preferences of the user and is not decided by the system. Users are free to organize their personal workspaces as they see fit.

Rooms will have doors which will connect the rooms to each other. Users move between rooms via doors. As in the real world, users can be in only one room at a time, they are free to move objects from room to room, and they can hear activity in other rooms (or the same room). There may potentially be many people in a given room. This last trait raises interesting possibilities of collaboration between users in a distributed rooms space. Sighted and unsighted users could collaborate through their respective Rooms implementations.

Like real rooms, each Audio Room will have a name associated with it. Users assign names to rooms and may refer to them later via these names. Users are free to use a given room for whatever purpose they deem it most fit. The system itself does not enforce a certain functionality to be associated with a given room.

Table 10.1. *Characteristics of real rooms*

Physical	
Shape	Quality
Size	Quality
Closet	Attribute
Windows	Attribute
Acoustic ambience	Attribute
Floor covering, color, wallpaper	Attribute
Objects	
Manipulation	Action
Three-dimensional layout	Quality
Permanence	Quality
Navigation	
Doors	Attribute
Hallways	Attribute
Layout	Quality
People	
Located in exactly one room	Quality
Can move between rooms	Action
Can carry objects between rooms	Action
Can hear events in other rooms	Quality
Rooms can contain more than one person	Quality
Other	
Names	Attribute
Functionality	Attribute
Configuration	Action

Typically, as in visual Rooms, users will create a room for a given purpose (such as an editing room or a mail reading room) and then place objects within that room which support that purpose.

Trait misses are traits which are either present in real rooms but not present in Audio Rooms, or traits which are present in Audio Rooms but not real rooms. We classify the two types of trait misses as either subset misses (meaning that the trait is present in the metaphor but not in the implementation) or superset misses (meaning that the trait is present in the implementation but not in the metaphor).

First we deal with subset misses. There are several characteristics of real rooms which either do not map well into our interface or which basically serve no purpose for us. For example, we have eliminated the concept of windows in walls, as the ability to view the outside world has no meaning in our applications. Similarly, we can safely ignore such room characteristics as floor covering and wallpaper. In a visual system these traits may serve to give visual cues as to the room's identity, but in an auditory system they are useless. Auditory cues such as the acoustic ambience of the room will aid the user in identifying a room.

We also chose to ignore the shape characteristics which real rooms may have. In Audio Rooms all rooms have the same shape, primarily for ease of navigation. Room shape does play a role in the acoustic properties of a room, but for our purposes size will serve as the sole acoustic determiner.

In a real room, objects may be laid out in three-dimensional space (for instance, a painting may be hanging on the wall directly over a sofa). In Audio Rooms room contents are restricted to being laid out in a two-dimensional plane. Again, this is primarily for ease of navigation and object selection within a room. There are few good three-dimensional input devices, and those that do exist are quite expensive.

Finally, Audio Rooms ignores the concept of hallways. Doors are the sole means of transferring location from one room to another. In our environment, hallways would be essentially an entity with the characteristics of both rooms and doors. We felt that the interface metaphor could be simplified by omitting hallways.

There are also several superset misses. For various reasons, it is often useful to include traits in an interface which are not present in the real world system which the interface attempts to model. Usually these superset misses are added to bring about a more usable and powerful interface.

Audio Rooms is enhanced by the addition of several of these superset traits. Most of these traits are also present in the graphical Rooms implementations, and research has shown them to be useful. For example, in Audio Rooms it is possible for the same object to be present in more than one room. A useful example of this feature would be a new-mail indicator program, which would be present in each room. The user could be in any room in the system and be informed when mail arrives.

Another example is the ability to "teleport" directly from one room to another. In some circumstances it may be annoying to have to maneuver through a series of rooms to reach a desired destination. While the concept of rooms maintains that users will typically install doors between rooms in order to move between them, there is still the need to provide a mechanism for instantaneous transportation to a new location. It should be noted that while most of us do not experience the teleporting phenomenon in our own lives, the concept is still easily understandable. The idea of instantaneous transportation is common in both science fiction movies and video games, and its inclusion in the Rooms metaphor certainly does not disrupt the model to the point of making it unusable.

Two other traits are present in Audio Rooms which are not found in our daily experience. First, the Rooms system is easily extended by its users. A user may choose to add a new room to support some type of activity or to hold the work related to a particular project. The user may then establish doorways from this new room to chosen existing rooms. In real life, systems of rooms are not so easily extended. Also the Audio Rooms environment provides a more complex system of user customization options than real rooms do (such as changing the acoustic properties of a room, ordering the automatic enunciation of a room's name upon entering, and so forth).

At this point, we have not identified any direct conflicts between the Rooms metaphor and the behavior of our environment. User testing will undoubtedly uncover some conflicts. In general we feel that Rooms provides a good interface metaphor which has useful traits for interfaces at large. Table 10.2 contains the characteristics of rooms which we identified earlier. Each characteristic is labeled as a match, subset miss, or superset miss.

Sound

The Audio Rooms environment is designed for users whose primary means of gathering information is hearing. Hearing is a powerful perceptual process. We constantly monitor our environment by listening to the sounds around us. For example, right now I can hear the hum of my computer, the dishwasher running in the kitchen, my dog walking down the hallway, and my colleague talking on the phone. Often we are not even aware of the constant stream of auditory information that we are processing. Our perceptual abilities mean that hearing is naturally multitasking. For example, we can monitor multiple conversations at the same time. This phenomenon is known as the "cocktail party effect." (Cherry, 1953). In contrast, vision could be thought of as a focused single-task process that relies on fast context switching to compile complex information. We gather information about what we are currently looking at, and we can look at only one place at a time. For these reasons, we believe that sound can capture the multitasking properties of computer systems as well as or better than graphical output. For example, many graphical interfaces signal the appearance of a dialogue box or message with a beep to guard against the user's failing to notice its appearance on the screen.

Computer-generated sounds can be divided into two classes: synthesized speech and nonspeech audio. Current systems for computer access for blind users are dominated by the use of synthesized speech. We believe that the use of nonspeech audio can provide a much richer and more powerful interface, in the same way that graphics can convey more information than text.

Speech

The invention of computer synthesized speech made it possible for blind computer users to interact with computers in a reasonably fast and efficient manner. We believe designers using synthesized speech should strive to meet the following requirements:

- The speech should be understandable and a large vocabulary should be supported.

Table 10.2. *Comparing real rooms and Audio Rooms*

Physical	Match	Subset miss	Superset miss
Size	✓		
(Dynamic size)		✓	
Closets	✓		
Windows		✓	
Acoustic ambience		✓	
Floor coverings, wallpaper		✓	

Objects	Match	Subset miss	Superset miss
Three-dimensional layout		✓	
Permanence	✓		
Same object in multiple rooms			✓
User specified placement	✓		
Navigation			
Doors	✓		
Hallways		✓	
Dynamic layout			✓
Teleports			✓

People	Match	Subset miss	Superset miss
Located in exactly one room	✓		
Can move between rooms	✓		
Can carry objects between rooms	✓		
Rooms can contain more than one person	*		

Other	Match	Subset miss	Superset miss
Names	✓		
Functionality	✓		
Configuration	✓		

* Although not included as part of our initial design, a multiuser version of Audio Rooms would support the notion of multiple people in one room, perhaps collaborating or working independently of each other.

- Variable speed is necessary so that information can be scanned at a rate much faster than a natural speaking pace.

- Different voices and inflections should be provided. A variety of voices can differentiate different types of messages in the same way that color and other graphical devices add meaning to textual information. The use of inflection patterns can signal that more textual information is available or that the computer is waiting for some input or that the computer is informing the user of a serious malfunction.

- The vocabulary should be context sensitive. For example, a phone number should be read as "eight nine four dash three six five eight," not as "eight hundred ninety-four hyphen three thousand six hundred fifty-eight." An Internet mailing address should be read as "beth at c c dot g a t e c h dot e d u" (beth@cc.gatech.edu).

Many of these features are now appearing in software based speech synthesis systems. Refer to Chapter 16 for further information on design criteria for speech synthesis systems.

Synthesized speech is a requirement for any accessible system, since even with GUIs computers still primarily convey textual information. But speech as a form of output has its limitations. Although we can monitor multiple conversations at a time, it is doubtful that we would want multiple applications talking to us at once for the same reason that we do not want multiple people talking to us at once. Speech requires directed attention. Also speech, like text, is bulky. Text and speech are both serial in nature; that is, they must both be processed from beginning to end, whereas graphic images are processed as a whole. Furthermore, graphic images are powerful because one picture can be used to replace a lengthy text description. In the same fashion, nonspeech audio cues can replace long streams of synthesized speech.

Multidimensional nonspeech sound and auditory motifs

Most work with nonspeech audio has focused on the manipulation of dimensions of sound such as pitch and volume and on the use of auditory motifs to carry information. Most studies have found changes in pitch to be the easiest to perceive (Bly, 1982). Mapping information onto the different dimensions of sounds has been used with some success for multivariate data analysis (ibid.; Buxton, Gaver, & Bly, 1991). Sounds can carry information even when a graphical representation of the same data would be impossible to comprehend or even produce.

Blattner introduced the term "earcon" for auditory motifs that can be used to carry information. Different sources of information in a computer application could have recognizable motifs. Different types of messages could follow different patterns in pitch and rhythm (Sumikawa, Blattner, Joy, & Greenberg, 1986).

Although auditory motifs are intriguing, in our implementation of the Audio Rooms metaphor we will concentrate on the manipulation of dimensions of sounds to convey some forms of information. But what sounds will we use?

Everyday sounds

Computers and other man-made devices emit a variety of beeps, buzzes, and other artificial noises. Conversely, we typically hear things crumbling, things sloshing, things colliding – we hear the results of objects interacting. When asked to describe a sound, we tend to describe it in terms of the objects that generated the sound: a door slamming, stairs creaking, or glass breaking. In other words, we describe sounds in terms of their sources, not in such terms as pitch and duration.

What this realization means to an interface designer is that we can use sounds to make users think of familiar objects in the same way that icons in GUIs characterize commonplace objects. Gaver (1989) first introduced the term *auditory icon* with his interface called SonicFinder. SonicFinder added cues to the graphical Finder environment on the Macintosh. Dragging a file icon with the mouse sounded like dragging something along the floor. Dropping an icon into the trash can sounded like dropping a large object into a metal trash can.

These concepts can be exploited to the full in the Audio Rooms environment. Going through a door can sound like opening a slightly creaky door. A copying operation can sound like a copying machine. When the user sends a file to the printer, the sound of a laser printer will be heard. And when the printing is completed, the sound will stop, creating an unobtrusive notification that the print job is finished.

Some sounds will be artificial. A computer application does not have an associated everyday sound, but it can have a standard metallic base sound. Each room can also have a distinctive sound that is partially determined by its size.

The point is to create a recognizable environment with the use of common symbolic sounds. One problem remains: how to sort through these sounds so that the interface is more than a cacophony.

Spatialized audio

In everyday life, humans perceive sounds in their environment as emanating from some source in space. The ability to determine the position of the sound source in relation to the listener is referred to as *localization*. It is in large part the ability to localize sounds which enables us to parse a volume of different sound sources and attend to individual sources as desired.

It is possible to exploit localization abilities in the interface. The process of filtering an audio signal to introduce synthetic localization cues is termed *spatialization*. These localization cues are largely the result of three effects:

- Interaural time delays – the difference in time between an audio signal striking one ear and striking the other.

- Head shadowing effects – some sound components are dampened as a lateral sound passes through the head and upper torso.

- Pinnae effects – the human pinnae (outer ear structures) impose a unique signal "fingerprint" on a sound source at a given azimuth and elevation.

These effects are fairly well understood and can be synthesized by a computer (Antonious, 1979; Blauert, 1973; Oppenheim, 1983; Oppenheim & Schafer, 1975; Rossing, 1990; Wolfram, 1988). The chief problem currently is the computational time required to perform the spatialization. Current hardware solutions (such as the Crystal River *Convolvatron*) are quite expensive (Wenzel, Wightman, & Foster, 1988). In the near future, however, software solutions will be possible on general purpose computers (Burgess, 1992).

How will this synthetic spatialization be used in the interface? We feel that the use of spatialized audio would be most beneficial in aiding users to determine the layout of objects in rooms. Just as in a real room, where each object in the room has a particular location, in Audio Rooms each application or file has a particular location. Spatialized audio can be employed to inform the user of the location of objects relative to his or her position.

Note that this technique is quite similar to virtual reality systems in which users are, in effect, placed "inside" a computer-generated environment (Foley, van Dam, Feiner, & Hughes, 1990). In Audio Rooms, users are free to wander through their room's layout and manipulate objects at will. The environment should sound like an actual room environment.

The Mercator project

Many of the ideas described above are currently being implemented by the Georgia Tech Multimedia Computing Group in a system called Mercator. The goals of the system are twofold:

- Provide an elegant, powerful environment for navigating through the computer system and its applications and files.

- Provide access to existing graphical applications.

The first goal is being addressed using the Audio Rooms approach described in this chapter. The second goal will result in the construction of a system for retrieving and presenting relatively high level semantic structures from applications.

Our platform for the project is Unix workstations running the X Window System. We believe that the system, when finished, will allow users with visual disabilities to work using an environment that is every bit as natural and productive as the graphical systems used by their sighted co-workers. Furthermore, we hope to provide access to existing X applications so that all members of a work group, both sighted and nonsighted, can use the same tools to accomplish their work.

Our research up to this point has resulted in the Audio Rooms metaphor presented in this chapter. Of course much user testing and evaluation will be necessary to validate or reject the metaphor and variations on its implementation. We plan to conduct extensive user testing.

During the course of the project we are conducting research into the generation and use of spatialized audio. We are now able to generate high quality spatialized audio in real time using current generation workstations. Further research concerns the use of everyday sounds in purely auditory interfaces.

The Mercator project is being conducted at the Georgia Institute of Technology and is funded by Sun Microsystems and the Nasa Marshall Space Flight Center (Grant no. NAG8-194). In addition to the two authors, other people working on the Mercator project include Dave Burgess, Ian Smith, and Tom Rodriguez from the College of Computing and John Goldthwaite from the Center for Rehabilitation Technology.

References

Antonious, A. (1979). *Digital filters: Analysis and design*. New York: McGraw-Hill.

Blauert, J. (1973). *Spatial hearing*. Cambridge, MA: MIT Press.

Bly, S. (1982) Presenting information in sound. In *Human Factors in Computer Systems: Proceedings of the ACM conference Chi '82,* ed. M. Schneider. New York: ACM Press (pp. 371–375).

Boyd, L. H., Boyd, W. L. and Vanderheiden, G. C. (1990, December). The graphical user interface: Crisis, danger and opportunity. *Journal of Visual Impairment and Blindness*, pp. 496–502.

Boyd, L. H., Boyd, W. L., and Vanderheiden, G. C. (1991). Graphics based computers and the blind: Riding the tides of change. In *Proceedings of the CSUN Technology and Persons with Disabilities Conference,* Los Angeles, CA.

Burgess, D. (1992). Low cost sound spatialization. In *Proceedings of the Conference "User Interface Software and Technology (UIST)."* New York: ACM Press.

Buxton, W. (1986). Human interface design and the handicapped user. In
    Proceedings of the ACM conference Chi '86, ed. M. Mantei and P. Orbeton
    (pp. 291-297).

Buxton, W., Gaver, B., and Bly, S. (1991, May). *The use of non-speech audio at
    the interface*. Tutorial presented at the ACM Conference Chi '91, New
    Orleans, LA.

Card, S. K., and Henderson, D. A., Jr. (1987). A multiple, virtual-workspace
    interface to support user task switching. In *Proceedings of the ACM
    CHI+GI'87 Conference on Human Factors in Computing Systems and
    Graphics Interfaces*, ed. J. M. Carroll and P. P. Tanner. New York: ACM
    Press (pp. 53–59).

Carroll, J. M., Mack, R. L., and Kellogg, W. A. (1988). Interface metaphors and
    user interface design. In *Handbook of Human–Computer Interaction,* ed. M.
    Helander. Amsterdam: North-Holland (pp. 67–85).

Cherry, E. C. (1953). Some experiments on the recognition of speech with one
    and two ears. *Journal of the Acoustical Society of America, 22*: 61-62.

Foley, J., van Dam, A., Feiner, S. and Hughes, J. (1990). *Computer graphics:
    Principles and practices*. Reading, MA: Addison-Wesley.

Fox, J. (1991, March). Unlocking the door: PCs and people with disabilities. *PC
    Today,* (pp. 43–51).

Gaver, W. W. (1989). The SonicFinder: An interface that uses auditory icons.
    Human–Computer Interaction, 4(1): 67–94,.

Henderson, D. A., Jr., and Card, S. K. (1986). Rooms: The use of multiple virtual
    workspaces to reduce space contention in a window based graphical user
    interface. *ACM Transactions on Graphics 5*(3): 211–243.

Kane, R. M., and Yuschik, M. (1987). A case example of human factors in
    product definition: Needs finding for a voice output workstation for the
    blind. In *Proceedings of the ACM CHI+GI'87 Conference on Human
    Factors in Computing Systems and Graphics Interfaces*, ed. J. M. Carroll
    and P. P. Tanner. New York: ACM Press (pp. 69–73).

Oppenheim, A. (1983). *Signals and systems*. Englewood Cliffs, NJ: Prentice-
    Hall.

Oppenheim, A., and Schafer, R. W. (1975). *Digital signal processing*.
    Englewood Cliffs, NJ: Prentice-Hall.

Rossing, T. D. (1990). *The science of sound*. Reading, MA: Addison-Wesley.

Sumikawa, D. A., Blattner, M. M., Joy, K. I., and Greenberg, R. M. (1986).
    Guidelines for the syntactic design of audio cues in computer interfaces.
    Lawrence Livermore National Laboratory Technical report UCRL-92925.

Vanderheiden, G. C. (1989, October). Nonvisual alternative display techniques
    for output from graphics based computers. *Journal of Visual Impairment
    and Blindness, 83:* 383–390.

Wenzel, E. M., Wightman, F. L., and Foster, S. H. (1988). A virtual display system for conveying three-dimensional acoustic information. In *Proceedings of the Human Factors Society 32nd Annual Meeting.* Anaheim, CA: Human Factors Society (pp. 86–90).

Wolfram, S. (1988). *Mathematica.* Reading, MA: Addison-Wesley.

11

Multiple modalities in adapted interfaces

**Alistair D. N. Edwards, Ian J. Pitt, Steve A. Brewster, and
Robert D. Stevens**

Introduction

Since the advent of interactive computing in the 1970s, almost all interaction has
been based on a keyboard and a visual display. Latterly the mouse has been
added, but still the communication has been essentially through two simple
"narrow bandwidth" channels. Advances in the technology have recently made it
possible to think in terms of much richer interfaces. This is seen by many as the
means of solving many of the problems of human–computer interaction. Not
least, it may help to solve some of the problems disabled computer users have.
As pointed out in Edwards (1992), having multiple communication channels
available opens up the possibility of *redundancy,* and it is the redundancy which
is inherent in most human-human communication which makes interaction with
people with sensory disabilities possible.

Currently the greatest obstacle to the exploitation of the variety of
communications channels now available is our lack of understanding of how to
use them. As Alty (1991) pointed out, we know very little about how to use any
of the new modalities in isolation, and far less about how best to use them in
"multi-modal" combinations. This chapter provides a critical presentation of
work carried out at the University of York. Mostly it has been concentrated on
one channel, hearing. We have attempted to see how much use can be made of
nonspeech sounds to substitute for the visual channel which is missing for a blind
person.

Soundtrack, an auditory user interface

The advent of the graphical user interface (GUI) has been the most significant
advance in human–computer interaction since the introduction of the personal
computer – for the majority of computer users. Unfortunately, it may be the
worst thing which could have happened for one group: those who are blind. (See
Chapter 10 for a much more complete description of the problem.)

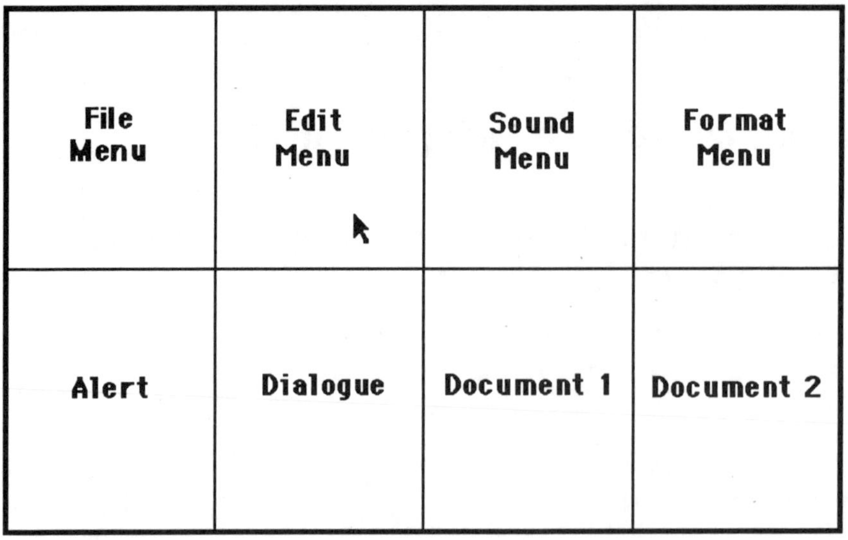

File Menu	Edit Menu	Sound Menu	Format Menu
Alert	Dialogue	Document 1	Document 2

Figure 11.1. The Soundtrack screen layout, a grid of auditory windows.

Work has been undertaken which shows promise of alleviating many of the problems of current interfaces (Edwards, 1991b; Schwerdtfeger, 1991) and, as reported in Chapters 9 and 10, work is under way which aims to ensure that the needs of blind people are addressed today in the development of tomorrow's interfaces. However, *Soundtrack* predates all of that work. Soundtrack is an experimental word processor with an auditory interface. It was not intended to be another word processor for blind people but rather a vehicle for research, a means of testing some ideas. Ultimately the hope was to develop adaptations which could be applied to existing visual interfaces.

The details of Soundtrack are fully reported elsewhere (Edwards, 1989a, 1989b, 1991a), but it is worth discussing it in this chapter in terms of the lessons learned. An idea of how Soundtrack works can be given by the following example of its use.

The screen of Soundtrack is laid out as shown in Figure 11.1. Each of the rectangles on the screen is called an *auditory window*. Each one has a name, as marked in the diagram, and a tone. As the cursor moves into a window, its tone is sounded. The tones are sine waves and vary in pitch, rising from left to right and bottom to top. In fact most of the tones are chords, as explained below. The edges of the screen are also marked with a distinctive tone. The user can navigate between windows using the tones: if he or she requires more exact information on the current position, pressing the mouse button at any time will elicit the name of the current window in synthetic speech.

There are two levels of interaction. Having located the required window, the user *activates* it by double-clicking the mouse button. This causes the window to reveal its contents. These are effectively a set of buttons, which operate in essentially the same way as the windows; in other words, each has a name (which can be spoken) and a tone based on the same pattern. The tones of a window's contents form the chord of the window when unactivated. The top four windows (Figure 11.1) have the role of menus. The activated File menu is shown in Figure 11.2. To select a command from that menu, the user would locate it using the tones and speech, as above, and then double-click on it.

Soundtrack was evaluated with the assistance of nine blind testers. The broad conclusion was that it was usable; people were able to learn to accomplish quite complex word processing tasks with it. However, it was in some ways quite difficult to use. The load on the user's memory is high. One of the attractions of graphical user interfaces is that they relieve users of having to remember many details, allowing them to rely instead on recognition (Mayes, Draper, McGregor, & Oatley, 1988) but that is not the case with Soundtrack. All computer users who are blind have to memorize a lot – the keystrokes corresponding to the commands – without any easily accessible aide-mémoire (such as a menu or on-screen help). It is necessary to learn, for instance, that the command to close a document is CTRL+K D. The information Soundtrack users had to learn was different. For example, the command to close a document is called "Close" – but it is in a menu called "File." The file menu is in the top left-hand corner, and "Close" is the third item down in that menu. The information is perhaps more

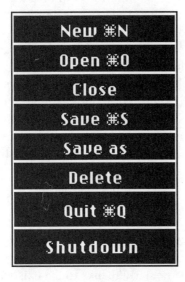

Figure 11.2. The Soundtrack auditory File menu.

structured, but it is more complex and has a spatial component.

There is good evidence that significant amounts of information can be conveyed in nonspeech sounds (see e.g. Bly, 1982; Smith, Grinstein, & Bergeron, 1990). It may be that if more information-rich sounds were used, the user's memory load can be reduced. Simple sounds were used in Soundtrack mainly because it was not clear what additional information would be useful and how it should be encoded in sound.

Two approaches to designing nonspeech sounds are advocated by Gaver and by Blattner. Gaver proposes the use of "auditory icons" composed of "natural" sounds: ones which sound like the object or event they represent. This approach works well in multimedia interfaces where the sound is a supplement to a visual representation, such as Gaver's *SonicFinder* (Gaver, 1989) and *Arkola* (Gaver, Smith, & O'Shea, 1991). However, in an interface which relies on its auditory representation (such as one for use by blind people), the limitations of this approach are apparent. What natural sound sounds like the "Find" command in a word processor, for instance?

The other approach is to use symbolic sounds and to have the user learn what they mean. This is going to be practical only if there is some structure to the sounds, so that the user can learn, and remember them and analyze their semantics. That is essentially the basis of the *earcons* proposed by Blattner and colleagues (Mansur, Blattner, & Joy, 1985; Blattner, Sumikawa, & Greenberg, 1989). Unfortunately, the ideas behind earcons have not yet been tested very extensively. Jones and Furner (1989) did carry out a comparison of earcons, auditory icons, and speech. They found that most subjects preferred speech cues, followed by earcons; auditory icons were least preferred. With regard to making associations between the cue and its meaning, speech was again the best, but auditory icons scored better than earcons. More recently at the University of York we have been carrying out some experiments in the utility of earcons but have yet to produce any conclusive results.

A significant gap in most of the existing work on symbolic nonspeech sounds is the lack of a systematic approach to the control of *timbre*. Timbre is one of the most significant properties of a sound. Whereas many variations in sounds are perceived only by people with musical training, variations in timbre are apparent to most people; only a musician might recognize that two notes played on a piano are an octave apart, but most people will notice the difference between a note on a piano and the same note on a trumpet. The problem is that the perception of timbre is very subjective and does not yet lend itself to mathematical description (Brewster, 1991).

This is a very good example of the sort of ignorance which is currently impeding the development of multimedia interfaces. The technology exists to control arbitrary sounds by computer (particularly thanks to the existence of the Midi standard), but very little is known about how to use sounds to convey information.

Mice and navigation in an auditory space

Many people have suggested that it is quite inappropriate to expect a blind person to use a mouse at all, and other developers working on the GUI problem have got around the need to use the mouse and have substituted a keypad. However, there are arguments that access to a mouse is necessary or desirable even for blind people. For one thing, an adapted mouse based interface is closer to the visual one used by sighted colleagues. Also, there are some interactions which are very natural with a mouse (or similar pointing device, stylus, trackball, etc.) and extremely awkward with any other device. Any application involving drawing is the obvious example – although any form of drawing presents a significant challenge in itself to blind people.

One of the objectives of the Soundtrack project was to see how successfully mouse interactions could be realized in an auditory interface. All of the operations used in a visual interface were included (targeting, clicking, dragging). The results of the Soundtrack evaluation might be interpreted as suggesting that the mouse is not a practical device, but perhaps mouse interaction was inefficient in Soundtrack because it was badly implemented. As explained above, the sounds used in Soundtrack were very simple. It was therefore decided to follow up the project with a series of experiments to explore how sounds might best be used in mouse interaction.

The fundamental mouse interaction is locating a target; there is no point in being able to click or drag an item if one cannot find it in the first place! An inherent property of GUIs is that there are a large number of graphical items on the screen at any time, any one of which may be the target of the user's next interaction. The system has essentially no knowledge of the user's next move. The system cannot therefore guide the user to a particular object (if it could, then the user action would be redundant, and the system could make the selection automatically). The interface designer must therefore ensure that all the items are accessible and that the user can find any one of them. It is up to the user to decide which is the next target and to locate it.

It is often assumed that, whereas vision is essentially parallel, sound is serial. This is not true. Buxton (1989) describes how we routinely monitor a number of different sounds when performing the task of driving a car. Given this ability to handle multiple sounds and the need to give access to a screen containing several potential targets, it might be possible to have a sound associated with each object by which the user can be guided.

Single-target experiments

First it is necessary to ascertain how best to guide the user to a single target. That was the objective of the first of the experiments in which we set out to provide *distance* information by means of sound. A music synthesizer was set up to produce the sound of a cello playing middle C (a fundamental frequency of 261.6

Hz), and volume change commands were sent to it from the computer using a serial Midi interface. The system was arranged so that the sound varied according to the distance between the cursor and the target, being at its quietest when the cursor was farthest from the target and reaching full volume when immediately adjacent to the target area. The intended analogy was that of the cursor acting as a microphone, picking up more sound when moved close to the target and less sound when moved farther away. When the cursor entered the target area, the sound changed to that of a ringing alarm. The program incorporated a facility whereby the route taken by each subject while attempting to locate the target could be recorded for later examination.

In preliminary experiments constant and pulsed tones were used. Two types of pulsing were tried, constant frequency and varying with distance such that the pulses got faster and merged into a single tone as the target was approached. It was found that pulsing made no appreciable difference to targeting speed, but it was important in that it made it easier to distinguish different sounds. This is because the wave envelope is important to differentiate sounds.

The tests were run using a group of five subjects, all of whom had normal eyesight and were regular users of GUIs. They were allowed to practice on the system as often as they wished until their scores showed no further improvement, and they were then tested at approximately weekly intervals performing 25 runs. The sound was generally relayed via headphones, although a few trials were also made using loudspeakers (which produced no significant effect on the results).

It was found that after a little practice subjects could quite reliably locate the target using aural information and that the time taken was approximately the same as that for visual location using distance information only (as ascertained in a preliminary experiment). See Table 11.1.

Analysis of these traces showed that subjects often moved the cursor to within a short distance of the target quite early during each run but then took a comparatively long time to fix on the target. Accordingly the program was modified so as to provide additional information close to the target. This involved increasing the ratio between the maximum and minimum volume levels available and then using this extra dynamic range to provide a sharper change of volume as the cursor got closer to the target. The modified system was tried using the same group of subjects again, and it was found that using a nonlinear range did indeed produce a small but consistent increase in the speed of target location. No attempt was made at this stage to determine the effect of other nonlinear volume changes.

Having shown that distance information could successfully be provided via auditory cues, we made efforts to provide the user with at least rudimentary directional information. An obvious means to do this is through the use of stereo (or more correctly in this case, *binaural*) sound. The system was again modified so that the sounds arriving at each ear of the listener could be independently controlled. In keeping with the existing analogy (i.e. the target emits sound, and

Table 11.1. *Target location speeds (pixels/second) for auditory location under different conditions. Visual location using directional information only is also included, by way of comparison.*

	Visual location, distance-only	Mono, standard dynamic range	Mono, expanded dynamic range	Stereo, standard dynamic range	Stereo, expanded dynamic range
Mean location speed	66	60	64	75	79

the cursor acts as a microphone), the system was set up such that the sound would appear more strongly in the left ear when the target was to the left of the cursor, and vice versa.

These experiments demonstrated how, by combining several modes of auditory information (direction, loudness, etc.) in a single signal, performance in an auditory navigation task was improved. It is suggested that a level of performance was attained which would be acceptable for a blind person undertaking *some* mouse based interactions. However, the speed of the interaction was still so much slower than that of a sighted operator that it is likely that a non-mouse based alternative would still be appropriate in some circumstances, at least when the use of a mouse is not particularly appropriate for some other reason.

Multiple target experiments

The next stage was to investigate whether the same sort of signal could be used to guide the user to one of a set of targets. We addressed several questions about the design of mouse based auditory interfaces. One frequently asked question is whether nonspeech sounds are appropriate. Do they have any advantage over speech? Another question is whether the largely unconstrained two-dimensional layout of most visual GUIs can be translated into a graphical form, or whether it would be better to constrain the interface so that most interactions are one-dimensional – essentially a series of selections from linear menus.

There is also a question as to how many auditory targets the user can cope with, though for technical reasons we were restricted in these experiments to a maximum of eight. Broadly the experiments consisted of a number of targets (between two and eight) being displayed, and the user locating a specified one.

Word processor
Drawing
Database
Graphics
Compiler
Statistics
Spread sheet
Game

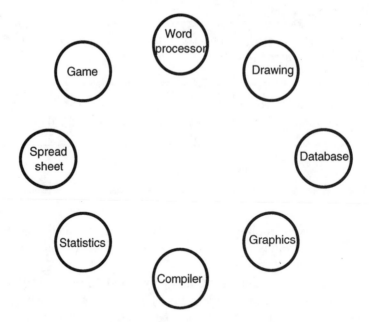

Figure 11.3. The two-dimensional layout of targets.

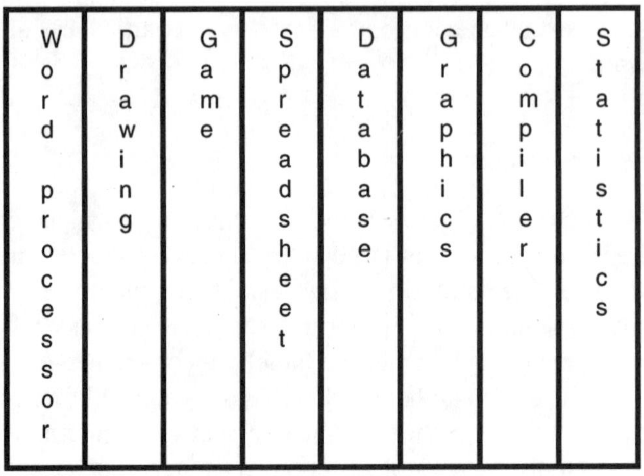

Word processor
Drawing
Game
Spreadsheet
Database
Graphics
Compiler
Statistics

Figure 11.4. Targets laid out as a one-dimensional menu.

Table 11.2. *Comparison of the two speech and nonspeech targeting speeds (mean speeds in pixels /sec)*

Screen arrangement	Single voice speech	Multiple voice speech	Nonspeech
One-dimensional	118	120	93
Two-dimensional	14	16	14

This was done using the following layouts:

1. targets displayed in two dimensions (Figure 11.3);

2. targets arranged as a one-dimensional menu (Figure 11.4).

Notice that the menus (Figure 11.4) were laid out horizontally, so that use could be made of stereo sounds (see below). Vertical movements of the mouse were ignored in this setup.

Speech and nonspeech sounds were used. The speech was digitized natural speech. In one series of experiments a single voice was used (simulating a system using a high quality single-voice speech synthesizer), while in another series a variety of voices were used. The nonspeech sounds were generated by a music synthesizer, a unique sound being allocated to each target.

In the one-dimensional condition, only the target currently under the cursor made its sound; to hear the others the user had to move the cursor, whereas in the two-dimensional condition all targets made their sounds simultaneously, distance information being given through loudness and direction through stereo (as in the final single target experiments). (Another experiment has been undertaken in which the targets were laid out as a menu, with all the targets making their sounds simultaneously, and loudness varying with distance. However, the results of the experiment under this condition are not yet available.)

For each test a number of targets (between 2 and 8, arranged as in the figures) would be displayed. At the beginning of each test in the one-dimensional case, the cursor was automatically placed randomly within the menu (i.e. in one of the targets). In the two-dimensional condition the cursor was automatically placed in the center of the targets. The subject was then asked to locate one of the targets, chosen at random. In the speech experiments the subject would be given the name of the target ("Word processor" or whatever). Before the nonspeech experiments the subjects were played each of the sounds they would hear and were asked to assign each a name. Those names chosen by the subject were then used as the labels in the experiment. For instance the experimenter might ask, "Please find the bird tweet."

The results of these experiments are summarized in Table 11.2. Evidently the speech sounds were better than the nonspeech sounds and furthermore the multiple voices were better than the single voice. That the nonspeech sounds were slowest appears to be due to the extra cognitive processing involved: The subjects had to perform a mapping from the name to the sound which is not necessary when the name *is* the sound. Errors of subjects locating the wrong target occurred in the nonspeech condition, showing that mismappings were occurring.

It is interesting that the results in the single voice condition were so good. In the early stages of the experiment it was thought that this condition might prove to be impractical. The sounds tended to merge and be indistinguishable. Indeed, it was found that the choice and selection of voices were critical, some voices being much more noticeable and insistent. A similar problem was found with the nonspeech sounds. The sounds used were chosen somewhat arbitrarily, and in fact the experiments had to be restarted using a new set of sounds, as early subjects found difficulty in distinguishing them. This reinforces the conclusion mentioned earlier that the effective design of nonspeech sounds is retarded by lack of a systematic approach to the description and manipulation of timbre.

Absolute speed is not a useful measure in the serial case. Since the user can only hear the current item, there is really no concept of the distance to the target. Nevertheless a comparison can be made between the serial and parallel conditions in that the speeds are proportional to the time taken to locate a target (given that the distances to the target were the same every time in the two-dimensional condition). It appears that for the untrained subjects, serial one-dimensional search is as fast as the parallel arrangement. However, there was evidence that subjects learn to use other cues in the parallel two-dimensional search, suggesting that with practice it could become a more efficient method. To test this the researcher who had done most of the work in the experiments (IJP) – who was the most highly trained in the task – was himself tested in the parallel condition. Averaging across the three auditory conditions (single voice, multiple voice, and nonspeech), his mean speed was 27 pixels/sec as compared with a mean speed of 15 pixels/sec for the other subjects. Evidently significant improvements in performance are attainable with training. Nevertheless it must be borne in mind that these speeds are much slower than for a comparable visual targeting task. (See the discussion of Fitts' Law in Chapter 2 of Card, Moran, & Newell, 1983.)

One subjective result of these experiments which must not be ignored is the degree of fatigue reported by some of the test subjects. No attempt was made to assess levels of fatigue during the experiments, but several subjects complained of tiredness during or immediately after the single target trials, and others later admitted to having experienced fatigue at some time during those experiments. It is possible that this was largely due to the artificiality of the experiment. Each subject had to repeat the identical target location task many times, whereas in a real life interaction one would move on to another task after locating the target. However, it could be that effects caused by the choice of sounds or the unusual auditory intensity of the task are significant. Such effects must be monitored in future experiments, because even the most efficient interface will not be used if it induces discomfort. It may be significant that no such effects were observed in the multiple target experiments. It may be that this is a less artificial environment and the concentration required less intense – which may be a significant result in itself, suggesting that parallelism is indeed a natural part of communication.

Although the design of the sounds we used evolved during the study, all the possibilities are far from being exhausted. In particular, technology has recently been developed whereby sounds can be "placed" anywhere in a three-dimensional space (Wenzel, 1992). Obviously such a facility is likely to be much more effective than the one-dimensional variation offered by the binaural stereo variation used in the experiments above. There is likely to be further scope for improvement, therefore.

The question of speech versus nonspeech sounds in this context has not been fully resolved. One definite conclusion is that using one voice to pronounce different messages simultaneously is impractical. This is significant, because most current speech synthesizers (at least the affordable ones) are incapable of producing different voices. Speech has the obvious advantage that the mapping of sound to meaning is inherent, but we still have a long way to go in investigating how easily the meaning of symbolic sounds can be learned, remembered, and used. (Work is continuing at York in this area.)

Alternative pointing devices

While the need for blind people to have access to a pointing device has been acknowledged, there remains a question as to whether the mouse is the appropriate device. Whereas it has been shown to be the most efficient pointing device for sighted people (Card, English, & Burr, 1978), no comparison of alternative devices has yet been undertaken for blind people. It would seem likely that a device which uses the finger as the pointer would be more appropriate. Blind people are used to relying on tactile information from their fingers, particularly if they are braille readers. The extra feedback through the finger tip about distance traveled may be significant. Experiments at the University of Calgary confirmed the suggestion that this form of interaction is successful with blind users (Döhrn, 1984).

There are a number of problems in providing finger based input. One is that the finger is a rather fat, inaccurate pointer; a finger is several pixels wide, while for many applications single-pixel accuracy is required. A second problem, when simulating mouse input, is the requirement to simulate one (or more) mouse buttons. For a one-button mouse, the ideal is a touch pad with two levels of sensitivity, one level signifying a pointing action (the equivalent to the user holding, and possibly moving, the mouse) and the second level signifying a button press.

The device used by Döhrn consisted of a graphics tablet which is normally used in conjunction with a stylus or a puck containing a coil. For the purposes of the experiments the users wore the coil attached to a ring on a finger. This meant that the finger tip was in direct contact with the pad and gave quite an accurate reading of the finger's position. An overlay of tangible lines was added to the pad to give the user enhanced tactile feedback. Within the experiment, no "mouse button" input was required.

On this basis, it was decided to repeat the auditory navigation experiments using a tactile input device. A commercially available touch pad, the *UnMouse*,[1] was used. This consists of a tablet with a touch sensitive area of 4.5 × 3 in. (11.2 × 7.4 cm) which is spring loaded. Plugged into a mouse port of a Macintosh, a finger touching the pad can act as if it were the mouse and pressing the finger causes the surface to depress, registering a mouse button click.

There were a number of problems in using the UnMouse. First it is very small, compared to the large screen being used (approximately 16 × 12 in. or 40.6 × 30.8 cm). This means that a small movement of the finger translates into a large movement of the cursor, exacerbating the problem of the large finger tip (approximately 0.4 in. or 1 cm diameter). Also the UnMouse appears to work by detecting changes in capacitance. This means that any item coming near to its surface (not necessarily touching it) may be detected. Thus, for instance, users may not hold their wrists well above the tablet causing other fingers to come near to its surface and be detected. This may cause the cursor to jump from the position corresponding to their pointing finger to some other point – which may seem somewhat random to the users, unaware of the effect of their other fingers. A further problems is with the clicking mechanism. The distance of travel is significant (about 0.1–0.2 in. or 3–4 mm), but being spring loaded over a comparatively large area the pressure required to activate the switch is not uniform across the surface. This leads to a variety of errors including clicks not being registered and "bouncing," leading to a double click when a single one was intended.

These problems led us to the conclusion that the UnMouse was not a suitable device to test the efficacy of finger input. However, the device can be used with a stylus in place of the finger. While the tactile feedback is lost, the stylus ameliorates some of the above problems and there are still possible advantages in using the UnMouse since it is an absolute pointing device and gives the user a fixed frame of reference. Hence, the above experiment using stereo expanded dynamic range and the parallel screen arrangement was repeated with subjects using the UnMouse with a stylus.

---

[1] UnMouse is manufactured by MicroTouch Systems Inc., 55 Jonspin Road, Wilmington, MA 01887.

Table 11.3. *Results of the UnMouse experiments (speeds in pixels/sec)*

Pointing device	Screen arrangement	Single voice speech	Multiple voice speech	Non-speech sounds
Mouse	Two-dimensional	14	16	14
UnMouse	Two-dimensional	13	14	13

The results are summarized in Table 11.3 (which includes some of the results already seen in Table 11.2, for comparison). As is apparent, the UnMouse turned out to give marginally slower speeds but they are not very different from the mouse condition. Evidently using the UnMouse with a stylus gives performance similar to using a mouse. This appears to bear out earlier informal results of using a stylus and bitpad with Soundtrack (Edwards, 1989b)

The question remains open as to whether a finger-sensitive device like the UnMouse, but without its problems, would give better performance. As yet the UnMouse appears to be the only such device commercially available for Macintoshes.

Soundtrack was the first attempt to make the Macintosh accessible to blind people and was effectively based on adapting the mouse-based interaction. Since those early days, a lot of progress has been made. Outspoken (Chapter 4) is commercially available and other work (including that reported in Chapter 10) has continued to try to make graphical user interfaces accessible by obviating the need to use a mouse. Nevertheless, it has been argued that access to a mouse – or at least an equivalent pointing device – is necessary. Hence the experiments described in this section. However, the most significant developments in this area are currently under way within the Guib project. (Much of the work reported in Chapter 9 was undertaken within this project. See also Petrie, Heinila, & Ekola, 1993.)

Another potentially significant technological development is that of the *Pantograph*, a pointing device with force feedback.[1] This device would enable users to feel virtual objects of different textures and constructions. For instance it can simulate impassable walls as well as tactile lines which offer a small resistance, but can be crossed. Combined with auditory feedback in three-dimensional space a very powerful nonvisual interface might be constructed.

---

[1] At the time of writing Pantograph was available only in prototype form. It is being developed by Robosoft Inc, 308 Pinetree Crescent, Beaconsfield, Quebec, Canada H9W 5E1.

Sounds and access to complex information

The rate of transmission of information – in both directions – between the computer and the user is often referred to as the *bandwidth*. The visual bandwidth is relatively large. This means that the designers of visual interfaces can cram a lot of information onto a computer screen, all (or most) of which is constantly visible to the user. This vastly parallel presentation of information is not overwhelming because the user can rapidly switch attention to the current point of interest and ignore or filter out extraneous information. Problems occur when the bandwidth is not sufficient for a particular application.

The basic problem of adapting any visual interface for blind people is that none of the other senses has the same bandwidth as vision. It was suggested above that a great deal more work will have to be done before we start to make anything like full use of the potential bandwidth of nonspeech sounds. Yet even when something like that full bandwidth has been realized, it will still not match what is available in vision. There are two possible approaches to this problem. One is to reduce the amount of information presented – to filter it. The other is to attempt to broaden the bandwidth by making use of other senses in combination with hearing. The hope is that the whole will be greater than the sum of the parts: that in combining media and modes of presentation, new channels of communication will be discovered.

Work is under way within the European *Maths* project (Mathematical Access for Technology and Science) to look at how hearing and touch should be combined in such a way as to be complementary. At the same time more developmental work is under way designing interfaces to other forms of complex information. Mathematics is a highly visual language. In order to be able to communicate, mathematicians always resort to visual communication (algebra, diagrams, etc.). Indeed, most people can follow only the most simple of mathematical proofs without the *external memory* of a piece of paper or a blackboard.

Obviously this channel of communication is not available to blind people, and hence they tend to be excluded from the study and application of mathematics. Even though they may have the intellectual ability to think mathematically, they cannot (easily) write down their thoughts. This may not seem a serious handicap, but mathematics is the basis of so many other disciplines in science and technology that the lack of a good background in it must exclude many blind people from important career and educational possibilities. In particular, the advent of adapted computers has meant that many blind people have become skilled in using computers and very much interested in them. However, if they should wish to pursue this interest, perhaps to the level of a degree in computer science, they are likely to find that a mathematical qualification is a prerequisite. The Maths project (which involves the University of York and four other European collaborators) is addressing textual representations of mathematics.

There is also a smaller scale continuing project at the University of York concerned with translating simple diagrams (line graphs) into sounds.

Auditory presentation of mathematical information

Mathematicians have to use algebra to communicate because they have to be able to convey a great deal of information, and it must be precise. Whereas in conversational speaking or writing, the odd word misheard does not generally affect understanding, one symbol missed in algebra can completely alter the meaning of the expression. Written algebra relies on the reader's ability to scan, move backwards and forwards, and focus on the relevant terms; in other words, it relies on all the properties which make vision so powerful. In translating algebra into a nonvisual form, it is desirable to substitute for as many of these properties as possible. It is not sufficient to send a stream of text to a speech synthesizer and have it spoken as one long utterance. There must be the ability to *control* the way the expression is scanned and spoken. The objective of this project is to see how to exploit a variety of communication modes to present algebra in a meaningful manner. This involves not only using several auditory modalities, but also designing the interaction such that the person is aware of the structure of the expressions being viewed.

In written algebra, the form helps the reader in several ways. The two-dimensional nature of algebra notation delimits syntactic groups by their spatial location. Exponents and fractions are good examples of this. These are visually obtrusive parsing markers. Additionally, the spacing of the symbols on the page aids parsing in a more implicit way. The order of precedence of algebraic operators can be correlated with the spatial arrangement. This "visual syntax" (Kirshner, 1989) helps a significant number of readers to parse an expression. A reader can review an expression and quickly focus attention on any part. The ability to perceive the expression as a whole has implications for its manipulation. A user's perception of an expression's structure will guide his or her strategy in solving the problem. (Lewis, 1981).

In most teaching situations, a teacher's verbal presentation of algebra only assists a visual presentation. In a purely verbal delivery, several problems arise. The most apparent are standard symbol names and syntactic ambiguity. Speech is essentially a linear form. In many situations the lack of spatial cues in the speaking of an expression can lead to ambiguity in the spoken form. The facility to gain an overview, to relate one part of an expression to another, is an opportunity not available in a purely verbal presentation. And a fundamental problem arises in trying to manipulate the expression. The physical and mental representation of the acoustic signal exists only transiently. Retention and integration of all the information given in an expression is an impossible task for all but the simplest, very familiar expressions. Simply speaking an expression in full will often overwhelm a listener.

A reader of print is able to control the information flow by browsing an expression. This facility needs to be offered to the person who "reads" an expression with speech. Vision is very well adapted to this kind of filtering, because attention can be focused on the salient parts. To present the same information in an auditory form it is necessary for the computer to perform the filtering task. However, this filtering must not be prescriptive: The reader must maintain control over which parts of the information are revealed at any time but must never be denied access to any part.

Two problems need to be addressed. One is to devise facilities which will give the user access to all the information available in a visual system. The second is, having identified the forms in which to present the information, to enable the user to control access. In this section we describe progress on solving the former problem in the context of the presentation of algebra, but as yet there is little to be said about the latter. As explained above, the amount of information available is very large, and once it is available in auditory form, the interface through which it will be controlled is necessarily complex. Where reading is an active process, listening is a passive one. Reading aloud is relatively slow, and a listener is liable to lose concentration. However, in a one to one situation, a listener may be able to take a more active part in the reading process. A skilled reader, using meaningful symbol names and unambiguous speech, can interpret the structure of an expression to deliver it in a controlled and comprehensible manner. In such cases a listener can interact and direct the reader in the same process.

It should be possible to replace the human reader with an interactive computer system. Such a system must be able to speak an expression via a voice synthesizer in a consistent and unambiguous way. The listener becomes a reader and should be able to use an overview of an expression's structure to guide his or her interaction. This interaction must enable the user to comprehend the macrostructure and detail of an expression and the relationship between its structural components, much as the reader of print is able to.

The first decision in speaking algebra notation is what type of information to give the reader. The written form gives the reader a literal meaning for an expression. The interpretation of that expression to something of more focused mathematical meaning relies on the user's knowledge. For instance, the expression

$$ax^2 + bx + c = 0$$

can simply be judged as a set of relationships between items unless the reader's mathematical knowledge recognizes it as a quadratic equation. It is the literal meaning of an expression that should be presented, not any interpretation. However, the expression should be presented in such a way that the reader can apply his or her knowledge to the information and make an interpretation.

The guidelines devised by Chang (1983) are used by many readers to make spoken mathematics consistent and unambiguous. Chang offers a set of standard names for symbols. However, the principal component of Chang's system is to delimit certain groups of symbols within an expression by the use of key words and phrases. These groups of symbols are those delimited, in print, by spatial location or visually obtrusive markers, such as fractions and parentheses. For example, parentheses are replaced with the words "the quantity" and "end quantity." The phrases: "the fraction," "the numerator," "the denominator," and "end fraction" are used to delimit the scope of a fraction line. Such phrases replace such parsing markers as parentheses (a word difficult to say) and such spatial cues as superscripts and vertical juxtaposition in fractions. A listener is given the structure in an unambiguous fashion as the speaker explicitly starts and ends certain syntactic structures.

The idea of simple and complex notation can be introduced to explain the use of the delimiting phrases. Complexity arises when grouping symbols is needed to prevent syntactic ambiguity in an expression written in a linear form: for example, $x^{(n+1)}$. Here the parentheses explicitly place both terms following the x into the superscript, and the phrase "end power" is needed in the spoken form. In contrast to this complex example, a single term in the superscript requires no explicit termination. Similarly, a simple fraction like

$$\frac{x}{y}$$

can be spoken as "x over y." A complex fraction

$$\frac{x + y}{x - y}$$

needs to have verbal tags inserted (see above).

Such guidelines for the speaking of algebra solve only one aspect of the problem and may exacerbate another. The addition of many verbal tags could increase the – already large – cognitive load on a listener, preventing a proper reading of the expression. This point reinforces the need for the listener to be able to control the information flow.

Another important feature of spoken algebra must be introduced at this point. The intonation pattern or prosody of a person's voice contains important information above the purely lexical content. Perceived pauses and pitch changes within speech divide the utterance into "units of information, new and given" (Halliday, 1970) and focus attention on certain items within those units. Prosody can give structure to an utterance, indicating major syntactic boundaries. A preliminary investigation has revealed some relatively simple rules for the prosody of algebra. Pauses are inserted at major syntactic boundaries; speed and pitch change also emphasize a change in structure. The use of these cues in spoken algebra could aid the process known as chunking. Additionally, some of the verbal tags could be replaced with prosodic cues. Another significant prosodic feature seems to be a sharp decrease in the pitch contour at the end of an expression. This feature could be useful to indicate the end of an expression.

As the complexity of an expression can indicate where to place verbal cues within the expression, it can also guide the control of information flow.

Besides the full uttering of an expression, three modes of browsing an expression can be distinguished. These are unconstrained browsing, staged release, and unfolding. A full utterance is adequate when the amount of information is small enough to be retained and integrated; that is, it is "simple." When the expression becomes too complex, through length or syntactic construction, other views need to be presented. Unconstrained browsing allows movement through an expression, character to character, term to term, into and out of complex items, and so on. The reader can ask for a range of views to be spoken. These include character term, superscript, level, complex structure, and so on. This browsing style allows a detailed examination of an expression.

If a reader finds a spoken expression too long to remember, a staged release strategy may be used. Each term is spoken in turn upon request. This control enables the expression to be broken into manageable units, ones that the reader can retain and integrate at his or her own pace.

The last browsing type is an unfolding strategy. In this method a series of views, ever more complex, are given to the reader. In each view simple syntax is spoken until a complex structure is found. This complex item is referred to by its type: "quantity" or "fraction." At the next signal from the reader, the complex item is spoken as before. At the end of the complex structure, speaking commences again at the previous level upon a signal from the reader.

The choice between full utterance (unconstrained browsing), unfolding, and staged release is the choice of how to filter the information flow. The different browsing strategies reflect the structural nature of an expression, and the presentation type reinforces that structure for the user. The control also enables the reader to read at his or her own pace.

To make a sensible choice among browsing strategies, a reader has to have some idea of the overall structure, complexity, or macrosyntax of an expression. This is one aspect of the very information the reader is attempting to acquire. The verbal reader needs a glance at, or summary of, the essential features of an expression in order to make that choice. The ability of prosody to impart the syntactic structure of an expression indicates the possibility of imparting an overview to a listener. In essence, by giving the listener the prosodic structure of a skilled speaker's utterance, the speaker reveals the algebraic structure. Just as spatial organization aids the parsing of a written expression, so can the pattern of pauses, pitch, and speed change in a spoken expression. This idea of "prosody without speech" can be achieved using nonspeech audio. These abstract representations of prosodic structure are called algebra earcons, based upon earcons as discussed above.

An interactive computer implementation of this reading method is currently being developed. The *Mathtalk* program can present the core of algebra notation to an arbitrary complexity. The speech style, based on Chang, is consistent and unambiguous. The unconstrained, unfolding, and staged release browsing strategies have also been implemented. Algebra prosody and algebra earcons have yet to be implemented.

The system as a whole should enable a listener to read an expression more actively. Selection of a browsing strategy based on the complexity of an expression presents a series of expression views best suited to convey the syntax of the expression. The prosody of algebra plays two roles in the system.

Once algebra has been transformed into an auditory format, as described, there remains the problem of providing the user with an interface through which to control access to the information. All the information of the visual format is retained. In fact, there is redundancy in that the same components of an expression can be viewed in different ways, using the alternative browsing strategies. Given that amount of information, the interface to it is necessarily going to be complex. A command language has been developed to enable the user to control the presentation of information. Two words make one command; the first is an action and the second a target. The initial letters of these command words are mapped mnemonically onto the keyboard. Action words include "next," "previous," "current," "start," and "quit." These actions work upon targets such as "character," "term," "level," "sub-expression," and "expression." This command language is universal within the system. For example, in the main menu, "next+expression" moves to the next expression in the list. The action "start" with the target "unfolding" will put that user into the browsing mode. The command "quit+expression" removes a user from a browsing mode.

In developing this system, wider questions of computer interaction by visually disabled users will have to be tackled. These include command selection, feedback, navigation, and orientation.

Presentation of information about the system by the system is difficult. To select a suitable command from a menu is necessarily slow in speech, where only one item is visible at a time. The reading process needs to be quick, and the command process (issue and feedback) needs to be as transparent as possible. A principle followed in this design is not to let issuing commands interfere with the presentation of the algebra. A careful design of the presentation should allow the spoken algebra to provide appropriate feedback for the user. For example, movement right would be associated with a relative fall in pitch, as is the case with a human speaker.

Nonspeech audio also has a role to play in indicating the start and end of levels and movement between levels. Nonspeech audio feedback for errors by earcons would decrease the need for disruptive speech messages.

The transient nature of speech means that review of preceding information is difficult. A consequence of this may be a lack of orientation, within both the system and a browsed expression. Suitable context-giving functions will be developed for the system. A combination of algebraic prosody, the browsing

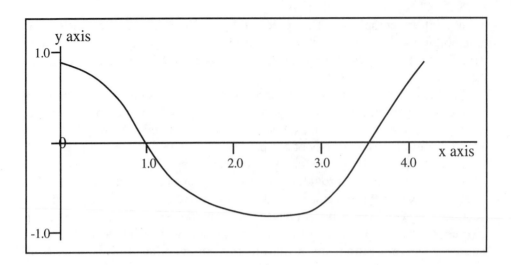

Figure 11.5. A typical line graph. This comprises a lot of information, but a sighted person is able to cope with all of it by focusing on whichever aspect is pertinent to his or her current needs.

functions themselves, and nonspeech audio should be able to ameliorate problems of orientation and navigation.

Another visual format for the presentation of mathematical information is the *line graph*. A diagram, such as the one in Figure 11.5, conveys a great deal of information. As with GUIs (and to a lesser extent algebra), part of the power of such displays is due to the fact that the user can select the portion of the information contained within it which is pertinent to current requirements. For instance, in order to answer certain queries it may be the point at which the curve crosses the *x* axis which is important, whereas in another context the minimum *y* value may be critical. Sound graphs (Mansur, Blattner, & Joy, 1985) are an attempt to provide access to such graphical information through the use of nonspeech sounds. The idea has been implemented as a software package (*Soundgraph*)[1] at the University of York (Pitt & Edwards, 1992).

The basic idea of a sound graph is that the *y* value of the curve should be represented by the pitch of a tone, the *x* axis essentially being represented by time. Graphs can be played to a listener, giving an indication of their shape, but they can also be examined interactively so that the user can locate points of interest, such as turning points. The coordinates of any point on the curve can be

[1] Soundgraph is available from the Research Centre for the Education of the Visually Handicapped, School of Education, University of Birmingham, PO Box 363, Birmingham, England B15 2TT.

obtained in speech. To make the package accessible to blind users, speech (through a standard screen reader) is also used as the basis of the interaction.

Soundgraph is multimodal in that it combines speech and nonspeech sounds. It also has a visual display. This was included in order to make the software usable by partially sighted (and indeed normally sighted) people. It turns out that this combination may be significant. Partially sighted people need aids which enable them to make full use of their residual vision. Hence most of them prefer not to use nonvisual interfaces (such as those which are purely speech based). In this case, however, they can use a visual interface (possibly with the assistance of a screen enlarger), but they also receive the auditory feedback, which seems to be a helpful augmentation.

The Soundgraph software was designed to be distributed to schools and colleges and to be accessible on as wide a range of computers as possible. It was therefore implemented on a PC, using no special graphics or add-on sound cards. That means that the visual display and sound output are crude. Work is continuing on the production of an enhanced version which will allow users who have a sound card the option of using it. This will allow the possibility of experimenting with further use of nonspeech sounds. For instance, a curve can be represented by a sound of varying pitch, as described above, but that sound can now be augmented by another note representing the first derivative of the function. This richer sound contains more information and makes it easier to locate turning points, for example.

Conclusions

Most of the work described in this chapter has been based on the use of sounds to replace visual communication in interfaces adapted for use by blind people. Several points are illustrated by these examples. The fact that no adaptation yet exists which gives the blind user equal access to applications with GUIs demonstrates that there is still a great deal to be done. Furthermore, the interfaces described are all crude in their use of sounds, but this merely reflects the current state of knowledge. There is a need for considerable research – at a quite fundamental level – into how sounds might better be used.

At present the auditory channel is not being used to its full potential capacity. At the same time, it has to be conceded that – even in ideal use – it does not have the broad bandwidth of vision. It is therefore apparent that greater use should be made of other nonvisual channels in adapting interfaces for blind users. Again some fundamental work is required to learn, first, how to communicate via these novel underutilized (within HCI, at least) channels and then how best to use them in combinations.

Acknowledgments

The work described in this chapter has been supported by various grants, including SERC Research Studentships 90310837 (Steve Brewster), 91308897 (Robert Stevens), and 92567838 (Ian Pitt); SERC Research Grant GR/E 71136; and an award from the Viscount Nuffield Auxiliary Fund. Further work has been supported by a Student Research Bursary from the Nuffield Foundation.

References

Alty J. L. (1991). Multimedia – What is it and how do we exploit it? In *People and computers VI: Proceedings of the HCI '91 Conference,* ed. D. Diaper and N. Hammond (pp. 31–46). Cambridge: Cambridge University Press.

Blattner, M. M., Sumikawa, D. A., and Greenberg, R. M. (1989). Earcons and icons: Their structure and common design principles, *Human–Computer Interaction, 4*(1): 11–44.

Bly, S. (1982). *Sound and computer information presentation,* PhD thesis, University of California, Davis.

Brewster, S. A. (1991). *Providing a model for the use of sound in user interfaces.* Technical Report YCS169. University of York, Department of Computer Science.

Buxton, W. (1989). Introduction to the special issue on nonspeech audio, *Human–Computer Interaction, 4*(1): 1–9.

Card, S. K., English, W. K., and Burr B. J. (1978). Evaluation of mouse, rate-controlled isometric joystick, step keys, and text keys for text selection on a CRT, *Ergonomics, 21*(8): 601–613.

Card, S. K., Moran, T. P., and Newell, A. (1983). *The psychology of human–computer interaction.* Hillsdale, NJ: Erlbaum.

Chang, L. A. (1983). *Handbook for spoken mathematics (Larry's Speakeasy).* Technical report. Livermore, CA: Lawrence Livermore Laboratory.

Döhrn, C. (1984). *The Speech-Pad: Direct manipulation computer access for the visually disabled based on speech and touch.* Unpublished MSc thesis, University of Calgary.

Edwards, A. D. N. (1989a). Modelling blind users' interactions with an auditory computer interface. *International Journal of Man–Machine Studies, 30*(5): 575–589.

Edwards, A. D. N. (1989b). Soundtrack: An auditory interface for blind users. *Human–Computer Interaction, 4*(1): 45–66.

Edwards, A. D. N. (1991a). *Speech synthesis: Technology for disabled people.* London: Paul Chapman.

Edwards, A. D. N. (1991b). *Evaluation of Outspoken software for blind users.* Technical Report YCS150. University of York, Department of Computer Science.

Edwards, A. D. N. (1992). Redundancy and adaptability. In *Multimedia interface design,* ed. A. D. N. Edwards and S. Holland. Heidelberg: Springer-Verlag (pp. 145–156).

Gaver, W. W. (1989). The SonicFinder: An interface that uses auditory icons. *Human–Computer Interaction, 4*(1): 67–94.

Gaver, W. W., Smith, R. B., and O'Shea, T. (1991). Effective sounds in complex systems: The Arkola simulation. In *Reaching through Technology: Proceedings of the ACM Conference Chi '91,* ed. S. P. Robertson, G. M. Olson, and J. S. Olson, New York: ACM Press (pp. 85–90).

Halliday, M. K. (1970). *A course in spoken English: intonation.* Oxford: Oxford University Press.

Jones, S. D. and Furner, S. M. (1989). The construction of audio icons and information cues for human computer dialogues. In *Contemporary Ergonomics: Proceedings of the Ergonomic Society's Annual Conference,* ed. E. D. Megaw (pp. 436–441). London: Taylor and Frances.

Kirshner, D. (1989). The visual syntax of algebra. *Journal for Research into Mathematics Education,. 20*(3):274–287.

Lewis, C. (1981). Cognitive skill in algebra. In *Skills and their acquisition,* ed. J. R. Anderson. Hillsdale, NJ: Erlbaum.

Mansur, D. L., Blattner, M. M., and Joy, K. I. (1985). Sound-Graphs: A numerical data analysis method for the blind. *Journal of Medical Systems, 9*:163–174.

Mayes, J. T., Draper, S. W., McGregor, A. M., and Oatley, K. (1988). Information flow in a user interface: The effect of experience and context on the recall of Macwrite screens. In *People and Computers IV: Proceedings of the Fourth Conference of the British Computer Society Human–Computer Interaction Specialist Group*, ed. D. M. Jones and R. Winder (pp. 275–290). Cambridge: Cambridge University Press.

Petrie, H., Heinila, J., and Ekola, H. (1993). A comparative evaluation of computer input devices for blind users. In *Proceedings of Ecart 2.* Hoensbroek, Netherlands: Ecart. p. II.

Pitt, I. J., and Edwards, A. D. N. (1992). *Final report on the Nuffield Project: Making line graphs accessible to blind students.* Unpublished report. University of York, Department of Computer Science.

Schwerdtfeger, R. S. (1991, December). Making the GUI talk, *Byte*, pp. 118–128.

Smith, S., Grinstein, G. G., and Bergeron, R. D. (1990). Stereophonic and surface sound generation for exploratory data analysis, In *Empowering people: Proceedings of CHI'90,* ed. J. C. Chew and J. Whiteside. Reading, MA: Addison-Wesley, pp.125–132.

Wenzel, E. M, (1992). Three-dimensional virtual acoustic displays. In *Multimedia interface design,* ed. M. M. Blattner and R. B. Dannenberg. Reading, MA: Addison-Wesley, pp. 257–288.

12

Travel alternatives for mobility impaired people: The Surrogate Electronic Traveler (*Set*)

Robert C. Williges and Beverly H. Williges

Introduction

Information work

The availability of work involving the manipulation of information is increasing rapidly. One estimate suggests that 50% of the current workforce in the United States is involved in information oriented work and that over 38 million computer workplaces are available. By the year 2020 information workers are expected to increase to 65% of the workforce (Giuliano, 1982). The information revolution is changing the nature of work from manual materials handling to computer based activities where application programs are used to manipulate information. The impact on job requirements is substantial since the primary focus of this computer based work is not programming but other activities, such as word processing, database retrieval, drawing, statistical analysis, and spreadsheet development. The workplace is becoming an electronic office that is computer controlled and computer managed (Naisbitt, 1982). In addition, businesses are becoming increasingly team oriented (Johansen, 1988).

In terms of electronic offices, current technology is in place to facilitate information work. Individual workstations can be networked to tie together workers within the same office or building and workers located anywhere in the world. In addition to the networking of these workstations, current communication technology allows integration of computers with voice and video conferencing. Together these technologies are used in electronic offices for the management and communication of information.

Employment impact for disabled workers

Of the 12 million working age Americans with disabilities, more than 8.5 million are unemployed. More than half of these individuals indicate that their disability wholly prevents employment. Only 35% of the disabled population participates in the labor force as compared with 88% of the able-bodied. In many cases one can assume that were it not for the disability, these individuals could be employed productively. In fact, disabled individuals who are employed hold jobs and earn incomes similar to their nondisabled counterparts. Many disabling conditions occur in persons under 35 years of age, leaving persons who are relatively young to face a lifetime of disability. These individuals represent a large untapped resource for American business (Bowe, 1987; U.S. Bureau of the Census, 1982, 1985).

Disability expenditures are costly. From 1978 to 1985 the cost of worker's compensation benefits in the United States tripled, with little impact on the injured worker's income. This cost does not include the financial loss to society from reduced productivity and the lower tax base that results when part of the population is unemployed. Significant economic savings could be realized if employment of disabled people were facilitated.

Because so many jobs require the manipulation of information rather than materials, it is essential to provide an approach to developing an office environment compatible with specific special needs of workers. Several accessibility considerations must be addressed in designing the electronic office for this population of workers. Current federal legislation speaks to this issue. In October of 1986 the U.S. Congress reauthorized the Rehabilitation Act of 1973 as amended by Section 508 of Public Law 99-506, which mandates that computers must be equally accessible to able-bodied and disabled workers in the electronic office environment. The General Services Administration issued an initial set of guidelines, and procurement procedures became effective September 30, 1988. This legislation should influence the design of electronic office hardware and software in that the capabilities and limitations of disabled workers must be considered (U.S. General Services Administration, 1988).

However, people with physical disabilities also must be concerned with obstacles to mobility and travel required in work related activities. Beginning in July 1992, the Americans with Disabilities Act (ADA) covers all businesses with at least 25 employees. Among other provisions the ADA legislation requires employers to make reasonable accommodation for disabled workers. Complying with the new federal law could be costly for some employers unless low cost accommodations that yield productive employees are available. Specific areas of the ADA legislation include reasonable accommodation in terms of employment, public accommodations and transportation (U.S. Senate, 1990).

As early as 1978 Overby (1978) discussed the importance of computer telecommunications technology in bringing jobs to people with disabilities. Electronic alternatives to solve mobility problems for workers with physical disabilities are finally becoming available. There are two approaches that can be taken to address mobility problems. First, remote work facilities can be established for these individuals to minimize commuting time and avoid the inconvenience of traveling back and forth to an office (M. H. Olson, 1983). Second, surrogate travel can be used in some situations to minimize the need for

Table 12.1. *Conferencing technology*

Audio Terminals	Cukier, 1986; Olgren & Parker, 1983
Bridges	Cukier, 1986
Telephone conferences	Christie, 1985
Voice messaging and annotation	Parker, 1987; Rice & Shook, 1990
Audiographics (facsimile, electronic blackboards, remote slide projectors)	Egido, 1990; Hiltz, 1984
Slow scan video (still video snapshots)	Cukier, 1986
Satellite broadcast	Cukier, 1986
Conferencing theaters	Cukier, 1986
Electronic mail	Hiltz & Turoff, 1978
Computer networking	Gido, 1985; McAleese, 1989
Computer-supported cooperative work	M. H. Olson & Bly, 1991

actual travel. With surrogate travel, only the information travels, not the employee.

Purpose

The purpose of this chapter is to review conferencing technology that can support surrogate travel, describe the hardware–software interface design of an electronic alternative to physical travel, and discuss two research challenges relating to electronic office analysis and communication research supporting shared work activities.

Traditional conferencing technology

Current conferencing technology is used for training, electronic meetings, and shared work. The hardware technology can be divided into audio, video, and computer conferencing. Each of these areas provides a variety of technological implementations, as shown in Table 12.1. Together these three technology areas can provide an electronic office for information management and communication worldwide. These conferencing technologies can be used to develop a travel alternative for the mobility impaired office worker.

Audio conferencing

Audio information exchange can be asynchronous using video messaging hardware/software, or synchronous using teleconferencing. Rice and Shook (1988) noted that audio communication was most useful when there was a need to retain affect in communication. Audio conferencing in the form of conference telephone calls is common. For people with physical impairments, speaker telephones are quite helpful. Audio teleconferences are often used for discussion among a small group of colleagues who know each other well. However, the use of audio teleconferencing must deal with various types of communication protocols among speakers, such as the order in which people talk and speaker identification. Further, sound quality may be unacceptable once the audio conference exceeds three or four participants.

Video conferencing

Video conferencing is available in several forms. Asynchronous information transmission can include an exchange of videotapes when there is a need to depict real-time motion. A facsimile of hardcopy graphics or pictorials transmitted over telephone channels can also be used. Telewriters such as AT&T's electronic blackboard transmit to remote monitors graphics drawn on an electronically sensitive tablet. Sometimes these forms of communication are referred to as *audiographic teleconferencing,* since they involve the telephone communication link and the transmission of pictorial materials (Egido, 1990). Synchronous video conferencing usually involves television transmission from a teleconferencing center through uplink to a satellite and a downlink to another teleconferencing theater. Real-time television transmission, however, requires a very high communication bandwidth and is relatively expensive. Recent advances in conferencing technology combine video and computer technology to allow for virtual workspaces (e.g. the *Cruiser* project at Bell Communications Research and *Polyscope* and *Vrooms* at Rank Xerox EuroPARC). These systems provide audio and video using a virtual space metaphor or video window to encourage casual communication among workers who are physically dispersed (Borning & Travers, 1991).

Computer conferencing

A third medium considered for conferencing is the computer. The existence of computerized workstations makes this approach feasible because of low cost, availability, and processing power. Asynchronous types of computer communication are widespread. Electronic mail is readily accepted and used in modern electronic offices today for rapid message transmission. Finhold, Sproull, and Kiesler (1990) reported that ad hoc work groups that frequently used electronic mail outperformed work groups that did not use computer communication. In addition, electronic bulletin boards and conferences have been used to provide information exchange for a group of people sharing a common interest. However, current interactive technology in computers opens up many possibilities for synchronous conferencing.

Advances in hypermedia allow one to consider different strategies and different alternatives for mixing media and finding flexible pathways through information structures. *Ribis* is a real time group hypertext system where a distributed set of users can simultaneously browse and/or edit multiple views of a hypertext database augmented by voice communication through a conference call using speaker phones (Rein & Ellis, 1991). Digital video interactive technology can be used to digitize video signals and present them on digital computers. This media has probably been used most effectively with geographically proximal groups to enhance presentations to small groups. The presentation is made via a computer that is controlled locally or long distance through networking and modems.

Synchronous computer conferencing is beginning to be used in computer supported cooperative work (CSCW) environments for tasks such as jointly authoring a paper or putting together a presentation where the individuals involved are at different work facilities. Current CSCW research encompasses a large body of scientific research and innovation in technology and software: for example three-dimensional CSCW tools to support computer conferencing in multiuser virtual reality systems. (For more information, see papers published in *CSCW '90*, 1990; Turner & Kraut, 1992; and *Human Factors in Computing Systems*, 1993.)

True computer conferencing differs from electronic mail in that participants share files that change dynamically based on the contributions of conference participants. Issues that must be addressed in the design of such systems include the dialogue for the user interface, access control, concurrence control, and the ability to move data in and out of the conference environment (Sarin & Greif, 1985). The NSF *Expres* project is an attempt to create a system for the interchange of editable documents (including animation, video, and voice) using a range of hardware and software. A limited amount of real time simultaneous conferencing capability is built into the system so that individuals at separate work sites can collaborate on a single document. Bikson and Eveland (1990) point out that the unique capability of electronic technology to integrate data processing, text processing, and communication provides new opportunities for information sharing and coordination in group work not available with other technologies.

Surrogate Electronic Traveler

At some point in the future, teleconferencing facilities may be ubiquitous and follow standard interfacing specifications. In the interim, electronic travel may be facilitated by providing the mobility impaired office worker with a set of software and hardware components that can be shipped to the meeting site. Based on the variety of audio, video, and computer conferencing alternatives, an appropriate mix of these existing technologies can be configured into a portable, low cost interface to allow remote participation in meetings. The resulting device can provide an electronic alternative to physical travel. This system is called the Surrogate Electronic Traveler (*Set*). Whenever conferencing capabilities are needed, the Set is shipped to a meeting site. Consequently, only the information, not the mobility impaired individual, travels. The worker remains at a remote site such as a home office and participates in CSCW activities through tele-conferencing technology.

Several specific requirements of the CSCW environment exist for surrogate traveling by disabled users. The Set would be used primarily for planned rather than casual communications among colleagues. The resulting configuration must use a low cost computer that is affordable to users, who often have quite limited financial resources. The configuration must support a variety of computer platforms in order to provide the most flexibility. In addition, a variety of computer media must be available to support a large number of presentation requirements. And, finally, the CSCW configuration must accommodate the special needs of the disabled user in terms of accessibility for presentation development and delivery.

Set configuration

The Set configuration is a physical interface based on specific design goals to facilitate electronic management and communication of information. As shown in Figure 12.1, both the communication requirements and the design goals must be considered in determining the final hardware and software of a Set configuration.

Communication requirements. In order to design the Set configuration, several issues related to communication tasks, media, and hardware and software requirements need to be addressed, as shown in Figure 12.1. Communication tasks include issues such as support for structured versus unstructured communications, two party versus multiparty conversations, and required type of communication (i.e., presentation, discussion, persuasion, etc.). Various computer media are available to support a Set configuration. For example, requirements for text, video, graphics, picture, animation, sounds, voice, gesturing, and pointing need to be specified.

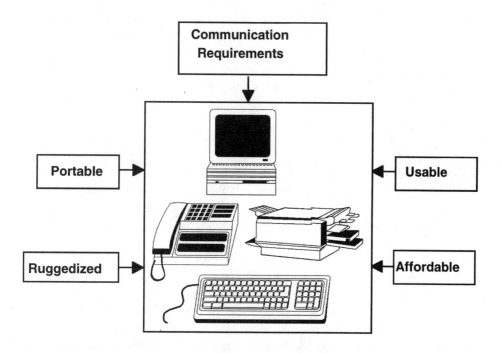

Figure 12.1. Design characteristics of the Set hardware/software configuration.

Requirements for communication software and hardware also need to be detailed. Special purpose application software is being developed to support computer based conferencing. For example, software to allow synchronous control of a remote computer, presentation software, group consensus software, and groupware applications to support simultaneous editing of computer files across several users are being developed to support CSCW activities. This special purpose software, as well as standard application software to support word processing, graphics, databases, spreadsheets, and so on, needs to be considered in the Set configuration to support the necessary level of communication.

Network cabling, such as satellite television, ethernet, fiber optics, and twisted pair, need to be specified to support the appropriate bandwidth requirements. Telephone configurations such as speaker phones, computer modem speeds, and telephone switching protocols (e.g., PBX, ISDN, ATM, and SL-1) also need to be considered. Multimedia computer terminals, fax machines, printers, computer projection systems, electronic presentation boards, and electronic conference tables need to be specified as needed to support the appropriate level of communication interface for a Set.

Design goals. Figure 12.1 depicts four major design goals for a Set configuration. The equipment must be portable, that is easy to move, self-contained, and requiring a minimum of space. It must be ruggedized to withstand shipping. To minimize cost, existing technology should be used. Finally, an overriding design goal is that the configuration must be usable in terms of ease of assembly and operation.

Hardware and software. The resulting hardware and software of a Set configuration is a combination of a microcomputer, modem, software application programs, and communication support tools. Specifically, the hardware may include such components as a speaker telephone, external speakers, telephone modem, microcomputer, color monitor, CD-rom, videocassette recorder/player, fax machine, and laser printer. Software includes standard application software as well as special purpose synchronous communication software.

The choice of appropriate hardware and software is not straightforward. In fact, Williges, Williges, and Koushik (1993) suggested that an expert system may be useful in configuring a Set for a particular user. The advice from the expert system needs to include a central database of currently available networking capabilities, software, workstation configurations, and cost data. This central database needs to be combined with information on current office configurations, required level of interaction, structure of the remote meeting, and special needs related to the disabilities of the user in order to develop a composite knowledge base for the expert system adviser.

Set design process

The Set configuration is a mixture of currently available audio, video, and computer conferencing technology. The overall design requires a user centered systems approach. As shown in Figure 12.2, such a systems approach involves user participation throughout the needs analysis, the initial as well as revised designs of the workstation, and usability testing. The Set is designed in a closed loop, iterative fashion to result in a truly workable operational system. Williges, Williges, and Elkerton (1987) noted that iterative design should include the three major stages of initial design followed by formative and then summative evaluation. They summarized a variety of methods and techniques which can be used in each of these iterative design stages.

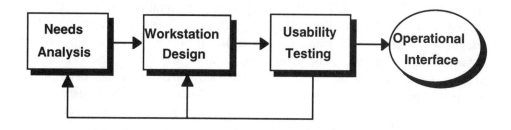

Figure 12.2. Systems approach to the iterative design of Set.

Set evaluation

Research is needed to determine the proper mix of audio, video, and computer conferencing modalities. For example, Green and Williges (1993) evaluated writing efficiency of dyads using three alternative communication media (i.e., audio only, audio plus video, and face to face) with and without the use of group editing software. Participants preferred having the groupware editor; but the face to face video views may not be necessary in highly structured communication tasks. Other researchers have evaluated task centered versus face to face video views and have concluded that there is little support for face to face views, but participants did use views that gave access to shared work objects (Gaver, Sellen, Heath, & Luff, 1993). The interaction of conferencing media alternatives with communication requirements in group work must be evaluated in the design of the Set. Of central importance is the effectiveness of the Set as the only electronic member of an otherwise person to person conference.

A simulated electronic office environment provides the most flexibility for conducting the subsequent communication research in a controlled research laboratory setting. This simulation includes a flexible arrangement of individual workstations and small group working conferences with a facade of alternative audio, video, and computer communication links. Standard benchmark tasks representative of electronic office environments can be used to facilitate research comparisons. Several dimensions must be considered in the evaluation of the Set. They include the level of expertise required to use the system, the ease of installation, the size of the group that can be accommodated, the flexibility of the system for use with various types of group work, and the cost of implementation.

Considerable support for the notion that the Set might be an effective means of remote communication for the mobility impaired employee stems from the success of Media Space, used to connect Xerox design teams in Palo Alto and Portland laboratories of the Systems Concept Laboratory (SCL). Media Space consisted of a network of video, audio, and computing technologies. The cross-site technological connection started with hard copy mail and individual audio (telephone). Over time the following were added: group audio (speaker telephones), 56K computer data link for a shared file and E-mail, a 56K video data link for group video, computer screen sharing for shared windows, and a video switch to provide individual video. The distributed design team determined a set of support tools necessary for adequate interaction. These researchers concluded that the SCL experience was not less than face to face interaction but something different that needs further exploring (M. H. Olson & Bly, 1991).

Research challenges

Two related research challenges need to be addressed before the Set becomes a reality. First, a comprehensive taxonomy of electronic office tasks needs to be developed in order to determine the appropriate information management and communication activities which can be performed by a Set. Second, aspects of group work which are most amenable to the Set need to be investigated.

Electronic office analysis

An analysis of information work requirements coupled with consideration of the proper mix of electronic media is necessary to yield a system that enhances work related interpersonal communication. The electronic office job analysis must provide a taxonomy of information work activities, the resulting communication requirements, and an assessment of the capabilities of the physically impaired worker. As shown in Figure 17.1, Casali and Williges (1990) provide a general model for selecting the appropriate computer hardware/software accommodative aid for users with special needs. This model couples the information task activity with the user's residual capacity in order to select the appropriate accommodation. Although Casali describes a general approach for assessing residual motor capacity in Chapter 17, a detailed task analysis of electronic offices is still needed to use the Casali and Williges (1990) selection model.

Unfortunately, no generally accepted detailed taxonomy of information work activities exists. Helander (1985) suggested that a taxonomy of electronic offices must take into account types of office interaction, human attributes, office tasks, and office automation tools. Czaja (1987) provided a preliminary evaluation of tasks involved in office automation. These tasks include document preparation, meeting and conferencing, filing and retrieving, communicating, decision making, and transacting. Additionally she recommended office automation features that are best suited to perform these information tasks.

Short, Williams, and Christie (1976) developed a taxonomy of meetings based on verbal descriptions of meetings provided by management personnel in business and government. The resulting taxonomy involves three dimensions: (1) function of the meeting (task allocation, information giving, dismissal of an employee, presentation of a report, problem discussions, appraisal of services/ products, review of subordinate's work, tactical decision making, advice giving); (2) activities of the meeting (conflict, gathering background information, problem solving, bargaining, work related gossip, generating ideas); and (3) atmosphere of the meeting (informal, cautious, constructive, or angry). A review of 1,791 face to face meetings (ibid.) confirmed that the two most common types of meetings were to solve a problem or exchange information. Note that this taxonomy includes only managerial meetings and does not consider intellectual or design group work.

As shown in Table 12.2, information work involves the broad categories of both the management and the communication of information, and a preliminary taxonomy of task activities can be stated for each category. Such a taxonomy needs to be developed in detail and validated across a variety of information work applications in order to provide a better understanding of potentially effective electronic information support systems. The information task activities most directly related to group work should receive primary consideration to evaluate the possibilities for electronic traveling.

Group work

Working in face to face groups involves (1) open communication where every member of the group is connected simultaneously with every other member via all modalities; (2) no response lag in communication; (3) all members of the group known to all other members; and (4) communication protocol governed by a culturally established set of rules (McGrath, 1990). This type of proximal work group is typical of many work situations. However, when one or more members of the work group are not located with other members of the group, communication must occur using some alternate form of communication media, as shown in Table 12.3.

Notice that each of the alternate communication media is distance spanning, but they vary in the time domain and in level of communication or interactiveness. The use of these alternate media can modify group communication in many ways, including the structure of the group, the information value of communication constrained by restricted modality media, the rules followed for communication protocol, and the impact of time lags on effective communication. For example, research indicates that electronic work groups have more difficulty initiating and planning work than do face to face work groups (Galegher & Kraut, 1990) and that group members participate more equally than do the members of groups meeting face to face (Kiesler, Siegel, & McGuire, 1984).

If a person with a mobility impairment is the only remote member of the group, new methods will be needed to achieve full integration of face to face and electronic participants in information work activities. Krauss and Fussell (1990)

Table 12.2. *Preliminary taxonomy of information tasks and task activities performed in electronic offices*

I. Information management

1. Planning
   a. Notetaking/reminders
   b. Appointments/meetings
   c. Work scheduling
   d. Budgeting
   e. Decision support

2. Control
   a. Environmental control
   b. Security/priority
   c. Purchasing/billing
   d. Payroll/personnel appointments

3. Search and retrieval
   a. Bibliographic databases
   b. Equipment inventory
   c. Personnel records
   d. Document filing

4. Analysis
   a. Spreadsheet layout
   b. Statistical data
   c. Financial/ accounting

5. Design
   a. Drafting
   b. Computer-aided design
   c. Computer-aided engineering
   d. Architectural design
   e. Simulation/modeling
   f. Software development

6. Document preparation
   a. Outlining
   b. Word processing
   c. Graphics/charting
   d. Drawing/painting
   e. Scanning
   f. Page layout
   g. Copying
   h. Printing
   i. Mailing

II. Information communication

1. Presentation
   a. Slide/overhead preparation
   b. Lecture presentation
   c. Multimedia preparation

2. Conference
   a. Audio conferencing
   b. Video conferencing
   c. Computer conferencing

Table 12.3. *Communication media appropriate for group work*

Communication media	Level of communication	Time domain	Space domain
Face to face groups	Two-way	Synchronous	Proximal
Letters	Two-way	Asynchronous	Distance spanning
Videotapes	Two-way	Asynchronous	Distance spanning
Reports or books	One-way	Asynchronous	Distance spanning
Fax transmission	Two-way	Asynchronous	Distance spanning
Television broadcasts	One-way	Synchronous	Distance spanning
Electronic mail	Two-way	Asynchronous	Distance spanning
Voice mail	Two-way	Asynchronous	Distance spanning
Computer conference	Two-way	Asynchronous	Distance spanning
Two-way closed circuit TV	Two-way	Synchronous	Distance spanning
Telephone conference	Two-way	Synchronous	Distance spanning
Online computer conference	Two-way	Synchronous	Distance spanning

Source: McGrath, 1990.

indicate that one component of group work essential for effective communication is mutual knowledge or common ground. This mutual knowledge is used to formulate messages appropriate for the knowledge level of various group members, to establish a common semantic basis for communication, and to integrate the distributed knowledge for problem solving. The establishment of common ground may be more difficult when most of the group have face to face contact and have established a "mini-culture" unknown to the remote participant(s). The remote participants also have little opportunity for informal communication and limited opportunity for spontaneous communication. Allen (1977) reported that as geographic distance between potential communicators increased, the number of communications decreased logarithmically. Even when group members are co-located, as in the *Colab* project at Xerox Parc, users required tools to coordinate their conversational actions and to specify the objects and actions they were discussing in the workspace (Tatar, Foster, & Bobrow, 1991). These tools may be even more critical when some group members are remotely located.

Some of the dialogue issues facing designers of groupware include (1) a choice between personalized and *wysiwis* (what you see is what I see) views of the work, (2) how and when to notify users of the actions of other members of the group, (3) how to degrade to a single-user system, and (4) whether to embed aspects of social protocol such as conversational turn taking into the software. Examples of other communication research issues that need to be addressed include the matching of the type of group work with specific conferencing technology, the effect of time lags on communication effectiveness in both synchronous and asynchronous forms of group communication, the role of interpersonal content in group work, and the usability of software interfaces that facilitate shared work activities and support appropriate social interaction protocols.

Conclusions

Electronic travel provides an alternative for the mobility impaired information worker, and the Set provides one configuration for accomplishing this travel. Research dealing with the development of a taxonomy of information tasks in automated offices, characteristics of group work, and the appropriate design of the Set configuration and its use in group work are needed before this alternative becomes a reality. Electronic travel by mobility impaired employees should not be viewed as a direct substitute for face to face meetings. In many cases the availability of electronic travel will mean the difference between participation in group work and exclusion of the disabled employee from such work. Barriers to group work participation not only discriminate against the disabled work but reduce the productivity of the overall workforce.

Acknowledgments

Support for this research was provided in part by a contract from the Center for Innovative Technology of the Commonwealth of Virginia and a grant from the Core Research Program of Virginia Polytechnic Institute and State University. The financial support from these two sponsors for this activity is gratefully acknowledged. The authors also appreciate the helpful comments made by Sara A. Bly on a preliminary draft of this chapter.

References
Allen, T. J. (1977). *Managing the flow of technology.* Cambridge, MA: MIT Press.
Bikson, T. K., and Eveland, J. D. (1990). The interplay of work group structures and computer support. In *Intellectual teamwork,* ed. J. Galegher, R. E. Kraut, and C. Egido (pp. 245–290). Hillsdale, NJ: Erlbaum.

Borning, A. and Travers, M. (1991). Two approaches to casual interaction over computer and video networks. In *Reaching through technology: Proceedings of the ACM Conference Chi '91,* ed. S. P. Robertson, G. M. Olson, and J. S. Olson. New York: ACM Press (pp. 13–19).

Bowe, F. (1987). Making computers accessible to disabled people. *Technology Review, 90*(1), 52–59.

Casali, S., and Williges, R. (1990). Databases of accommodative aids for computer users with disabilities. *Human Factors, 32*(4), 407–422.

Christie, B. (1985). *Human factors of information technology in the office.* New York: Wiley.

CSCW '90. (1990). *Proceedings of the Conference on Computer-Supported Cooperative Work.* New York: Association for Computing Machinery.

Cukier, W. (1986). Teleconferencing. In *The ergonomics payoff: Designing the electronic office,* ed. R. Lueder (pp. 110–131). Toronto: Holt, Rinehart and Winston of Canada,.

Czaja, S. J. (1987). Human factors in office automation. In *Handbook of human factors,* ed. G. Salvendy (pp. 1587–1616). New York: Wiley.

Egido, C. (1990). Teleconferencing as a technology to support cooperative work: Its possibilities and limitations. In *Intellectual teamwork.* ed. J. Galegher, R. E. Kraut, and C. Egido (pp. 351–371). Hillsdale, NJ: Erlbaum.

Finhold, T., Sproull, L. and Kiesler, S. (1990). Communication and performance in ad hoc task groups. In *Intellectual teamwork.* ed. J. Galegher, R. E. Kraut, and C. Egido (pp. 291–325). Hillsdale, NJ: Erlbaum.

Galegher, J., and Kraut, R. E. (1990). Computer-mediated communication for intellectual teamwork: A field experiment in group writing. *Proceedings of CSCW 90,* 65–78.

Gaver, W. Sellen, A., Heath, C., and Luff, P. (1993). One is not enough: Multiple views in a media space. In *Bridges between worlds: Proceedings of Interchi '93* ed. S. Ashlund, K. Mullet, A Henderson, E. Hollnagel, and T. White (pp. 335–341) Reading, MA: Addison-Wesley.

Gido, J. (1985). *An introduction to project planning* (2nd ed.). New York: Industrial Press.

Giuliano, V. E. (1982). The mechanization of office work. *Scientific American, 247*(3):148–165.

Green, C. A., and Williges, R. C. (1993). Using a group editor with alternative communication media in a co-authoring environment. In *Proceedings of the Human Factors and Ergonomics Society 37th Annual Meeting.* Seattle: Human Factors and Ergonomics Society.

Helander, M. G. (1985). Emerging office automation systems. *Human Factors, 27*: 3–20.

Hiltz, S. R. (1984). *Online communities: a case study of the office of the future.* Norwood, NJ: Ablex.

Hiltz, S. R. and Turoff, M. (1978). *Network nation: human communication via computer.* Reading MA: Addison-Wesley.

Interchi '93. (1993). *Bridges between worlds: Proceedings of Interchi '93,* ed. S. Ashlund, K. Mullet, A Henderson, E. Hollnagel, and T. White. New York: ACM Press.

Johansen, R. (1988). *Groupware: Computer support for business teams.* New York: Macmillan.

Kiesler, S., Siegel, J., and McGuire, T. W. (1984). Social psychological aspects of computer-mediated communication. *American Psychologist, 39*: 1123–1134.

Krauss, R. M., and Fussell, S. R. (1990). Mutual knowledge and communicative effectiveness. In *Intellectual teamwork.* ed. J. Galegher, R. E. Kraut, and C. Egido (pp. 111–145) Hillsdale, NJ: Erlbaum.

McAleese, R. (1989). *Hypertext: Theory into practice.* Norwood, NJ: Ablex.

McGrath, J. (1990). Time matters in groups. In *Intellectual teamwork.* ed. J. Galegher, R. E. Kraut, and C. Egido (pp. 23–61). Hillsdale, NJ: Erlbaum.

Naisbitt, J. (1982). *Megatrends.* New York: Warner.

Olgren, C., and Parker, I. (1983). *Teleconferencing technology and applications.* Dedham, MA: Artech House.

Olson, G. M. and Atkins, D. E. (1990). Supporting collaboration with advanced multimedia electronic mail: The NSF EXPRES Project. In *Intellectual teamwork.* ed. J. Galegher, R. E. Kraut, and C. Egido (pp. 429–451). Hillsdale, NJ: Erlbaum.

Olson, M. H. (1983). Remote office work: Changing work patterns in space and time. *Communications of the ACM, 26*: 182–187.

Olson, M. H., and Bly, S. A. (1991). The Portland experience: A report on a distributed research group. *International Journal of Man–Machine Studies, 34*: 211–228.

Overby, C. M. (1978). Some human factors and related socio-technical issues in bringing jobs to disabled persons via computer-telecommunications technology. *Human Factors, 20*(3), 349–364.

Parker, M. F. (1987). *The practical guide to voice mail.* Berkeley, CA: Osborne McGraw-Hill.

Rein, G. L., and Ellis, C. A. (1991). rIBIS: A real-time group hypertext system. *International Journal of Man–Machine Studies, 34*: 349–367.

Rice, R. E., and Shook, D. (1988). Usage of, access to and outcomes from an electronic messaging system. *ACM Transactions on Information Systems, 6*: 255–276.

Rice, R. E., and Shook, D. E. (1990). Voice messaging, coordination and communication. In *Intellectual teamwork.* ed. J. Galegher, R. E. Kraut, and C. Egido (pp. 327–350) Hillsdale, NJ: Erlbaum.

Sarin, S., and Greif, I. (1985). Computer based real-time conferencing systems. *IEEE Computer, 18*(10), 33–45.

Short, J., Williams, E., and Christie, B. (1976). *The social psychology of telecommunications.* New York: Wiley.

Tatar, D. G., Foster, G., and Bobrow, D. G. (1991). Design for conversation: Lessons from Cognoter. *International Journal of Man–Machine Studies*, *34*: 185–209.

Turner, J., and Kraut, R. (eds.) (1992). *Proceedings of the Conference on Computer-Supported Cooperative Work.* New York: Association for Computing Machinery.

U.S. Bureau of the Census. (1982). *Current population reports,* No. 922. Washington, DC: GPO.

U.S. Bureau of the Census. (1985). *Statistical abstract of the United States: 1900–1985.* Washington, DC: GPO.

U.S. General Services Administration. (1988). *Managing end user computing for users with disabilities.* Information Resources Management Division, 1. Washington, DC: GPO.

U.S. Senate. (1990). Subcommittee on Disability Policy. *Americans with Disabilities Act of 1990.* Washington, DC: GPO.

Williges, R. C., Williges, B. H., and Elkerton, J. (1987). Software interface design. In *Handbook of human factors*, ed. G. Salvendy (pp. 1416–1449) New York: Wiley.

Williges, R. C., Williges, B. H., and Koushik, G. (1993, August). *Assistive technology to facilitate surrogate electronic traveling for physically disabled workers.* Paper presented at the American Psychological Association Symposium on Overcoming Barriers to Work: Interactions of Social and Technical Systems, Toronto.

13

Input and integration:
Enabling technologies for disabled users

Robin Shaw, Anne Loomis, and E. Crisman

Introduction

To date the field of HCI research has largely bypassed the issues involved in making computers accessible to handicapped people. This limits the promise that modern technology holds for people with disabilities. Not only can dedicated control devices and adaptable software help handicapped users gain access to computers but the computer can also be pressed into service to help disabled people attain new measures of freedom and efficiency in their daily and professional activities.

Our objective has been to explore and expand the possible uses of the computer in control systems for people with severe physical disabilities. At the most fundamental level, disabled users have far more limited means of interacting with the computer than do most people. Common input devices such as the mouse and the keyboard are inaccessible to people with such disabilities as high level quadriplegia, advanced multiple sclerosis, and central motor control dysfunction. Thus it is necessary first to provide disabled users with an appropriate input device. Yet alternative input devices alone, even the most sophisticated, are not sufficient to allow disabled people to use existing mass market applications; very few are adapted for anything but mouse or keyboard input.

Software, as a means of transforming input to output, provides the ideal mechanism for extending and customizing the possible range of binary inputs available from current input devices. As well, it is through software that a single piece of hardware, the computer, is transformed into a powerful integrated system able to accept input from a variety of different sources and, in turn, direct that input to control multiple peripheral output devices. Applying existing software and hardware technology to the design of control systems for disabled users will not only improve the comfort and flexibility of systems available but will provide a dramatic increase in the range of activities currently possible for disabled individuals.

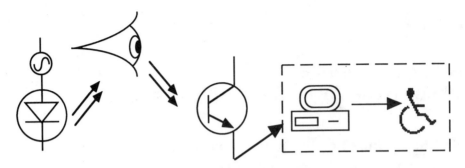

Figure 13.1. Diagram of basic EWCI concept. The state of each eyelid is detected by a pair of infrared detectors (infrared light is reflected off the corner of each eye by IR diode-transistor detection). This information is fed to the computer. The computer analyzes the state of each eyelid over time to interpret possible commands and issue the corresponding output directive to the wheelchair.

In this chapter we describe the *Eye Wink Control Interface* (EWCI). The unit is designed to enable severely disabled persons to control mechanical and electrical devices by using eye winks of varying duration. Sequences of left and right eye winks detected through infrared eyelid reflections are used as input to a battery powered portable computer. The control software serves to expand the range of this otherwise simple input device, dramatically increasing the range of possible commands. The computer interprets the sequences and issues the corresponding control signals to the device (see Figure 13.1). Initially we have focused on integrating the EWCI with a powered wheelchair. In a proof-of-principle study, a prototype system was developed and tested with two subjects: a person with C3–4 quadriplegia[1] and a stroke victim with "locked-in syndrome" who is restricted to voluntary control of a single eyelid (Crisman, Loomis, Shaw, & Laszewski, in press).

Together the EWCI and its associated control software and the user interface provide a concrete paradigm for exploring a more centralized role for the computer in systems developed for disabled people. Ultimately we intend to extend the EWCI system to provide users with access to computer software and to centralize environmental controls. We are investigating the use of graphical user interfaces to create control modules for many different types of peripheral

---

[1] A condition of "C3–4 quadriplegia" indicates paralysis of all four limbs as a result of spinal cord injury between the third and fourth cervical vertebrae. People with such injury typically have full voluntary control of muscles above the neck. (See also Chapter 2.) The photographer with C3–4 quadriplegia mentioned in this chapter sustained his injury when he dove headfirst into shallow water.

devices, such as light switches, televisions, and telephones. We hope to demonstrate that it is possible to replace the plethora of hardware controllers with a more flexible, intuitive, and "user friendly" set of software tools accessible to disabled persons.

Current input devices

Most existing wheelchair and environmental controls for severely disabled individuals are mechanically based. Traditional interfaces fall into one of three categories: pneumatic devices, joystick controllers, and body (paddle) switches. The popular "sip–puff" pneumatic device operates from a pressure switch controlled with the mouth. Operators have been known to control as many as ten switches triggered by either blowing or sucking on the mouthpiece with varying degrees of pressure (Gunderson, 1985). More common, however, is a pneumatic two switch controller (Technical Aids and Systems for the Handicapped, 1989). There are several variations of the joystick control interface. One unit attaches the shaft, via a suction cup, to the operator's chin. Another requires the manipulation of the joystick by pressure from the chin or with a mouth grip. Operators with sufficient muscle coordination may use proportional force joystick controllers, and discrete joystick controllers are available that command up to five binary switches. Users also have the option of simple head actuated switches, often positioned in a manifold surrounding the back half of the head. Though other control interfaces exist, they are mostly variations of the simple and multiple two position (binary) switch controls represented by the pneumatic and joystick types described.

Advances in processing optical and acoustic frequency information coupled with high speed microprocessors have created a new generation of interfaces under development for disabled users. Electromagnetic and mechanical (sound) waves allow users to issue commands without being in physical contact with the controlling device. Unlike the traditional interfaces described above, devices that employ optical or sound waves do not require the operator to touch and manipulate a control. Such advances have resulted in some benefits to the user with respect to aesthetics and comfort.

Voice controlled interfaces have also been commercially developed for both powered wheelchair and environmental control devices. Voice control offers the advantage of a nonphysical contact with the interface and the potential for a relatively sophisticated command set, but, to date, fully integrated environmental control applications have not been developed. For example, existing specialized word processing modules do not offer equally effective television and radio control. Voice control systems are growing increasingly sophisticated but they are still too technically difficult for widespread application. At present voice controlled interfaces have the reputation of unreliability and complexity among practitioners in the field. Further collaboration among disabled users, occupational therapists, and engineers is required to develop more user friendly systems.

Infrared (IR) light has long been used in conjunction with both eye wink and eye gaze detection. In 1977 Rinard and Rugg used light emitting diode and photodiode arrays to detect the boundary of the pupil relative to the sclera (Rinard & Rugg, 1977). Such gaze detection was applied as both a communications aid and an interface to a powered wheelchair. Eye winks were used to signal the selection of the command on which the gaze was fixed; however, the primary control emphasis was placed on where the user was looking. A similar optical transducer is used in the *Eye Com* system. This technology was advanced, via the limbus reflection method (ten Kate, Frietman, Stoel, & Willems, 1980), to increase speed and range selection. Using eye wink detectors developed for the United States Air Force (O'Brien, 1987), Energy Optics Corporation developed a wheelchair controller based on a single switch visual scanning system. This system, however, once again fixes head position and eye gaze when used as a wheelchair control.

The most popular and advanced eye gaze position transducer is LC Technologies' *Eye Gaze Computer System*, which resulted from the commercialization of an HCI system developed by Huchinson, White, Martin, Reichart, and Frey (1989). This well integrated computer system and user interface facilitates both computer and environmental control, the latter transmitted throughout a dwelling via the house wiring. The system features an autofocusing video camera and infrared light source able to track head motion, and hence eye position, for a range of 16 in. (41 cm) horizontally and 12 in. (30.5 cm) vertically. Unfortunately, at present it is a stationary system, prohibitively expensive and not feasibly integrated with a mobile wheelchair.

Restrictions of current devices

Today many individuals with severe motor impairments are able to control a powered wheelchair successfully. However, the rigid positioning of the controls places cumbersome restrictions on the operator. Popular present day controls, such as the sip–puff pneumatic interface and chin-strapped or mouth-held joystick, restrict the motion of the user's mouth and head. Thus, while the chair is being operated, the body parts over which the operator has voluntary control are immobilized, making it nearly impossible to look around or communicate with either spoken words or gestures.

The commercially available input devices still consist of simple and multiple switches, which transmit the user issued command direct to the wheelchair or environmental control device. The recent development of dedicated on-chair integrated electronics allows for some customizing of performance features but the coupling of input devices to computer control electronics has yet to be accomplished in a cost effective manner. As a result, existing computer control input devices rely upon physical manipulations that restrict combinations of head, speech, or eye movements. Most are both aesthetically unappealing and quite tiring.

The majority of devices also intrude into an operator's workspace, hindering recreational and vocational activities. One participant in our pilot study with C3–4 quadriplegia is an avid (and published) photographer. This man is able to control his photography equipment, mounted on his wheelchair desk, by using plastic mouth sticks. He is able as well to pull in and push away his chin operated joystick via a mouth stick. However, in functional position, the joystick impedes his use of the photography equipment. But with the joystick pushed aside hc is rendered immobile. This is exhausting and frustrating for a photographer seeking the proper angle and perspective. It is a problem often faced by disabled individuals pursuing vocational and recreational independence.

Eye detectors in general have been developed in lieu of eye wink detectors for the perceived increase in command input range. Yet current sensors of this type still carry three limitations.

1. Eye gaze is dedicated to command input, so while controlling a powered wheelchair, users are unable to look in any direction other than where they wish to go. An eye gaze switch scanning system actually fixes both head and eye position.

2. Detector positioning is not robust. While traveling, the operator has to wear a cumbersome helmet for extended periods to maintain the crucial spacing between detector and eye position. This is at the very least unattractive and uncomfortable.

3. The command set, while potentially extensive, remains limited to the operations prescribed by the manufacturer.

As with the research in eye gaze tracking, technological developments in the field of alternative control devices for persons with severe motor impairments have focused on expanding the variety of sensors through which operators can issue commands (e.g. voice recognition and brain wave tracking). Although these systems have succeeded in their immediate goals, cost, technical complexity and reliability still limit their acceptance.

There is a tremendous need for well designed control devices developed around input systems which do not require the full attention of the operator but still provide a complete range of command options. Controlling an on-chair dedicated computer with a less restrictive but simple binary switch input device is one viable way of fulfilling that need. Users adept with existing input devices should achieve the same or greater range of control commands but with a much less restrictive and intrusive input and control device. Such an integrated system should also allow persons limited to single switch input (such as users with locked-in syndrome) access to controls previously beyond the range of a single binary switch operation.

The Eye Wink Control Interface

The promise of the EWCI and devices like it lies in the union of relatively simple binary switch inputs with a dedicated portable computer. The computer, relying only on the position of one or both eyelids, obviates the necessity of a great number of independent switch inputs. Instead, combinations of left/right eye open/close plus the length of time closed are used to select more complex sets of instructions programmed into the software. A few binary switch signals, integrated with a programmable personal computer, can do the work of even the most sophisticated input and control devices developed to date (head positioning sensors, eye gaze detectors, and the like). The concept of using portable personal computers to extend simple binary inputs to control more complex sequences should be a major advance toward improving the quality of life for the disabled individuals we have been describing.

The EWCI registers eye winks – timed closings of one or both eyelids – electronically via two pairs of infrared photosensors. The sensors are attached to the earpieces of a normal pair of eyeglass frames (Shaw, Crisman, Loomis, & Laszewski, 1990). We have used as sensor elements both off-the-shelf infrared light emitting diodes (IR-LED) and photo transistor (PT) pairs and a commercial equivalent proximity detector. The sensors, one for each eyelid, continually pass the status (UP or DOWN) of the respective lid to a dedicated computer. The

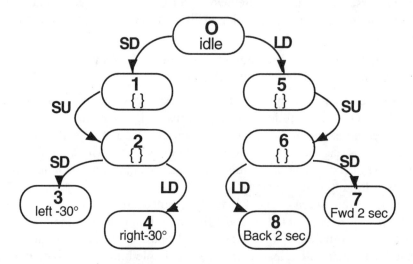

Figure 13.2. State diagram of the FSA for user with control of a single eyelid. Abbreviated commands refer to the single lid, e.g. SD – SHORT DOWN. All sequences start at the initial state, which is idle mode for the chair, and default back to the initial state if any type of wink is issued other than the expected one.

Table 13.1. *FSA state transition matrix for Figure 13.2*

State	Input				
	SU	SD	LU	LD	Other[a]
0	0	1	0	5	0
1	2	—	0	—	0
2	—	3	—	4	0
3	0	—	0	—	0
4	0	—	0	—	0
5	6	—	0	—	0
6	—	7	—	8	0
7	0	—	0	—	0
8	0	—	0	—	0

[a] Covers all commands of time length less than SHORT and greater than LONG.

computer times the period when the status of both eyes remains unchanged. The timed period is categorized, by the length of time that the eyelids remain in one position, as BLINK, SHORT, LONG, or SUPER LONG. Any reflex eye blinks are timed out by the computer. The computer also provides audio feedback to aid the user in timing input. Commands are defined as a combination of the status of the eyelids and the length of time that status was held (e.g. BOTH DOWN – SHORT, LEFT DOWN – LONG, etc.). With four possible time lengths and four possible states of the eyelids (two eyes, two positions) sixteen commands are possible.

Directives to the output device are issued via command sequences (i.e. commands issued in series). The command sequences, as well as the delineating milliseconds for each time category, may be customized for each user. Data sets of command sequences are read in by the control software when the computer is booted up. Each data set is modeled after a Moore Finite State Automaton (FSA) (Figure 13.2) to allow general table driven control (Table 13.1) of the relationship between wink input and wheelchair (or other peripheral) output. Output from the computer to the chair's electronics emulates that of a sip–puff pneumatic switch, thus the output controls are reduced to four commands.

The commands described above are discrete. They are registered only by a change in the eyelid status. For example, when both eyes are open for a LONG period of time and then the right eye closes, it is only at the instant the right eye closes that the BOTH UP – LONG command is registered. In practice, we extend

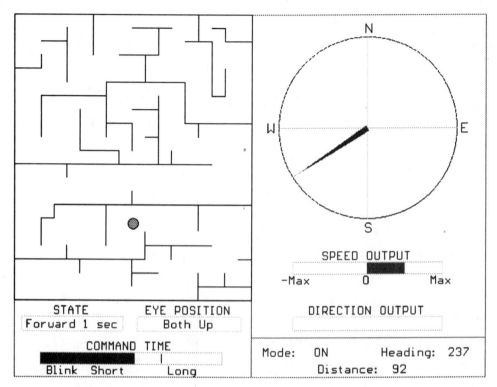

Figure 13.3. One level of the simulation software.

the FSA to allow for dynamic commands (commands in progress). The command input range is therefore doubled from sixteen to thirty-two. Using the dynamic commands for the user with C3–4 quadriplegia, we incorporated sequences that permit left and right turn control of the chair by simply holding down the left and right eyelid respectively.

Simulation software

Before users attempt to control a powered chair, they train with the interface via a graphical simulator. The simulation is a vehicle for allowing the user some familiarity with the interface and an opportunity to learn the custom command sequences. The monitor displays a rectangular movement area and directional, speed, distance, command time, and state feedback. The movement area contains an icon used to represent the user in the chair. When the user is comfortable controlling the icon within the movement area, mazes of increasing complexity are superimposed on the movement area. These mazes are designed to test and improve coordinated control, not cognitive ability. Only after the user has become proficient at navigating the advanced mazes is control of an actual powered chair attempted. Figure 13.3 illustrates one level of the simulation software.

A sample study

In the prototype, an Invacare *Power Rolls Arrow* wheelchair was used with the EWCI. Signals from the eyeglass frame–mounted wink detectors were converted to digital information and received by the computer through a digital I/O board which communicated with the Invacare electronics. The motor control signals were transmitted to the Invacare chair through the same plug normally used to connect the sip–puff pneumatic control electronics option. The computer, an 80286 based machine running MS-DOS, was selected to be compatible with mainstream microcomputers. The built-in VGA display capability was used only for initial program installations. Power for the computer was obtained from the wheelchair batteries. All software was contained on the hard drive, and once the control software was uploaded into ram, the hard drive was parked to prevent damage.

The user with quadriplegia (Subject A) and the user with locked-in syndrome (Subject B) were selected to represent opposite ends of the spectrum of users for whom the EWCI would be particularly useful as an input device. Subject A, the photographer mentioned earlier, is a person disabled with quadriplegia who is quite dextrous at manipulating his powered wheelchair with a chin manipulated joystick but finds the control mechanism itself a hindrance in his everyday activities. He was graduated to the powered chair after approximately six hours of practice with the training system and was able to control the chair with the EWCI. The command sequences designed for him incorporated the use of both eyes and a "latched forward" mode option. This user has found the EWCI to be both less obtrusive and more flexible as a control device than his current joystick. Prior to our project, the user had achieved limited success as a professional photographer and currently controls his equipment via mouthsticks and oral triggers. A control interface that does not limit head movement or dedicate mouth control promises him considerably more flexibility and independence in pursuing his profession.

After four three-hour sessions, Subject B was able to navigate his icon through the first-level computer generated maze. Despite a reduced concentration span, the user demonstrated every indication of progressing through the stage of control of the powered chair – an unprecedented accomplishment for an individual with his level of motor impairment. The command sequences developed for Subject B involved a minimal command set: left turn, right turn, and timed forward mode. As described earlier, the command sequences are entirely software based and can therefore be readily modified. By modifying the control software, we can easily convert the command set from a system customized for a person with full head and eyelid control (Subject A) to one customized for a person retaining autonomous control of only a single eyelid (Subject B).

In essence, the EWCI is composed of four parts exclusive of the powered wheelchair. These are:

1. the sensor platform consisting of the emitter and detector sensors, the mounting frame for the sensors, and the connecting cable to the computer interface;

2. the computer input interface, consisting of electronic circuits to power the sensors and condition the signals from them, and the interface card on the computer that translates the signals from the sensors into the digital form recognized by the computer;

3. the computer with control software; and

4. the computer output interface which provides the motor control signal to the wheelchair (and which varies from manufacturer to manufacturer).

A key element of the Eye Wink Control Interface is the marriage of a simple sensing scheme with a programmable computer. When the EWCI is applied to control of a wheelchair, or ultimately to environmental control, the presence of the computer will permit custom command sequence libraries to be developed by the operators themselves. Since the timing and command interpretation for the EWCI is software based, users will be able to customize and add to the initial set of commands by creating macros that will provide shortcuts for common actions. For example, from the entrance of the dining room, the chair could be programmed to travel forward 10 feet to the table, rotate clockwise 90°, and then inch forward another 2 feet to position the user right at the table.

Extending the EWCI paradigm

Computers are used to perform a variety of tasks that previously had to be done with specialized hardware. An office no longer needs drafting boards, typewriters, adding machines, and so forth. All of their functions can be performed by one piece of hardware plus many pieces of software. Solving a problem with software is much cheaper than solving it with hardware. It requires a smaller development investment, and the software is more easily put together, more easily debugged, more easily changed, and more easily customized. Instead of buying many specialized pieces of hardware, customers can now buy one generic machine and many specialized applications for that machine. However, this type of integration has not yet been applied to systems for disabled users, where the potential advantages transcend mere convenience and could provide truly enabling technologies.

The software industry today is already moving toward achieving greater systems integration. Multimedia applications are one example in which users can control a variety of devices, such as videodisc players or CD-rom drives, directly from the computer. As well, such programs allow users to create and display data in a variety of media, such as graphics, sound, and animation, within the same presentation. Operating systems under development promise support for allowing today's isolated applications to communicate with each other and to combine in creating specialized solutions to user needs.

In the future, we hope to see control systems for disabled people that are modularized in much the same way that the software industry hopes to integrate its applications. Users will no longer be required to purchase monolithic and highly specialized input devices or control systems but rather will be able to interchange components, including input devices, computer applications, and peripheral devices, in order to create a flexible accessible environment.

Currently software interfaces for disabled people are quite specialized in order to accommodate the particular input device being used. While it is important that the user interface be carefully designed in order to accommodate the most restricted set of inputs, ideally the software should be flexible enough to accept input from a variety of different devices, based on the user's needs and desires. Rather than developing user interfaces for all of the different input devices, we can redirect our efforts to developing principles which can be applied toward allowing many different types of input devices to "plug into" the same program. A program developed for the EWCI today should be equally accessible to a disabled person who uses a dual output sip–puff controller and one who uses a joystick. Likewise, as exciting new input technologies become increasingly reliable and affordable, the user should be able to replace his or her existing input device with a voice recognition system or a gesture based input system.

As a future goal of the EWCI project, we also intend to extend the software interface to allow inputs from devices other than the eye wink sensor mechanism, as well as to develop software drivers for other wheelchairs currently on the market. Such modifications will allow users the flexibility to connect the interface they feel most comfortable with to the computer control system, and use it to control their current wheelchair or any number of other peripheral devices. Most electrical appliances can be manipulated using computer actuated switches, input/output cards, and limited interface circuitry. Environmental control systems already allow disabled users to control peripheral devices such as light switches, radios, and televisions; it would be a simple matter to connect these devices to the computer, which would then serve as a single hardware device through which users could gain access to peripherals via different software modules.

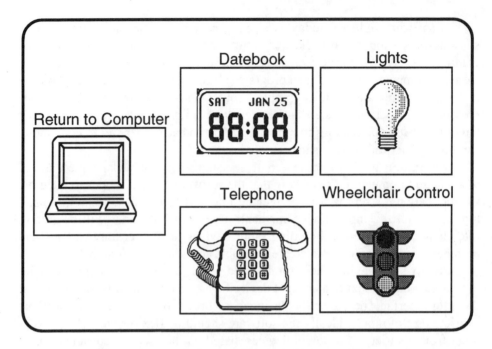

Figure 13.4. What an icon screen might look like for a typical set of peripherals linked to the computer for control.

We intend to investigate the use of icon driven graphical user interfaces to create control modules for many different types of peripheral devices, such as light switches, television/VCR controllers, telephone dialers, word processing programs, and so forth. Even though the EWCI has a limited set of input options, with a computer these inputs can be utilized for different purposes and even extended. Software programs can take advantage of "modes" to extend the user's options at a given moment. In "wheelchair mode," a left eye blink might indicate a left turn; on the computer screen a left eye blink might move a cursor one unit to the left. For example, Figure 13.4 is a representation of what an icon screen might look like for a typical set of peripherals linked to the computer for control. Selections would be made by steering around the on-screen "bug" with eye winks. Choosing the telephone icon with the EWCI would result in the second level, shown in Figure 13.5, at which point further action, such as "Smith–DIAL," could be selected by moving the bug to those positions in that order.

To add peripheral appliances to such a system, one need only install the software driver for it and then connect the peripheral to the output board. Thereafter, to turn on a light switch, for example, the user would select the lightbulb icon from the graphical choices on the screen and then the particular light fixture on the next screen (front door, bedroom ceiling, etc.). Not only

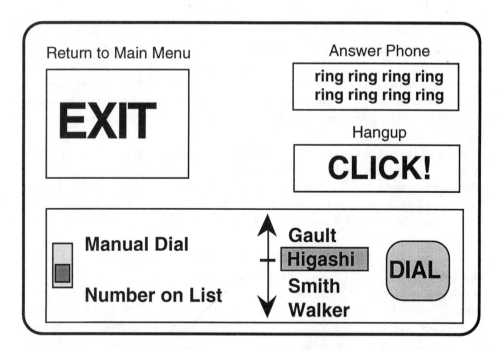

Figure 13.5. Second level interaction.

would the user be able to turn the units on and off but dimming and timer controls could be incorporated into the lightbulb module without extra hardware.

Electronic aids that help people with daily tasks are constantly being developed, and the amount of electronic information available is growing exponentially. New applications and services to take advantage of this are springing up all over: kiosks in malls, automated teller machines, and so on. As a disabled person's environmental control devices are centralized in the computer, this will allow severely disabled people – who are often isolated from the mainstream of society – to participate in the electronic world and the vast network of electronic services rapidly evolving. These include not only today's applications, such as electronic bulletin boards, fax machines, and electronic mail and news services but future developments such as home banking, electronic books and libraries, and entertainment digests distributed through television networks.

Conclusions

The wheelchair control software developed in parallel with the eye wink detection interface provides us with the means to explore a more centralized role for the computer in improving independence and quality of life for the disabled. A major thrust behind the development of the Eye Wink Control Interface is to develop a simple yet powerful input device that frees persons with high level quadriplegia from restrictions on their speaking, head positioning, movement, and gaze direction during the act of controlling motorized wheelchairs or other peripheral devices. The EWCI will provide an unobtrusive and inexpensive control input device. The dimensions of the IR pickup allow for eyeglass frame mounting, thereby providing a significant increase in aesthetics and comfort over traditional interfaces.

As well, the EWCI provides a first generation example of an integrated system. The on-board computer manages the chair's operations through software controlled command sets. Because they are software based, the chair operator will be able to dynamically edit and add to the existing command set. The software can be updated periodically to take advantage of state of the art graphics and microcomputer technology.

One goal of the personal computer industry has always been to empower the individual user. It is unfortunate that the class of users most often forgotten in the development of state of the art software is the group whose quality of life could perhaps be the most dramatically affected by the power of modern technology. Today software and control systems for the disabled lag a generation behind mass market applications. Research is being done in exciting new input devices and in improving access to standard applications for disabled people but the technology exists today to improve the performance of current input devices greatly. The same principles of systems integration that began with the proliferation of software developed to extend the functionality of the computer in business can be applied to provide disabled people with centralized access to wheelchairs, software applications, and various other peripheral devices.

Acknowledgments

Development of the Eye Wink Control Interface has been supported by the United States Department of Veterans Affairs Rehabilitation Research and Development Program. The authors are grateful to Hil Anderson, Kenneth Davis, Melissa Gold, Carson Roberts, and David Simons for their assistance with this project.

References
Crisman, E., Loomis, A. T., Shaw, R., and Laszewski Z. (in press). Using the Eye Wink Control Interface to control a powered wheelchair. In *Proceedings of the 13th Annual International Conference of the IEEE Society for Engineering in Medicine and Biology,* Orlando, FL.

Gunderson, J. R. (1985). Interfacing the motor-impaired for control and communication. In *Electronic devices for rehabilitation*, ed. J. G. Webster, A. M. Cook, W. J. Tompkins, and G. C. Vanderheiden. London: Chapman and Hall (pp. 190–230).

Huchinson, T. E., White, K. P., Jr., Martin, W. N., Reichart, K. C., and Frey, L. A. (1989). Human-computer interaction using eye-gaze input. *IEEE Transactions on Systems, Man and Cybernetics, 19*(6): 1527–1533.

O'Brien, P. M. (1987). Eyeblink monitoring as a means of measuring pilot physiological state. In *Proceedings of the SAFE 25th Annual Symposium.*

Rinard, G. A., and Rugg, D. E. (1977). Current state of development and testing of an ocular control device. In *Proceedings of the Annual Conference on Systems Devices for the Disabled.*

Shaw, R., Crisman, E., Loomis, A., and Laszewski, Z. (1990). The Eye Wink Control Interface: Using the computer to provide the severely disabled with increased flexibility and comfort. In *Proceedings of the Third Annual IEEE Symposium on Computer based Medical Systems,* Chapel Hill, NC.

Technical Aids and Systems for the Handicapped. (1989). Product catalog. Ontario, Canada.

ten Kate, J. H., Frietman, E. E. E., Stoel, F. J. M., and Willems, W. (1980). Eye-controlled communication aids. *Medical Progress Technology, 8*: 1–21.

Practice

The other sections of this book have described the current state of the art, in terms both of what is currently available and the research which will lead to tomorrow's developments. The purpose of this section is to set out practical advice which will be useful to designers of today's systems and adaptations.

It was pointed out in Chapter 2 that the term handicap applies to the effects a person's limitations have on the ability to function in his or her environment. Chapter 14 explores that concept in a very important direction. It advances the proposition that the average human–computer interface is so badly designed that *anyone* who uses it is handicapped by it. Moreover, it suggests a way to respect the user, based in the theory of computer science. It should therefore appeal to the computer scientists and programmers who design interactive systems. This is an interesting perspective from a writer who works in the mainstream of HCI research but has always been aware of the broad range of capabilities of potential users.

Chapter 15 makes the point that, whereas computers have been a boon to many people, to some disabled people they have represented a veritable revolution of opportunities, through the possibility of their accessing information sources online. It is suggested that the design which succeeds in being accessible and "friendly" to a disabled user will almost certainly be highly convenient for most nondisabled users. Hence if the designers of the interfaces to online services can learn some of the requirements of disabled potential users, they are likely to design much better, more accessible systems. A number of existing designs are cited where what to the designer probably seemed like almost inconsequential decisions (such as how to lay out a screen) have had a major effect on some disabled users. It is to be hoped that books like this one will heighten the awareness of interface designers so that this will not happen in future.

Many of the authors in this section have unusual and incisive perspectives on their subjects. Harold Thimbleby (Chapter 14) has already been mentioned. Norman Coombs (Chapter 15) also has a unique outlook. He is a history professor who relies on information technology in his work because he is blind. The availability of this technology makes it possible for him to do things from which he otherwise would probably be precluded. For instance, he is able to communicate with and teach a student who is deaf by using a computer to mediate their communication. In this chapter he explains how *redundancy* is the key to this broad communication and how the level of redundancy available can aid or hinder the process.

Paul Blenkhorn writes in Chapter 16 about the design of a speech synthesizer from a particularly informed position, since he developed one of the most successful such devices. Braille is a long established medium of textual communication for blind people. (Some of the more recent developments in computer generated braille are described in Chapter 9.) However, braille is not as useful as is often assumed, mainly because only a very small proportion of blind people learn to read it. The advantage of speech is that no training is necessary to understand it. However, just because it is possible to generate understandable synthetic speech does not mean that all the problems have been solved, as Paul Blenkhorn's chapter illustrates.

The chapter deals quite specifically with the speech synthesizer, which is one of the most significant developments in the emancipation of disabled people through the adaptation of information technology. However, it also highlights the sorts of consideration which must be taken into account when designing for a special population and illustrates that these are not always the ones which seem most obvious to the (usually able-bodied) designer.

As pointed out in Chapter 1, whereas most HCI designers target an "average" user, there is no such person amongst the population of people with disabilities; all are "extra-ordinary." Hence there have to be a number of different interfaces available, so that, instead of matching the interface to the user, there is often a problem of matching the user to the interface because of the vast range of adapted interfaces from which to choose.

Current methods used to select computer hardware and software for users with disabilities are unsystematic and often fail to provide aids which maximize the user's productivity. A new approach to equipment selection is presented in Chapter 17. The approach considers the physical capabilities of the user as well as his or her task functions when matching user needs with equipment characteristics. A physical skills assessment test was developed to measure the skills needed in using cursor control devices. An empirical study was conducted to determine the test's ability to predict an individual's capability of using such devices efficiently.

A valuable corollary of the results of the study described is that the majority of adaptations required have a very low cost. Employers are often wary of taking on workers with disabilities because they fear that accommodating them will be expensive. This work helps to show that that is usually not the case.

Chapter 18 illustrates the need for more and better research into the design of interfaces for disabled users by presenting some statistics which highlight the incidence of disability in the population and by describing the market – or potential market – for adaptive information technology. It then goes on to suggest how the sort of approach conventionally taken in human–computer interaction development might be applied in the design of interfaces for people with disabilities, illustrating this with a case study. The approach will be familiar to most HCI designers, but the context may be new and some of the questions raised novel and thought provoking.

The motivation behind a lot of the current interest in adapting computers for disabled users arises from the adoption of legislation in the United States. These laws are outlined in Chapter 19, which also presents a collection of resources upon which the developer may draw.

14

Treat people like computers?
Designing usable systems for special people

Harold Thimbleby

Introduction

Three true stories:

- An old and disabled woman makes a special trip to visit her electric utility to make a payment on her monthly credit book. The clerk refuses to accept payment because the date for the next installment is tomorrow, and the computer cannot process early payment. The woman goes to the local newspaper, and the story that gets printed includes the clerk's manager's complaints about the computer system: It is not only badly designed for customers but it also disables staff in how they can handle customers.

- I am recording a live TV broadcast on my video recorder. The adverts come on, so I press PAUSE to stop the recording. When the adverts finish, I press the wrong button, and the VCR does something I've never seen before. I get confused. The frustration I feel is so intense that I do not wish to waste my time with this gadget ever again; effectively disabling myself from gaining its possible benefits in the future.

- The ticket regulations for traveling on British Rail are so complex that passengers can often be seen anxiously trying to understand their tickets, as the Senior Ticket Collector for the train announces that only he is qualified to answer queries. The ticket regulations are so complex that they disable people.

Thus badly designed systems handicap all users. Attitudes, too, handicap users: Users are generally blamed for their own difficulties. Didn't they know? Didn't they read the manual? Are they too old for this technology? The designers thereby avoid any responsibility for the users' difficulties. Their attitudes handicap users and deflect attention from the engineering design of systems.

In this chapter it will be argued that improvements should be sought in better engineering and that there are the means to do so. This chapter may make the reader question who is handicapped and what is the cause of that handicap.

Inevitably this chapter complains about the disabling design of interactive systems, although a longer chapter would also include disabling designs in intelligent homes for the elderly, and indeed, all areas of interactive technology. If the reader thinks that such complaints are overdone or that the problems complained of are obvious, then why are such problems so common? Why do designers or manufacturers not notice them and not avoid them? *They cannot be so obvious to designers; or perhaps designers, despite knowing, do not know how to recognize or avoid the problems.*

As well as providing ammunition for people who want to complain about the problems, this chapter will make two central constructive contributions. First, I will point out an analogy with automobile safety: Informed consumer pressure can change things, and usability (drivability and safety) is an engineering issue. Second, I will point out an analogy between user and computer: Designers (who can program) implicitly know how to do the engineering properly. I discuss the imbalance whereby computers get better treatment than users, to the point of making the almost outrageous suggestion that if humans were treated with at least as much care as computers are, then computer users' lives would be improved.

The automobile analogy

In 1963 the American Association of Casualty and Surety Companies reported a common fault found in many cars, that they sometimes ran back against the parking brake. The solution they suggested was to educate the driver to get into the habit of putting his foot on the foot brake pedal when pulling on the parking brake. The foot brake would apply a greater force on the brake shoes than could be applied by hand alone, thus ensuring that the shoes engaged properly and the parking brake held. The advice they provided was that there was no problem – if drivers train themselves to do this. Put like this, the solution clearly lay in the area of driver psychology: Most drivers, for instance, did not read the car manual. How could drivers be educated to drive properly?

This problem was reported in Ralph Nader's now classic book *Unsafe at Any Speed* (1965). But looking back, with the benefit of the consciousness raised by Nader's book it is now obvious that a proper solution would have been to solve the engineering problems in the parking brake. The parking brake should have worked properly and not have required the additional assistance of the foot brake! The solution was not in getting the driver to read the manual but in designing the system so that no comment ever needed putting in a manual. This point of view is now widely accepted. Yet in computer systems, we can see from the standard warranties provided with proprietary software that designers or manufacturers are not and do not *want to be* responsible (Thimbleby, 1990a, 1990b). The purchaser is given no effective comeback on product defects, of which there are many. There is a veil of secrecy over crippling product defects.

Today computers, whether PCs or embedded inside domestic products and other machines, are designed quite as badly as 1960s cars. Most are partially unusable. They rely for their apparent success on the long sufferance and dogged perseverance of the user. The similarity between the poor design of cars thirty years ago and modern computing systems is indicated by the agony columns in many computing magazines and the sorts of solutions to readers' problems that are suggested there. Hence the title of an article, "You're Right About the Cure: Don't Do That" (Thimbleby, 1990a), reflecting on a piece of agony column wisdom where a reader was told that the only way around a bug was to give up and avoid a useful facility.

Computers are (occasionally!) useful, and users are very often justifiably pleased with what they can achieve with their help. Indeed, the more so the less the user could do previously in comparison with what can now be done with computer support. That may explain why users tend to put up with computer limitations without complaining: On balance, users are better off with computers than without them. When a computer crashes (due to a software error), the user, like a laboratory rat, soon learns not to do whatever caused the crash; that is, if the user is fortunate enough to see any discernible reason why the crash occurred. Soon the user will learn how to work the computer reliably or modify his or her work so that only reliable parts of the computer system are required.

Another reason why users tend to downgrade usability problems is that the computer represents a major investment in financial terms and training time. Admitting problems is tantamount to admitting having wasted time and money. It is easier to believe that the computer is all right, and that with even more effort, more money, or more training, one will get used to it. With today's consciousness, it seems easier to admit being technically incompetent than to admit wasting time and money.

This is the same user oppression as the 1960s driver example: Engineering problems are passed off as user handicaps, and the users acquiesce.

If problems are the user's handicaps, who is responsible for the problems? Not the designers, manufacturers, or dealers! Should we have a government initiative in technology literacy, so that users can better put up with the oppression? Should users (perversely) feel proud of the sophisticated skills they learn (Thimbleby, 1993)?

It is a truism that we as humans are all handicapped with respect to our potential. The discussion above indicates that everyone is reduced by current technology. If you start off being handicapped, you are made much worse off, in ways that are not always obvious, but in ways that both manufacturer and user conspire to conceal and deny.

The exploitation of users is technically avoidable. Although improvement will result from action at all levels – political action, consumer action, litigation, human factors consciousness – the aim here is to argue that technology itself has better to offer users. Improvement will result from better engineering and a more professional attitude from designers.

The computer analogy

A user has to put up with poor systems. A user has to adapt work patterns to fit in with or avoid quirks and bugs. Yet if the human user was instead a computer and had any such problems, then obviously the designers would have to fix the problem. A computer cannot choose to do other than what it is told, and therefore it is obvious that its problems (say, dividing by zero) must be *caused* by bad programming. It is not sensible to criticize or blame a computer for being uninformed, stupid, old, or incapable. Its problems *have* to be fixed by the programmer responsible. When a user has problems, however, responsibility is evidently not so obvious.

In all of the many millennia before the age of computers, people were talking to each other without worrying too much about their own idiosyncrasies, their grammatical errors, their interruptions, their ways of resolving misunderstandings, and so forth. All humans share the same skills and the same defects, and so they are hard to see. We often do not realize just how limited and error prone we really are.

Today many people interact with computers, but computers have *very* different skills and defects from humans. Thus when ordinary people interact with computers they become acutely aware of the mismatch between their skills and the computer's. The very human skills of conversation repair do not help with computer defects any more than a computer's skill helps it cope with human quirks. The computer makes no concessions to the differences and incompatibilities: Always, it seems, it is the human who has to adapt to the idiosyncrasies of the computer.

We must ask, "What is common to both computers and humans, and how can we ensure that interactive computer systems are designed to be at least up to the common baseline?" At least the first part of the question is a familiar and foundational issue in computer science. There is a standard and uncontentious answer, and it provides a rigorous standard for what is minimally acceptable behavior in programmable systems, whether human or computer. I will briefly discuss the standard answer, and then I will be able to argue that this standard is *higher* than present computer systems manage to achieve; yet because the standard is so straightforward and well researched, there are very many practical opportunities to improve the state of the art. Otherwise, until systems are routinely designed to this standard, humans will be brought down to the subhuman standards of badly programmed computers.

Turing Machines were defined (by Alan Turing) specifically to get rid of the distraction of special and particular skills to determine exactly what, in a formal sense, a person could do. People are Turing Machines.

If we say that humans are Turing Machines, we run the risk of being misunderstood. Turing Machines sound like robots, and people are certainly not robots. However, an anatomist would have little problem understanding a human as a particular sort of mechanical machine whose levers are bones. A physicist, going to a further extreme, would have little problem understanding a human as a point whose only characteristic is mass. Neither view demeans the human. Likewise a computer scientist should have little problem understanding a human as a Turing Machine. Saying this is no more contentious than saying "Drivers are point masses" to a physicist. People obey the laws of mechanics in quantifiable ways; ergonomics is the discipline that uses their mechanical properties to make people's environment and work more comfortable and effective for them.

The Church–Turing Thesis posits that all forms of computation are fundamentally equivalent. There is considerable weight of evidence for the Church–Turing Thesis, and it has the standing of a natural law. Perhaps there may be an experiment (as yet to be devised) that refutes it, but until then we may believe that everything, whether computer, human, or otherwise, acts in accordance with the laws of computation.[1] The important point is that what is impossible for a Turing Machine to do is impossible for any other concept of computing, *including* human beings, be they disabled or exceptional. Such problems are termed noncomputable, in contra-distinction to the computable problems that computers can solve.

When a car designer makes a car that does not protect the driver from minor collisions, the designer is implicitly hoping that the driver can miraculously escape the consequences of physical laws. The unfortunate driver who obeys the law of conservation of momentum – and he cannot do otherwise – has an unfortunate tendency to fly through the windshield or to hit the steering wheel. (One wonders why safety belts took so long to be adopted.)

Likewise, by accepting the Church–Turing Thesis, we are able to make a distinction between two sorts of usability problem. There are designs that merely *hinder* users, and there are designs that try to make users break the natural law by requiring them to do something noncomputable. It happens rather more often than might be expected. (Perpetual motion machines are continually being invented, and some of them run for an impressive time before succumbing to reality!)

---

[1] There is a technical quibble about quantum mechanics. But nobody is suggesting that to rely on quantum mechanical effects at the human level would be advisable. The same goes for intuition and spiritual aspects: These are subtle human qualities that computers apparently do not share, but to rely on them would generally be a burden to impose on users.

The consequences of setting humans noncomputable tasks is as disabling as ignoring the conservation of momentum in the design of car safety features. There is no argument: Designers must give users computable systems. It follows that users must have or be given an algorithm (i.e. a "program that does something computable") to operate the system; the algorithm may of course be constituted in a vague way from the user's world knowledge, or it can be more precisely defined in a manual or operator's guide.

Styles of computation

The Turing Machine is only one of many equivalent ways of formulating computability. Strictly, I should have been writing "Turing Machine Equivalent" above, since I am not trying to impose the Turing Machine's *particular* approach to computation as an approximation of human computation. Indeed, since Turing Machines are formal conceptualizations, they conjure up a rather idiosyncratic approach to computation that would never be used for practical computation. The point, which is easily made, is that in principle all models of computation, including human, can be reduced to Turing Machine configurations. The fact that mechanics can be reduced to a few basic types of lever does not mean that every machine is a heap of levers.

The Turing Machine approach is imperative – to some extent a Pascal style of computing. There are several alternative nonimperative approaches, represented, for instance, by the computer programming languages Prolog (declarative), ML (functional), and others. Just as a programmer chooses an appropriate computational model from this wide choice, we intend an interactive systems designer to make a similar wide choice about the style of interaction based on the user and the user's specific tasks.

For an example, see Thimbleby (1990b, chapter 15) which includes a discussion of logic programming applied to user interface design. For exactly the same reasons that logic programming is promoted as an approach to programming, for user interfaces it provides additional flexibility.

What impact for design?

A precise and brief summary of the discussion above is that systems that are meant to be used by people should support computable algorithms for their use. (For some tasks, like education, one might want mystery and surprise, but they should be introduced deliberately rather than by default, whatever the user is supposed to be doing.) Without algorithms, systems are far harder to operate or more error prone than they need be.

I give some examples now of the change in perspective this view brings to user interface design. None of the examples is pursued in much depth, nor is the repertoire by any means exhausted by this short list. The purpose of the examples is to show the potential of the approach, and secondly to stimulate the reader.

Physical disability

Various forms of physical disability reduce the speed and energy that can be put into conversation and typing. There are many algorithms for text compression: If typing is a burden for the user, there are algorithmic approaches to improve the user interface. It is pleasing, then, to report on the success of some recent work motivated in this way (Darragh & Witten, 1992, and see also Chapter 6); that is, an application of computing theory to usability.

A word processor

Few word processors distinguish the way they display spaces, tabs, and nothing at all (e.g. the nothing beyond the end of a line). All are blank regions on the screen, yet they behave differently. Suppose a user wishes to move the word processor's cursor from where it is to a position he or she has in mind, perhaps to correct a spelling. Because blanks can be different things, the user is in principle unable to work out (that is, is unable to *compute*) how to move the cursor to the desired goal. Word processors that use a mouse have a similar problem, and one that is sometimes more mysterious. There are places on the screen where the mouse can be positioned, yet where it is not possible to type. How does a user detect such places without wasting time?

This is a very simple, but common, example of a user interface's assuming that the user can somehow circumvent the limitations of computability. In practice, the user must experiment: Try to move the cursor to where it is wanted, and if it ends up somewhere else, try to move it from there to where it should be. As a rule, the user will be able to do this, so the way the cursor moves will not be that surprising. Nevertheless, the word processor requires the user to solve a problem that a computer would fail at. (It would be amusing to challenge a programmer to write a program to use a word processor via the standard user interface of that program.)

Software designers get away with nonsense (as the example illustrates), and everyone else gets so used to it that we even start to expect it. Indeed, many expert word processor users may fail to see the problem as described so briefly here. Users, and some designers, are evidently being trained to be masochists. It is an impressive brain washing maneuver that makes handicapped users feel proud of skills that keep them handicapped.

The proper solution to the word processor problem is trivial: Design the system so that the cursor motion is not affected by what the cursor is moving over (then the UP arrow key, for instance, will always move directly up, which is reasonable). There are many other solutions (Bornat & Thimbleby, 1989). The point is that users put up with a little unnecessary mental effort, some surprises, and some unnecessary but unavoidable experimentation, in this example, to get a cursor exactly where they want it. A computer would not readily tolerate such unpredictability. Why should a human?

A modern programmer, writing a program not for a human but for a computer to do the editing, would say that tabs or spaces is a detail of implementation and not the concern of high level operations. Abstract data types and encapsulation are standard tools for programming computers; why are they not standard tools for user interface design? Why do the underlying Ascii code details intrude into the user's editing task if such an intrusion would be avoided for the computer's sake?

Dementia

Persons with dementia who are hospitalized or moved to a new home can become disoriented and may deteriorate seriously. Part of the reason for this is the lack of familiar cues in their surroundings: They are literally lost.

Computers do not so much get lost as never knew where they were to start with. Thus any algorithm for a computer to move around in a conceptual space (a data structure) must provide for keeping track of what places have been visited and what places looked promising for future exploration. There are very many algorithms for doing this systematically, two of the simplest being breadth-first search and depth-first search (Thimbleby, 1991b).

No current hypertext systems provide algorithms for their users to avoid problems of getting lost. Instead, users have to rely on memory, and they become disoriented – a phenomenon called "getting lost in hyperspace."

If this is what happens to people with dementia, they might be helped in a similar way: by being given the cues that a computer would need to do their tasks. The advantage of the computer analogy is that it makes abundantly clear what cues are necessary, though in practice more alternatives might be needed.

In an institution with lots of confusing passages, radio devices could be used not only to say where one was but also to say where one had been – just as one would provide flags (or whatever) to stop a computer from getting stuck in a loop. In fact, demented people live in the past and would probably not be able to benefit from such novel technology. But maybe it should not be novel; maybe it is time that as direction aids (say, for car navigation) become more widely available they should be better designed along these principles. This would improve them and would help their users as they age and start to rely on their facilities for day-to-day living.

Permissiveness

Most people are right handed. Although left handed people grow accustomed to an awkward right handed world, a person with a stroke can suddenly lose the use of the right hand and find things very difficult. Such persons are additionally disabled by any device, such as a door knob, that assumes that the correct way to be operated is to be manipulated in a right handed fashion. More generally, the underlying assumption is that there is *one* correct way of doing things: in this example, the right handed way. Users have to conform to the "correct" way chosen by the designer.

Suppose we are designing a network program, or an algorithm for computers to talk to each other. We cannot assume that another computer will work the way we deem to be correct. Any compatible program must cater for several ideas of correct protocols. The successful network program has to be designed so that it can cater for various protocols. If we called the protocols left and right handed, the point would be clear: Computers never learn or adapt (change handedness), so we have to cater for both.

The assumption that there is just one correct way to design any human facility, even for disabled people, is so deeply entrenched that it is useful to have a word for deliberately avoiding narrowness. A system is *permissive* if it permits itself to be successfully used in more than one way.

The video recorder example we started this chapter with required the user to press the correct button. Different manufacturers make different design decisions about which button is correct. In a permissive video recorder, any of the buttons that at this point do not do anything could be used. Then whatever a user did would be correct, whether the PLAY, RECORD, or PAUSE button was pressed.

The user of a permissive system need not even know that there are alternatives. The old lady (of the chapter's first example) faced a nonpermissive credit control system; railway travelers (the third example) face a nonpermissive and obscure set of ticket regulations.

(Even human factors experts may assume that there is one right design and users must know it. A case in point was a permissive system that provided users with alternatives, yet the system design was criticized on the basis that users did not know how to use it properly if they knew only one of the alternatives!)

Know the user

Few programmers would try to make a program they called efficient without knowing about the computer it was running on. Few competent programmers would try to optimize a program without first making measurements of its performance. Why then do programmers make systems they call usable without knowing about the users the systems work with?

Viewing user interfaces as the realization of algorithms naturally suggests exploring the many standard books on algorithms (such as Sedgewick, 1988) for ideas for developing quality user interfaces. This is the first step in making user interfaces more usable. The second step is to find out about the specific users.

The myth that children can use things adults can't

Finally, it is claimed that children can cope with modern technology better than adults. Children can programme video recorders when their parents cannot. This point of view is disabling, for it suggests that adults are incompetent.

There is very little evidence in support of this. When one considers that children have not paid for the video recorder, are not worried about breaking it, and generally have more time on their hands (they don't have a mortgage at the back of their minds), then their putative skills with video recorders look less dependent on age. Maybe the rest of us are not too old! Adults might be too busy, but few people are oppressed by being made to feel too busy rather than too old.

There is another possibility that I want to suggest, one that is amenable to serious study. That is that children handle technology better than adults because they *don't* understand it. Adults have problems because they understand things "too well," and the technology fails to live up to their (quite reasonable) expectations.

In one simple real experience, my colleague Ian Witten and I expected a digital clock to work to the 24 hour clock: It certainly gave clues that it was a 24 hour clock, like being able to count from 00:00 to 24:59, even to 99:99. We were wrong (actually, the *designers* were wrong) and stuck, but the clock did not tell us.

Experiments showed that if one made no assumptions about how the clock worked – if buttons were pressed at random – then the clock could be got working in just nine or ten button presses on average (Thimbleby & Witten, 1993). This is much quicker than we were: We took almost an hour. Since we had "misunderstood" the clock, we would have been better off flipping a coin to decide what to do rather than thinking carefully about it. Tossing a coin, acting randomly, might have led us to do the wrong thing some of the time, but we wouldn't consistently have done the wrong thing all the time and be stuck – it might have been – forever.

It therefore seems plausible that children are successful with technology not because they are cleverer, but because they do not understand what they are doing, nor do they persist in doing any one thing. They play randomly, and that is a good way of learning how the world works, including digital clocks and video recorders. Adults, having spent most of their childhood playing, may prefer to work rather than play; certainly errors with a cooker clock or video recorder are rarely playful.

It is in the manufacturers' interest to encourage us all to believe that we are inadequate when we cannot use their products. I was told I was too old when I complained that I could not use my video recorder. If I believe that, then my problems are my own fault, and I am handicapped.

Why engineering first? Why not human factors first?

When the functions of a product have been decided and perhaps a prototype built, it is common for designers (stylists) to design a suitable appearance. Users will experience certain sorts of problems that would be ameliorated by the provision or removal of certain features. However, given the pressures of manufacturing in a competitive marketplace, by the time anything is known, the engineering effort will have been completed, and the product is ready to ship. Just when users can contribute to product evaluation, it is already too late to rectify design flaws. The solution can only be to add another feature.

When the same thing happened with cars, it was termed "the gadget approach to safety" by Ralph Nader. It was easier for car manufacturers to add gadgets (or let component manufacturers supply them to an after market) than to make a well designed car. There was an after market in antisway bars for the General Motors Corvair that greatly improved the handling of the car. General Motors should have made the car stable in the first place, or at least taken responsibility for fixing the stability problem the manufacturer had created. Once a car is built, however, gadgets are all that can be provided. Likewise, there is a gadget approach to usability, whereby the more features a system has, the easier to use it is assumed to be. Whatever the user wants, there is a feature available to do it. The marketing term for this is "feature bouquet." The bouquet approach not only misses opportunities for systematic design and rationalization that might even reduce the number of features while increasing usability, but it also encourages the provision of third party products to correct defects in the original product. When manufacturers rely on this approach, they soon have less incentive to design properly in the first place. Specific examples of how an engineering approach would impact user interface design have been developed and discussed elsewhere (Thimbleby & Witten, 1993).

Conclusions

Systems can be made easier to use, and there are rigorous technical standards available. A start in the right direction is to treat the user at least as well as a computer would be treated: to make the user interface computable and to provide algorithms for users to succeed in their work with the system. Present systems do less than this and thereby exploit users; and there is a culture to keep things this way. Sadly, users are caught up in this culture and blame themselves for not being clever enough, not being young enough, and not having read and understood the manual; they are not even qualified to comment.

In reality, rather too many usability problems are straightforward engineering problems. Car parking brakes should be designed properly. It is obviously not the drivers' responsibility to learn workarounds or to read agony columns about driving techniques in order to avoid dangerous features. Yet when it comes to working with computers or video recorders or microwave cookers, the user lives in a world of restrictions and enforced workarounds. When a user becomes pleased with his or her technological prowess, a manufacturer has profoundly handicapped somebody.

How can we encourage designers to respect users a little more? Even to respect them at least as well as they would computers? (The current standards of usability are substandard from a computer's point of view.) When we take the Church–Turing Thesis seriously we see that by treating users as noncomputers we are treating them as far *less* than human. In other words,

> To treat humans as less than computers is disabling, and it is avoidable.

Humans are Turing Machines (and more besides) and are only held back by poor interfaces to bad technology.

Designers should work out algorithms to ensure that their designs are usable, at least in the computability sense. Only then should they go to human factors consultants to finish the design. Otherwise the necessary human factors contribution will only palliate or camouflage engineering defects, or even condone workarounds. Too often cosmetics (including gratuitous features) are used to gloss over fundamentally unusable designs.

In aircraft cockpits, we may talk of computer encouraged error (Race, 1990), but the pilot is still blamed. In cars, radios have caused accidents, and this is hardly surprising when you look at one and try to understand it. Many have over twenty buttons with meanings that depend on what text 2mm high says. What driver can read that while concentrating on driving? Not to put too fine a point on it, accident survivors are often disabled for life. Such observations are poignant when seen in the context of Ralph Nader's efforts of thirty years ago to improve car safety. The mechanical engineering has improved, but the interactive usability has decreased.

References

Bornat, R., and Thimbleby, H. (1989). The life and times of Ded, Display Editor. In *Cognitive ergonomics and human–computer interaction*, ed. J. B. Long and A. Whitefield (pp. 225–255). Cambridge University Press.

Darragh, J. J., and Witten, I. H. (1992). *The reactive keyboard*. Cambridge University Press.

Nader, R. (1965). *Unsafe at any speed*. Pocket Books.

Race, J. (1990). Computer-encouraged error. *Computer Bulletin*, ser. IV, *2*(6): 13–15.

Sedgewick, R. (1988). *Algorithms*. Reading, MA: Addison-Wesley.

Thimbleby, H. (1990a). You're right about the cure: Don't do that, *Interacting with Computers*, 2(1): 8–25.

Thimbleby, H. (1990b). *User interface design*. Reading MA: Addison-Wesley.

Thimbleby, H. (1991a). The undomesticated video recorder. *Image Technology: Journal of the British Kinematograph, Sound and Television Society*, *73*(6): 214–216.

Thimbleby, H. (1991b). Can humans think? *Ergonomics*, *34*(10): 1269–1287.

Thimbleby, H. (1993). Computer literacy and usability standards? In *User needs in information technology standards*, ed. C. D. Evans, B. L. Meek, and R. S. Walker (pp. 223–230). Butterworth-Heinemann.

Thimbleby, H., and Witten, I. H. (1993). User modelling as machine identification: New design methods for HCI. In *Advances in human–computer interaction*, ed. D. Hix and H. R. Hartson (vol. 4, pp. 58–86). Norwood, NJ: Ablex.

15

Interfacing online services, alternative inputs, and redundant displays

Norman Coombs

Introduction

In recent years there has been a rapid growth of online information services, which bring information to the user instead of the user's having to travel to the information source. This fact, along with the advent of adapted computer systems, means that the user with disabilities becomes an *enabled* user, not a disabled user. The development of the personal computer with adaptive software and/or hardware has been one of the most liberating innovations for handicapped persons in modern times. The ability to take this new powerful tool and connect it to a modem and telephone can bring the world to serve one's needs. Computer telecommunications are rapidly providing access to numerous commercial and educational services and also to an expanding variety of information sources. These include online education, access to reference works, full textbooks and periodicals, and a wide variety of databases for education and business as well as shopping services.

While accessing information resources from a computer at home is convenient for most people, this ability provides an entirely new opportunity for the otherwise handicapped. Information is power, and the computer user, whether disabled or not, has a competitive edge in today's highly competitive world. Interfacing this information goldmine provides exciting creative potentials for both the disabled and nondisabled computer user. These online services, however, may present two kinds of problems to the disabled computer user: inconvenient user input requirements and displays that may be difficult to access. These difficulties could often be overcome by more careful design: permitting alternative user inputs and presenting display information in redundant forms. Designers of systems will want to make their facilities widely accessible to the otherwise handicapped and "friendly" to the maximum number of nondisabled patrons. Many of the considerations which will further open this world to the their databases for a small audience of disabled computer users as it is at helping them realize that while they are meeting some of these special needs they will be developing an information source which will at the same time be opened up to the maximum possible number of consumers.

Online access to information services of whatever kind has two advantages for disabled computer users: not having to travel, and using already familiar computer systems. Persons with mobility impairments may find commuting to a library, a school, or some other information provider difficult and sometimes impractical. In a world where driving an automobile is freedom and independence, the visually impaired or blind person is also greatly restricted. Instant access to data resources from home is far more than a convenience to these users. It is freedom and power. (See Chapter 12 for a fuller discussion of the possibilities of using information technology as a means of "surrogate" travel.)

Besides the travel problem, working online means that the person can use equipment with which he or she is familiar. There exist a wide variety of adaptive access systems, each with its own unique command structure and function. When a disabled user arrives at an information provider such as a library or school, the access system will undoubtedly be different from the one normally employed by this user. Working from home both overcomes the travel barrier and lets the user continue to use familiar adaptive hardware and software.

However, the design of online systems can make this access easier or harder. In fact, the design itself can make a difference as to whether such services continue to be accessible or not. I will approach the topic from three perspectives. First, the chapter will provide some examples of the opportunities made possible to disabled computer users using online services. Second, it will give some examples of difficulties which also exist in some of the present systems. Third, it will make suggestions to maximize online accessibility for disabled users and simultaneously, increase system "friendliness" for many other users. It is hoped that this discussion will help designers of future online systems create a product which will be liberating and enabling to many persons with physical impairments and also adapt such systems to meet the various work styles and preferences of the general computer using public. Better design will benefit all.

The world at my fingertips

As a blind history teacher, I have found online services opening exciting teaching channels for me, and advancing learning opportunities for students with and without disabilities. As a researcher and scholar, I have been given access to facilities which are familiar to most people but which are exciting new opportunities to a disabled person.

When I began teaching in 1961, some of my professional reading was available to me in braille or on recordings, but most of it was not. I depended heavily on human readers to keep up on professional materials as well as to read the exams and term papers of my students. Now all student papers and essay exams are turned in to me using electronic mail on the college's Vax cluster. My PC and speech synthesizer do the reading. No longer do I need to schedule such work to fit someone else's time. I can connect both from the office and home and am wholly in charge of when I choose to work. The advantage to the students is that their grades and my comments are returned in Vax mail – and usually within 24 hours. Becoming familiar with doing work through telecommunications also prepares students for such systems when they graduate and find employment.

Since the middle 1980s I have been using a computer conference system to fill the role of classroom discussion for a "telecourse" in American history. This class never meets face to face. Originally it did meet for an orientation and introduction to the computer presentation, but we now deliver this material in print and supplement it with an audio conference by telephone.

The Rochester Institute of Technology (RIT) has as one of its constituent colleges the National Technical Institute for the Deaf. Some of its students have found that a class using a computer conference opened more possibilities for their participation in class discussions. It became an ideal format for mainstreaming some students, especially those who had lost their hearing as youths or young adults. In the same class with traditionally able students, there are often a blind teacher and some hearing impaired students. On the computer screen we all are equal. More than one of the deaf students has told me that this was his or her best course at RIT. "I have felt so left out of it in other classes," one woman confided. "I really enjoyed having class this way because it allowed me to participate in a hearing class," she exclaimed and concluded, "By that I mean I was able to get your opinions firsthand so to speak – and the opinions of the other students."

In the fall of 1991, RIT was joined by Gallaudet University in Washington, DC, more than 400 miles away, to conduct two courses using computer conferencing in which half of the students in each class are on each campus. Both courses rely on captioned videos and movies along with text readings to present course content. However, the group discussions and personal interactions between student and teacher take place via computer. I am teaching a course in black civil rights using Vax Notes on an RIT Vax system, and J. S. Schuchman is conducting a course in mass media and deaf history using a similar system on a Vax at Gallaudet. Half of my students are at Gallaudet and connect to the RIT computer over the Internet data network. Similarly, half of Schuchman's students are at RIT and use the Internet to enter class discussions on the Gallaudet computer. Some of the students are hearing impaired, and some are not. We are using computer telecommunications to transcend both physical distance and physical disabilities. Clearly this system is also liberating for persons with other physical disabilities like motor and mobility impairments.

Online services have also expanded my world as a scholar and researcher. I vividly recall the excitement with which I connected to the college library catalog. The first thing I did was to see if my book really existed. It did! That made me feel like a genuine author. Now, while sitting at home, I have accessed library catalogs from New York to California as well as in England and Australia, and I did it all by myself. Previously I had to be accompanied by a reader on a visit to a local library to browse in the catalog. Our college library is exploring online access to its CD-rom products. This brings a rapidly growing number of reference tools online where I can use them to facilitate both research and course preparation.

The same online menu which interfaces the local facilities of the college's library also interfaces RIT faculty and students with some of the facilities of the Dow Jones system. For me, it was amazing to have independent access to an online encyclopedia. Although I had earned a Bachelor of Science, a Master of Science, and a doctorate and had been teaching for some 30 years, I had never had such an opportunity before. Using the Dow system, I can also read the latest headline news as soon as a story breaks. Previously I gained most of my news from radio or television.

While I have not made extensive use of the more expensive commercial databases, I have used *Dialog* in searching for some scholarly information. There are several important information sources available especially related to legal and medical research. Others are being planned to meet the needs of varying disciplines. Business people use data communications to follow stocks and to make financial transactions.

Data networks and computer bulletin boards host active discussions on any and every topic imaginable. I belong to several Bitnet and Internet discussion groups primarily related to my professional interests in history, education, and telecommunications. Online services connect me on a daily basis with information resources, students, and other professionals. My work output has expanded dramatically. The online world has turned me into a much more productive teacher and scholar. My case is not unique, but it is the one I know best.

Problems in accessing online services

Online services, however, may present two kinds of difficulties to the disabled computer user: inconvenient user input requirements and displays that may be difficult for a physically impaired person to access.

The online services I have used require two different kinds of user inputs: keystrokes and manipulating a highlight bar on the menu. For some motor impaired users, complicated keystroke combinations can be difficult or even impossible to implement. When the keystroke demands the user's holding two keys simultaneously, this can make a system unusable. Some systems require the use of function keys or other special keys, and differing communication packages may not send the expected code through to the host computer. *Isaac*, for example, is a bulletin board system for teachers, and until late 1991 it restricted itself to discussing the uses of IBM computers in education. Members were sent free copies of the Kermit communications system to access Isaac. The software came configured ready to pass function key codes through to the host in the expected manner.

Like many other users, I generally do my online work using *Procomm*. While there is a way to reconfigure Procomm to do the job, it requires complicated work by the user. Personally I object to having either to learn a second program or to reconfigure mine. Being required to use special software to access an online service seems to me to be like having to borrow a different automobile to be able to access a drive-in restaurant. Restricting or complicating access to an online service would appear to be self-defeating. However, during the time this chapter was being written, Isaac reconfigured its system. It can now be accessed by a very broad spectrum of communications programs. It has also changed its menu keystroke requirements to standard keys. It has become more accessible and friendly. Users may now interface with Isaac without changing software.

Manipulating a highlight bar can present problems of a different kind. Manipulating and clicking a mouse can prohibit its use by some motor impaired persons. The highlight bar can be utilized by blind users, but it frequently causes unnecessary complications. Before the user can manipulate the bar, he or she has to be able to locate it. Most speech output software can identify items that are highlighted, but it usually requires extra work by the user. Sometimes an extra keystroke will tell the software to look for such items; in other cases, the user has to listen to the menu with the speech software inserting words like "normal" or "bright" in front of each item spoken, which can be both distracting and annoying. Although visually impaired users can access menus built around this approach, such cumbersomeness can discourage them from accessing these systems unless they contain material that is vital and cannot be procured elsewhere.

Inconvenient displays are a second area of access difficulty. Obviously the discussion above regarding manipulating highlight bars is also an example of a display problem. Interfaces which rely heavily on graphics for their menus and other outputs are also a serious access problem for the blind. Speech access software is normally designed to work with Ascii text. The U.S. commercial *Prodigy* system, as another example, not only requires the user to learn its unique access software, but it is, at this point at least, inaccessible by speech output software. Not only has this service needlessly prohibited blind users from accessing it, but its graphics dependence also limits which computers can access it. In the name of presenting an attractive product, the proprietors are restricting their consumer audience. Many of Prodigy's users also complain about the slowness resulting from the graphics orientation.

Other displays which are text oriented can also become needlessly complicated. The CD-rom products which our college library is making accessible online provide another example. Not only does each of several producers have an entirely different menu style and command set, but some of the designers have made their menus confusingly and annoyingly complex. It almost appears that they believe blank space on a screen is a sin. These spaces are filled up with equal signs, asterisks, and other symbols which are supposed to enhance the appearance of the product. However, they can make quick location of one's choice more difficult for any user. For a blind user with speech output, hearing 80 equal signs being spoken is maddening. The producers of one of these CD-rom products fills the opening screen with literally dozens of occurrences of the name "Wilson Disk." Besides driving a listener to distraction, when accessed online, even at 2,400 baud, the system takes an inordinately long time to map the screen, which is frustrating to any user.

Other users of online services than myself may have more items to include or better examples to make these points. My intent was not to cover all the problems or to point a finger at particular culprits. I wanted to use my own experiences to help focus attention on the kinds of problems which do occur with some online services. These problems, however, are not part of every service and are not necessary features. The last portion of this chapter will suggest possible solutions and point out examples of systems which do function well without such features.

Alternative inputs and redundant displays

Providing online service users with the choice of alternative input systems and simultaneously presenting the displayed material in redundant formats will go a long way to overcoming the problems mentioned here. Some disabilities make one kind of input easier to use, while another disability may function better with an alternative choice. Similarly, differing output displays will benefit different people. Not only is this true of the obviously disabled user, but so-called normal users also have varying work styles and preferences. What may be included in computer software design in order to achieve access for otherwise handicapped consumers will be found beneficial to mainstream users as well. If these considerations are taken into account in early design stages, they will not require much extra effort and will produce a product with appeal to a wider audience.

Accessing sophisticated and complicated information resources does not preclude the use of simple-appearing interfaces. In fact, it probably makes their use even more desirable. Two of the more complex data sources I have used are the Dow Jones system and the Dialog database. Both have simple and clean menus and a straightforward input system. The Dow uses menus with numbers next to each item. The user inputs the relevant number to make a selection.

While I do not recall using an online service with redundant displays, I have had software on my personal computer which had a highlight bar to indicate menu choice but also had every menu item identified with a number or a letter. Computers with advanced graphics capability might want to continue to utilize highlight bars, but they could easily put brief text beside the icon. A picture of a wastebasket could have "del" beside it. Often icons are not as communicative as is supposed. Recently a friend told me that when she booted her computer it did not function normally but did present her with a picture of a spinning disk and a question mark. She had absolutely no idea what that was intended to convey. Perhaps phrases like "i/o error" fail to communicate too, but the icon was no improvement. Whether an icon and brief text would have helped in this case depends on the icon and text as well as on the user's previous knowledge.

If providing redundant outputs sounds like creating twice the work, remember that software is seldom produced from scratch. Programmers are normally using a set of predefined tools. Certainly they are not drawing a picture of a pencil or wastebasket every time they create a menu with icons on it. So the extra work is involved only in creating the original set of predefined symbols and tools. Thereafter the effort involved will be the same. The more information that can be presented quickly and simply, the more the user can comprehend the meaning of the display.

The obvious accompaniment to redundant display is permitting the user a choice of two or more input methods. The display concept suggested here could readily interface with a user manipulating a mouse, tapping UP- and DOWN-arrow keys, or inputting a brief command through the keyboard. While allowing such diversity of access may make the difference as to whether a person with motor impairments can use the system or not, it also lets a user access a variety of systems using a similar input method. At present, users have to manipulate highlight bars on one system and input keystrokes on another. Instead of forcing standardization on users and programmers, the kind of system having choice built into it would let a user continue to work with whichever method was preferred, no matter what facility was being accessed.

When the content of the information source is essentially graphics data, there would seem to be no way around the problem. A blind user may have to accept the need for another person's help when he or she needs information that is contained in a picture or a map. Requiring an information source to include a lengthy description of such items would be a hardship and most likely would not be satisfactory in any case. There is work being done to have a computer assist a visually impaired user to access complex charts and diagrams. Professor David Lunney of East Carolina University and the Science Institute for the Disabled is developing a system which combines speech output with patterns of musical notes to communicate difficult three-dimensional material. Perhaps someday such a system will be tied into an online access system. In the meantime, there will have to be some limits to accessing information of this kind. However, the hope is that such problems will result only from the nature of the information itself and not from the inaccessibility of the online interface.

Interfacing with online services is at present even more complicated than mastering different display outputs and command sets. The entire structure of various databases can be different and can require quite different strategies for searching and retrieving information. An exciting new project to transcend this problem is *Wais,* which stands for Wide Area Information Server. It is the result of a cooperative venture sponsored by four leading information corporations: Thinking Machines Corporation, which has developed high-end information retrieval engines; Apple Computer, well known for its user interface expertise; KPMG Peat Marwick, with an information-dependent user base; and Dow Jones and Company, emphasizing business information sources.

Wais functions between the user's access program and the information databases. The user can work using any one of a variety of front end programs. It might be one written especially to interface with Wais. It might be a search program originally developed to access a large research library catalog at a university like Yale or Harvard. Wais uses a common protocol to transmit questions and retrieval requests. The user has the advantage of working on a familiar system, often one which is user definable, and yet searching several information sources with different requirements and structures. The user inputs his request in a plain English format, remaining oblivious to all these complications, and lets the machine do the confusing work.

Wais also permits a user to use *relevance feedback*. When the system has found something the user wants, he or she indicates that articles similar to the one found would be relevant. The system uses this information to refine and extend its search. While Wais is not primarily concerned with the user inputs and the display, it is a gigantic step toward making the machine fit human needs instead of making the user learn how several different electronic information sources function. Wais has special value for disabled users, but it is also another step in adapting the machine to human needs.

Summary: A plea to designers

The bottom line in this chapter is a plea for the software developers to remember the user. There clearly is a tendency to want to show off the high tech capabilities of a system. Moving highlight bars around a screen looks impressive and provides the appearance of advanced design. Yet it may require a user to move the bar down several rows by tapping the DOWN arrow or dragging the mouse, when a simple keystroke could more easily select an item far down the menu. The question is less "How does the computer work?" or "How can it be made to work?" "How does the human work?" In the early years of computers, humans had to learn how they worked in order to use them. We are now in an era where we can make the computer conform to our functioning. The fact is that people are different. Not only are some physically impaired and others not, but all of us work differently. Some of this difference is that we think and perceive differently from one another. Some of us are right brain oriented, and some are left brain. Some of us think in a linear fashion, while others approach objects in a more holistic manner. When it comes to accessing a computer, some people are oriented to text and keyboard inputs. Others intuitively respond to icons and the mouse. Designers need not select between these two systems. They can let users choose for themselves.

The next generation of personal computers will be faster than those we use today, and they will have much more memory available for software features. Building a system from the ground up with redundant outputs and able to accept alternative inputs will neither slow down the machine noticeably nor take enough extra memory to be significant. If the concept is built in at the beginning, it will not mean significant design expense. The end result will be a human–computer interface suited to the needs of more people. Creating redundant displays and permitting alternative inputs, while providing access to a growing number of disabled computer users and offering them an enhanced personal and professional life, will suit a larger population of nondisabled computer users as well.

16

Producing a text-to-speech synthesizer for use by blind people

Paul Blenkhorn

Text-to-speech synthesis

A text-to-speech synthesizer is a device which will accept data in standard Ascii format which is transformed by predefined rules such that it can be spoken by the device. Generalized text-to-speech conversion implies that the device can speak anything sent to it. In other words, it has an unlimited vocabulary. This is in contrast to *copy synthesis* systems, which have a number of stored words or phrases which can be played back.

Specific algorithms for conversion of text to speech are not the concern of this chapter, and so for purposes here a traditional text-to-speech system can be simply described in terms of processing the text through several stages:

- A preprocessor converts abbreviations and numbers into textual form. For example: Mr. → mister, 1992 → nineteen ninety two, 1st → first.

- A text-to-phoneme stage converts words to phonemes (sound elements); for example: coin → K OY N, the → DH UH or DH EE (depending on whether or not the next word begins with a vowel sound).

- A prosodic component decides upon both the pitch and the duration of each phoneme, depending upon the type of the current sentence (or phrase) and the surrounding phonemes.

This well marked phonetic data is then passed to a lower level system which chooses precisely which sounds to use and how to join them together. This description is something of an oversimplification; with all languages there are nontrivial problems associated with most of the stages above, and with English there are difficulties at *every* stage. For a comprehensive summary of text-to-speech synthesis, see Klatt (1987). Text-to-speech systems are constructed of hardware and software, but the better quality speech synthesizers are mainly hardware based.

Uses of text-to-speech synthesizers

For illustration it is convenient to consider blind people using text-to-speech synthesizers in two broad and somewhat overlapping areas, which will be termed personal data processing and external data processing. The use of a synthesizer in the education of blind people, and particularly its use with blind children, will not be considered in this chapter.

Personal data processing. Here the blind person will be using such software as a word processor, a database, or a spreadsheet. The user will be entering and editing data in a highly interactive manner and will be reading information which is probably quite familiar. In most cases this will involve using a screen reader with the synthesizer. A screen reader is a piece of software and/or hardware which "hooks into" the operating system of the computer and sends information to the synthesizer which enables the blind person to use the program. For further discussion of screen readers see Blenkhorn (1993), Blenkhorn and Caulderwood (1992), Meyers and Schreier (1990), Schreier, DeWitt, Goldberg, and Leventhal (1987). Some clients will have their synthesizers built into a portable battery powered device, giving them, at a minimum, note taking facilities.

External data processing. In the case of a user accessing external data, it will be taken to be in such areas as reading a book using an optical character reading (OCR) system (Converso & Hocek, 1990; Hazan & Hunt, 1990; Schreier & Uslan, 1991) or accessing a remote database such as Prestel (King, 1989; Omotayo, 1984) or teletext, such as Ceefax and Oracle (Blenkhorn & Payne, 1985). These facilities may be provided by custom built hardware or again by using a screen reader with a computer adapted to perform the appropriate task, for example with a teletext card installed. In this case the client is normally taking a much more passive role and, although interacting with the system, will be spending a much greater proportion of the time just listening.

An application which has been gaining importance has been the use of CD-roms for storing and accessing information (Dixon & Mandelbaum, 1990; Kendrick, 1991). It is worth noting that in this case the style of interaction will depend very much on the information on the CD-rom being used. So, for example, in reading an article from the CD-rom, the mode of interaction will be much the same as in external data processing, as described above. However, if the user is interrupting word processing to look something up in a thesaurus, the mode of interaction is taken to be a supplement to the personal system and can be assumed to be much more interactive.

The current state of systems

It is somewhat speculative to try come up with figures, but there are probably several thousand blind people with such systems in the UK alone. Most of these people will be using the computer for personal applications, predominantly word processing, but possibly also access to online services such as those discussed in the previous chapter. This is probably not a true reflection of the priorities of blind people. A greater need is for access to print, which is possible with the use of OCRs. It is likely that the current low use of OCRs is due to their relatively high cost and the difficulty of using them – a human–computer interface problem still to be addressed.

Most users of screen readers will be using fairly low-cost personal systems which have been developed specifically for disabled people. The quality of the voice on these systems will generally not be as high as on the "top-of-the-range" synthesizers or as good as research synthesizers. However, it should be made clear that most clients very quickly get used to their synthesizer, often in spite of the quality of the voice. In fact, having become accustomed to a particular synthesizer, some users are very loathe to change to a "better" system. However, with novices it has been found that an improved quality of voice does make a system less forbidding than one which they cannot, at first, understand very well.

Points to consider

In producing a device such as a text-to-speech synthesizer, many factors must be taken into consideration. These will, of course, each have a greater or lesser part to play in the final decision of what to implement. Criteria will be considered here in three overlapping groups: issues relating to the voice, physical requirements, and marketing considerations.

Issues relating to the voice

There is no clear dividing line between the speech synthesizer and the driving software – the screen reader – particularly in software based synthesizers. This has always been something of a problem in defining interactive talking systems (Morford, 1983), and it complicates discussion of voice related issues. However, regardless of where these issues are addressed, they can still be described from the user's point of view. Several categories of facilities can be identified as being of relevance.

Interacting with speech. When using a highly interactive system, and particularly one with a screen reader, the feedback from the synthesizer can have a significant influence on how quickly a blind person can work. Clearly if the synthesizer can be used at a higher speed and still be understood, then work can proceed more rapidly. A high speed can also be used to skim parts of text, the synthesizer then being slowed down for more careful work. In fact, with practice many blind people use synthesizers at extremely high speeds; some demanding systems speak at well over 500 words per minute (Chong, 1987). It should be noted that the speed of spoken English is typically between 150 and 250 words per minute.

It should be possible to silence the voice instantly and for the software driving the synthesizer to know on which word the voice has been stopped. The voice should respond quickly when information is required, either because the user has requested the information or because the screen reader has determined that some information should be given, for example an error message appearing at a given position on the screen.

Other facilities which can prove useful include putting pauses between words, which can be particularly helpful to people who are just getting used to the voice; being able to spell words either in the normal way ("Ay," "Bee," "See," etc.) or phonetically ("Alpha," "Bravo,," "Charlie," etc.); to have the data being typed echoed either as characters or as words or not at all; to have some or all punctuation spoken or to have it just indicated by the intonation of the voice; and to be able to distinguish whether parts of the text are either upper or lower case by using sound effects or by changing the pitch of the voice appropriately.

In many ways this category, more than anything else, highlights the differences between what seem to be the current aims of the speech research community and the needs of blind people. Research synthesizers, and the commercial synthesizers which have been developed from them, tend to have a good quality voice which is quite easy to understand. Sadly, in almost every case they also do not speak at a very high rate and are slow to respond. An interesting anecdote, although one from which it would be a little unfair to generalize, is that several blind users have commented that they would not use a leading high quality synthesizer even if they were given one for free because of poor interactive facilities which would restrict them when using their screen reader.

The quality of the voice. The voice quality is one of the first characteristics of the synthesizer a user encounters. A good voice can make understanding the synthesizer much easier, particularly when the user is getting accustomed to using the system. What is often meant by a high quality synthesizer is one that sounds more natural, more like a person. A more natural voice may have some bearing on how tired a person gets working with speech, and it can be especially useful when accessing external data, for example reading a book. Of paramount importance in all synthesizers is that the voice be consistent, clear, and, even if some training is required, understandable. There are a number of well known tests which are often used to gain a measure of the intelligibility of synthesizers – for more information see Allen, Hunnicutt, and Klatt (1987). (It is interesting to note that with earlier synthesizers people used to comment about the "robotic" or "dalek like" quality of the voices, whereas now they are more likely to comment on the accent.)

Most text-to-speech synthesizers are quite clearly male, even when they supposedly have female voices, but they are increasingly being provided with facilities to switch between different voices. This can prove most effective in indicating different contexts to the blind user. For example, a voice can be used for error messages different from the one used for the standard writing mode.

It should be noted that when a synthesizer is used at high speed, as described above, the voice is no longer natural.

The pronunciation of words. Clearly if a client wants to read a document, and particularly if he or she wishes to check something that has been written to be sent to another person, it is of some significance that the spelling of text be correct, and this is best accomplished if the pronunciation of the words is correct. (In English at least, this is not completely achievable.) A statistic which helps to illustrate part of the problem is that in the USA the Social Security Administration (1985) has estimated that there are over 1.7 million different last names in its files, and to pronounce many of them correctly would involve some understanding of each of the countries of origin of the names – if, indeed, the country can be identified from the current form of the name. A pragmatic solution to the problem of mispronounced words is to include the facility for the client to have his or her own *exceptions dictionary* where individualized pronunciations can be stored. It is hoped that this area will improve. But – to defend current systems a little – with many synthesizers consistently pronouncing words incorrectly, the user gets accustomed to this and can treat it as just another aspect of the synthesizer's accent.

Multilingual aspects. Cost is dealt with in a later section; it is appropriate here to point out that having access to several countries with a multilingual synthesizer can result in greater sales and can help to reduce cost. Increasingly, and especially outside the UK, blind people will be using more than one language. In some cases there are a large number of people who may use up to four languages (in Switzerland, German, French, Italian, and English). So a synthesizer must not just be able to speak several languages but should also have be able to switch between languages quickly and easily.

This has serious implications, as the underlying structures of the text-to-speech algorithms must cope with different character sets, such as Roman, Greek, and Cyrillic. It is also helpful if those structures permit new languages to be readily constructed out of existing ones. In the commercial world one can often justify spending quite a lot of time on major European languages. It is hoped that languages with a smaller potential market, such as Irish or Welsh, can also be implemented and supported.

Physical considerations

There are several, sometimes conflicting, requirements in considering the uses of synthesizers for blind people. The synthesizer should:

• be small enough to be included in battery powered portable computers;

- be able to fit inside a desktop computer so that the user does not end up with a tangle of wires;
- be portable and capable of running on battery power, so a client working on several machines can carry it between them and easily install it;
- have different interfaces so that users can connect the synthesizer to different computers, for example a PC-compatible or an Apple – this generally implies that it should have a choice of parallel and serial interfaces;
- be readily upgradable if the manufacturer comes up with an improved algorithm;
- be robust, considering that it may well be carried around.

It is not expected that a single configuration can meet all of these physical requirements for a text-to-speech synthesizer for blind people, and so it will be useful to have a range of synthesizers to choose from. They should all have the same voice, so that a client with several systems to meet different needs will need to become accustomed to just one type of voice.

Often users will want to hear the speech through headphones so that they will not disturb their neighbors, but usually they will also want the option of being able to use loudspeakers.

In time it is expected that software-only synthesizers will make consideration of many of these physical characteristics irrelevant. However, that may still be some time away, especially as software-only systems have a tendency to take up memory, and more important, can slow down the computer and hence the interaction.

Marketing considerations

It is fair to state that the current markets for speech synthesizers all seem to be quite specialized, with the mass market still to come. It is probably the case that the market of disabled people is a significant part of the total market if one includes educational software, *augmentative communications* systems for people who cannot speak, and systems for blind people. Looking to the future, though, it is prudent to note that some of the more serious research in this area is being conducted by telecommunications companies, who see computer generated speech as being of importance in their market.

One of the major considerations for most people buying a synthesizer is the cost. Not surprisingly, addressing many of the features described above can involve investment of a great deal of research and development time and money. This clearly implies some level of compromise, but it can be greatly alleviated if the product can be sold in sufficient quantities. Again it is difficult to come up with figures, but a reasonable estimate of the present potential world market for text-to-speech synthesizers for blind people is going to be several thousand a year – perhaps as many as 5,000. In terms of, say, transistor radios, that is a tiny quantity (especially since synthesizers may have to be produced in several forms and then be continually updated as computer manufacturers change their models and interfaces).

It is probably necessary to expect to sell the same models of synthesizers for some years, which means that a continuation of supply for their components, without too great an increase in unit costs, is required. This has proved difficult on occasion in the past, with specialist speech chips either being withdrawn or, more recently, rumored to be withdrawn, which made planning difficult. This is of decreasing importance as more synthesizers are being developed which are based on general purpose digital signal processors (DSPs); they are expected also to be used in other markets for a considerable time to come.

Of significant importance to many people already selling equipment to disabled people, and also to clients using existing products, is whether a new synthesizer will work with their software. For example will the synthesizer work with other manufacturers' screen readers? It is quite unfortunate that there are no widely accepted speech synthesiser interface standards or protocols. The issues of one manufacturer supplying synthesizers to other software manufacturers and of standard interfaces is further complicated by the fact that these people may well also market their own hardware and so may not be very keen to sell or support those of other companies.

A related issue is support of the hardware, although in many ways this is not always the problem that it seems at first. As long as a product is reliable and easily upgradable, the main problem is supporting a client who uses it. With a synthesizer, a client is in many ways in much the same position as someone buying a printer to go with a word processor; as long as the word processor is set up appropriately for the printer, the support requirements of the user are largely related to the word processor.

Conclusions

Some criteria of relevance to producing a text-to-speech synthesizer for blind people have been discussed. These may be of use to current and future designers and manufacturers of synthesizers but may also be of interest to HCI researchers in illustrating some of the requirements of synthesizers beyond speech quality.

It is hoped that in time the price and quality of speech of text-to-speech synthesizers will be such that they are available to many more users, assuming of course that performance is not sacrificed where high performance is appropriate.

References

Allen, J., Hunnicutt, M. S., and Klatt, D. (1987). *From text to speech: The MITalk system*. Cambridge University Press.

Blenkhorn, P. (1993). Requirements for screen access software using synthetic speech, *Journal of Microcomputer Applications* 16(3):243–248.

Blenkhorn, P., and Caulderwood, D. (1992). Access to personal computers using speech synthesis: A review of the past decade. *The New Beacon – The Journal of Blind Welfare, 76*(898): 185–188.

Blenkhorn, P. L., and Payne, B. (1985). Teletext for the visually impaired. *The New Beacon – The Journal of Blind Welfare*, 69(819): 197–198.

Chong, C. (1987, October–November). What do blind consumers want from a speech synthesizer? *Braille Monitor*, pp. 453–457.

Converso, L., and Hocek, S. (1990). Optical character recognition. *Journal of Visual Impairment and Blindness*, *84*(10):507–509.

Dixon, J. M., and Mandelbaum, J. B. (1990). Reading through technology: Evolving methods and opportunities for print-handicapped individuals. *Journal of Visual Impairment and Blindness*, *84*(10): 493–496.

Hazan, R. and Hunt, A. (1990). For once the blind came first: The history of the Kurzweil 1970–1990. *British Journal of Visual Impairment*, 7(2): 45–47.

Kendrick, D. (1991). CD-ROM spells efficiency for some, equality for others. *Tactic*, 7(2): 8–11.

King, R. W. (1989). Layout processing, user control and prosody insertion in an on-line synthetic speech system. *Proceedings of Conference Eurospeech '89*, Paris, vol. 1, pp. 121–124.

Klatt D. H. (1987). Review of text-to-speech conversion for English. *Journal of the Acoustical Society of America, 82*: 737–793.

Meyers, A., and Schreier, E. (1990). An evaluation of speech access programs. *Journal of Visual Impairment and Blindness, 84*(1): 26–38.

Morford, A. R. (1983). How to select a talking terminal. *Aids and Appliances Review*, *9*:6–10.

Omotayo, O. R. (1984). Performance of Videotex-to-speech converter. *IEE Proceedings*, *131*(5): 328–333.

Schreier, E. M., DeWitt, J. C., Goldberg, A. M., and Leventhal, J. D. (1987). An evaluation of synthetic speech software programs. *Journal of Visual Impairment and Blindness, 81*(2): 70–74.

Schreier, E. M., and Uslan, M. M. (1991). An evaluation of PC-based optical character recognition systems. *Journal of Visual Impairment and Blindness*, *85*(3): 131–135.

Social Security Administration. (1985). *Report of distribution of surnames in the Social Security number file*. Social Security Administration Pub. No. 42-004. Washington, DC: Department of Health and Human Resources.

17

A physical skills based strategy for choosing an appropriate interface method

Sherry Perdue Casali

Selection of an appropriate computer access method

Computer technology has the potential to offer individuals with physical limitations greater levels of independence and increased opportunities for meaningful employment; however, the maximum benefit of a computer system can be realized only when the individual can interact as efficiently as possible with the computer.

Available access methods

In addition to the standard input and output techniques available for computer systems, literally thousands of adaptive devices and special programs to assist individuals with disabilities in using computers have been developed and are available (Berliss, Borden, & Vanderheiden, 1989; Closing the Gap, 1990). For example, a number of solutions are available to help in typing. There exist a variety of keyguards which fit over the keyboard to make the selection of a particular key easier, enlarged keyboards to help those who have difficulty selecting the small keys of a standard keyboard, and reduced keyboards to augment the skills of individuals with severely limited range of motion or the use of only one hand. There are aids which allow a user to select keys with a pointer held in the mouth or fixed to a headstrap, and others which imitate keyboard entry by the activation of a single switch mounted so that it may be operated by some functional body member (Chapter 13). There are also methods of inputting information by speaking (Chapter 7), and systems which monitor a person's gaze to determine the item on the screen being viewed. There are a host of aids to assist visually impaired persons as well. The computer's screen can be magnified, and the output can be presented in the form of braille (Chapter 9) or artificial speech (Chapter 16).

Adaptive hardware must often be accompanied by special software. Programs are available which allow a user to enter simultaneous keystrokes sequentially.

Users of a headstick or mouthstick or a single switch, for example, would otherwise be unable to accomplish functions which require pressing two keys simultaneously, such as entering a control code. A variety of programs are available to help increase the keying entry rate. Some programs allow the user to enter user defined abbreviations for frequently used blocks of text, and many programs also have word predictive capabilities which allow the user to type only the first few letters of a word before the program completes that word, based on the frequency of occurrence of particular words (Chapters 6 and 5). Literally thousands of adaptive hardware devices and software programs exist which can make computers more accessible to persons with all types of disabilities.

Sources of information on accommodative aids

Although many aids are available to provide easier computer access, it is often difficult to know where to begin to find information about them so that those best suited to a particular individual can be selected. A number of organizations provide services which promote computer access by persons with disabilities. Assistive device centers maintain a large stock of different types of aids for a client to try. However, the expense associated with acquiring the equipment and employing specialists limits the number and usefulness of such centers. Workshops and conferences often include presentations by vendors describing new products and ideas as well as exhibit areas where products are demonstrated; however, travel to them may not be practicable.

There are a number of electronic bulletin board services (BBS) for computer users with disabilities. While this type of service offers the unique advantage that one can often communicate directly with a current user of a product, the list of products is not comprehensive, because the primary purpose of the BBS is not to be a product resource directory. There are also a number of catalogs and databases which list and describe the available aids. Several such databases exist and are reviewed in detail in Casali and Williges (1990). They differ slightly from one another with respect to organization and range of products covered but are similar with respect to the type of product information available. Most simply list the product name, product class, a short narrative description, and the vendor's name and address. Some contain information regarding product cost, size, and weight. Refer also to Chapter 19 for information on sources of information.

Current selection methods

The goal when selecting accommodative aids is, of course, to select the hardware and software configuration that will maximize the efficiency of a person with a given physical limitation in performing a predetermined set of tasks. This naturally involves a correlation between the task requirements of the user and the functionality of the equipment. It also involves a correlation between the physical capabilities of the user and the physical skills required to operate each piece of equipment.

At present, the approach taken to device selection is "pseudo-systematic and subjective" (Kondraske, 1988, p. 14). Although most clinicians administer standardized (although subjective) evaluations of muscle strength and range of motion as well as tests of hand function, the resulting data are generally not used when selecting computer equipment. Instead, the clinician usually assesses the client's skills subjectively by watching the client perform these and other standardized tests and activities. With this information, the counselor may choose aids available at the center for the client to try until a workable solution is discovered. Alternatively, where aids are unavailable to try, the clinician may review descriptions of products and choose one which appears to be of use to the client. With this procedure, however, only after purchasing the aid can the client evaluate specific product functions and operational techniques to determine if the device will indeed meet his or her needs. Currently, then, a successful match depends on the clinician's expertise in assessing the client's functional abilities and task needs as well as on the clinician's breadth of knowledge of the currently available devices (Kondraske, 1988).

As stated by Lee and Thomas (1990), "when only a few options existed, the trial and error method, or 'trying-on' of access systems was feasible and practical. Now, this same approach would be inordinately time-consuming and costly for the clinician and fatiguing for the client." Similarly, the choices are far too great for a clinician to be familiar with the capabilities and requirements for use of all. As a result, counselors must rely on manufacturers' information to become familiar with products. This type of information, however, is generally not sufficient to ensure selection of a device which the client is capable of using. Typically the only quantitative data describe the size of the device. Guidelines for the strength, speed, vision, dexterity, and so forth, needed for operation are not available. As suggested by Kondraske (1988), this is akin to "purchasing clothing from a catalogue without size information." Even if detailed product information were available, no systematic method currently exists for equating the results of a physical assessment and the predicted performance of a device with given characteristics. Further, the assessment of the user's task needs is often incomplete and hence results in the selection of equipment which fails to meet the function requirements.

Prescription of an inappropriate aid may result in inefficient use of the computer system and correspondingly low productivity of the individual. In extreme cases it may even result in the client's inability to use the system at all. Better tools and a systematic method of evaluating each product for a particular end user are clearly needed.

A systematic approach to device selection

Background and rationale

Because of the increasing difficulty in selecting an accommodative aid, attention within the field of computer applications for users with disabilities is turning toward the *process* of device selection. For example, Lee and Thomas (1990) have developed the Control Assessment Protocol (CAP), a step-by-step procedure for selecting computer based technology. The procedure leads the clinician through a nine-stage process:

- gather background information;
- observe the client;
- survey client skills;
- investigate ideal access system characteristics;
- propose access system;
- personalize access system;
- set goals for instruction;
- implement the system, and
- monitor progress.

The procedure encourages the clinician systematically to consider different control options (e.g. direct selection versus scanning versus encoding) and control sites (head, hand, foot, etc.) and to include in the decision process other influential factors such as proper seating and appropriate stabilizers. While such protocols offer a much needed global approach to device selection, they were never intended to address the issue of the need for detailed information regarding specific equipment or how such information could best be used. The clinician must still rely on his or her own judgment to suggest candidate access methods, and on trial and error to choose a specific device.

The literature offers a few examples of efforts to compare the operating requirements for devices with a user's physical skills. Minkel, Zeitlin, and Masiello (1988) developed a system to aid in the selection of switches. An individual's optimal target size and possible actuation force are measured and compared with the requirements for operation of commercially available switches. If the switch size and actuation force information are available, a switch can be selected which is operable by the user. Similarly, Rosen and

Goodenough-Trepagnier (1989) developed a system for choosing an appropriate keyboard actuated augmentative communication board for motor impaired nonvocal individuals. A specialized assessment board measures a client's ability to choose different sized targets located at different distances from one another. This information is then used to predict client performance (in terms of the communication rate possible) on various commercially available augmentative communication boards with different selection key layouts.

While these efforts are extremely valuable, they are somewhat limited in application, in that a given test, relying on specific test equipment, assesses only the specific skills needed for operating a given type of equipment. A less restricting approach, and one which would thus be more widely applicable, would be to associate performance on different pieces of equipment with the results of a generic assessment of physical skills. This type of approach has not yet received much attention.

A systematic selection system

Figure 17.1 illustrates a systematic approach to selecting the most appropriate computer aids for a computer user with a disability. A detailed description of the approach and the supporting rationale can be found in Casali and Williges (1990). Briefly, the system includes a database containing detailed information on currently available hardware and software; a means to assess the physical skills of the client; a means to determine the task functions to be supported; a method to integrate the various sources of information and select the appropriate combination of aids; and an iterative process of usability testing to evaluate the selections.

Hardware and software database

Although current databases provide extremely valuable information concerning the availability of accommodative aids, they provide only a brief description of the products' functions and generally no information concerning the physical skills required for efficient operation. Without such information, it is difficult to predict whether a particular product will meet the client's specific task needs, whether it is operable by the individual, given his or her physical limitations, whether it can easily interact with other products, and so on.

For example, concerning objects that must be physically manipulated, the size, shape, and weight of the object, as well as the specific action required (e.g. lift, slide, grasp, push), are critical when assessing whether an individual has the skills needed to operate the device. Such information should therefore be included in the product description. Similarly, software descriptions should include such information as visual requirements (e.g. object sizes, text fonts),

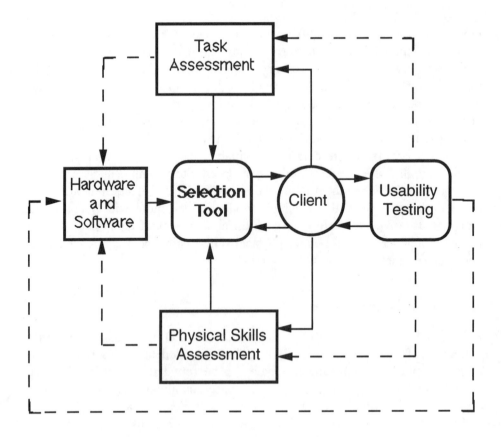

Figure 17.1. Schematic diagram of the proposed selection system. (Reprinted with permission from *Human Factors*, Volume 32, No. 4. Copyright 1990 by the Human Factors Society Inc. All rights reserved.)

auditory requirements (e.g. volume and frequency of auditory cues), and input requirements (e.g. keyboard size and shape, key spacing, size of targets).

Physical capabilities assessment

In order to choose equipment which does not require physical abilities beyond those the client possesses, a comparison must be made between the client's physical skills and those required for device operation. This of course requires that the physical skills necessary in operating the product be identified and described and that the ability of a client to accomplish those actions be determined.

Task needs analysis. A structured approach for determining the specific tasks an individual wishes to be able to accomplish must also be employed. Given that a detailed description of the function of hardware and software products is available in the database, a match can then be made which will meet the functional requirements of the individual.

Selection tool. Selecting appropriate computer aids requires the comparison of information regarding the task requirements and physical capabilities of the user and the functionality and operational requirements of currently available hardware and software aids. When the task needs of the user are compared with the function of each device, a list of products that provide the necessary functions can be generated. Next, when the physical skills needed to operate each piece of equipment are compared with the capabilities of the client, the product or products which can most easily be operated by the client can be determined.

Two key elements in such a selection tool are the link between the description of a client's task needs and the functions of the equipment and the link between the description of the client's physical abilities and the operational requirements of the equipment. In order to make the necessary comparisons between the client's needs and the functions of the equipment, a common language and decision rules are needed. One potentially promising method is to create a detailed taxonomy of office-type tasks. This taxonomy could be used (either by the manufacturer or the database maintainer) when providing information concerning the functions of each device. The client and/or clinician could review this same list when indicating the tasks the client will need to perform. A match could then easily be made between equipment functions and user needs.

Similarly, a common language is needed when comparing the physical actions required to operate a device with the physical capabilities of the client. The database should contain a description of the physical capabilities needed for each device (supplied by either the manufacturer or database maintainer). The physical capabilities of the client should be expressed in the same terminology used to describe the product requirements. Again, a promising method is to create a taxonomy of actions required to operate electronic equipment. This taxonomy can be used in describing products as well as in describing the capabilities of users.

The difficulty in developing an expert system based on objective comparisons, however, lies in specifying the knowledge base needed by the system. Decision rules for choosing equipment with certain characteristics for persons with specific characteristics must be developed.

Usability testing. Usability testing, as applied to this system, consists of an iterative process involving initial selection of possible aids, formative evaluation of the various alternatives, and a final, or summative, evaluation of the selected aid (Williges, Williges, & Elkerton, 1988). These evaluations need to be conducted with the actual user of the aid while performing representative benchmark tasks in the real work environment. One does not necessarily expect to be able to select the best accommodative aid initially. This type of selection procedure would first narrow the alternatives to a workable subset. The subset can then quickly be reduced to the single most useful aid which matches the requirements of a particular disabled client. If such a rigorous usability assessment procedure is followed, a truly workable computer interface in which the appropriate accommodative computer aid is chosen can be determined efficiently. Usability testing can also be used to improve the components of the selection process itself. As shown by the dashed feedback lines in Figure 17.1, both the task assessment and disability assessment methodology can be improved by the results of usability testing. In addition, the usability analysis may suggest the need for hardware and software accommodative aids that do not currently exist.

A supporting study: Matching a user's physical capabilities with input device requirements

As noted, a key element of the proposed selection system is the set of decision rules linking the results of a physical skills assessment with an individual's expected performance when using a piece of hardware or software. An assessment strategy was developed such that the results of the test can be used directly to indicate whether an individual has the physical capabilities needed to use a particular device efficiently. An empirical study was then conducted to evaluate this assessment strategy in terms of its ability to predict an individual's performance with a particular device.

In particular, an assessment test was developed to measure the skills needed to operate a number of manual computer input devices. Individuals who had experienced either partial or total loss of hand function were assessed and were then tested using several input devices. The results of both measures were used to determine the usefulness of the assessment strategy in selecting appropriate computer input devices.

Cursor control and users with disabilities

With the growing popularity of direct manipulation interfaces, choosing an appropriate cursor control device is of increasing importance in general, and may be more so for persons with disabilities. Electronic pointing devices require considerable fine motor control. As a result, typical performance differences among input devices may be magnified for users with impaired motor control. A control device must be selected based on the disabled individual's physical strengths and weaknesses. Not only is it important to choose a device that an individual is able to use, but it is also important to choose one from among those devices which will allow the maximum possible productivity.

Although empirically derived information is available to guide in the selection of an appropriate input device for nondisabled individuals, it is of little value in choosing input devices for persons with physical disabilities. Little empirically derived information exists regarding the performance of individuals with upper extremity motor impairments using cursor control devices. Consequently no data are available to help clinicians choose between various devices or to develop the decision rules.

The current research study has attempted to develop a means of predicting an individual's performance with a set of computer cursor control devices based on descriptions of the device and of the individual's hand skill. Both a standardized method of describing the actions required in operating these devices and an assessment test to measure an individual's ability to accomplish each of these actions were developed. Empirical tests were then conducted to determine how well the assessment test predicts performance. Specifically, the strategy should indicate whether an individual is capable of operating a given device. The test should also be capable of identifying specific areas of difficulty which would be encountered when operating a device, thereby suggesting areas where modifications to the device or an accommodative aid may lead to better performance. Finally, the test results may provide an indication of the level of performance that can be expected with each device. The ability of the assessment strategy to meet each of these three objectives was determined.

Method

Subjects. Both nondisabled and functionally limited persons participated. Twenty persons currently undergoing therapy at a rehabilitation center served as subjects with physical limitations. Based on the expert judgment of trained occupational therapists, persons who would be considered candidate users of such input devices yet who had limitations which would be likely to affect device operation were involved. The participants were also required to have no detectable cognitive impairment. The resulting 20 participants were all quadriplegics but had vastly different levels of residual hand and arm functionality. Table 17.1 describes the level of injury (including completeness) and time since injury of the 20 participants with disabilities. In addition, 10 nondisabled persons from the university community participated.

Experimental apparatus. A Macintosh SE was used to present the computer based tasks and to record time and error data. Specially developed programs running under HyperCard were developed and used. The cursor control devices used were the Macintosh SE expanded keyboard directional cursor keys, a

Kensington Turbomouse trackball, the standard Macintosh mouse, a Kurta 12" × 12" (30.5 × 30.5 cm) graphics tablet (operated in absolute mode), and a Kraft joystick. These particular devices were chosen because of their tremendous popularity as well as the range of physical capabilities which they require for operation. For each device, the control/display ratio setting was chosen according to the manufacturer's general recommendations.

Experimental procedures. Each participant performed a functional assessment test designed to measure his or her ability to perform the types of actions used in operating each of the cursor control devices. He or she also performed a computer based task (target acquisition task) using each of the five cursor control devices. The methods for acquiring the computer based task performance data and the physical skills measurements are discussed separately.

Assessment test development. Physical and occupational therapists have for years used a number of functional tests to assess client skills. For example, the Jebsen Hand Function Test (Carlson & Trombly, 1983), Nine Hole Peg Test (Mathiowetz, Weber, Kashman, & Volland, 1983), Purdue Pegboard (Tifflin, 1968), and the Box and Block Test (Mathiowetz, Volland, Kashman, & Weber, 1985) are among the many functional tests of hand and finger dexterity. These tests require the client to manipulate objects and are objectively scored (usually in terms of time to complete a set of tasks). Although the resulting data are typically used to indicate a need for treatment as well as to track client progress in a therapy program, the tests otherwise serve primarily to provide the client with a standardized exercise that can be observed by the therapist. Relationships between performance on such tests and performance in a functional activity have not been explored or well documented (Mathiowetz et al., 1985). However, after we identified the motions and actions required to operate each of the input devices, we determined that none of the tests reviewed would efficiently measure the actions required for this particular activity. Virtually all subtests of these functional hand tests require the individual to grasp and move objects. However, the ability to grasp objects is not required to operate many cursor control devices (e.g. cursor keys, trackball). Therefore, these tests did not appear to be sensitive enough at lower levels of physical hand/arm skills to determine an individual's ability to perform the types of activities required in operating cursor control devices.

Table 17.1. *Description of subject sample*

Subject no.	Age (years)	Level of injury [1]	Complete/ incomplete	Time since injury (years)
1	33	C6–7	C	2.5
2	42	C5–6	C	0.5
3	27	C3–4	C	8.0
4	18	C5–6	I	0.5
5	26	C5	C	1.5
6	64	C6	I	11.5
7	18	C5–6–7	I	0.5
8	36	C3–4	C	20.0
9	51	C5	C	1.5
10	38	C7	I	0.75
11	37	C4–5	C	2.5
12	27	C5–6	I	10.0
13	28	C4–5	I	7.0
14	34	C5–6	C	4.5
15	35	C5	C	10.0
16	27	C6–7	C	2.75
17	24	C6–7	I	2.5
18	36	C6	C	8.0
19	20	C6	I	0.25
20	20	C4	I	1.25

[1] See Chapter 2 for a description of levels of spinal injury.

Therapists also commonly use a set of standardized tests to evaluate gross muscle and range of motion. The evaluations consist of rating the force and range of motion of various movements. These tests, too, are typically used to indicate a need for treatment and to track client progress in a therapy program rather than as a means of predicting performance in other tasks. Measurement of individual muscle strength and joint range of motion is typically not an adequate indicator of functionality thanks to the ability of an individual to transfer control from the more likely muscle groups to control by a more controllable group of muscles (McPhee, 1987). For example, an individual who has no controllable movement of the lower arm or fingers would be unable to operate a trackball in the conventional fashion. However, he or she may instead use the palm as the point of contact and move the arm about the shoulder to roll the ball. To predict performance based on an evaluation of strength and range of motion would require the counselor to consider all possible methods of performance.

Table 17.2. *Action categories and associated descriptors*

Action category	Attribute
Reach (or "point")	Target size
	Target distance
Slide	Resistance
	Target size
Lift/move	Object size
	Object shape
	Object weight
Place	Object size
	Object shape
Repetition speed	
Reaction time	

An alternative assessment strategy is to construct an assessment test which measures specific *actions* required in the activity of interest. A new assessment procedure was developed which measures the specific actions needed in operating cursor control devices and contains elements which differentiate among levels of extremely limited hand skill (i.e. little or no finger or manual dexterity). In addition, the test was developed so that the results would be directly usable by a selection system such as that described previously. As mentioned before, such a selection system requires that a common language be available for describing the actions needed to operate a device and the physical capabilities of the potential user. Because it is desirable that nonspecialists be able to provide device action requirements, the description should not be based on a physiological description of the motor control involved. It should be based instead on simple observable actions. To maintain consistency, the terminology used to describe these observable actions should be standardized. Therefore a taxonomy of actions required in operating such devices was first developed. The assessment test was then developed so that it measures the ability to accomplish (and the resulting degree of proficiency) each of these basic actions.

Each input device being considered was first analyzed with respect to the actions needed for operation. This analysis was based on the methods engineering approach of motion and time study. It involved observing persons using each of the devices and breaking down their physical actions into elementary components. Once the elementary actions required in using the five devices were identified, they were organized into action categories, and appropriate attributes for each category were identified.

The resulting set of action categories and attributes is shown in Table 17.2. Note that not all possible attributes are included for each action category. For example, distance of the move is of course an important attribute of the action

Table 17.3. *Action categories and attribute levels for the reach subtests*

Reach subtest	Target distance, center to center (in.)	Target size (in.^{2})
R1	1	0.5
R2	2	0.5
R3	2	1.0
R4	5	0.5
R5	5	1.0
R6	11	0.5
R7	11	1.0
R8	11	2.0

"Move." However, in order to keep the testing time reasonably short, certain assumptions regarding the interrelationships of the actions had to be made. In this case, for example, it is assumed that if a person can reach long distances and can move an object a short distance, then he or she can move that object a long distance. Therefore, distance is not varied in the "Move" action. If such assumptions were not made, and each action were tested using every combination of all possible descriptions, the time needed to administer the test would quickly become impractically great.

Once the action categories and appropriate attributes were identified, appropriate levels of each attribute to be tested were decided. A representative sample of what was thought to be a practical range for each attribute of each action in a wide range of tasks was chosen. For example, Table 17.3 shows the levels of each attribute to be tested for the "Reach" category. Once the actions and attributes were identified, a subtest was developed which mimicked the action and appropriate level of each corresponding attribute.

For the test to be of practical value to clinicians, it should not only be reasonably short in duration but should also be easy and inexpensive to construct and administer. With these points in mind, the subtests were constructed to involve:

- reaching/pointing to targets of various sizes and spacings drawn on large sheets of paper;
- sliding wooden blocks of various sizes and resistances onto targets of varying sizes (so as to test levels of precision);
- grasping and lifting wooden and metal blocks of various sizes and weights;
- putting objects of various sizes and weights through various sized templates (testing levels of precision);
- repetitive tapping; and
- a measure of reaction time.

Standardized instructions were developed and used, and performance was measured using a stopwatch. The test includes six action categories (point/reach, slide, lift/move, place, reaction time, and repetition speed), with several levels of numerous attributes for the first four, resulting in a total of 39 subtests. Finally, each device was again considered, and the subtests were identified which were thought best to represent those actions identified as being essential for operation of each device. Accordingly, performance with a given input device should be a function of the performance on the set of relevant subtests for that device.

Input device performance measurement. To measure an individual's actual ability to operate each device, each subject performed a generic computer task (i.e. a cursor positioning/target acquisition task) with each of the five cursor control devices. Independent variables were device, trial block, target size, target distance, and "button mode." Button mode (or select mode) had two levels: button up and button down (or what are commonly referred to as "point and click" and "drag" modes).

The target acquisition task required the subject to move the cursor from one target area labeled "Start" to a second target area, using the cursor control device, and then confirm the selection by pressing and/or releasing the select key associated with the input device. Each target was square in shape. Four target sizes were used: 0.1, 0.21, 0.42, and 0.84 in (0.27, 0.54, 1.07, and 2.14 cm). Three target distances were used: 0.79, 1.57, and 3.15 inches (2, 4, and 8 cm). These target sizes/distances are representative of the range typically encountered in many graphics and word processing task environments (Epps, 1986). The direction of movement was randomized.

Each trial block consisted of one selection of each of the target size × target distance combinations (3 × 4), for a total of 12 target selections. Half of the trial blocks involved button up moves (point and click) while the other half involved button down moves (drag). In order to reduce the length of testing as much as possible (because of the possible endurance limitations of many of the subjects), the smallest number of blocks needed to reach asymptotic performance was desired. However, the time required for performance to asymptote for users with physical limitations has not been estimated and may vary from that of nonimpaired users. Given these considerations, six blocks of 12 trials (or 72 trials) were used for each button mode, virtually assuring asymptotic performance while maintaining a reasonable testing time.

As mentioned previously, the Macintosh directional cursor keys and *Easy Access* program, *Turbomouse*, standard Macintosh mouse, Kurta graphics tablet, and Kraft joystick were tested. Because determining the effectiveness of the assessment strategy in suggesting areas for possible device modification was of interest, the mouse was available in three configurations: off the shelf, modified with a strap handle, and modified with a toggle type button (via the toggle up/down keys associated with the directional arrow keys on the keyboard). The strap handle aids those individuals who have difficulty picking up and moving the mouse, while the toggle button aids those who have difficulty simultaneously holding down the button and sliding the mouse (i.e. dragging). In addition, the tablet was also available in two configurations: the standard configuration and with a strap attached to the stylus to fit around the user's hand. This strap securely attaches the stylus to the user's hand, eliminating the need to grip the stylus firmly. Each individual with a disability first attempted to use the standard configuration of each device. If he or she was unable to use it comfortably, then the alternative configurations were tried. Each individual used only one configuration of each device for actual testing. Hence the device has five levels. The primary dependent measure was task completion time per target acquisition trial (measured in hundredths of a second).

Each subject was tested on the computer task either in a single session or over multiple sessions, depending on his or her schedule and endurance limitations. Presentation order of the devices was balanced using a Latin squares design. Each subject was pretested with each mouse and tablet configuration just prior to actual testing, and only the best configuration was tested for each person. Before actual testing, each participant received a practice trial during which he or she could (with the experimenter's aid) reposition himself or herself or move the device so that the setup was most comfortable, and could experiment with different control strategies. Within each trial block, presentation order of the 12 target selections was randomized.

Data analysis

Input device composite performance measure. For each individual, a single measure of performance for each of the input devices was first computed. The target acquisition time (TT) data were first analyzed across trial blocks to determine the learning effect associated with each device, so that the single measure of performance would include only those trial blocks where asymptotic performance had been realized. An analysis of variance (Anova) and subsequent post hoc tests indicate that performance was stable for all devices after just one block for persons without disabilities, and after two blocks for the group with disabilities. Hence the single measure of performance was computed for each individual with each device as the mean target acquisition time collapsed across all independent variables, for the last four trial blocks. (A complete analysis of the cursor control device performance data can be found in Casali, 1992.)

Assessment test validation

Before the assessment test was evaluated to determine its ability to predict whether an individual with a disability can or cannot operate a given device efficiently, an analysis was conducted to estimate the validity of the test. Specifically, the analysis estimates the extent to which performance on those subtests which are thought to be representative of the actions needed in operating a given device (i.e. relevant subtests) is actually related to the performance with that device.

A series of regression procedures using data from the nondisabled participants were employed. Ideally a separate multiple regression for each of the five devices, in which the dependent variable is the individual's composite measure of input device performance and the regressors are the individual's scores on the 39 subtests, should yield a set of significant regressors for each device that correspond to the set of subtests considered to be relevant for that device. However, because of the small sample size ($n = 10$), such a procedure was not possible. As an alternative, 39 simple regressions were performed for each device, generating one equation for each of the 39 subtests. Results indicate that in the majority of cases those subtests which represent actions which had been thought to be relevant for a particular device were found to be significant regressors.

Next, multiple regression equations were generated describing the performance of each input device in terms of only those subtests (i.e. regressors) which were thought to be relevant for that device and had also been shown to be significant regressors in the simple regression analyses. The results are shown in Table 17.4. Each regressor is labeled according to the abbreviated name of the subtest it represents (e.g. R1 is the first subtest involving the reach action). Considering that only 10 observations were available and thus that the power of the tests was quite low, the resulting R^2 values for the multiple regression equations are remarkably high, particularly for the trackball, keys, and tablet. Thus, despite the fact that not all subtests which were thought to be relevant subtests were found to be significant regressors, the large number which were, along with the high predictive power of the multiple regression equations, strongly suggests that the assessment test as a whole measures the appropriate actions, the correct subset of actions (i.e. relevant subtests) for each device was chosen, and that each subtest sufficiently measures the intended action. Hence these results suggested that the test should indeed be capable of providing an indication of whether a person with a disability can use a given device, and of giving an indication of the level of performance which can be expected.

Table 17.4. *Multiple regression equation for each input device*

Device	Equation	R^2	p
Mouse	Perf = 1.3035 + 1.0863R2 + 0.1539R4 - 1.3899R5 + 0.1686R7	0.77	0.0734
Track ball	Perf = 2.2497 + 0.0673R1 + 1.2228R2 + 0.7536R4 - 2.2259R5	0.85	0.0253
Keys	Perf = -10.9645 + 0.5699R1 + 0.3764R3 + 38.0016React	0.86	0.0055
Joystick	Perf = -3.2975 + 0.3663R3 + 20.2439React	0.52	0.0724
Tablet	Perf = 0.4630 - 0.2462R1 + 0.5427R2 + 0.0472R4 - 0.2849R5 + 0.3775R6 - 0.1958R7 + 0.2406L11 - 0.1627P7	0.98	0.0424

Assessment test – Generation of device–performance relationship

Given that the assessment test was shown to measure adequately an individual's ability to accomplish the actions used in operating the input devices considered in this study, the next phase of the analysis was to:

1. determine whether a disabled individual's scores on the subtests can be used to indicate whether he or she can operate a device;

2. determine whether the test scores can be used to indicate where device modifications or aids can be provided to allow an individual to use a device who may otherwise be unable to do so; and

3. determine if the assessment test results can be used to indicate the level of performance that can be expected from an individual using a particular device.

Score normalization. To make both the device performance scores and the assessment test subtest scores intuitively meaningful and comparable, both sets of scores were first normalized with respect to the mean of the nondisabled subject sample. First, the mean score on each of the five input devices for the group of nondisabled subjects was calculated (using the single measure score for each subject as generated previously). The single measure score for each device for each participant (both nondisabled and disabled) was then converted to a "percent normal" score (i.e. original single measure score divided by the mean nondisabled score times 100). The same procedure was used to normalize each individual's scores on each of the 39 subtests. In this manner, each score itself carries immediate meaning (e.g. a score of 20 means the individual scored 20% of "normal.") And the relationship between the scores on the devices and the scores on the "relevant subtests" should be apparent.

Objective 1. The first objective of the assessment test was to be able to use an individual's test scores to predict whether he or she will or will not be capable of operating a given device. Recall that for each device a list of actions needed in operating that device was constructed. The scores on the subtests of the assessment test indicate what actions a person is capable of accomplishing. If a person can *proficiently* perform all of the necessary actions, one would predict that the person could operate the device. If some of the necessary actions are outside a person's repertoire, one would predict that he or she could not operate the device. The results of the study show that the assessment test is in fact quite effective in identifying these "missing actions." In all cases, if an individual was unable to perform a necessary action, then he or she was also unable to operate the device.

Consider the tablet as an example. As described previously, two configurations of the tablet were available: the standard configuration and with a cuff which fits around the user's hand to hold the stylus. Only 7 of the 20 subjects with disabilities were able to use the standard configuration of the tablet, but each of the remaining 13 participants was able to use the modified version. Tables 17.5 and 17.6 contain the distributions of scores for the relevant subtests for users of configurations 1 and 2, respectively. Specifically, listed within the tables themselves are the number of individuals whose score on a given subtest fell within each category, where the categories are expressed in terms of a percentage of the normal score. Subtests labeled L11 and L12 ("lifting" subtests) and P6 and P7 ("placing" subtests) represent actions which are necessary when using the tablet in the standard configuration but are not necessary when using the modified device (configuration 2).

First, compare the scores on all 15 subtests of the group which was able to use the standard tablet (Table 17.5) with the scores of those who were unable to it (Table 17.6). Immediately apparent is the fact that no one who was able to use the standard tablet was unable to perform any of the necessary actions. In fact, no one who used the standard configuration of the tablet scored below 30% of normal on any subtest. On the other hand, the scores of the individuals who were not able to use the standard tablet reveal several instances where a subtest could not be performed, and many others where the subtest could be performed but the resulting score was quite low. Examining the individual scores (not shown) indicates that 2 of the persons who were unable to use the standard tablet were unable to accomplish four of the necessary actions. This result immediately suggests that these persons would be unable to use the tablet in the standard manner. In addition, 7 of the 13 users scored in the teens or below on at least two of the subtests, while 11 of 13 scored in the twenties or below on two or more subtests. Only 3 people scored above 30% on more than one subtest, and only 1 person scored above 40% on more than one subtest. On the other hand, 5 of the 7 participants who could use the standard configuration scored 50% or better on every subtest.

Table 17.5. *Distribution of scores for the disabled subject sample for the tablet relevant subtests (configuration 1) (n = 7)*

Sub -test	0	1-9	10- 19	20- 29	30- 39	40- 59	50- 59	60- 69	70- 79	80- 89	90- 99	100 +
R1	0	0	0	0	0	0	1	3	0	2	1	0
R2	0	0	0	0	0	0	0	2	1	2	0	2
R3	0	0	0	0	0	0	1	0	1	2	1	2
R4	0	0	0	0	0	0	0	0	1	1	3	2
R5	0	0	0	0	0	0	0	0	2	3	2	0
R6	0	0	0	0	0	0	0	1	1	1	1	3
R7	0	0	0	0	0	0	0	0	1	2	1	3
R8	0	0	0	0	0	0	0	1	0	3	1	2
S1	0	0	0	0	2	1	0	2	2	0	0	0
S2	0	0	0	0	0	0	0	2	3	0	1	1
S3	0	0	0	0	0	0	0	1	0	2	2	2
L11	0	0	0	0	1	1	1	3	1	0	0	0
L12	0	0	0	0	0	0	3	4	0	0	0	0
P6	0	0	0	0	1	0	0	2	3	1	0	0
P7	0	0	0	0	1	0	2	2	2	0	0	0

Table 17.6. *Distribution of scores for the disabled subject sample for the tablet relevant subtests (configuration 2) (n = 13)*

Sub -test	0	1-9	10- 19	20- 29	30- 39	40- 49	50- 59	60- 69	70- 79	80- 89	90- 99	100 +
R1	0	0	1	1	3	4	3	1	0	0	0	0
R2	0	0	0	0	1	2	8	2	0	0	0	0
R3	0	0	1	0	2	7	1	2	0	0	0	0
R4	0	0	0	1	0	5	4	2	1	0	0	0
R5	0	0	0	1	0	6	3	2	1	0	0	0
R6	0	0	1	0	0	5	5	1	1	0	0	0
R7	0	0	0	1	1	5	3	1	1	0	0	0
R8	0	0	1	1	3	3	4	1	0	0	0	0
S1	0	0	6	4	0	2	1	0	0	0	0	0
S2	0	0	1	4	2	3	3	0	0	0	0	0
S3	0	0	0	0	2	4	4	2	1	0	0	0
L11	2	0	5	4	1	1	0	0	0	0	0	0
L12	2	0	3	6	1	1	0	0	0	0	0	0
P6	2	2	3	1	4	1	0	0	0	0	0	0
P7	2	2	1	5	2	0	0	0	0	0	0	0

The assessment test was clearly able to differentiate between persons who would be able to operate a device with little difficulty and persons who were lacking the ability to perform one or more actions needed to operate a device. However, the results also demonstrate that merely knowing that an individual is able to perform all of the necessary actions is not sufficient to conclude that the individual can operate the corresponding device. An individual need not only be able to perform each of the required actions, but must be able to perform each action with a given degree of proficiency before we can conclude that he or she can operate the corresponding device. Establishing criteria for acceptable performance for the actions may not be easy.

Realistically, development of specific predictive relationships between assessment test results and device performance should not rely on the empirical testing of users. Although empirical testing may result in the best decision rules, such an approach is simply impractical. It is not feasible to test every available device empirically to determine the relationship between its use and the results of an assessment test, particularly given the difficulties associated with acquiring a large sample of individuals with similar types of functional impairments. Alternatively, a single prevailing guideline (e.g. an individual must score x percent on each of the necessary actions) applicable for all devices within a device class could be established. To do so empirically on a small sample of the devices being considered would not be prohibitively difficult. Although the resulting decision rules may be less accurate, the extreme disadvantages of establishing empirically derived rules for each device may make the method preferable.

In order to estimate the amount of predictive power lost by using a global rule rather than specific rules, both methods were applied to the data from this study. The results from each configuration of each of the five devices were studied separately to estimate the minimum score necessary on each subtest that would suggest that an individual can use the corresponding device. Table 17.7 summarizes these decision guidelines. For each configuration of each device, we give the minimum score on the relevant subtests that would result in the recommendation that an individual would be capable of using that device. For example, the results suggest that, in addition to being able to perform each relevant subtest, an individual should be able to score 40% of normal or better on at least four of the five subtests if he or she is to use the trackball. Note how similar the resulting guidelines are to one another. This would suggest that a single guideline for all devices of a particular type (e.g. manual cursor control devices) may be sufficient. Therefore, these guidelines were also consolidated to form a global guideline for manual cursor control devices, also shown in Table 17.7.

The degree to which these guidelines would result in a correct decision was measured by applying the guidelines to the data from the assessment test scores of the participants in this study and comparing the predicted outcome with the actual outcome obtained when each participant attempted to use each device. For

Table 17.7. *Summary of decision guidelines*

Device	Minimum score necessary to result in a Yes decision
Trackball	40% on 4/5 subtests
Keys	40% on 4/5 subtests
Joystick	40% on 4/5 subtests
Mouse (1)	40% on 6/8 "reach" AND 50% on all "lift" AND 40% on 2/3 "slide" subtests
Mouse (2)	40% on 6/8 "reach" AND 40% on 2/3 "slide" subtests
Mouse (4)	40% on 6/8 "reach" subtests
Tablet (1)	40% on 6/8 "reach" AND 40% on all "lift" and "place" subtests
Tablet (2)	40% on 6/8 "reach" subtests
Overall	40% or better on 75% of the relevant subtests

example, the guidelines correctly suggest that 6 of the 7 individuals who were able to use the tablet in the standard configuration would be able to do so but incorrectly suggest that 1 of them would not. Of the remaining 13 who proved to be unable to use the tablet without modification, the guidelines were accurate in suggesting that all 13 would not be able to operate the device unaided. Hence the guidelines were correct for 95% of the individuals tested. Similar results were obtained for the other four devices. Using the specific guidelines, a correct decision (either that a person would be able to use a device when he or she was indeed able to use it, or that a person was not able to use a device when he or she was unable to use it) was reached for each device for at least 85% of the individuals.

When the global rule was applied for each device, only small declines in accuracy were realized. Correct decisions were reached for 80% of the individuals for the mouse and trackball and for 90% of the individuals for the keys, joystick, and tablet. Very little information was lost by aggregating the guidelines into a single guideline. One would suspect that a global guideline derived in such a manner would also apply well to other similar devices, but this should be verified.

Objective 2. The second objective of the assessment test was to provide results which will indicate, for individuals who are unable to operate a given device, the specific actions inhibiting access. By identifying those actions necessary for device operation which the individual cannot proficiently perform, the practitioner may be able to either suggest aids which might allow the person to perform the particular action better or suggest modifications to the device which may eliminate the need to perform the difficult action.

Again using the tablet as an example, consider the first eleven and the last four subtests separately. Recall that the last four subtests are those which represent actions necessary when using the standard configuration of the tablet but unnecessary when using the modified version. The scores of the participants who were able to use the standard tablet (Table 17.5) indicate that none had difficulty performing these four subtests. The assessment test scores suggest that these individuals have the physical skills needed to operate the standard tablet. However, the participants who were unable to use the standard tablet (Table 17.6) show much lower scores on these particular subtests, not only suggesting that these persons do not have the physical skills required for using the standard tablet but also indicating the specific actions which are needed but unavailable. The modified configuration of the tablet was designed to eliminate the last four actions. In all 13 cases where an individual scored very low on one or more of these last four subtests but scored well on the remaining subtests, the individual was indeed able to use the modified version of the tablet. These results suggest that the assessment test scores are useful not only in indicating whether an individual can or cannot operate a device but also in indicating which actions are required but unavailable at the necessary proficiency levels. With this information, an aid or modification can be provided to assist the individual in using the device.

Objective 3. The third objective of the assessment test was to be able to estimate, from the scores on the test, an individual's expected level of performance when using a particular device. Several approaches were considered.

Developing a regression equation for each of the devices, using the performance scores of the persons with disabilities as the dependent variable and their scores on the relevant subtests as the regressors (similar to the approach described previously for validating the assessment test), initially appears to be appealing. However, the approach has several limitations. As noted previously, empirically derived relationships based on data collected from a sample of subjects with disabilities are impractical. Second, the appropriateness of a regression approach using a group of individuals with varying levels of hand skill must be questioned. Although the same actions are required of each individuals, the motor performance of these individuals varies greatly, thereby affecting the percentage of total time spent on each of the relevant actions. Hence the relative "importance" of each of the actions may vary greatly within such a heterogeneous group, and hence the regression equation may not adequately predict performance for any given individual.

Two approaches were attempted which do not require collecting data on a sample of disabled subjects in order to generate a description of the relationship between the performance on the relevant subtests and the device. First, it was

Table 17.8. *Pearson Product Moment correlation coefficients of actual performance versus predicted performance, using regression equations*

Device	N	R	p
Mouse	4	0.1655	0.8345
Trackball	20	0.3727	0.1056
Keys	20	0.6028	0.0049
Joystick	20	0.4934	0.0270
Tablet	7	0.4686	0.2889

thought that, with the help of the regression equations generated previously, using the data from the group of nondisabled subjects to estimate the performance of an individual with a disability might at least result in a rough estimate of his or her performance levels. This approach is not as limiting as using a subject sample of persons with motor limitations to build regression equations, since obtaining and collecting data on a group of individuals without disabilities is not prohibitively difficult or time consuming. For each of the 20 individuals with disabilities, predicted performance on each device was estimated using the regression equations given in Table 17.4. (Note that for each device only the data from the subjects who used the device in the standard configuration were used, since the other configurations have a different set of relevant subtests and therefore a different regression equation.) This predicted performance score was correlated with the actual performance achieved, using a Pearson Product Moment correlation. The results are shown in Table 17.8. As shown, the correlations are not particularly high and are significant for only the keys and joystick.

Finally, an even more appealing approach is to determine the relative weights of each of the subtests based on "expert judgment," as opposed to empirical data. The primary advantage, of course, is that to generate the predictive relationship for a device requires only a careful analysis of the device and no data collection. For each configuration of each device, the relevant subtests were weighted by the experimenter according to the estimated importance of each to the operation of that device. The predicted performance for each individual was calculated as the linear sum of the relevant subtests, appropriately weighted. Again, the correlation between the predicted performance and actual performance was determined; the results are shown in Table 17.9. With the exception of the trackball, the correlation coefficients were low and nonsignificant.

The results of this analysis were disappointing. Although it is reasonable to suspect that a relationship exists between the level of performance on the assessment test and the level of performance on a particular device for persons with disabilities, several methods were unsuccessful in defining that relationship.

Table 17.9. *Pearson Product Moment correlation coefficients of actual performance versus predicted performance, using estimated weights*

Device	N	R	p
Mouse (1)	4	0.6802	0.3198
Mouse (2)	10	0.2725	0.4462
Mouse (3)	6	0.5425	0.2661
Trackball	20	0.7381	0.0002
Keys	20	0.0818	0.7318
Joystick	20	0.3208	0.1679
Tablet (1)	7	0.1328	0.7764
Tablet (2)	13	0.4432	0.1293

Discussion and conclusions

Current methods used to select computer hardware and software for persons with disabilities are time consuming and do not always result in a successful user–device match. No systematic method of matching user skills with hardware or software requirements previously existed. The proposed selection system, which has the potential to be automated, systematically considers both the physical skills of the user and the task requirements when choosing hardware and software.

Specifically, to consider physical skills in the selection process, one must know the physical skills required by the hardware and/or software. The method of describing these skills should be standardized, and such information for currently marketed products should be cataloged and made easily accessible. Standardized assessment procedures would yield results that could be used directly to indicate whether or not an individual could use a given device efficiently. Such a strategy should eliminate the needlessly long trial-and-error procedures and/or the purchase of inappropriate equipment that are typical of current selection processes.

The results of the empirical study described here suggest that the proposed approach is feasible and has utility. The assessment strategy suggested relies on a very simple analysis of candidate devices. Hence, in a product directory such as those that currently exist, it is not impractical to include a description of each product in terms of the "actions" required for operation. Similarly, the assessment of an individual's physical skills does not rely on expensive equipment or complicated techniques; therefore, the assessment test itself is not impractical.

Most important, the assessment strategy appears to yield results that can be used to predict performance with a device. In cases where an individual cannot perform a relevant subtest, he or she also cannot operate the device requiring that action. In cases where an individual scores well on a set of relevant subtests, he or she is also able to use the device requiring that set of actions. When an individual can perform each action, but not necessarily very well, decision rules can be generated to determine how good the performance must be on each action before one concludes that the person can operate the device. When the assessment test reveals that an individual has difficulty accomplishing a given subtest, an aid or modification can be provided. In many cases this will allow the participant to operate the device.

When the assessment scores were used to try to predict the level of performance that could be expected with a device, the results were disappointing. No clear, easy-to-apply method resulted in even a rough estimate of the actual performance levels obtained. However, through further analyses it may be possible to develop a method which demonstrates a relationship between the two sets of scores. It must be noted, however, that the method would be infeasible in the field if it required a complex manipulation of the data or required the collection of data from a large number of persons with disabilities.

Although the assessment strategy presented here may not yet offer a "cookbook" method of choosing the optimal input device, it does guide the clinician to systematically consider the physical skills of a user and the physical actions required by the device. It also appears to have great potential for eliminating devices that individuals will not be able to operate, so that the only devices left for serious consideration are those that individuals at least have the capability to operate.

It is also very interesting to note that although participants in the study represented a tremendous range of physical skill levels, all participants were able to use each of the five devices with only very simple modifications. Each modification was essentially cost-free, and did not permanently alter the workstation. (Modification costs and inconvenience to others are typical concerns of employers who consider hiring persons with disabilities.)

Much of the description of the assessment strategy has been couched in terms of the example used for empirical testing. However, it must be remembered that the assessment strategy is more general than matching a user's physical hand/arm skills to the requirements of operating manual input devices. The same strategy applies to other human capabilities as well: matching a user's visual capabilities with the visual requirements of a software/hardware configuration, or matching a user's vocal skills with the speech requirements of a voice recognition system. In all cases, the requirements of the system must be specified, and then the capabilities of a user to accomplish the necessary actions must be measured.

Finally, it should be noted that although the emphasis throughout this chapter has been on creating a systematic process for choosing computer related hardware and software for persons with disabilities, the idea of considering the physical requirements of a piece of hardware or software in the selection process may have advantages for the nondisabled population as well.

Acknowledgments

The research was completed at the Human–Computer Interface Laboratory at Virginia Tech and was partially supported by the Center for Innovative Technology of the Commonwealth of Virginia under contract INF-89-004 and the Cunningham Dissertation Fellowship program at Virginia Tech. I wish to thank Robert C. Williges and Beverly H. Williges for their significant contributions throughout the project, Joseph C. Chase for his efforts in developing the software used in this study, and the staff and students at Woodrow Wilson Rehabilitation Center, Fishersville, VA, for providing the staff, facilities, and time necessary for data collection. Preparation of this chapter was supported by Management Systems Laboratories, Department of Industrial and Systems Engineering, Virginia Polytechnic Institute and State University.

References

Behrmann, M. (1989). *Development of an expert system for assistive technology identification.* Presentation at Closing the Gap Conference, Minneapolis, MN.

Berliss, J., Bordon, P., and Vanderheiden, G. (Eds.). (1989). *Trace resource book: Assistive technologies for communication, control, and computer access.* Washington, DC: Resna Press.

Carlson, J., and Trombly, C. (1983). The effect of wrist immobilization on performance of the Jebsen Hand Function test. *American Journal of Occupational Therapy, 37*(3): 167–175.

Casali, S. P. (1992). Cursor control device performance by persons with physical disabilities: Implications for hardware and software design. In *Proceedings of the 34th Annual Meeting of the Human Factors Society,* Santa Monica, CA: Human Factors Society.

Casali, S. P., and Williges, R. (1990). A review of databases of accommodative aids for disabled users of computers. *Human Factors, 32*(4): 407–422.

Closing the Gap. (1990). Closing the Gap resource directory. *Closing the Gap Newsletter, 8*(6).

Epps, B. (1986). *Comparison of cursor control devices on target acquisition, text editing, and graphics tasks.* Unpublished doctoral dissertation, Virginia Polytechnic Institute and State University, Blacksburg.

Kondraske, G. (1988, September). Rehabilitation Engineering: Towards a Systematic Process. *IEEE Engineering in Medicine and Biology Magazine.*

Lee K., and Thomas, D. (1990). *Control of computer based technology for people with physical disabilities.* Toronto: University of Toronto Press.

McPhee, S. D. (1987). Functional hand evaluations: A review. *American Journal of Occupational Therapy, 41*(3): 158–163.

Mathiowetz, V., Volland, G., Kashman, N., and Weber, K. (1985). Adult norms for the Box and Block Test of manual dexterity. *American Journal of Occupational Therapy, 39*(6), 386–391.

Mathiowetz, V., Weber, K., Kashman, N., and Volland, G. (1983). Adult norms for the Nine Hole Peg Test of finger dexterity. *Occupational Therapy Journal of Research, 5*(1): 25–36.

Minkel, J., Zeitlin, D., and Masiello, R. (1988). An evaluation tool for switch selection. In *Proceedings of ICAART 88 (International Conference of the Association for the Advancement of Rehabilitation Technology)* (p. 152). Washington, DC: Resna Press.

Rosen, M. J., and Goodenough-Trepagnier, C. (1989). The Tufts–MIT prescription guide: Assessment of users to predict the suitability of augmentative communication devices. *Applied Technology, 1*(3): 51–61.

Tifflin, J. (1968). *Purdue Pegboard examiner manual*. Chicago: Science Research Associates.

Williges, R. C., Williges, B. H., and Elkerton, J. (1988). Software interface design. In G. Salvendy (Ed.), *Handbook of human factors*. New York: Wiley.

18

Technology for people with special needs: HCI design issues

Kate Howey

Introduction

As we have seen in previous chapters, assistive technology devices can help a wide range of people with differing physical impairments to improve their communications ability and to extend the range of tasks they can perform, and can also provide access to computer and telecommunications technology. Despite an increasing proliferation of such devices, access to computer and other information technology (IT) products by these user groups is not as extensive as might be expected (Mintel, 1992). This is especially noticeable in the workplace (where increasing computerization may have been expected to benefit physically disabled workers), because the predominant requirement now is for intellectual rather than physical skills. However, accessing a computer is a physical skill in itself, and there are other reasons why the potential for an equalization of access to technology has not resulted in an equalization of job opportunities between disabled and able-bodied workers (Howey, 1988).

In 1976, for example, 13.6% (75,857) of registered disabled people in the UK were unemployed, compared with a national average of 5.4% (Thorpe-Tracey, 1976). A more recent survey in the UK states that only 31% of all disabled people under pensionable age are in work (Martin & White, 1988). In the United States, two thirds of the disabled population (i.e. 12 million skilled disabled people) are unemployed, making these people the biggest and most impoverished minority group in the USA (World Congress, 1991). This is despite the diminishing size of the general workforce and the many national programs and projects to incorporate disabled people into economic and social life.

There are many factors contributing to this situation, and they must be seen in the wider social, political, and economic context of the disabled person. They include a basic lack of assistance with the tasks of daily living (such as getting dressed), lack of mobility assistance (getting to work), and the costs of assistive technology (technological aids and adaptations to the workplace). The low incomes of many disabled people also contribute to their disadvantaged position.

343

Although many disabled people can use standard commercially available systems, they often need specialized interfaces, equipment, or additional support, which can be costly and set them apart from other people. One of the reasons for the high cost of assistive technology is the need for specialized designs. Another is the inaccessibility of many standard technology products, which has the effect of further increasing the reliance of people with disabilities on special equipment.

Even where disabled people have appropriate assistive technology available to them, this is often not sufficient to ensure social integration. For example, employers can be unclear about how to restructure jobs to meet the needs of disabled people. The provision of guidance to supervisors and other colleagues to ease integration on the ground is often not forthcoming. As a result, disabled people can suffer from a "disability apartheid" which unwittingly excludes them from work and society. These attitudes can carry over into design.

Often disabled people themselves are not included in the user specification process in product design, nor are they asked what it is that they require of technology. Part of the problem is a lack of confidence on the part of designers about speaking to disabled users. Some government agencies in the United States have overcome this lack of confidence between able-bodied and disabled people by providing training in the workplace (e.g. by teaching able-bodied people to use sign language so that they can talk to their deaf colleagues). Similar confidence-raising methods could be applied to the design situation. More disabled people need to be included in the design process and in user trials of prototype equipment.

Bringing a human perspective to technology design can help us to understand the requirements of disabled people. We need to understand both their priorities for improved designs and the problems they have in using existing products in order to ensure that we produce useful equipment for the majority of users. In this way standard products can be made more widely available to all user groups.

Increases in the population of elderly people in the West mean that new markets are opening up for manufacturers who are interested in addressing these problems. Designing for people with age related impairments may become increasingly lucrative as the buying power of elderly people increases (Engelstad, 1989). Improved designs may also benefit people with impairments similar to those of elderly people by reducing reliance on special aids.

This approach to design raises some challenging issues for the discipline of human–computer interaction (HCI), as Newell and Thimbleby point out in their chapters in this book. Practitioners are being asked to extend the baseline for their designs away from what is currently considered to be average and to take a more realistic look at the characteristics of the general population.

I aim here to focus on ways in which the HCI design community is addressing the use of technology by people with disabilities.

Use of technology by people with disabilities

Loss of hearing, vision, speech, motor control, or intellectual ability may affect people's ability to communicate with each other, to perform daily tasks, and (because of design constraints such as those mentioned by Thimbleby in Chapter 14) to operate advanced technological equipment, such as computer and telecommunications systems.

Physical, cognitive, and perceptual impairments may affect the ability to use domestic appliances, perform household tasks, and interact with such home technology systems as TVs, videos, and telephones. Unless design practice changes, the use of future home technology systems and services (such as home banking and home shopping) may also be restricted to only the most "able" of users. Losses in visual ability are particularly critical, as so much information today is received from the printed word or from computer displays and other interfaces and controls.

Not withstanding that functional impairments vary in their degree of severity between individuals, as many as 18 million people in the European Union (EU) countries have mobility impairments, 6 million from upper-limb disorders, and an approximately equal number have hearing and visual defects. A further 3 million are affected by speech disorders (Sandhu & Wood, 1990).

Existing assistive technology devices to some extent make up for the gap between functional ability and the design of technology goods and services aimed at the average consumer. They can be used to improve the communication ability of many visually, hearing, and speech impaired people by making it easier for them to read, write, and speak, either by replacing or enhancing their existing modes of communication. Special interfaces can also help physically disabled people (especially those with motor impairments) to gain access to IT systems, thus allowing them, in many cases, to carry out the same tasks as able-bodied people. Assistive technology can also help provide access to telecommunications systems and public information networks for people who would not otherwise be able to use them (e.g. text telephones for people who are deaf).

Many physically disabled people are able to gain access to IT systems by using standard technology (albeit in sometimes unconventional ways). Others require adaptations or specialized interfaces (such as braille keyboards) to computer systems; unfortunately, these can often result in a degradation of performance (such as slower operating times). Severely disabled people and those with multiple impairments have tended to require purpose-built systems, which cannot always perform the same range of functions or provide compatibility with standard systems. The low production volume of such systems also means that unit costs are high.

Howey (1986) suggests that existing technology can be used as follows:

1. It can be used "stand-alone" to improve a physically disabled person's communication capacities (e.g. microelectronic aids for people with hearing or speech impairments).

2.   It can link a disabled person with existing technologies (such as computer systems) to extend access to technology services (e.g. speech output devices can allow blind persons access to conventional computer systems).

3.   It can provide disabled persons with telecommunications services (e.g. to allow deaf people to make telephone calls).

How can we improve the design of technology systems for people with disabilities?

Dahlman (1989) says:

> *Functional problems are one way of describing a mismatch between human ability and the environment. The mismatch can often be eliminated by rearranging the environment . . . Some of the [problems] can be controlled and design is one of the tools.*

Engelstad (1989) suggests that existing designs for people with disabilities have tended to create environments which stigmatize and segregate aged (and disabled) persons from society, and says that specialized equipment can "humiliate" the user or make the person dependent on others for help in operating it. This is also true to some extent of computers (e.g. a motor impaired person may need help with loading paper into a printer). He goes on to say that these two factors must be overcome in the development and design of new technology and new technical equipment. One way of doing this is to integrate the needs of people with disabilities into the design of ordinary equipment.

For this to be possible, we need to know more about the characteristics of the disabled and elderly populations, what information is needed by designers of technology systems to meet the requirements of different impairment groups, and in what form this information should be presented to designers. There is an increasing need for studies of the ways in which "ordinary" people differ from people with disabilities and of how people within different broad impairment groups interact with hardware and software. This knowledge needs to be applied to general design situations in the form of clear design requirements.

Some recent European research initiatives, such as the Research and Development into Advanced Communications for Europe (*Race*) program and the Technology for the Integration of the Disabled and Elderly (*Tide*) program, aim to bridge this gap between disability experts, technology designers, and human factors personnel by compiling design guidelines advice on human factors aspects of technology use. This is often done by the adoption of user centered design practices requiring multidisciplinary teams and/or user groups representing people with differing disabilities in the product design process. Of particular note are the following Race projects: R1054 APPSN (Application Pilot Project for People with Special Needs), R1066 IPSNI (Integration of People with Special Needs in Integrated Broadband Communication), R1066 Tudor

(Tutorials about Users who are Disabled or Retired),[1] and the Tide *Ashored* project (see below). The functional requirements of people with different capabilities using telecommunications equipment, was considered in the *Cost 219* project (Frederiksen, Martin, de la Bellacasa, & von Tetzchner, 1989).

If experts in disability assessment, technology design, and human factors can find successful ways of working together, then future products can be improved and reach a wider market. The discipline of human–computer interaction has much to offer in this area, acting as it does as an interface between users and technologists. By providing a link between users, experts in disability assessment, and product designers, the techniques of user centered design can help to integrate knowledge of populations of people with disabilities into existing frameworks for product development. The techniques of user requirements analysis and task analysis for different groups can be applied successfully to the product design process. Information about the broad functional characteristics of different impairment groups and their special requirements for access to systems and products and for the performance of particular tasks or functions can be given to designers at appropriate parts of the design cycle. User trials can enable the evaluation of design solutions in line with the criteria set during specification. This in turn can improve the specifications, and therefore the usability of future systems and interfaces. This may facilitate the creation of "universal" solutions which put people with disabilities on a more equal footing with able-bodied users.

In this way, people with disabilities will no longer be treated as a subgroup of computer users with special requirements, but rather the concept of ordinary or mainstream users will be extended beyond the current (somewhat arbitrary) "norm." This may be of benefit to the wider user population, as everyone varies in the range of abilities, and all of us can be either temporarily or permanently disabled at some point in our lives through illness, age, or accident.

The integration of special needs requirements into mainstream design practice could have wider benefits:

- improved knowledge of the range of requirements of different user populations;
- encouragement of designers of technology to focus on real user needs, resulting in more useful and more successful products;
- improved user specifications;
- improved interface designs;
- improved social integration of people with disabilities in the community;
- lower priced products for users with disabilities.

[1] Further details of these Race projects are available from the Race Central Office, DG XIII, rue de Trèves 61, B1040, Brussels, Belgium.

Recurring issues for designers and manufacturers who want to take account of the needs of people with disabilities include the following:

1. *Estimating the market size of different impairment groups.* What proportions of the general population suffer from the different kinds of impairment, to what degree, and how does this affect the functions they can perform or the tasks they can carry out?

2. *Design requirements of different impairment groups.* What are the requirements of each impairment group for services, products, access, and interfaces to information technology products and domestic goods? That is to say, what percentage of each group can use existing standard products, how many have additional requirements, what are they, and how far can these be accommodated in commercial designs?

3. *What are the implications for design?* How can standard, commercially available information technology systems, consumer products, and public and private services incorporate the widest possible span of user ability and requirement into their designs, at an economic cost? In other words, what generic facilities will allow the widest range of users to access them?

4. *Users whose needs cannot be incorporated in improved designs.* What needs to be done for groups of people with very specific needs who cannot be catered for by producing improved standard designs, so that they are not excluded from use of goods and services? This group includes people with very severe disabilities or with multiple impairments.

Knowledge of the population of disabled people is obviously the first step toward answering these questions and broadening the baseline of design so that we avoid the mistake of continuing to design for an artificially defined standard human being. However, economic considerations will have an effect on the degree to which the overall requirements of all user groups can be met by this approach. Whereas small modifications to existing designs may expand target user groups to some degree at little additional cost, meeting the needs of more people by introducing more substantial modifications may also increase the costs of manufacture and the price of products. Addressing the widest possible range of user needs, although desirable, could increase the price of goods to an unacceptable level for ordinary consumers – an option that large manufacturers are unlikely to take. A trade-off is required between designing for the widest range of users and keeping costs to the consumer as low as possible. These issues are explored further in the following sections.

Characteristics of the market

Deciding which impairment groups to target is the first step in making products more accessible to a wider range of users. Priorities will have to be established whereby slight modifications to existing designs can have a sufficient impact on the numbers of users with impairments, without significantly increasing the costs of manufacture and the prices of products.

Sandhu and Wood (1990) have produced a market analysis which describes the numbers and economic characteristics of people in the EU countries with different forms of impairment. They have also produced detailed breakdowns of consumer expenditure on different kinds of products as a guide to the various market sectors for particular goods. This information is very useful for the prospective manufacturer of products aimed at the market of people with disabilities, who may not realize the true extent of the market for different kinds of products. Information on the size of disability groups can help in the selection of design priorities (those which will benefit the largest numbers). Also insight is required into the kinds of functional adjustments which need to be made for each user group, although it should be remembered that some of these user groups will overlap and that any individual may have multiple requirements.

Sandhu and Wood estimate the current population of the European member states at approximately 322 million, of which some 36–49 million (11.3–15.1% of the total population) have some form of disability. The number of elderly people alone (that is, over age 65) is estimated at 44 million and is expected to rise to 71 million by the year 2040. Both of these overlapping groups represent a significant market for consumer goods. Roughly a third of the disabled populations of the EU member states are over 60 and therefore may also be suffering from such age related impairments as impaired vision, hearing, and motor control. Design will have to take account of the specific impairments of younger people as well as of the changing abilities of people throughout the life cycle.

Sandhu and Wood point out that the greatest number of disabled people are those with a physical impairment of some type (some 24.8 million people suffer from upper and lower limb impairments – this represents 7.7% of the total European population), followed by those with perceptual impairments: hearing (8.7 million), vision (6.5 million), and speech (3.6 million). Some 7.4 million people suffer from some kind of intellectual impairment; designing for this group may be more complex than for those with physical disabilities, owing to the mixture of effects on cognitive and physical skills (see Chapter 7).

People with mobility impairments are by far the largest disability group (some 18.7 million people have lower limb impairments). Although they may have specific needs for transport and vehicle design, lower limb impairment does not generally affect the design of IT systems directly (unless, of course, these are used in vehicles in connection with other operating controls). Thus it would seem that designers of information technology systems should initially focus their attention on people with upper limb or motor impairments and on people with impairments to perception (especially hearing and vision) if they want to include the needs of as many people as possible in their designs for future products.

People with motor impairments to the upper limbs are likely to have special requirements for physical access to IT products (e.g. via specialized interfaces which limit the effects of uncontrolled motor movements) and may also require help with operating controls more generally (owing to weakness in the limb). People with perceptual impairments (especially vision) may need alternative or enhanced interfaces to IT systems to help with information processing. Those with hearing or speech defects may require additional assistance with communication (e.g. products involving speech, such as telecommunications). People with speech impairments may also suffer from physical limitations, as discussed by Newell et al. in Chapter 5.

Designers of mobility aids and of vehicle technology will primarily be concerned with impairments affecting the use of controls (i.e. people with upper and lower limb disorders or perceptual impairments where these affect control of a vehicle). The effects of perceptual impairments will be increasingly important in this context in the future as the use of communications and computer technology in vehicles increases.

Designers of home products and technology (such as TVs and videos) will need to consider all impairment groups, although the functional limitations of people with upper and lower limb disorders may be more relevant to designers of household appliances.

Although identification of the general needs and size of user groups is important, it should be remembered that these groups often overlap and that people within the different groups of impairment suffer from different degrees of functional loss. It may not be enough to design general purpose solutions to functional difficulties for each impairment group. Some scope for additional modification may be necessary. It is, however, likely that people with slight impairments (the biggest group of disabled people) will benefit most from general solutions.

Designing for people with different degrees of impairment and different levels of ability

In order to help designers understand how different levels of ability may be catered for in design, Sperling (1989) posits a "user pyramid" wherein he divides the general user population into people with "ordinary functional capacity," those with "light functional impairment," and those with "severe functional impairment."

Those with ordinary functional capacity are the largest group of users (and this includes the healthy aged). Those with light functional impairment can manage the activities of daily living on their own without help if the environment and equipment are carefully thought out. People with severe functional impairment generally require personal assistance and individually adapted technical aids. (See also Sandhu & Wood, 1990.) In general, the more severe the disability, the smaller the percentage of the population affected by it. Thus the majority of people with disabilities may require very little in the way of modification to equipment.

Sperling suggests that if the goal for the product is set at the level of light functional impairment, "The needs of critical users – those who are on the borderline between independent and dependent living – are provided for. At the same time the comfort and function increases for ordinary users." It may be possible that some modifications to equipment will not add to the costs of design if the requirements of the elderly and disabled are incorporated early enough.

Some users of technology systems will still be able to use standard, commercially available products, and more users can be included in the design of future products by extending the baseline for design. Indeed, some features for enhancing partial sight are already included in standard designs (such as the Apple Macintosh's *Close View* screen magnifying facility, which is incorporated into the operating software). Other users with more specialized requirements may be able to interface to these systems if high level facilities which allow them to gain access to them are provided, but some users will still require specialized systems and services. The more severely disabled a person is, the more likely it is that specialized systems will be needed.

With regard to human factors and ergonomic considerations, the concept of design requirements operating at different levels is particularly useful in studying people with disabilities. Howey (1986) suggests that while some requirements will be common to all users (e.g. ergonomic standards for ease of use), others will be specific to people in different impairment groups. Still other requirements will be user specific. So, although human factors concepts can be useful for distinguishing different user groups, we must not lose sight of the fact that they cannot provide a total solution in all cases and that some users will still require special facilities.

Enhancing future designs – The trend toward integrated systems

One way of combating variations in user ability is to present the user with integrated systems comprising modular solutions to different functional difficulties. There is an increasing trend toward the development of such systems, as they can provide yet another way of expanding the accessibility of standard systems and products to disabled people in the workplace and in the home. This trend is also being echoed in the design of transport systems and private vehicles.

Smart homes

Recent developments in "smart homes" have pointed the way toward the increasing integration of technology systems for use in the home. The European Race *DCPN* and Tide *Ashored* research programs, for example, are examining ways of improving the design of interfaces to increase the accessibility of domestic goods and consumer products to include people with a wider range of impairments. This includes access to washing machines and other white goods as well as TVs, videos, telecommunications, and home surveillance systems. Generally the smart home concept is to have several different systems based on computer and telecommunications technology running off a home network or "bus," controlled centrally from one or more points (e.g. via a TV monitor, a hand held remote control device, a personal computer, or some other form of centralized control panel). This can also allow remote control of domestic devices and of the home environment (e.g. door locking, heating, and ventilation systems) and control of surveillance and security alarm systems.

These developments can be particularly relevant for people with disabilities, as they can, for example, allow physically disabled people to control appliances remotely, and hearing impaired people to receive information visually via TV screens or computer monitors. Future external services such as home shopping and home banking will also be available through TV screens, thus increasing the availability of such services to those with mobility impairments. These developments aim to increase the independence of disabled and elderly people both inside the home and in interacting with the wider society.

Workplace technology

In the workplace, integrated systems are being seen as a solution to accessibility problems which disabled people may experience in relation to office technology. Government and commercial agencies in the USA actively encourage the purchase and installation of integrated systems and integrated office networks for disabled people. The impetus for developments in this area is the necessity for employers to be in compliance with recent American legislation for ensuring the widespread accessibility of electronic equipment and telecommunications systems (The Rehabilitation Amendment Law, Public Law 99-506, and the Americans with Disabilities Act, Public Law 101-336). This means that when purchasing IT systems, employers must ensure that they are capable of adaptation to the needs of all disabled people, and guidelines exist for this purpose (see Chapter 19).

Because integrated systems made up of components produced by different manufacturers are thought to increase user choice and quality, a lot of previously incompatible systems are now being put together to meet the needs of a wide range of users. For example, systems incorporating print enlargers, braille text entry devices, voice input and output, and tactile readers can all be combined. It is thought that designing accessibility into off-the-shelf, generic products will bring prices down, thus increasing the size of the consumer market. (This message should also be of interest to producers of home products.)

There is a need in both these areas for the development of minimum standards for interface design, regulations, and design guidelines. These, however, must still allow for innovation in the development of products with accessibility features.

Changes in office technology which allow networking or telecommuting and access to external services from the home are no substitute for mobility, and they may even increase the isolation and dependence of disabled people. For example, the Swedish *Tuffa* project (Breding, 1991) takes a holistic view in considering information technology requirements for disabled people in the workplace and includes a person's need to get to and from the home to the workplace as part of its remit. Mobility is also important if people with disabilities are to participate fully in life and to enjoy leisure pursuits and sociability in addition to access to income through employment.

Vehicle technology

In the design of vehicle technology too there is a trend toward designing integrated systems. Currently the needs of mobility and motor impaired people are met by mechanical adjustments to vehicle controls and by local adaptations to vehicles where possible. The needs of those with sensory impairments – loss of hearing, vision, and speech – are not, to my knowledge, provided for. The neglect of this group of users will become more significant as the use of IT devices (e.g. mobile telephony) becomes more widespread.

These issues are being addressed in European research initiatives such as the Dedicated Road Infrastructure for Vehicle Safety in Europe (*Drive*) program. The Drive *Telaid* project looks at how the requirements of disabled drivers may be incorporated into future vehicle designs; the Drive *Eddit* project looks at the needs of elderly drivers. These projects aim to ensure that the vehicle technology of the future will be available to more people with impairments than is currently the case.

Recommendations for the design of future vehicles will include configurations of the following, to produce integrated solutions for people with different impairments:

* *Vehicle ergonomics:* The general needs of different user groups for the design of the vehicle interior, e.g. access needs for getting in and out of cars, ease of door opening, seating arrangements, and storage of wheelchairs or luggage.

* *Vehicle control:* Consideration of the requirements of people who need alternative controls. This will predominantly affect those people with upper and lower limb impairments, although the use of Road Traffic Informatics (RTI) systems in combination will have different implications for different users.

- *Interface design:* Interfaces can be subdivided into *displays* and *tele-communications or computer interfaces.* Information displays on vehicle dashboards will predominantly affect the perceptually impaired, particularly those with visual defects. The needs of those with hearing or speech difficulties (or where the upper limbs are being used to substitute for the lower limbs) will particularly need to be taken into account in the design of telecommunications or computer interfaces.

The design of integrated solutions to the driving difficulties experienced by people with disabilities, along the lines suggested above, may well increase the numbers of disabled and elderly drivers on the roads. This will also mean that attention will have to be paid to the safety issues raised by these new systems and devices. It also means that it will be in the interest of manufacturers to cater for these expanding markets, thus increasing the mobility of certain groups of people with disabilities and helping them to become more integrated into society.

A design issues case study

As we have seen, people with disabilities are becoming recognized by designers as an important target group, and much is being done to improve the usability and accessibility of all forms of IT products for this group. In the broadest sense, design issues for people with disabilities in all these areas – the home, the workplace, and vehicle technology – are likely to be similar. The design of all kinds of IT products to increase their use by people with impairments is likely to focus on access via display technology, the usability of interfaces, and the provision of alternatives to conventional control modes.

For example, alternative modes of access for the visually impaired user are as important when considering access to a home based TV, personal computer, or security system as they are to the development of office based technology. The use of controls (whether for domestic appliances or in cars) is likely to involve similar problems of reach, grasp, strength needed to operate them, and so forth. Ways of ameliorating limitations in vision, speech, hearing, and the use of upper and lower limbs will all need to be considered. In each case there is a need to provide a choice of more than one mode of interaction with particular facilities, or to enhance existing modes.

In the following example of a domestic network, the central control function is performed through a remote control unit (RCU) in conjunction with a TV monitor. The application gives access to TV, video, personal computer, and surveillance systems. It is assumed that a telephone system and a telecommunications link to external services are provided.

Some suggestions for the design of an RCU and TV monitor to take account of the needs of visually impaired users follow. These recommendations are based on current research carried out within the Race Domestic Customer Premises

Network (DCPN) project by the Husat Research Institute (Maguire, Hirst, Allison, & Howey, 1991).

Recommendations for the design of an RCU

There are many kinds and degrees of visual disability. Most assistive technology is targeted at one of two groups: blind or partially sighted people (few people are wholly blind, and the causes and effects of partial sight vary considerably). The following suggests some ways in which lost vision may be replaced or partial sight enhanced in the use of standard home technology systems of the future.

Partially sighted users require that:

• Buttons or keys should be large and as few as possible.

• Lettering and numbering on keys or buttons should be large and in contrasting colors for different functions. Key shape and locator nodules on certain keys can also assist with locating keys correctly.

• If liquid crystal diode displays (LCDs) are used, there should be a good contrast.

• A zoom button could be very useful for enlarging text or parts of the screen.

These guidelines in themselves may also improve the usability of RCU devices for the general public.

Blind users require that:

• Braille buttons or keyboard overlays are provided. Ridges or raised markings on keypads are helpful. Alternatives to push button control (such as voice control) should be considered. Auditory feedback is needed to indicate the effect of actions.

TV monitor (including TV, computer system, display of pictures from surveillance cameras)

Partially sighted users:

• Software could include a magnifier as a standard facility (as on current Macintosh computer systems) to enhance the size of interaction dialogue/text.

Blind users:

- Gaining access to text and graphics is especially difficult for the visually disabled user. Graphical representations of the security system, icons, and menu driven selection modes would therefore be especially difficult for blind users. Indeed, graphical user interfaces are a growing problem for blind and partially sighted users of technology systems (World Congress, 1991; Chapter 10, above), as effective tactile or speech driven alternatives have not yet been found. However, voice controlled interactions may be adequate for simple dialogues.

- Control dialogue and system feedback could be provided (e.g. for use of menus) by including a voice output option in the system design.

- A speaker channel could provide an alternative to pictures. In the case of TV broadcasts, this would provide descriptive information.

- Computer systems software for translating graphics interfaces or icons into another mode is needed. Experiments in audio commentary to help clarify TV pictures and the graphics presented on displays are currently being explored (Emiliani, 1990). This is a difficult research area, as the special nature of graphical user interfaces may be difficult to express in other modes.

Links to other communication services – telephone, audio/videophone, surveillance system, alarm system

Partially sighted users:

- Surveillance cameras could include a "zoom" facility and/or a voice channel so that the caller can introduce him or herself.

Blind users:

- These users need greater audio stimulation and alternative (e.g. braille or other tactile) control buttons or overlays.

- Surveillance cameras could include a voice channel so that the caller can introduce himself or herself. A "smart card" alternative giving details of the caller may also be suitable here.

- Tactile alerting devices for alarm messages.

These examples of potential solutions to some of the problems posed by visual impairment show the variety of problems encountered by people in one impairment group, and thus indicate the challenge of designing something to fit all groups of people with disabilities. Even if general or core solutions could be found for each impairment group to cater for the variation within that group, problems arise when one attempts to find solutions across impairment groups. For example, loss of acuity in hearing and visual perception is often associated with ageing, and overlapping losses may make it harder to provide alternative modes of access.

Many general guidelines exist for incorporating special needs requirements into low technology products and equipment in order to make them both useful and acceptable to the user (e.g. Dahlman's [1989] report on the requirements of elderly people in their homes). However, useful as guidelines are for pointing out functional problems such as restrictions on reach, grasp, and so on at the ergonomic level, they are not intended to provide insights into the generic needs of groups of disabled people for technology systems. More work needs to be done on developing specific guidelines for technology systems.

Discussion

Some of the suggestions described above may require facilities which are still under development or of low quality. Alternatives to conventional interfaces must therefore be looked at carefully. The developmental status of many of the options suggested here requires that careful user testing and evaluation of designs be carried out. For example, broadband communications networks which allow for the transmission of text, image, voice, and graphics are being explored by the European Race research program (see Astbrink, 1990).

In some cases, design recommendations for different user groups may conflict. For example, flashing lights instead of ringers may be suitable for hearing impaired people but not for visually impaired users. The designers of technology products will not be able to incorporate all of the requirements of all the impaired user groups into all designs, and a cost effective trade-off will be necessary.

In my view, integrated design solutions (based on the needs of as wide as possible a user base) or the incorporation of extra-ordinary requirements into mainstream designs (by the provision of extra facilities which may also be useful to able bodied people, as suggested above) are more likely to provide effective solutions for people with disabilities than add-on devices, which may provide only a partial solution for the user, be cumbersome to use, and result in slower operating times, degraded performance, or increased cost for the user. (Multiple add-on devices may also result in a duplication of facilities.)

For some functions (such as telephone operation for hearing and speech impaired users), adaptive technology, special systems, and interfaces currently exist but may require users at both ends to have similar facilities. If purpose-built integrated design solutions do not prove to be cost effective at this stage (because technical developments are still in progress), then we must ensure as a first step that these specialized input and output devices can be used with standard technology. This requires compatibility between different systems. It is also important that hardware manufacturers allow for future developments (e.g. the transmission of lipreading and sign and symbol languages for TV programs and video recordings).

In formulating design advice for disabled users, we must study usage problems as part of the product design process. For example, although braille display technology can be of great benefit to the visually impaired, its use is different from the paper based reading of braille (discussed in Chapter 9). For cognition of the text ahead in document scanning, braille readers usually use both hands to scan the page vertically. Tactile displays allow only linear scanning, so the cues present on a braille page are missing on a screen. Also, braille displays often allow only 40 characters (half a screen) to be displayed at a time, making the checking of input for errors a laborious business for the visually impaired user. Increased numbers of studies of the ways in which disabled people actually use technology devices (and the associated training and support issues) are needed to refine user specifications of technology and produce a closer fit between user need and product design.

Conclusions

I hope that I have illustrated some directions that the design of technology systems may take to ensure that the systems of the future include the needs of user groups who are currently largely excluded from access to today's technology. Access to computers and home based technology will enable people with impairments to maximize their abilities and will minimize the handicapping effect of their impairments, thereby increasing the possibilities for self-sufficiency.

If we broaden the baseline of design and extend the design principles above to other fields, increased access to public transport systems, to urban environments, to public buildings, and to workplaces will follow. Thus people with disabilities will have greater control over their environments, improved mobility, and access to public information and communications networks.

Better designs will be more successful and reach larger markets. There are currently some 89 million disabled and elderly people in the EU member states. Understanding their needs for products and services can only improve the quality of design for the public in general. This will require closer collaboration among experts from the fields of disability assessment, technology design, and human factors. As HCI practitioners, we must ensure that information on user needs is presented to designers in optimal ways. This integration of knowledge and people can be achieved by broadening the focus of HCI design activities, and it is the major challenge of this discipline.

References

Astbrink, G. (Ed.). (1990). *Proceedings of the Second COST 219 European Conference on Policy Related to Telematics and Disability*. Luxembourg: Office for Official Publications of the European Communities.

Breding, J. (1991). The TUFFA Project – Technology for disabled people in working life. In *Europe: Markets and Politics: Proceedings of the British Computer Society Disability Programme Sixth Annual Conference* (pp. 76–78), ed. G. Watson. London: British Computer Society.

Dahlman, S. (1989). Declaration of intent, In *Design for Elderly, a Home of an Ageing Person: Design for Independent Living* (pp. 16–17). Final report of ICSID Long Term Project 2, Kristiansund, Norway.

Emiliani, P. L. (1990) In *Proceedings of the Second COST 219 European Conference on Policy Related to Telematics and Disability*, ed. G. Astbrink. Luxembourg: Office for Official Publications of the European Communities.

Engelstad, H. (1989). Mature age – from charity to privilege. In *Design for Elderly, a Home of an Ageing Person: Design for Independent Living* (pp. 4–6). Final Report ICSID Long Term Project 2, Kristiansund, Norway, .

Frederiksen, J., Martin, M., de la Bellacasa, P., and von Tetzchner, S. (1989). *The use of telecommunication: The needs of people with disabilities*, Fundesco and Telefonica. Published for the EEC by Fundesco (Spain) and Telefonica (Spain), as part of COST 219 (European Cooperation in the Field of Scientific and Technical Research, Future Telecommunications and Teleinformatics Facilities for Disabled People).

Howey, K. R. (1986). New technology work aids for the physically disabled. In *People and Computers II: Designing for Usability. Proceedings of the Second Conference of the British Computer Society Human–Computer Interaction Specialist Group* (pp. 501–526), ed. M. D. Harrison and A. F. Monk. Cambridge: Cambridge University Press.

Howey, K. R. (1988). Factors affecting the use of information technology and computer systems as work aids for the physically disabled. In *Information Technology and the Human Services* (pp. 39–49), ed. B. Glastonbury. Chichester, Sussex: Wiley.

Maguire, M., Hirst, S., Allison, G. and Howey, K. (1991). Adapting Electronic Home Products to the Needs of the Elderly and the Physically Disabled. In *User aspects and revised Design of DCPN user interface* (pp 35-49). Commission of the European Community RACE - DCPN (1015) project report, HUSAT Research Institue, Loughborough, UK

Martin, J., and White, A. (1988). *The financial circumstances of disabled adults living in private households*. Office of Population Census and Surveys (OPCS), Disability Survey, Part 2. London: HSMO.

Mintel (1992). Video and Leisure Market, *Leisure Intelligence,* 2. London: Mintel International.

Sandhu, J. S., and Wood, T. (1990). *Demography and market sector analysis of people with special needs in thirteen European countries: A report on telecommunication usability issues.* Race Tudor 1088. Special Needs Research Unit, University of Northumbria at Newcastle, Newcastle-upon-Tyne.

Sperling, L. (1989). Manual handling in the home. In *Design for Elderly, a Home of an Ageing Person: Design for Independent Living* (pp. 34–39). Final report of ICSID Long Term Project 2, Kristiansund, Norway.

Thorpe-Tracey, R. (Ed.). (1976). *Integrating the disabled.* National Fund for Research into Crippling Diseases, Vincent House, 1 Springfield Road, Horsham, West Sussex, England RH12 2PN.

World Congress on Technology. (1991). *The First World Conference on IT, Computerisation and Electronics in the Workplace for People with Disabilities.* Arlington, VA (unpublished mimeographed proceedings).

19
Resources

Alistair D. N. Edwards and Rex Hancock

Introduction

This book is not a recipe book of solutions and adaptations for extra-ordinary computer users with different special needs; such a book could not and should not be written. The commonest advice to the designer of any human–computer interface is "Know thy user." The greatest problem in following that maxim is that users are individuals, and to know one or some of them is not to know them all. If that is true of the "average" user, it is even more true of disabled users. To "design *the* computer interface for users with cerebral palsy" makes about as much sense as designing *the* car for Americans. The point has been made in several chapters that all people are a collection of skills and abilities. Any well designed interface will allow a user to make the best use of the communications skills he or she is good at. The differences for the users we have been addressing are that there may be no alternative communication channel and that even those which do work may be comparatively inefficient.

The book should have given an impression as to how solutions can be sought and developed. The current state of the art has been represented, as well as a glimpse into the future. (Another reason why packaged solutions cannot be presented is that they would be prescriptive, when what we need are novel – even radical – ideas.)

Nevertheless, the book would be incomplete if it did not attempt to equip the reader to know where to start in devising a solution to the access problems of individuals. To that end, this chapter will point the reader to sources of help and information which should be of assistance. Recall that one of the objectives of this book is to heighten the awareness of designers of all human–computer interfaces to the needs of a wider population. Such designers should also find these resources valuable in finding ways in which they can build greater flexibility into their designs.

Addresses of all the organizations mentioned are given at the end of the chapter. Comprehensive information on the availability of resources and information can also be found in Lazzaro (1993).

Legislation

The field of extra-ordinary HCI has been greatly influenced by the introduction of federal legislation in the United States. In 1986 the U.S. Congress passed Public Law 99–506, reauthorizing the Rehabilitation Act of 1973. The law, signed by President Reagan on October 21, 1986, contained a small amendment titled "Electronic Equipment Accessibility." "Section 508," as it has come to be known, has had a significant impact on the design of computer systems and their accessibility by users with disabilities.

The driving principle behind Section 508 can be found in Section 504 of the Rehabilitation Act of 1973, which states:

> *No otherwise qualified handicapped individual in the United States shall, solely by reason of his handicap, be excluded from the participation in, be denied the benefits of, or be subjected to discrimination under any program or activity receiving Federal financial assistance.*

Like other information based settings, the federal government has benefited from rapid advances in information technology. Section 508 was developed because it was realized that government offices were rapidly changing into electronic offices with microcomputers on every desk.

Section 508 does not specify what the guidelines should be, nor does it delineate a philosophy on which to base the guidelines. A committee made up of representatives of the government and the electronics industry as well as rehabilitation engineers and disabled computer professionals worked for a year developing the philosophy and guidelines which significantly affect the purchase of electronic office equipment, including computers and software, by the federal government.

This group worked in conjunction with the National Institute on Disability and Rehabilitation Research (NIDRR), the agency given lead responsibility for developing federal computer accessibility guidelines. Ultimately industry representatives, researchers, and the General Services Administration (GSA) cooperatively prepared guidelines to make access possible without setting rigid specifications. On November 19, 1987, the initial guidelines titled *Access to Information Technology by users with disabilities*, were published jointly by GSA and NIDRR. The purpose of the initial guidelines was to set a tone and to provide early guidance to industry on the direction in which the government planned to move in the months and year ahead.

After considerable response to the initial guidelines, the General Services Administration published on October 13, 1988, regulations for all federal agencies pursuant to Section 508 in its Federal Information Resources Management Regulation (FIRMR). This policy implements Public Law 99–506, Section 508 (29 USC 794d) regarding electronic office equipment accessibility. The FIRMR regulations inform federal agencies what they are required to do to comply with Section 508. It is worth stating the general policy under which federal agencies must operate:

> *Federal agencies shall provide handicapped employees and non-handicapped employees equivalent access to electronic office equipment to the extent such needs are determined by the agency . . . and the required accessibility can be provided by industry. In providing equivalent access to electronic office equipment, agencies shall consider:*
>
> *i.   access to and use of the same data bases and application programs by handicapped and non-handicapped employees,*
>
> *ii. utilization of enhancement capabilities for manipulating data (i.e., special peripherals) to attain equivalent end results by disabled and non-handicapped employees; and*
>
> *iii. access to and use of equivalent communications capabilities by disabled employees.*

Shortly after the implementing regulations were put in place regarding electronic office equipment accessibility, a related law was passed. Public Law 100–542, the Telecommunications Accessibility Enhancement Act of 1988, was put in place to ensure the accessibility of the federal telecommunications system for communications with and within the federal government.

In general, the regulations require that agencies of the federal government must assess the needs not only those of its current and potential employees with disabilities but of those citizens who need access to an agency resource. Agencies are instructed to incorporate appropriate functional specifications for meeting those needs into solicitations to vendors of information technology. To provide additional guidance, GSA published two FIRMR bulletins, C-8 and C-10 (originally Bulletins 56 and 63 respectively), for government personnel involved in acquiring, managing, and using information resources. The bulletins outline management responsibilities and provide functional specifications for equipment to assist agencies in achieving accessibility for their employees. These and other documents helpful to government buyers, vendors, and users are available in a guide titled "Managing Information Resources for Accessibility" (GSA, 1991).

To ensure across-the-board compliance, the GSA in its congressionally mandated role as an overseer of federal acquisitions of information technology has incorporated in its review of agency procurement practices the issue of equivalent access to those resources. Agencies are required to submit to the GSA a request for a delegation of procurement authority when acquisitions are over a specified dollar threshold. When the agency submits a request, it must include specific language for meeting the requirements of the disabled users affected by the acquisition. In addition the GSA conducts triennial reviews of federal agencies and their information resource acquisitions. Education is a large part of the effort to ensure access to the federal government's information processing resources. Technology fairs, management briefings, and training of persons charged with the acquisition of information resources is a continuing activity at many agencies.

As implementation proceeds, it is anticipated that accessibility related equipment and support services will become integral aspects of agency acquisitions. The responsibility then shifts to industry to outline a plan to meet agency requirements for accessibility when responding to agency requests for proposals. A number of government agencies have awarded multimillion dollar contracts which include Section 508 provisions for computer accessibility for their employees with disabilities. Many other agencies are in the process of preparing solicitations which include accessibility.

Users with disabilities will receive equipment, accommodation related software, hardware add-ons as necessary, training, and technical support equivalent to what is received by users without disabilities. In addition, it is anticipated that as end user needs evolve, the acquisition plans of federal agencies will increasingly reflect the total information processing environment of all individual end users.

Those who drafted the legislation were at pains not to prescribe solutions; in fact it is stated, "The government will welcome vendor creativity in responding to the functional requirements" (Gray et al., 1987, p. 11). The idea was to suggest that it is not possible to state that a particular adaptation is *the one* to be applied for a particular class of user. That sort of approach would not take account of the vast differences among individuals and would stifle the development of novel solutions.

Hence the legislation spawned a set of *guidelines* in the document *Considerations in the Design of Computers and Operating Systems to Increase Their Accessibility to Persons with Disabilities,* (Scadden & Vanderheiden, 1988), which was produced by the Industry/Government Cooperative Initiative on Computer Accessibility. This document analyzes the needs of computer users with different disabilities and outlines approaches which might be taken to accommodate them. It is available free from the Trace Center at the University of Wisconsin–Madison (see below), but the approach taken in it can be appreciated by examination of summary tables from it, which are included in Chapter 2.

Design guidelines

Scadden and Vanderheiden (1988) present one form of design guidelines enumerating particular impairments, the barriers to access that they constitute, and possible methods of overcoming them. However, it is worth considering design guidelines at a more abstract level. Any experienced HCI designer is likely to recognize most or all of the guidelines set out below. This simply illustrates the point that designing interfaces which are good for people with extra-ordinary needs will lead to designs which are good for all users. The point is that often the needs of a disabled user are more critical – there is less room for the user to adapt, and the interface should be molded to the user.

Know the user

This is surely at the top of any HCI designer's list of guidelines, but in this context the designer must remember that the user may vary to a great extent from the "average." It is vital to involve potential users in the design process so that their needs (and not the able-bodied designer's perception of their needs) can be addressed. It should always be remembered that *all* users have a range of ordinary and extra-ordinary abilities. As far as possible, the use of oversimplified categories should be avoided – the assumption should not be made, for example, that all people with hearing losses are the same.

While potential users clearly know their own needs best, it should not be forgotten that there are also others with valuable experience and knowledge, namely the professionals who work with such people. Teachers and social workers are obvious examples, and one should not forget those "professionals" who do not get paid – members of the users' families. Sometimes, though, it is as well for the designer not to pay too much attention to entrenched ideas of others. Innovative solutions may be overlooked if the designer always trusts the "expert's" opinion of what a client can and cannot do.

Clearly any adaptation must work around the limitations of users, and the designer must exploit their abilities. But at the same time the design should make the most of users' residual capabilities. An obvious example is partial sight. People with impaired vision will generally much prefer to make the most of the sight they have than to use nonvisual forms of interaction.

It is also important to remember that many people have multiple impairments. Sometimes these will have the same cause and hence quite commonly be associated, but often the combination will be unusual. It is impossible to be prescriptive, and so it is all the more important that the designer learns of the individual's requirements. It is also important to make interfaces as rich and as flexible as possible to facilitate the accommodation of people with unusual needs. (This is also relevant to the discussion on redundancy below.)

Use appropriate technology

This book is about human–computer interaction and therefore tends to concentrate on high level technology, but that should not obscure the fact that such technology does not always provide the answer and low technology can be more appropriate. For instance, a programmer approaching the problem of accommodating a user with limited manual dexterity may immediately think in terms of writing a modified keyboard driver customized to the user's style of keyboard use. However, it might well be that a piece of plastic drilled out to form a keyguard is a much more effective – not to mention cheaper and simpler – solution.

Know the technology

The technology of aids and adaptations for people with special needs is evolving at least as rapidly as any other area of information technology. It is therefore very important to keep up with the latest developments to ensure that you are making the best technology available. A frequent problem is that of reinventing the wheel, of developing an aid or adaptation which is very similar to one which someone else has already produced. This arises partly because people tend not to share their work – to publish it. They work on a device for an individual, meet his or her needs, and stop there – and probably do not want to seek any "publicity" for what they have done.

Media independence

Current interfaces are visually dominated. This immediately disadvantages users with visual disabilities and makes adaptation more difficult for the HCI designer. Particularly with the advent of multimodal interaction, interfaces should be specified in media-independent terms. The specifier should think in terms of the information to be conveyed and only at a later stage translate that specification into a particular form of information. For instance, the Apple user interface guidelines (1987) state, "Every action must have an effect which the user can *see*" (emphasis added). If this were rephrased as "Every action must have an effect which the user can *perceive,*" then the difficulties encountered by those who have tried to adapt the Macintosh for blind users might have been reduced (Chapter 4).

It is to be hoped that continuing developments in user interface management systems (UIMS) will lead to effective separation of the interface and application, possibly to the extent that one application may have a variety of interfaces bolted on, each using a different mix of modes of communication – a mixed visual– auditory interface for most users and a wholly auditory one for a blind user, for instance.

Redundancy

Again the evolution of multimodal interfaces is important in this context, in that it offers the possibility of redundancy in communication. As mentioned above, traditional interfaces tend to use one channel of output, the visual. However, natural communication contains redundancy. For instance, for the most part to a hearing person the lip movements of speech convey no useful information, but a deaf person may rely on them to understand the speech. In some circumstances, though, the hearing person may also lipread, such as when the auditory signal is ambiguous, perhaps because of background noise. By definition, a multimodal interface provides alternative channels. Under most cirmcumstances the user will concentrate on one of those channels (and under most circumstances that will be a visual channel) and will not be attending to the information on the other channels. However, when appropriate the user might switch to one of the other channels or start to heed another channel as well, splitting his or her attention between sources of information. This will lead to better, more efficient communication for the majority of users, and the presence of this redundancy will make adaptation for extra-ordinary users simpler – or even unnecessary.

There is another aspect of redundancy: the provision of alternative channels to the user with sensory impairments. As was mentioned earlier, there is something of a schism in the community of blind people between braille and speech users. However, this split would be seen as wasteful if people would accept that braille is good for some purposes and speech better for others. In designing an interface, therefore, as many channels of communication as practical should be provided, allowing the user to chose between them and to switch from one to another, depending on the task.

Adapt where possible

Cost is usually an important consideration, and one way of reducing cost is to provide adaptations of existing technology. For instance, it would be possible to develop a word processor with a switch based interface for a physically disabled user. However, if the user also wanted to use a database, then a completely new application would have to be developed – at great expense. If one built a switch based keyboard emulator, then two standard applications would be made accessible for the same cost.

Apart from those people who portray themselves as eccentric or colorful, most people do not want to stand out too much in a crowd. Or, to be more specific, we generally prefer to not be distinguished too much from colleagues at work. This is less possible for people with disabilities. From the very fact that they have been labeled as such, they are immediately highlighted as different. It is desirable to minimize differences, and adaptation can be part of this process. Given suitable adaptations, users with special needs can use the same systems and software as their colleagues.

Uniformity has other benefits. It means that workers can share data stored in the same format.[1] Also there is a good reason why there is such a variety of

---

[1] There is software available to convert files between formats, but as anyone who has used such programs is aware, they are often impractical, not providing the particular

software available. There must be hundreds of different word processors, for instance. Each has a variety of features which suit some users; hence people have a choice of the one they like best. It is only right that users with special needs should have the same choice. It would be no more possible to create (say) the *best* word processor for blind users than it would be to create the *best* visual word processor. With a successful adaptation, the whole range of applications should be accessible and the disabled user allowed the same choice.

Cultivate integration

Whereas in the past there was a tendency to isolate anyone who was different, to hide these people in institutions away from the rest of the population, there is now a movement toward integrated living. There is a recognition that – apart from some requirement for physical support – the needs of persons with disabilities are just the same as for anyone else and can be met in the same sort of way. Thus, their requirements for employment, housing, transportation and so on can all generally be met in the same manner as those needs are addressed for everyone else. Adaptation is one aspect of cultivating integration, but designers of aids and adaptations must keep in mind at all times the aims of integration.

A particular aspect of integration is that designers must be acutely aware of the aesthetics of any device they develop. They may invent some device of breath-taking functionality, but if it is going to make the user look odd and stand out in a crowd then it is likely not to be used. For instance, there is great interest in the possibilities of using global positioning by satellite (GPS) as a means of providing blind people with navigational information. A system which supplies the information that a blind person currently lacked would seem a great boon – but if its use requires the wearing of a satellite dish on the head it will not be used by many people; the fact that blind people cannot see themselves does not mean that they do not care how they appear to others.

Control must remain with the user

As discussed in Chapter 2, disability is largely concerned with loss of independence. Technology can be used to reduce dependence, to give some control back to the individual. This objective must be borne in mind in the design of that technology. A bald example is a computer which provides all sorts of new capabilities to a physically disabled person – but which has an on–off switch which he or she cannot operate. That person remains dependent on some person who has the power of allowing or denying access to the facilities.

---

mapping needed, and wasting time converting from format A to B and then back again to A for the original user, and so on.

As has been seen repeatedly in this book, often the fundamental limitation of the human–computer interface is that there is insufficient bandwidth. For example, the visual sense has a very broad bandwidth, and when that is substituted for, the alternative channel (sound and/or touch) has less capacity. Often the solution is to *filter* some of the information to reduce the bandwidth requirement. That is all very well, but is it *not* the designer's role to decide that a particular piece of information is not needed by the user and that access to it can therefore be denied. For instance, a status line on a computer screen may contain information which is usually of little value and is little more than a distraction to the user (particularly in a speech based interface). The adaptation designer may decide to hide that information *under normal circumstances*, but the designer must not make it wholly inaccessible. In other words, some means should be built in so that the user can access information if and when it is required. In that way the user retains control.

Of course this can make the interface more complex. Such a facility might be used only by an advanced user and may not even be taught to a novice. Nevertheless, the principle is an important one: The designer will not prescribe what the user is and is not allowed to access.

The need for testing

One resource required for anyone developing extra-ordinary human–computer interfaces is human subjects for testing and evaluation. That may sound obvious, but it is something which is often overlooked. It is all too easy for an able-bodied person to see a need and to go ahead and produce what he or she thinks is an ideal solution. However, it may well be that it turns out to be altogether inappropriate when presented to the intended user.

This can be illustrated by a specific example. A large number of electronic devices have been developed to help blind people navigate when walking – and yet the white cane remains the most popular navigation aid. The electronic devices generally consist of some sensor which detects obstructions and communicates their presence to the user by sound. To a sighted person, such a device might seem an ideal aid for someone with no sight, but the blind user may have objections which never occurred to the (sighted) designer. Blind people rely to a great extent on the natural sounds around them. To have those masked by electronic bleeps (possibly presented through headphones) is to cut off much more information than the device provides. As mentioned earlier, another potential problem with such devices is that they will be unacceptable on aesthetic grounds. Again consulting potential users at an early stage might obviate waste of effort developing a device which will not be acceptable on those grounds.

"Know the user" is a well known adage in human–computer interface design, and this is even more true for extra-ordinary users. Ideally users should be integrated in all the design and development stages, but at the very least regular testing and evaluation should be carried out during development. It can be difficult to find suitable testers. They must have the disability which the interface is designed to alleviate, and that means that the number of potential subjects may be small. However, it is not generally acceptable to simulate the disability. For instance, to test an adaptation to make a computer accessible to a blind person, a sighted person wearing a blindfold is *not* the same as a blind person. Only a blind tester can assess what it would be like to have to use the computer through that interface; sighted testers know that they would never actually use such an interface when the visual one with which they are familiar is available.

Participative design is in some senses the ideal. Who knows better about the design requirements of any product than a potential user? As the same time, this is sometimes an unattainable ideal because it may involve a paradox. For instance, those working on making GUIs accessible to blind people often have to use GUI based programming tools – which implies that the one person who cannot do that job is a blind person. Until the GUI has been made accessible the blind worker will not be able to use the necessary tools.

Evaluation is an example of an area in which cross-fertilization between HCI and extra-ordinary users may be very productive. On the one hand, evaluation is something which HCI developers have been doing for some time, which is very much needed (as explained above) as part of the development of adapted interfaces. At the same time, evaluation of the innovative interfaces developed with testers of very different abilities can present some novel challenges to the evaluator, which may in the long run enhance the discipline.

Organizations

Obviously the organizations represented by the authors of this volume are engaged in research and development and are excellent sources of information with regard to their particular specialties. There are a number of other organizations which can provide advice and assistance. As well as having information on devices which are currently available, they should be able to provide advice about the development of new adapted human–computer interfaces and how to accommodate a broader range of users' needs.

The Trace Center is a major center of research and development as well as a source of information on what is currently available. Most of the major computer manufacturers have responded to the need to provide access to computers to disabled users by the establishment of groups and centers focusing on that area. These can be contacted via the companies.

A large number of organizations stock selections of adaptations for evaluation purposes. People commonly need to assess what kind of equipment is best suited to their requirements and so need to try a variety of possibilities, perhaps even borrowing one or two examples for an extended period. Such organizations are often locally based or associated with particular organizations. In the USA, the

Trace Center would be the best source of information as to where the most suitable help can be found. In the UK, there is a national network, the National Federation of Access Centres, with establishments in a number of cities.

IBM has been particularly visible in this regard, having established a number of Support Centers for People with Disabilities. In the USA the center is in Atlanta, Georgia. Europe is served by a center in Belgium. The British Computer Society (BCS) includes the longest established professional group of computer users with disabilities, and the BCS Disability Programme has set up the Computability Centre in Warwick. Another source of information in the UK is the Handicapped Persons Research Unit (HPRU), based at The University of Northumbria at Newcastle. As well as doing research, this center maintains several databases of information on research and on hardware and software adaptations for users with disabilities.

Some of the work on adapting computers has been done under the auspices of established groups in the area generally referred to as *rehabilitation engineering*. This is a broad term, covering all kinds of prostheses. In the USA the principal organization in this area is Resna (Rehabilitation Society of North America).

Information is also available online on computer networks and bulletin boards. *Internet* is the largest computer network in the world, with over one million hosts internationally. Through it users can access *News*, which consists of a vast number of *news groups,* many of which contain discussions of interest to computer users with disabilities. The most general such group is probably *misc.handicap*, which will at least provide a good starting point. A query posted to that group will usually generate a sheaf of responses. Several of the databases available on bulletin boards are reviewed in detail in Casali and Williges (1990).

The International Federation for Information Processing (IFIP) is a body which operates largely through its working groups. Working Group 13.3, *Human–Computer Interaction and Disability,* has been established with the following aims:

1. To make HCI designers aware of the needs of people with disabilities.

2. To recommend guidelines for the design of human–computer interfaces to facilitate the use of computers by people with disabilities.

3. To monitor the latest developments in the design of human–computer interfaces and their impact on accessibility and usability.

4. To encourage the development of information systems and complementary tools which permit the adaptation of the human interface for each specific user.

Conferences

One of the objectives of this book is to encourage the dissemination of information on extra-ordinary human–computer interaction to a broader community, including mainstream HCI practitioners. As pointed out in Chapter 1, this work has not had a very high profile in the past in HCI conferences, but nevertheless it does exist. The annual ACM (Association for Computing Machinery) Chi conference is one example, as is the annual conference of the Human Factors Society. The ACM has a long established special interest group (sig) on computers and the physically handicapped, Sigcaph.

More of what has been published has been in rehabilitation engineering conferences. Principal among these is the annual Resna conference. In Europe there is a much newer regular conference, Ecart (European Conference on the Advancement of Rehabilitation Technology), which is biennial. Another newly established European based conference is the International Conference on Computers for Handicapped Persons. The second major annual conference is "Closing the Gap." Technology and Persons with Disabilities is a growing annual conference, hosted by California State University, Northridge (CSUN).

Journals

Apart from the conferences mentioned above, it is often difficult to find journals suitable for publication of this kind of research. Hopefully as extra-ordinary HCI moves more into the mainstream, journals such as *Human–Computer Interaction* and the *International Journal of Human–Computer Studies* (formerly the *International Journal of Man–Machine Studies* or *IJMMS*)[1] will become places where more of this kind of work is published. Journals aimed at potential users of extra-ordinary HCI are listed in Appendix C of Lazzaro (1993). A new publication is the journal *Information Technology and Disabilities*. It is unusual and exciting in that it is distributed electronically and thus accessible to anyone who can use a computer.[2]

Anyone interested specifically in research related to visually disabled people will find Gill and Peulevé (1993) an invaluable resource.

Conclusions

Making computer systems accessible to users with disabilities is a challenging problem requiring the cooperative efforts of the computer industry, third party

---

[1] *Human–Computer Interaction* is published by Lawrence Erlbaum Associates Inc., and *The International Journal of Human–Computer Studies* is published by Academic Press.

[2] To subscribe to the journal address an Email message to: listserv@sjuvm.stjohns.edu. Leave the subject line blank, and send the following one-line message:
sub itd-jnl John Smith (substituting your name for "John Smith").

vendors of adaptive devices, rehabilitation engineers, and computer users with disabilities. In many cases the solutions serve as a catalyst to the introduction of well designed technology innovations of benefit to all users. The development of Section 508, the initial guidelines, and the implementing regulations demonstrate that cooperation is possible. This law applies only to direct purchases by the U.S. government, where it is most easily enforced. Much more needs to be done, but the future seems brighter for a world where computers will be accessible to all regardless of disability.

Addresses

ACM
11 West 42nd Street
New York NY 10036

Computability Centre
IBM Warwick
PO Box 31
Birmingham Road
Warwick
England
CV34 5JL

The Human Factors Society
PO Box 1369
Santa Monica CA 90406

IBM European Support Center
    for Persons with Disabilities
135 chaussée de Bruxelles
La Hulpe
Belgium
B-1310

IBM National Support Center for
    Persons with Disabilities
PO Box 2150
Atlanta GA 30055

IFIP Secretariat
16 place Longemalle
CH-1204 Geneva
Switzerland

National Federation of Access Centres
Hereward College of Further Education
Bramston Crescent
Tile Hill Lane
Coventry
England
CV4 9SW

Resna
Suite 700
1101 Connecticut Avenue NW
Washington DC 20036

Trace Research and Development
    Center
S-151 Waisman Center
University of Wisconsin-Madison
1500 Highland Avenue
Madison WI 53706

The annual CSUN conference is
    organized by:

Office of Disabled Student Services
California State University, Northridge
18111 Nordhoff Street – DVSS
Northridge CA 91330

References

Casali, S., and Williges, R. (1990). A review of databases of accommodative aids for disabled users of computers. *Human Factors, 32*(4): 407–422.

Gill, J. and Peulevé, C. A. (1993). *Research information handbook of assistive technology for visually disabled persons.* London: Royal National Institute for the Blind.

Gray, D. B., LeClair, R. R., Traub, J. E., Brummel, S. A., Maday, D. E., McDonough, F. A., Patton, P. R., and Yonkler, L. (1987). *Access to information technology by users with disabilities: initial guidelines.* Washington, DC: General Services Administration.

GSA. (1991). *Managing Information Resources for Accessibility.* Washington, DC: General Services Administration.

Lazzaro, J. J. (1993). *Adaptive technologies for learning and work environments.* Chicago, IL: American Library Association.

Scadden, L. A., and Vanderheiden, G. C. (1988). *Considerations in the design of computers and operating systems to increase their accessibility to persons with disabilities,* Working document of the Industry/Government Cooperative Initiative on Computer Accessibility. Trace Center, University of Wisconsin–Madison.

Index

abilities, cognitive 4, 7, 9, 34
accent 310
acoustics 209, 211–213, 214, 235, 265
ADA (Americans with Disabilities
    Act) 19, 246
aesthetics 76, 265, 267, 276, 368–369
age and capabilities 8–20, 21, 33, 34,
    245, 246, 290, 292, 343, 344,
    346, 347, 349
aids 317, 318, 321, 322, 323, 336
    communication 45, 84, 91, 92, 107,
      137, 266
    mobility 26, 350
    navigation 92, 369
    physical therapy 141
    writing 114
algorithm 46, 95, 117–119, 135, 137,
    288–294, 307
    genetic 179, 180
    predictive 105
    text compression 137
    text-to-speech 311, 312
Alzheimer's disease 34, 169
American Sign Language (ASL) 170–
    174
animation 249, 250, 273
aphasia 8, 10
Apple Computer 59, 79, 109, 138,
    205, 304, 312, 351
    interface guidelines 72–76, 366
Arkola 224
arthritis 37
Ashored research project 347, 351
audio conferencing 248, 253, 256
auditory icons 216, 224
auditory images 152

auditory interface 72, 76
auditory navigation 195, 212, 225–
    232, 240
auditory output 40, 60, 61, 67, 76,
    160, 175, 176, 207–218, 221–
    241, 319, 355, 366, 367
augmentative communication 32–33,
    45, 85, 96, 137, 170, 312, 319
autocompletion 11
Autoprogramming Calculator 105,
    124–137

bandwidth 31, 46, 104, 144, 221, 234,
    241, 248, 251, 369
Bitnet 300
blindness (*see also* visual disability;
    visual impairment) 8–13, 20, 22,
    25–28, 35, 39, 45, 59–80, 142,
    183–199, 201–218, 221–241,
    279–280, 298–303, 307–313,
    346, 355–356, 366–370
body language 83
braille 10, 27–28, 39, 41, 59, 142,
    183, 187–199, 231, 280, 299,
    315, 345, 352, 355, 356, 358,
    367
    keyboard 195, 345, 355
    mathematics 183
    mouse 187, 188, 189
    music notation 183
braille display
    piezoelectric 186, 195
    polyvinyldifluoride (PVDF) 185
brain
    damage 30, 83, 169
    disease 34

calculator 13, 103, 105, 106, 124, 125,
    128, 137
  Autoprogramming 105, 124–137
captioning 40, 299
car navigation 290
cassette
  audio 11
  video 252
CD–rom 36, 137, 252, 273, 300, 302,
    308
cerebral palsy (CP) 30, 36, 51, 52,
    114, 141, 169–174, 181, 361
charity 4, 13
Chi (ACM) Conferences 4, 372
children 12, 14, 87–89, 94, 107, 141,
    169–181, 292, 308
chunking 152, 237
cognitive
  abilities 4, 7, 9, 34
  load 12, 34, 93, 104, 105, 123, 128,
      137, 147, 151, 161, 166, 167,
      230, 237
  processor 152, 156, 161
  prosthesis 46, 143
  psychology 154
Colab project 257
color blindness 38, 146
command language 239
commercialization 266
communication
  augmentative 32–33, 45, 85, 96,
      137, 170, 312, 319
  nonvocal 48, 56, 141, 319
  prosthesis 84, 96
  tactile 27, 28, 142, 186, 198, 231,
      233, 356, 358
computer conferencing 247– 256, 299
computer network 249, 300, 358, 371
conferencing
  audio 248, 253, 256
  satellite 247, 248
  technology 247–258

theater 247
video 253
consistency 71, 128, 236, 239, 310, 311
  user interface 34, 72–73
Convolvatron (hardware) 217
CP/M operating system 193
CSCW (computer-supported
    cooperative work) 249–251
CSUN (California State University,
    Northridge), conferences at 372–
    373
cursor routing 142, 189, 192–193,
    195–196

database 84, 91–93, 249, 252, 256,
    297–298, 300–304, 308, 316,
    319, 321, 367, 371
  navigation 84
dataglove 95
deafness 5, 8, 9, 11, 26, 29, 35, 40,
    146, 170, 174, 279, 299, 344–
    346, 367
Dectalk 94
dementia 34, 290
design by metaphor 205–207
desktop metaphor 71, 76, 205, 208
disability 20
  cognitive 7, 8, 9, 13, 21, 33, 34, 35,
      84, 85, 146, 323, 345
  physical 5, 7, 8, 10, 11, 21, 246,
      248, 263, 289, 298–305, 323,
      343, 345, 349, 352, 367, 368
  sensory 7, 21, 27–29, 143, 221,
      353, 367
  visual (*see also* impairment, visual)
      26, 29, 59, 209, 218, 355,
      356, 366, 372
DragonDictate 148–165
Drive (Dedicated Road Infrastructure
    for Vehicle Safety in Europe)
    353
dyslexia 12, 35, 88, 89, 141, 145–167

earcon 215, 224

Ecart (European Conference on the Advancement of Rehabilitation Technology) 372

Echo (Extra–ordinary computer–human operation) 85–95

education 12, 20, 22, 32, 83, 147, 234, 288, 297, 300, 301, 308, 312, 363
  literature on 35
  special 14, 51, 146

elderly people 7, 13–14, 284, 344, 346, 349–354, 357, 358

electronic mail (E–mail) 103, 113, 114, 211, 212, 215, 247, 248, 249, 254, 257, 275, 299

electronic travel 245–258, 297, 298, 316

employment 12–13, 142, 147, 245, 246, 253, 254, 258, 280, 299, 315, 339, 344, 352, 353, 363, 364, 368

engineering, rehabilitation 4, 13, 362, 371, 372, 373

enlargement 27
  print 352
  screen 38, 59, 241

epilepsy 40

ergonomics 287, 351, 353, 357

ethernet 251

evaluation 7, 11, 34, 45, 47–55, 60–80, 89, 91, 181, 205, 206, 207, 208, 218, 223, 225, 252, 253, 293, 317, 321, 322, 347, 357, 369, 370

EWCI (Eye Wink Control Interface) 264, 276

eye gaze input 31, 37, 95, 174, 266, 267, 268

eye wink input (*see also* EWCI) 22, 32, 41, 144, 264

eye–hand coordination 39

fax 251, 252, 257, 275

Fitts' Law 230

flow graph 152

Frank Audiodata 195

games, video 180–181, 212

gender 20, 35

gesture 83, 130
  input 94, 169–181, 250, 266, 273

global positioning by satellite (GPS) 368

glove 95, 174, 179

goms (goals, operators, methods) models 141, 152

Grabra 197, 199

graphical applications 176, 205, 217

graphics 41, 95, 120, 128, 129, 130, 133, 135, 204, 213, 215, 248, 250, 251, 256, 273, 301, 303, 328, 356, 357

graphs 178, 235
  line 240
  sound 240

GUI (graphical user interface) 45, 79, 80, 192, 202, 203, 204, 205, 207, 208, 210, 212, 213, 216, 223, 225, 227, 264, 274, 356
  and blind users 8, 22, 28, 59, 60, 193, 199, 201–218, 221–233, 301, 356, 370

Hamlet (speech synthesizer) 94

handicap 20, 27, 29, 143, 234, 279, 283, 284, 362

hearing 27, 28, 213, 221, 234, 357
  impairment 5, 7, 28, 29, 40, 146, 299, 345, 349, 350, 352, 353, 357

hypermedia 249
  HyperCard 79, 323
  hyperspace 290
  hypertext 91, 249, 290
  Ribis 249

IBM 60, 301, 371
    European Support Center for
        Persons with Disabilities 373
icons, auditory 216, 224
IFIP (International Federation for
    Information Processing) 371,
    373
images, auditory 152
impairment 20
    hearing 5, 7, 28, 29, 40, 146, 299,
        345, 349, 350, 352, 353, 357
    language 12, 13, 33, 96, 145, 147
    limbs 7, 29, 345, 349, 350, 353,
        354
    mobility 7, 9, 47, 56, 245–258, 298,
        299, 345, 349, 352, 353
    motor 105
    perception 33–34, 147, 349
    speech 48, 56, 141, 319
    visual 7, 8, 10, 13, 27, 38, 202, 207,
        298, 301, 303, 315, 354, 356,
        357, 358
independence 21, 30, 144, 267, 271,
        275, 298, 300, 315, 351, 352,
        368
input switch 31, 41, 95, 144, 265–273,
        316, 367
integration 95, 263, 272, 344, 346,
        347, 368
interface
    auditory 72, 76
    guidelines 72–76, 366
Internet 215, 299, 300, 371

joystick 141, 144, 170–180, 265, 266,
        267, 271, 273, 324, 328, 331,
        335, 337, 338

key, "sticky" 36
keyboard (*see also* Reactive
        Keyboard) 29, 30, 32, 34, 36, 37,
        38, 39, 46, 49, 50, 59, 84, 88, 94,
        191, 195, 202, 207, 221, 239,
        263, 303, 305, 315, 328

braille 195, 345, 355
    emulation 31, 367
    enlarged 315
    modified 31, 365
keyguard 30, 37, 41, 49, 50, 315, 366
Kurzweil reading machine 12

language 48, 49, 53, 112, 307, 311
    body 83
    disorder 83
    impairment 12, 13, 33, 96, 145,
        147
    natural 48, 55, 112, 120
    and "political correctness" 33
    processing skills 55
    processing system 147
    programming 124, 288
    reference to disability 19–21
    symbolic 171, 358
    visual 234
    written 146, 147
legislation 13, 19, 246, 281, 352, 362–
        364
line graphs 240
lipreading 358, 367
load, cognitive 12, 34, 93, 104, 105,
        123, 128, 137, 147, 151, 161,
        166, 167, 230, 237
locked-in syndrome 264

Macintalk (speech synthesizer) 67
Macintosh 59–80, 92, 106, 109, 111,
        114, 137, 148, 205, 232, 233,
        323, 328, 355, 366
    Close View 351
    Finder 73, 201, 205, 206, 216
mail
    conventional 256
    electronic (E–mail) 103, 113, 114,
        211, 212, 215, 247, 248, 249,
        254, 257, 275, 299
    voice 257
management
    briefing 364

information 48, 245, 247, 250, 254, 255, 362
  personnel 254
  workers with disabilities 363
mathematics 137
  access for blind people 234–241
  braille 183
Maths project (Europe) 234
Mathtalk program 238
Media Space 253
memory
  computer 189, 193, 305, 312
  external 234
  human 7, 54, 112, 119, 152, 223, 224, 290
  impairment 33, 34, 147, 156
  screen 39
  sensory 152
  spatial 209
Mercator project 201–218
Metamouse 106–135
metaphor
  Audio Rooms 202, 208–218
  design by 205–207
  desktop 71, 76, 205, 208
  interaction 76, 142, 202, 204
  nonvisual 207–208
  Room 142, 205, 208–213
  touch 134
  virtual space 248
  workbench 120
Microsoft Windows 60
Midi (Music Industry Digital Interface) 224, 226
Minicom 29
Minspeak 47–56
mobility 20, 22, 353, 354, 358
  aids 26, 350
  assistance 343
  impairment 7, 9, 47, 56, 245–258, 298, 299, 345, 349, 352, 353
Mosco 93
motor control 8, 322, 326, 345

motor impairment 9, 30, 36, 169, 263, 266, 267, 271, 299, 300, 301, 303, 319, 322, 323, 345, 346, 349, 353
motor processor 152, 156
motor skills 152
mouse 187, 192, 197, 202, 207, 221–233, 263, 289, 301, 303, 324–337
  braille 187, 188, 189
  click 192
  interrupt 195
  routing 193, 197
  tactile 188
  tracking 192, 197
mouthstick 30, 36, 271, 316
MS–DOS operating system 28, 59, 106, 108, 114, 137, 193–194, 271
multimedia 60, 142, 143, 224, 251
  applications 273
  preparation 256
multiple sclerosis 263
music 303
  braille notation 183
  synthesizer 225, 229
  training 224

Nasa 142, 188, 218
navigation
  aids 92, 369
  auditory 195, 212, 225–232, 240
  blind people 368, 369
  car 290
  database 84
network
  broadband 357
  computer 249, 300, 358, 371
  conferencing 247
  home 352, 354
  Internet 299
  Media Space 253
  office 245, 352
  public information 345

television 275
Usenet 114
networking 353
nonspeech sound 28, 61, 76, 201–215,
    221–241
nonvisual algebra 235
nonvisual channel 241
nonvisual interaction 22, 27, 39, 68,
    77, 142, 201, 209, 233, 241, 365
nonvocal communication 48, 56, 141,
    319

occupational therapy 51, 169, 265
OCR (optical character recognition)
    28, 35, 308–309
Optacon 28, 186–188
Oracle 308
output, auditory 40, 60, 61, 67, 76,
    160, 175, 176, 207–218, 221–
    241, 319, 355, 366, 367
Outspoken 45, 59–80, 233

Pal 87–90, 107
PalStar 87–89
Pantograph 233
paralysis 30, 34, 36, 113
paraplegia 30
Parc (Xerox Palo Alto Research
    Center) 208, 257
partially sighted people (*see also*
    impairment, visual) 27, 59, 241,
    355, 356
participative design 26, 370
PC 60, 114, 157, 176, 189, 193, 241,
    299, 312
perception of timbre 224
perceptions
    designers' 365
    of ability 20
phoneme 186, 307
phonetic alphabet 310
phonetic analysis 89
phonetic spelling 50, 52
phonetic symbol 141

phonetics 147, 166, 172, 307
photosensor 268
physical disability 5, 7, 8, 10, 11, 21,
    246, 248, 263, 289, 298–305,
    323, 343, 345, 349, 352, 367,
    368
physical therapy 51, 141, 180, 181
    aids 141
Pin–Matrix Device 189
Polhemus (3D tracker) 175
Powerglove 179
print enlargemnent 352
processor, cognitive 152, 156,
    161
Prodigy 301
programming
    by demonstration 129
    by example 124
    language 124, 288
    logic 288
    tools 290, 370
pronunciation and synthetic speech
    52, 311
prosthesis 19, 22–33, 46, 105, 145,
    371
    cognitive 46, 143
    communication 84, 96
    speech 47–57, 171
    speech recognition 146, 147, 161,
        166
    speech synthesizer 47–57, 171
    writing 151
psychology
    cognitive 154
    of drivers 284
    in design 145

quadriplegia 30, 51, 263, 264, 267,
    271, 276

Race (Research and Development into
    Advanced Communications for
    Europe) 346, 351, 354, 357
Reactive Keyboard 107–140

rehabilitation
    engineering 4, 13, 362, 371, 372, 373
    literature 11, 35
    technology 19
    therapy 323
Resna (Rehabilitation Society of North America) 96, 371, 373
    conference 372
Ribis 249
RK–button 106–114
RK–pointer 106–114
room metaphor 142, 205, 208–213
Rooms, Audio 202, 208–218

safety
    car 284, 288, 294, 354
    critical systems 96
    "gadget approach" to 293
satellite
    conferencing 247, 248
    global positioning (GPS) 368
    television 251
screen enlargement 38, 59, 241
Screen Reader (IBM) 60
screen readers 59, 142, 241, 308–313
sensor
    eye gaze 267
    eye wink 268–272, 273
    head position 268
    photo- 268
sensory disability 7, 21, 27–29, 143, 221, 353, 367
Set (Surrogate Electronic Traveler) 245–261
Sigcaph (ACM Special Interest Group on Computers and the Physically Handicapped) 372
sign languages 47, 48, 170, 344, 358
    American Sign Language (ASL) 170–174
    Makaton 93

simulation
    office 253
    powered wheelchair 270
sip–puff switch 31, 37, 41, 265–273
SonicFinder 216, 224
sound, nonspeech 28, 61, 76, 201–215, 221–241
Soundgraph 240, 241
Soundtrack 60, 221–225, 233
special education 14, 51, 146
speech
    impairment 48, 56, 141, 319
    input, DragonDictate 148–165
    prosthesis 47–57, 171
    recognition prosthesis 146, 147, 161, 166
    synthesis (*see* speech synthesizer)
    therapy 12, 48, 50, 51
speech synthesizer 13, 28, 35, 41, 52, 76, 84, 92, 93, 141, 169, 181, 185, 186, 213–215, 229, 231, 235, 236, 280, 299, 307–313
    articulator based 169
    Dectalk 94
    Hamlet 94
    Macintalk 67
    pronunciation 52, 311
    prosthesis 47–57, 171
    Touch 'n Talk 196
spinal injury 30, 325
spreadsheet 137, 206, 256
"sticky" key 36
stigmatization 33, 346
stroke 8, 30, 33, 34, 83, 264, 291
switch
    body 265, 315
    light 265, 273, 274
    on–off 368
    operation 94, 173
    selection of 318
    sip–puff 31, 37, 41, 265–273

syntax
    and dyslexia 148
    prediction 88, 136
    visual 235
synthesizer
    music 225, 229
    speech (*see* speech synthesizer)

tactile communication 27, 28, 142,
        186, 198, 231, 233, 356, 358
tactile marks 39
tactile sense 9
tactile tablet 188
TalksBack 92
TDD (Telecommunication Device for
        the Deaf) 29
Telaid 353
telecommunication device for the
        deaf (TDD) 29
telecommunications 95, 246, 297,
        299, 300, 343, 345, 346, 347,
        352, 354
    and Accessiblity Enhancement Act
        363
    companies 312
    organizations 95
telecommuting 353
teleconferencing 248, 250
telephone 11, 29, 35, 117, 119, 143,
        251, 254, 265, 297, 345, 346,
        354, 356, 357
    conferencing 247, 248, 257,
        299
    dialer 274
    directory 115, 137
    number 115, 215
    speaker 32, 248, 252, 254
    text 345
    video 356
Telesensory Inc 187
teletext 5, 308
television 248, 257, 275
    controls 265, 273, 274
    network 275

remote control 12
satellite251
subtitling 5, 11
tetraplegia 30–31
theory, computing 279, 289
therapy 167, 175–180
    occupational 51, 169, 265
    physical 51, 141, 180, 181
    rehabilitation 323
    speech 12, 48, 50, 51
Tide (Technology for the Integration
        of the Disabled and Elderly–
        European initiative) 60, 69, 346
timbre 224, 230
touch 27, 187, 234, 369
    constraint 129, 136
    metaphor 134
    typing 156, 160
Touch Talker 47, 56
Touch'n Talk 196
touchpad 36, 231
touchscreen 37, 39
    simulation 36, 39
trackball 225, 324, 325–338
training, musical 224
trauma 22, 83
travel, electronic 245–258, 297, 298,
        316
typing 37, 49, 70, 108, 114, 151169,
        190, 195, 206, 289, 315
    touch 156, 160

Unix 28, 59, 79, 106–123, 137, 201,
        218
UnMouse 232–233
Usenet 114

video
    camera 266
    captions 299
    conferencing 245, 247, 248, 252,
        253, 256
    data link 254

digital 249
games 180–181, 212
home use of 345, 350, 352, 354, 358
interactive 143
messaging 248
recorder 283, 291, 292–293, 294
slow scan 247
videodisc 273
video tape 257
virtual reality 174, 179, 217, 249
virtual space metaphor 248
visual disability 26, 29, 59, 209, 218, 355, 356, 366, 372
visual impairment , 7, 8, 10, 13, 27, 38, 202, 207, 298, 301, 303, 315, 354, 356, 357, 358
vocal tract 141, 169–172
voice mail 257

wheelchair 7, 22, 29–32, 53, 143–144
access 7
and airlines 143
curb cuts 29
EWCI 264–276
motorized 276
simulation 270
storage 353
Windows, Microsoft 60
workbench metaphor 120
writing
aids 114
prosthesis 151.
wysiwis (what you see is what I see) 257
wysiwyg (what you see is what you get) 76, 197

X Window 123, 142, 201, 218
Xerox Parc (Palo Alto Research Center) 208, 257